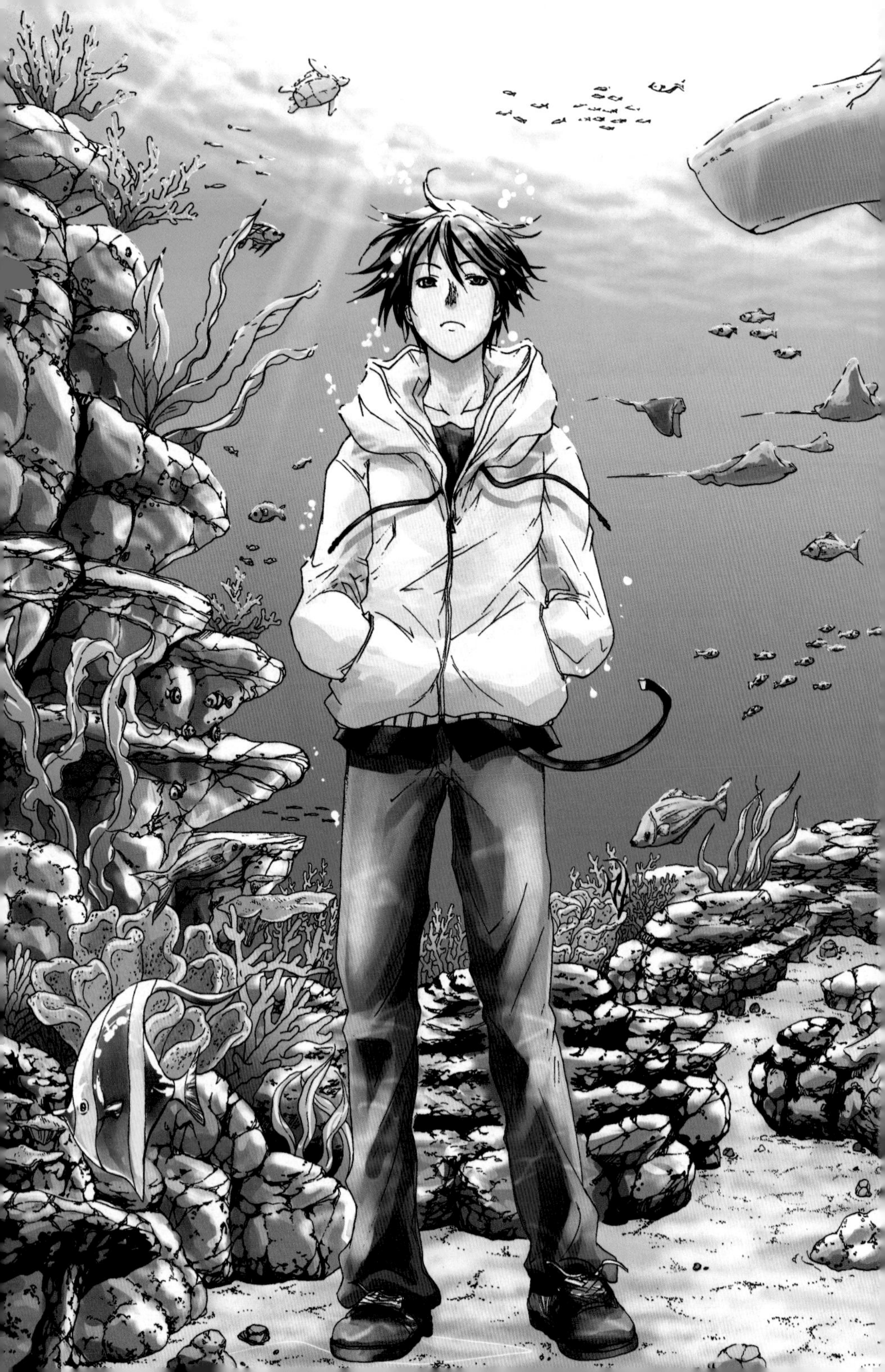

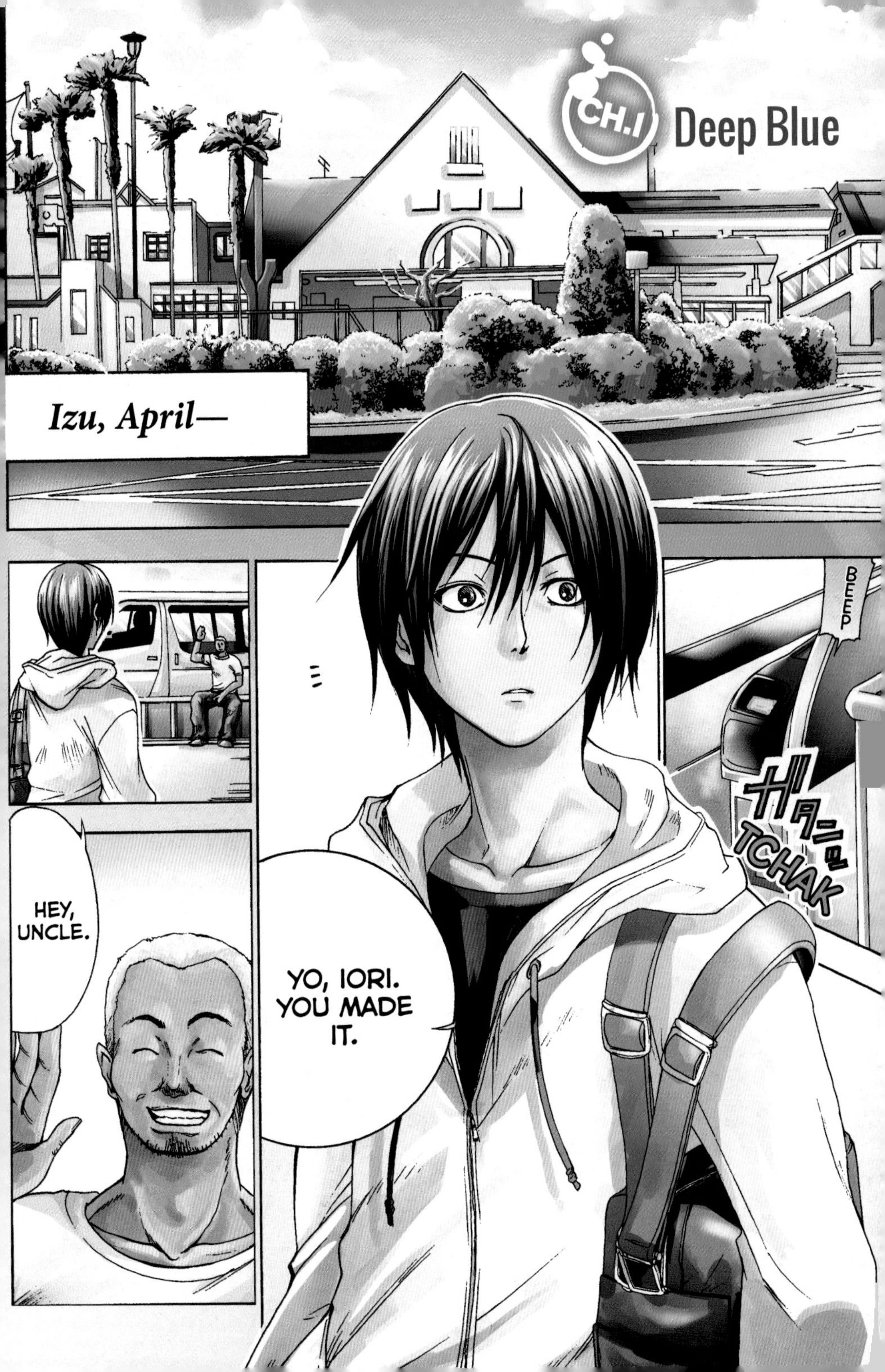
CH.1 Deep Blue
Izu, April—
BEEP
TCHAK
YO, IORI. YOU MADE IT.
HEY, UNCLE.

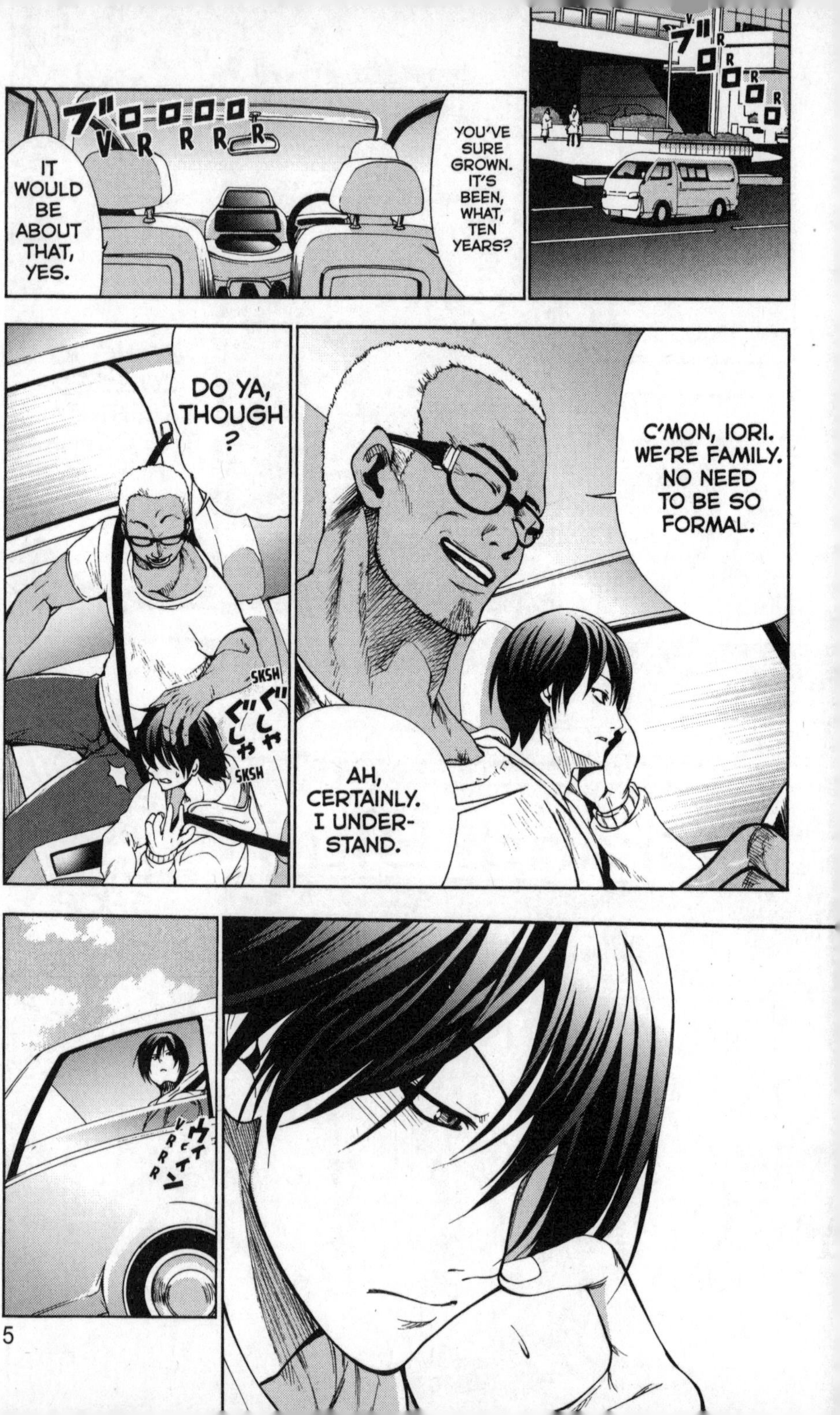
ブロロロロ
VRRRR
ブロロロロ
VRRRR
YOU'VE SURE GROWN. IT'S BEEN, WHAT, TEN YEARS?
IT WOULD BE ABOUT THAT, YES.
C'MON, IORI. WE'RE FAMILY. NO NEED TO BE SO FORMAL.
AH, CERTAINLY. I UNDERSTAND.
DO YA, THOUGH?
ぐしゃぐしゃ
SKSH SKSH
ウイィン
VRRRR

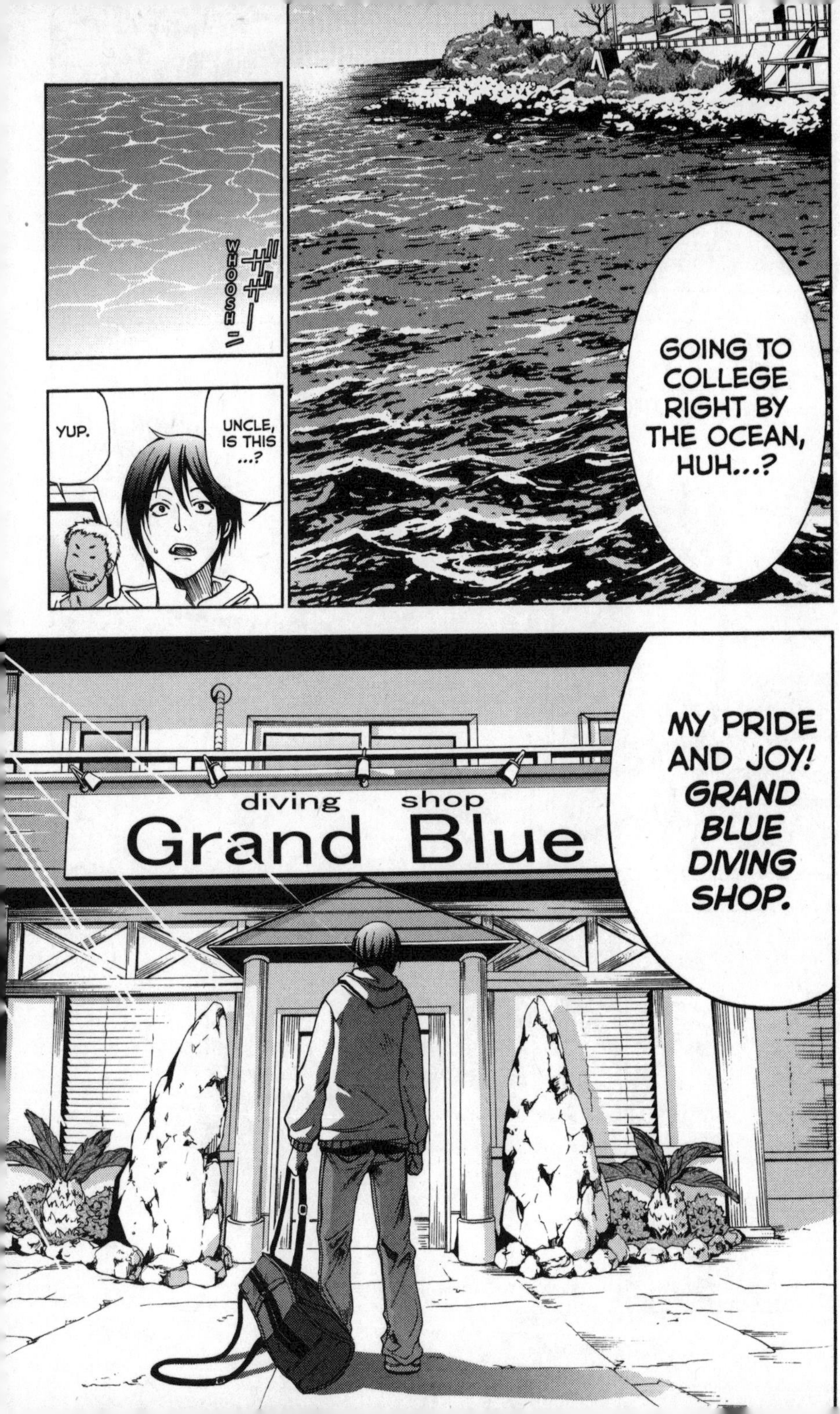
GOING TO COLLEGE RIGHT BY THE OCEAN, HUH...?
ザザー
WHOOSH
UNCLE, IS THIS ...?
YUP.
MY PRIDE AND JOY! GRAND BLUE DIVING SHOP.
diving shop
Grand Blue

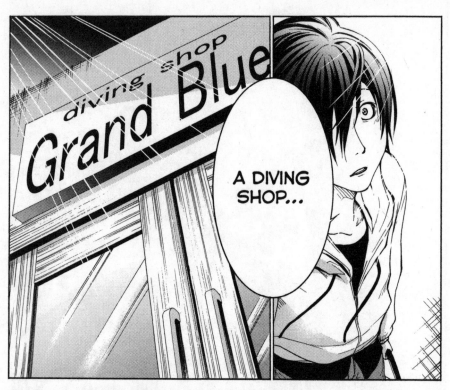

diving shop
Grand Blue

A DIVING SHOP...

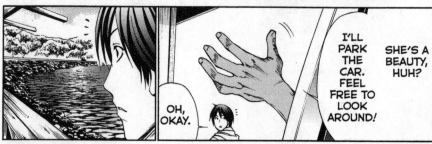

SHE'S A BEAUTY, HUH?

I'LL PARK THE CAR. FEEL FREE TO LOOK AROUND!

OH, OKAY.

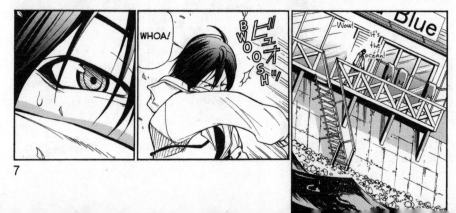

WHOA!

B W O O S H!!

Wow! It's the ocean!

Blue

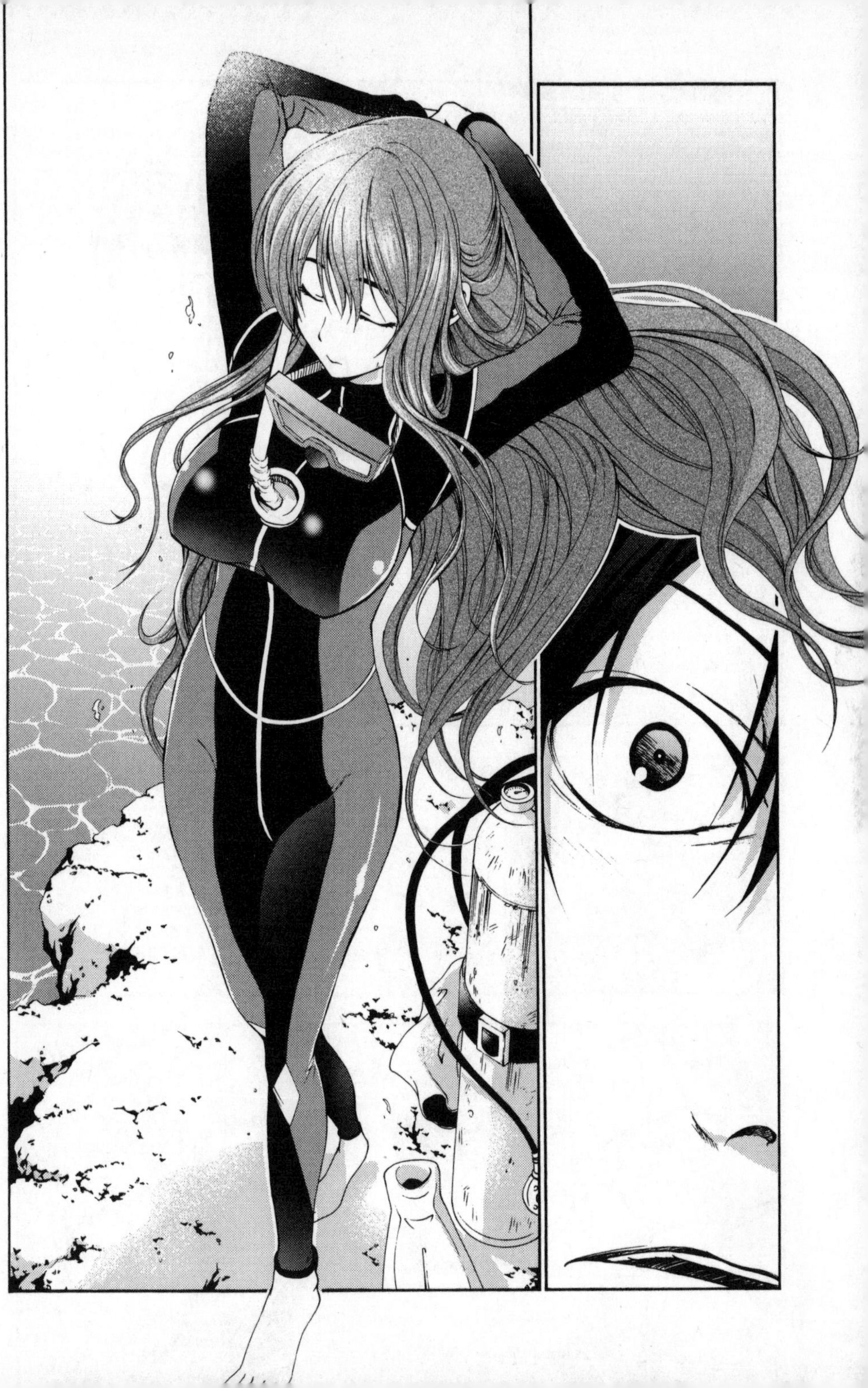

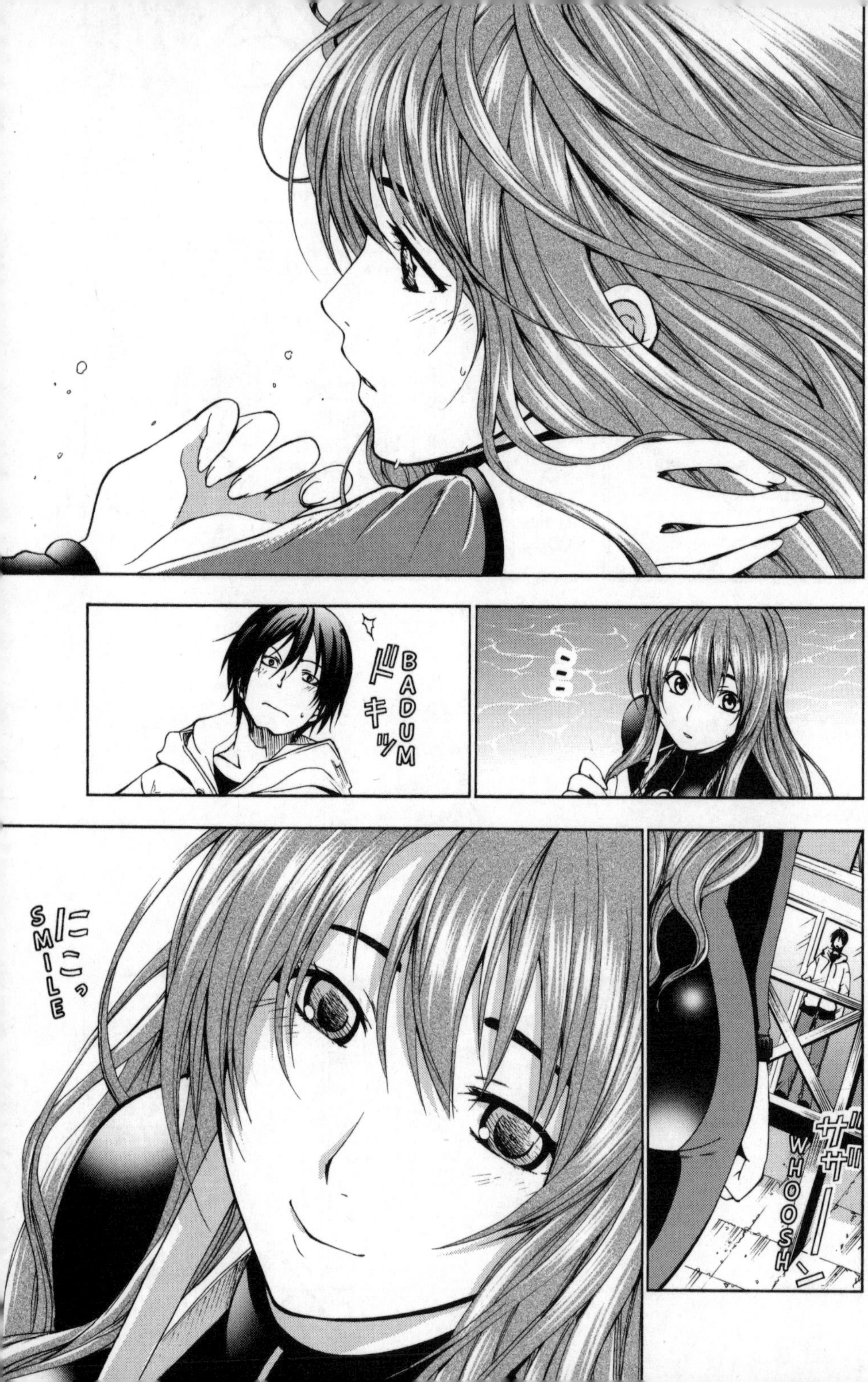
...
ドキッ
BADUM
ザザーン
WHOOSH
にこっ
SMILE

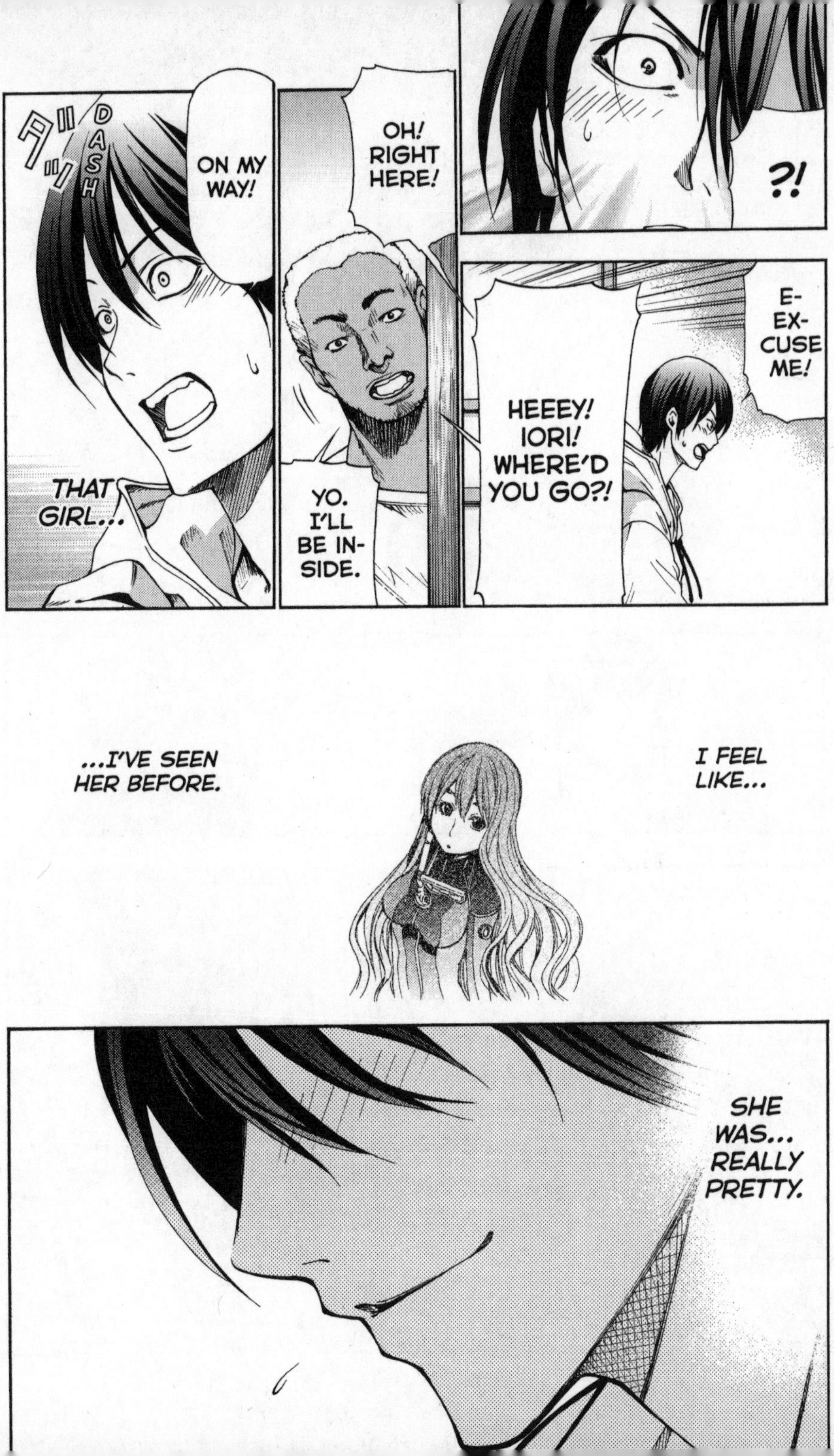
?!
E-EX-CUSE ME!
HEEEY! IORI! WHERE'D YOU GO?!
OH! RIGHT HERE!
YO. I'LL BE IN-SIDE.
ON MY WAY!
DASH
THAT GIRL...
I FEEL LIKE...
...I'VE SEEN HER BEFORE.
SHE WAS... REALLY PRETTY.

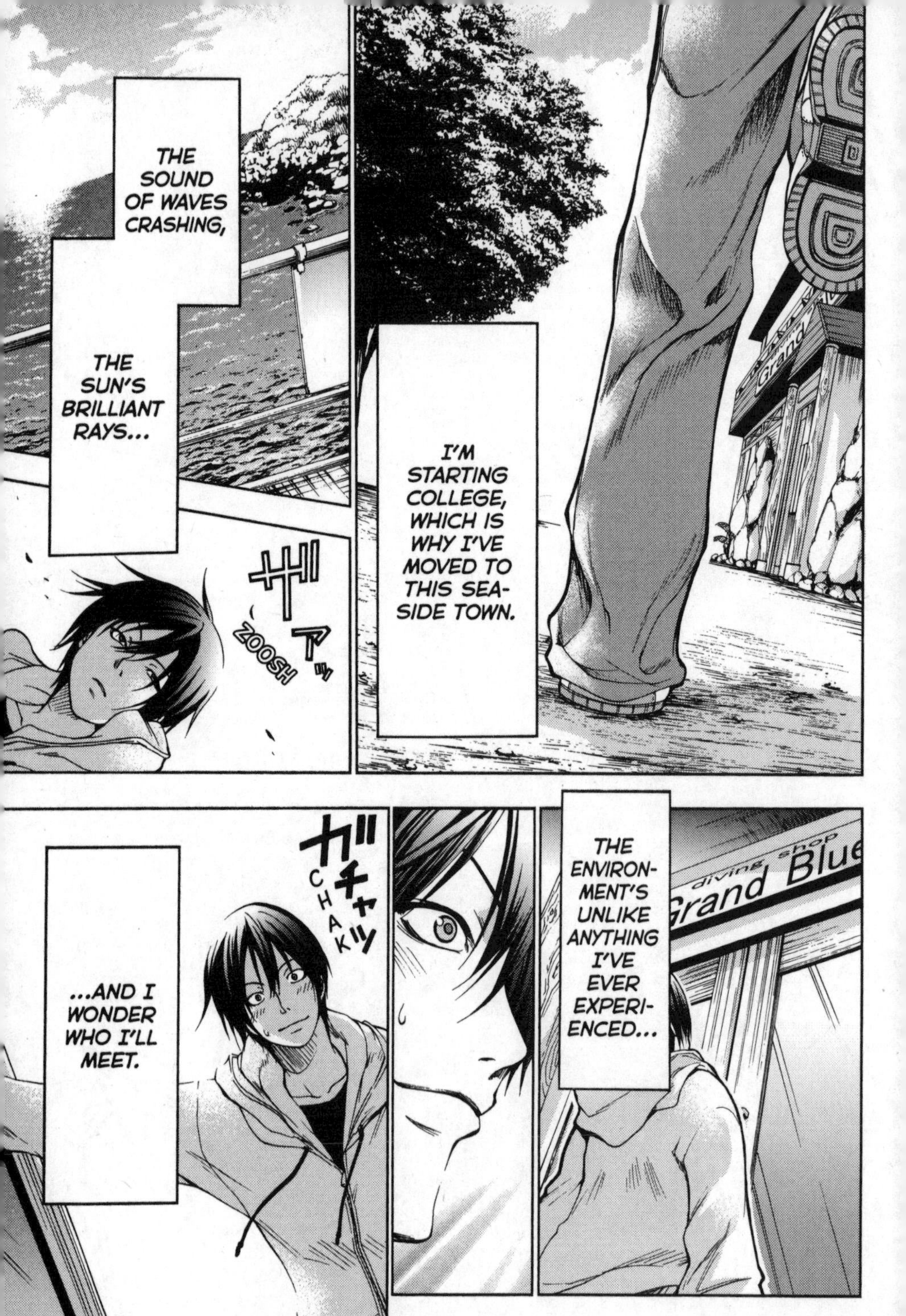

Grand
I'M STARTING COLLEGE, WHICH IS WHY I'VE MOVED TO THIS SEA-SIDE TOWN.
THE SOUND OF WAVES CRASHING,
THE SUN'S BRILLIANT RAYS...
ザアッ
ZOOSH
diving shop Grand Blue
THE ENVIRONMENT'S UNLIKE ANYTHING I'VE EVER EXPERIENCED...
ガチャッ
CHAK
...AND I WONDER WHO I'LL MEET.

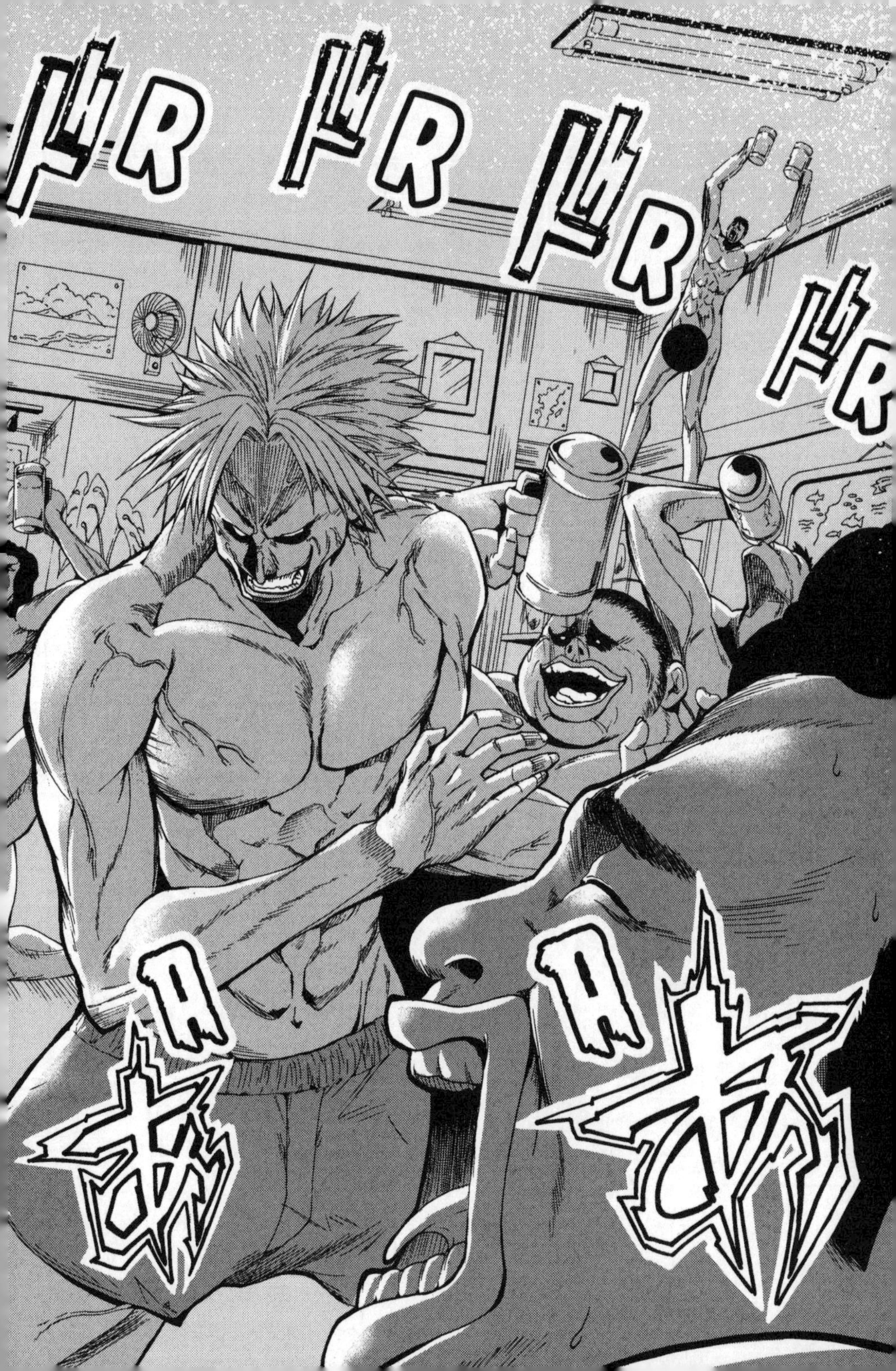
FUR
FUR
FUR
FUR
A
A

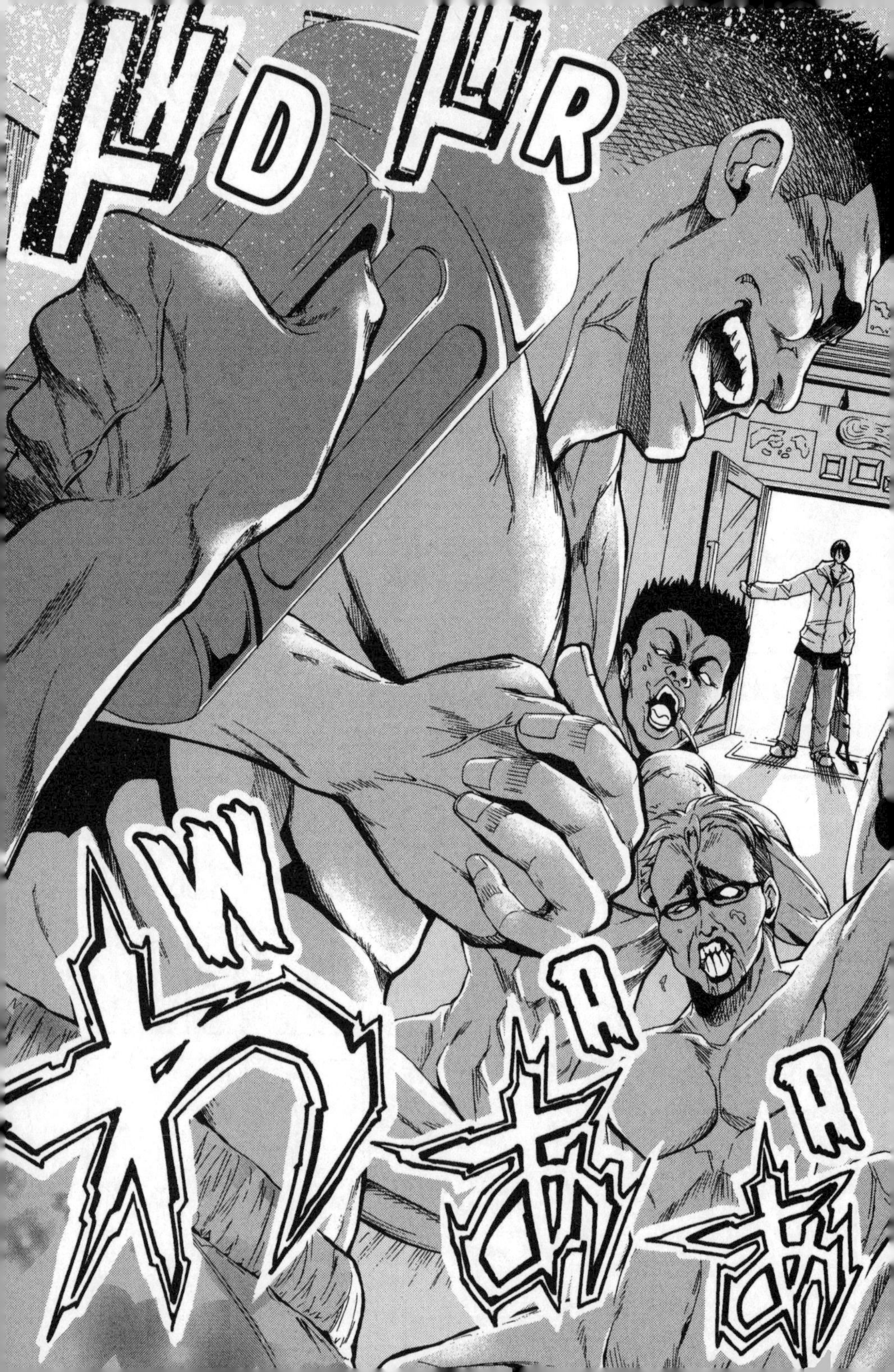
WAAA

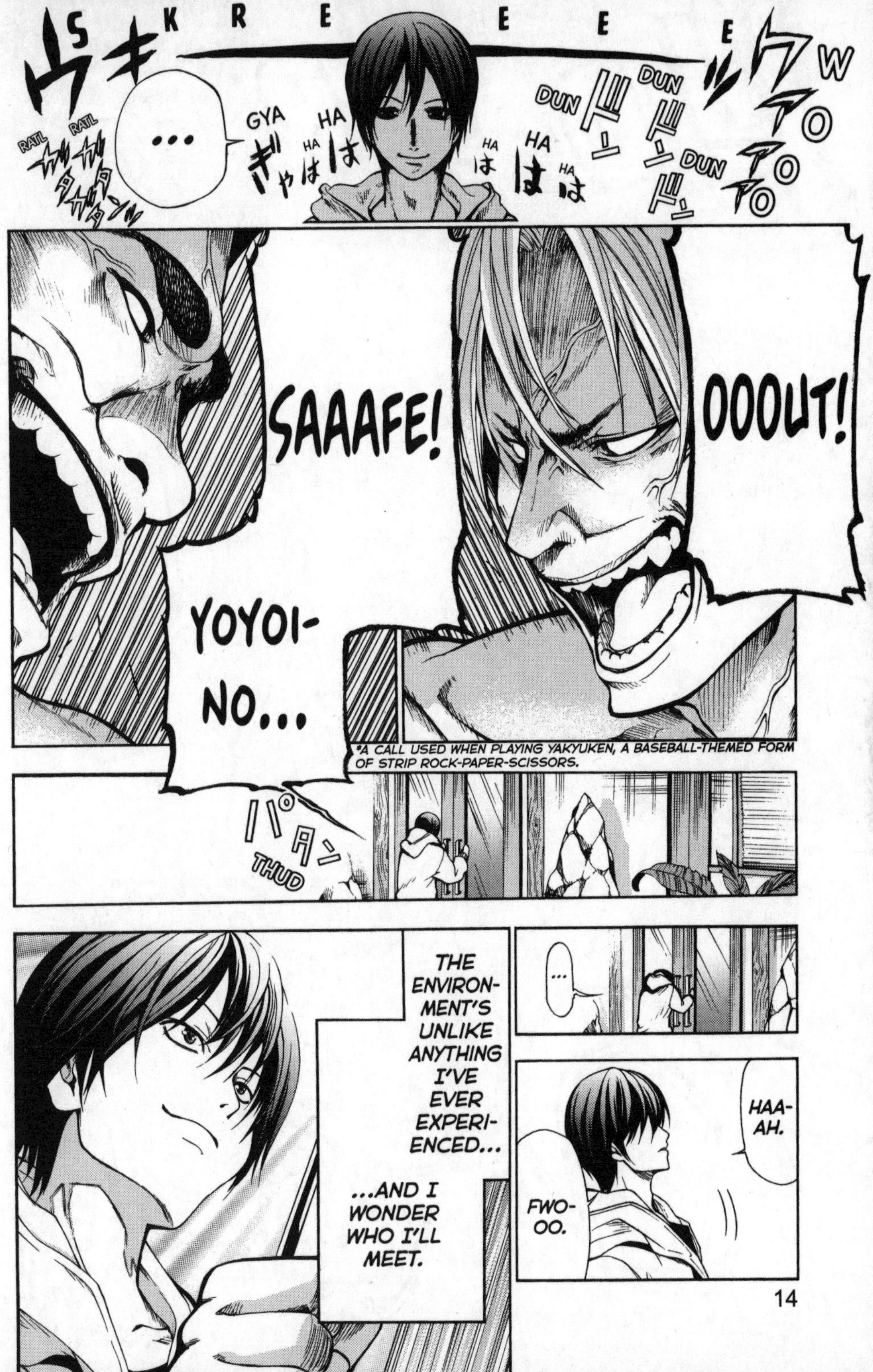
SKREEEEE
WOOOO
DUN DUN DUN
HA HA HA
GYA HA HA
...
RATL RATL
OOOUT!
SAAAFE!
YOYOI-NO...
THUD
...
HAA-AH.
FWO-OO.
THE ENVIRONMENT'S UNLIKE ANYTHING I'VE EVER EXPERIENCED...
...AND I WONDER WHO I'LL MEET.

*A CALL USED WHEN PLAYING YAKYUKEN, A BASEBALL-THEMED FORM OF STRIP ROCK-PAPER-SCISSORS.

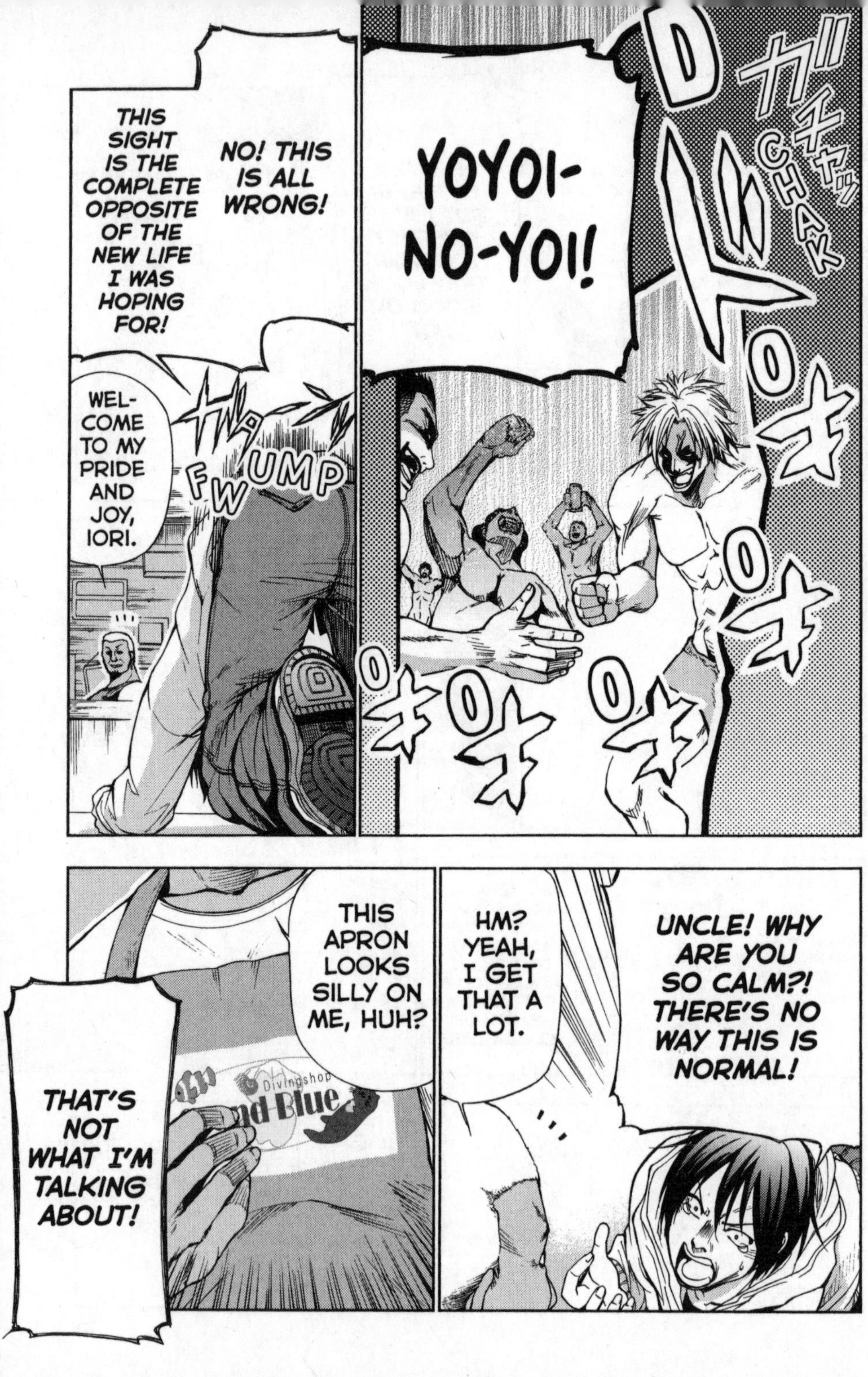
YOYOI-NO-YOI!
CHAK
NO! THIS IS ALL WRONG!
THIS SIGHT IS THE COMPLETE OPPOSITE OF THE NEW LIFE I WAS HOPING FOR!
FWUMP
WELCOME TO MY PRIDE AND JOY, IORI.
UNCLE! WHY ARE YOU SO CALM?! THERE'S NO WAY THIS IS NORMAL!
HM? YEAH, I GET THAT A LOT.
...
THIS APRON LOOKS SILLY ON ME, HUH?
Divingshop
THAT'S NOT WHAT I'M TALKING ABOUT!

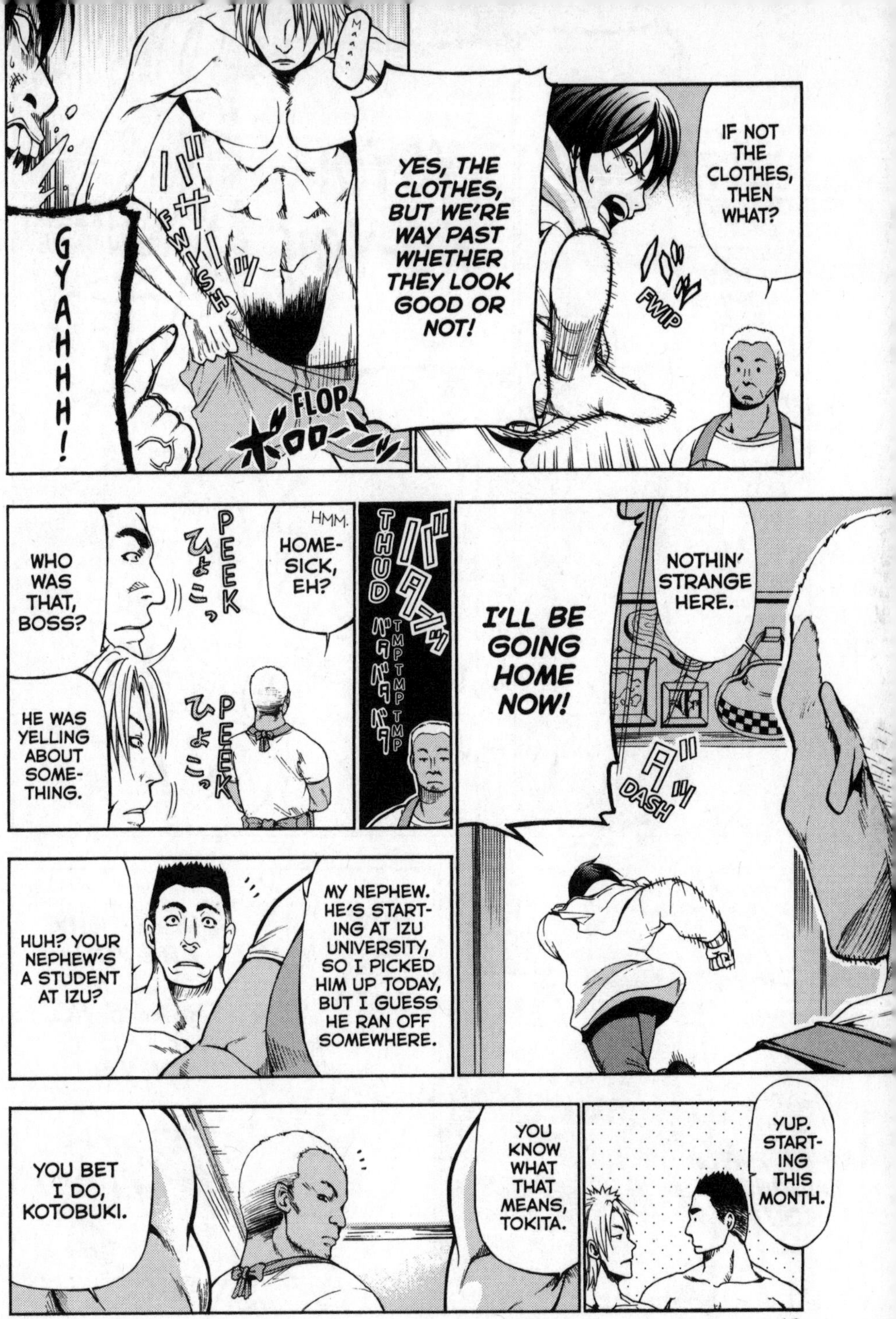
IF NOT THE CLOTHES, THEN WHAT?
FWIP
YES, THE CLOTHES, BUT WE'RE WAY PAST WHETHER THEY LOOK GOOD OR NOT!
Maaan.
FWISH
FLOP
GYAHHH!
NOTHIN' STRANGE HERE.
I'LL BE GOING HOME NOW!
DASH
THUD
TMP TMP TMP TMP
HMM.
HOME-SICK, EH?
PEEK
PEEK
WHO WAS THAT, BOSS?
HE WAS YELLING ABOUT SOME-THING.
MY NEPHEW. HE'S START-ING AT IZU UNIVERSITY, SO I PICKED HIM UP TODAY, BUT I GUESS HE RAN OFF SOMEWHERE.
HUH? YOUR NEPHEW'S A STUDENT AT IZU?
YUP. START-ING THIS MONTH.
YOU KNOW WHAT THAT MEANS, TOKITA.
YOU BET I DO, KOTOBUKI.

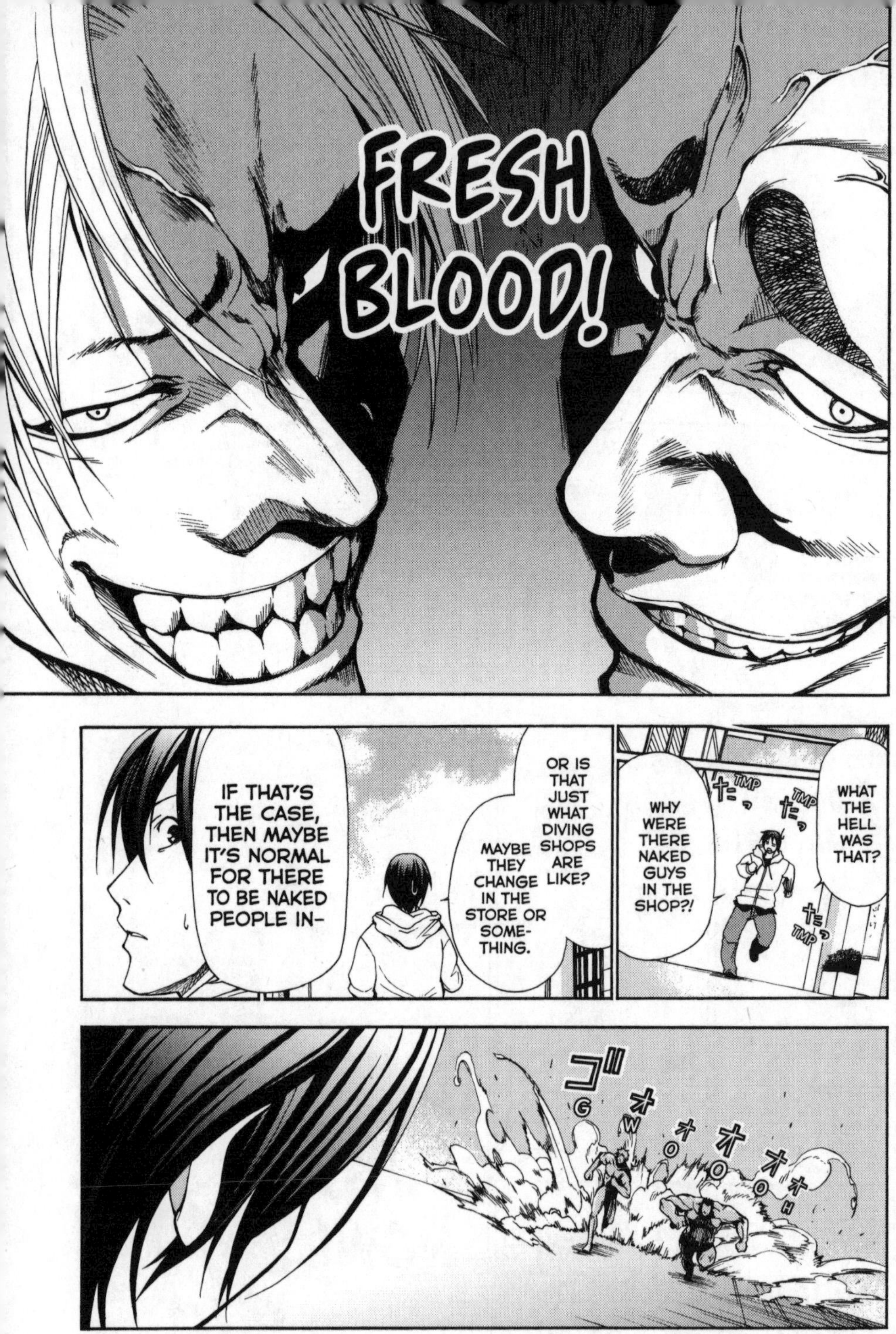
FRESH BLOOD!
WHAT THE HELL WAS THAT?
TMP
TMP
TMP
WHY WERE THERE NAKED GUYS IN THE SHOP?!
OR IS THAT JUST WHAT DIVING SHOPS ARE LIKE?
MAYBE THEY CHANGE IN THE STORE OR SOME-THING.
IF THAT'S THE CASE, THEN MAYBE IT'S NORMAL FOR THERE TO BE NAKED PEOPLE IN-
GWOOOH

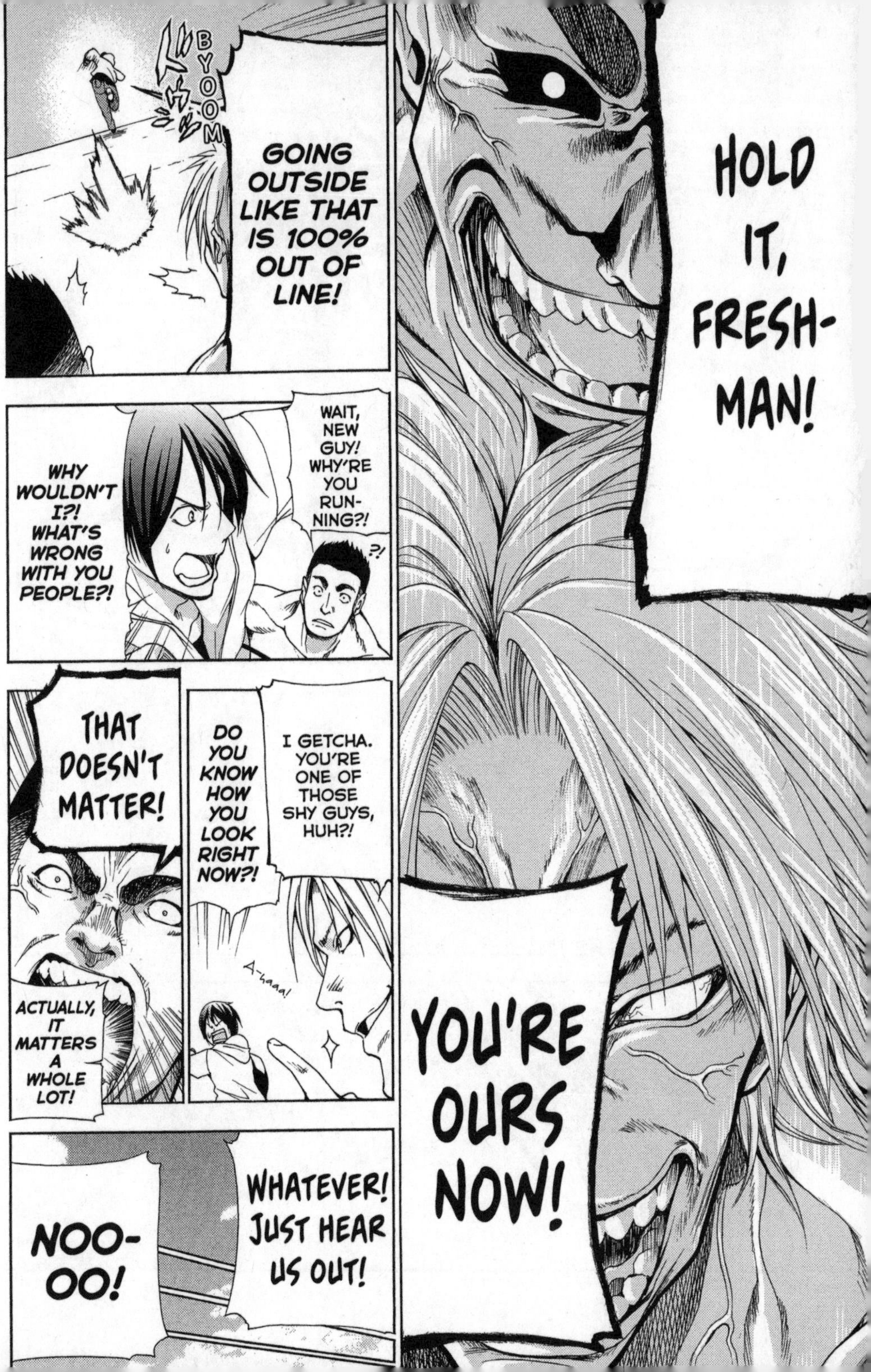

HOLD IT, FRESH-MAN!
YOU'RE OURS NOW!
BYOOM
GOING OUTSIDE LIKE THAT IS 100% OUT OF LINE!
WAIT, NEW GUY! WHY'RE YOU RUN-NING?!
?!
WHY WOULDN'T I?! WHAT'S WRONG WITH YOU PEOPLE?!
I GETCHA. YOU'RE ONE OF THOSE SHY GUYS, HUH?!
DO YOU KNOW HOW YOU LOOK RIGHT NOW?!
A-haaa!
THAT DOESN'T MATTER!
ACTUALLY, IT MATTERS A WHOLE LOT!
WHATEVER! JUST HEAR US OUT!
NOO-OO!

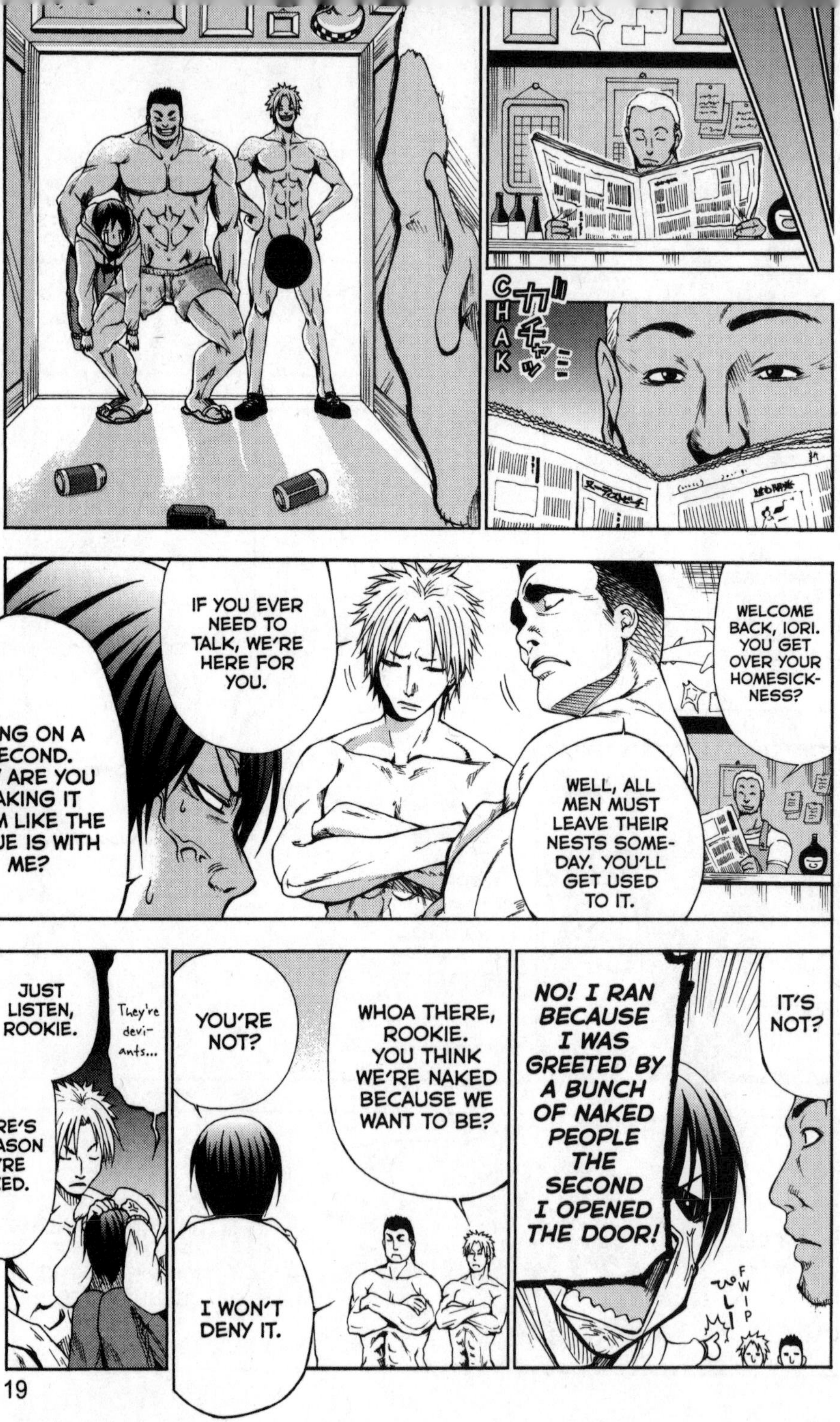
CHAK
WELCOME BACK, IORI. YOU GET OVER YOUR HOMESICKNESS?
WELL, ALL MEN MUST LEAVE THEIR NESTS SOMEDAY. YOU'LL GET USED TO IT.
IF YOU EVER NEED TO TALK, WE'RE HERE FOR YOU.
HANG ON A SECOND. WHY ARE YOU MAKING IT SEEM LIKE THE ISSUE IS WITH ME?
IT'S NOT?
NO! I RAN BECAUSE I WAS GREETED BY A BUNCH OF NAKED PEOPLE THE SECOND I OPENED THE DOOR!
FWIP
WHOA THERE, ROOKIE. YOU THINK WE'RE NAKED BECAUSE WE WANT TO BE?
YOU'RE NOT?
I WON'T DENY IT.
JUST LISTEN, ROOKIE.
They're deviants...
THERE'S A REASON WE'RE NAKED.

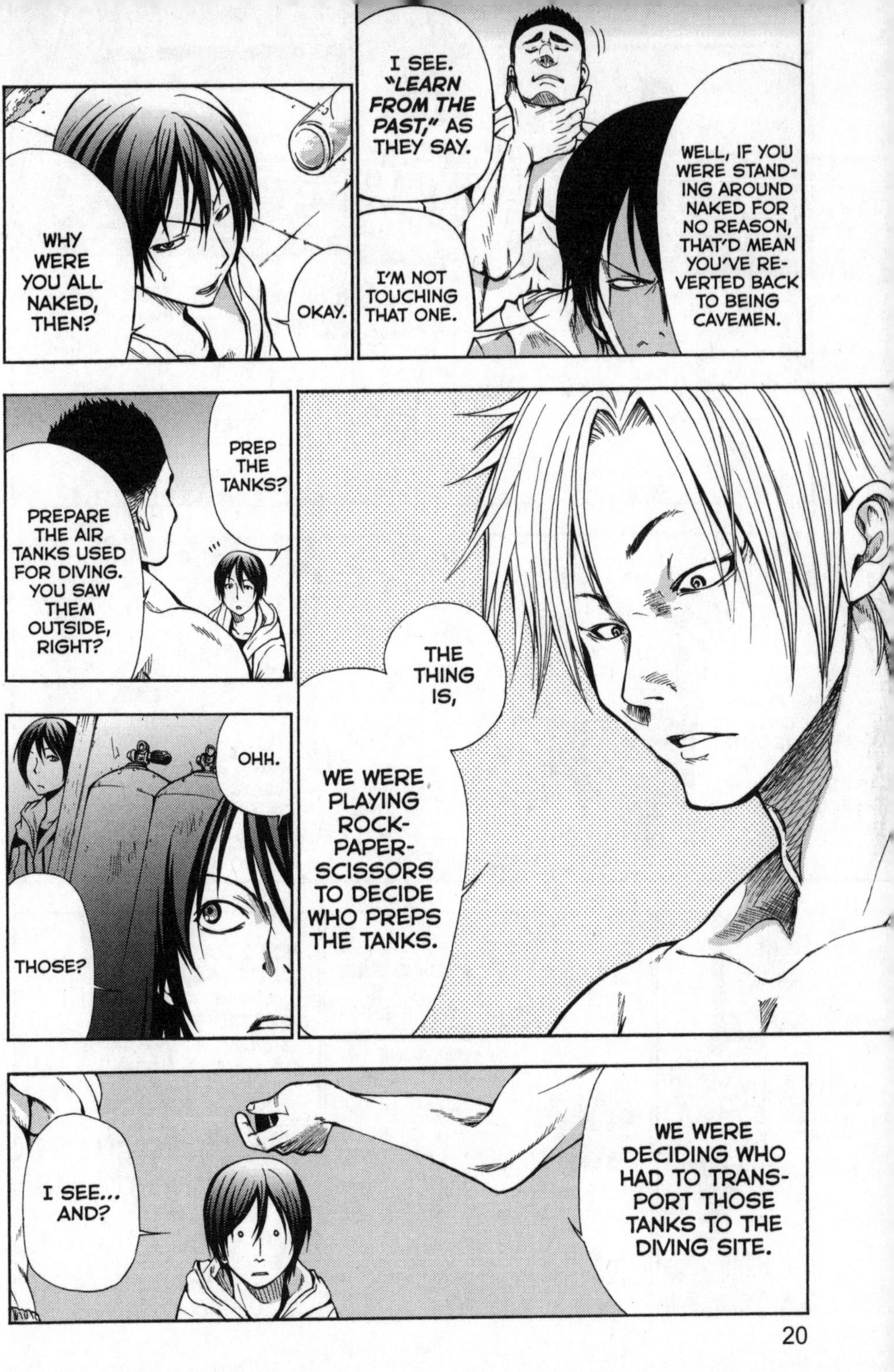
WELL, IF YOU WERE STANDING AROUND NAKED FOR NO REASON, THAT'D MEAN YOU'VE REVERTED BACK TO BEING CAVEMEN.
I SEE. *"LEARN FROM THE PAST,"* AS THEY SAY.
I'M NOT TOUCHING THAT ONE.
OKAY.
WHY WERE YOU ALL NAKED, THEN?
THE THING IS,
WE WERE PLAYING ROCK-PAPER-SCISSORS TO DECIDE WHO PREPS THE TANKS.
PREP THE TANKS?
PREPARE THE AIR TANKS USED FOR DIVING. YOU SAW THEM OUTSIDE, RIGHT?
OHH.
THOSE?
WE WERE DECIDING WHO HAD TO TRANSPORT THOSE TANKS TO THE DIVING SITE.
I SEE... AND?

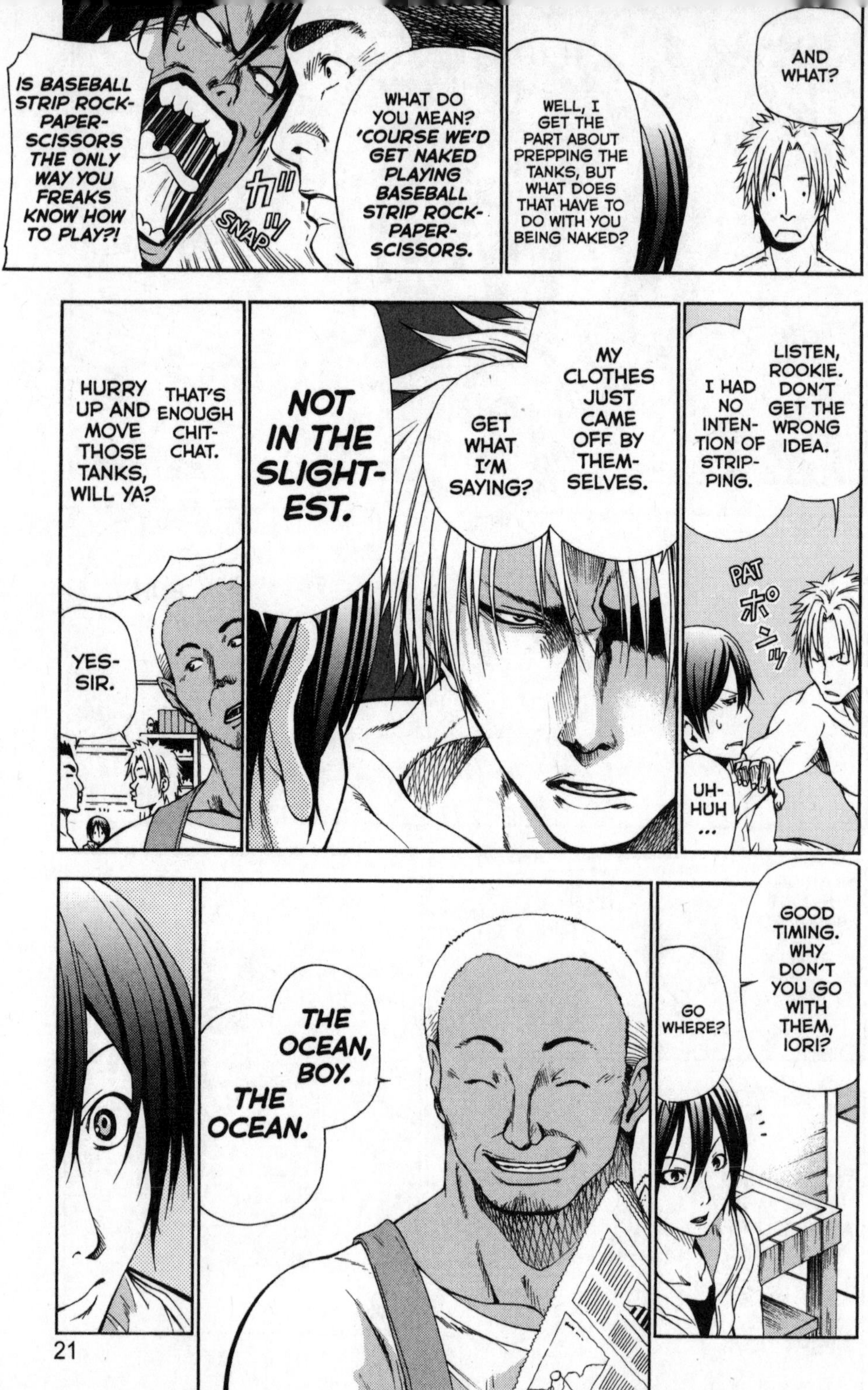
AND WHAT?
WELL, I GET THE PART ABOUT PREPPING THE TANKS, BUT WHAT DOES THAT HAVE TO DO WITH YOU BEING NAKED?
WHAT DO YOU MEAN? 'COURSE WE'D GET NAKED PLAYING BASEBALL STRIP ROCK-PAPER-SCISSORS.
SNAP
IS BASEBALL STRIP ROCK-PAPER-SCISSORS THE ONLY WAY YOU FREAKS KNOW HOW TO PLAY?!
LISTEN, ROOKIE. DON'T GET THE WRONG IDEA.
I HAD NO INTENTION OF STRIPPING.
PAT
UH-HUH...
MY CLOTHES JUST CAME OFF BY THEMSELVES.
GET WHAT I'M SAYING?
NOT IN THE SLIGHTEST.
THAT'S ENOUGH CHIT-CHAT.
HURRY UP AND MOVE THOSE TANKS, WILL YA?
YES-SIR.
GOOD TIMING. WHY DON'T YOU GO WITH THEM, IORI?
GO WHERE?
THE OCEAN, BOY. THE OCEAN.

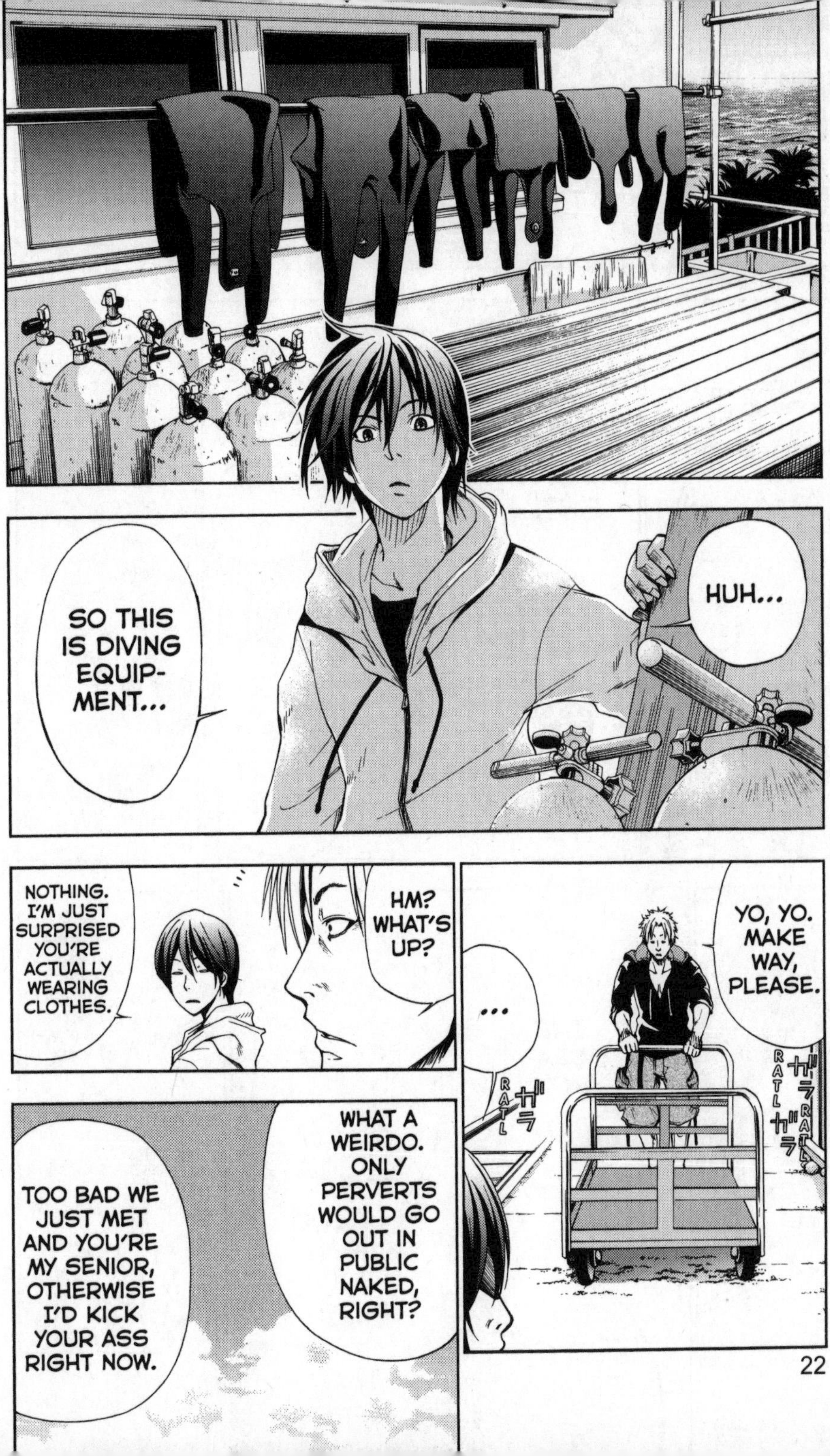
HUH...
SO THIS IS DIVING EQUIPMENT...
YO, YO. MAKE WAY, PLEASE.
RATL RATL
ガラガラ
...
RATL
ガラ
HM? WHAT'S UP?
NOTHING. I'M JUST SURPRISED YOU'RE ACTUALLY WEARING CLOTHES.
WHAT A WEIRDO. ONLY PERVERTS WOULD GO OUT IN PUBLIC NAKED, RIGHT?
TOO BAD WE JUST MET AND YOU'RE MY SENIOR, OTHERWISE I'D KICK YOUR ASS RIGHT NOW.

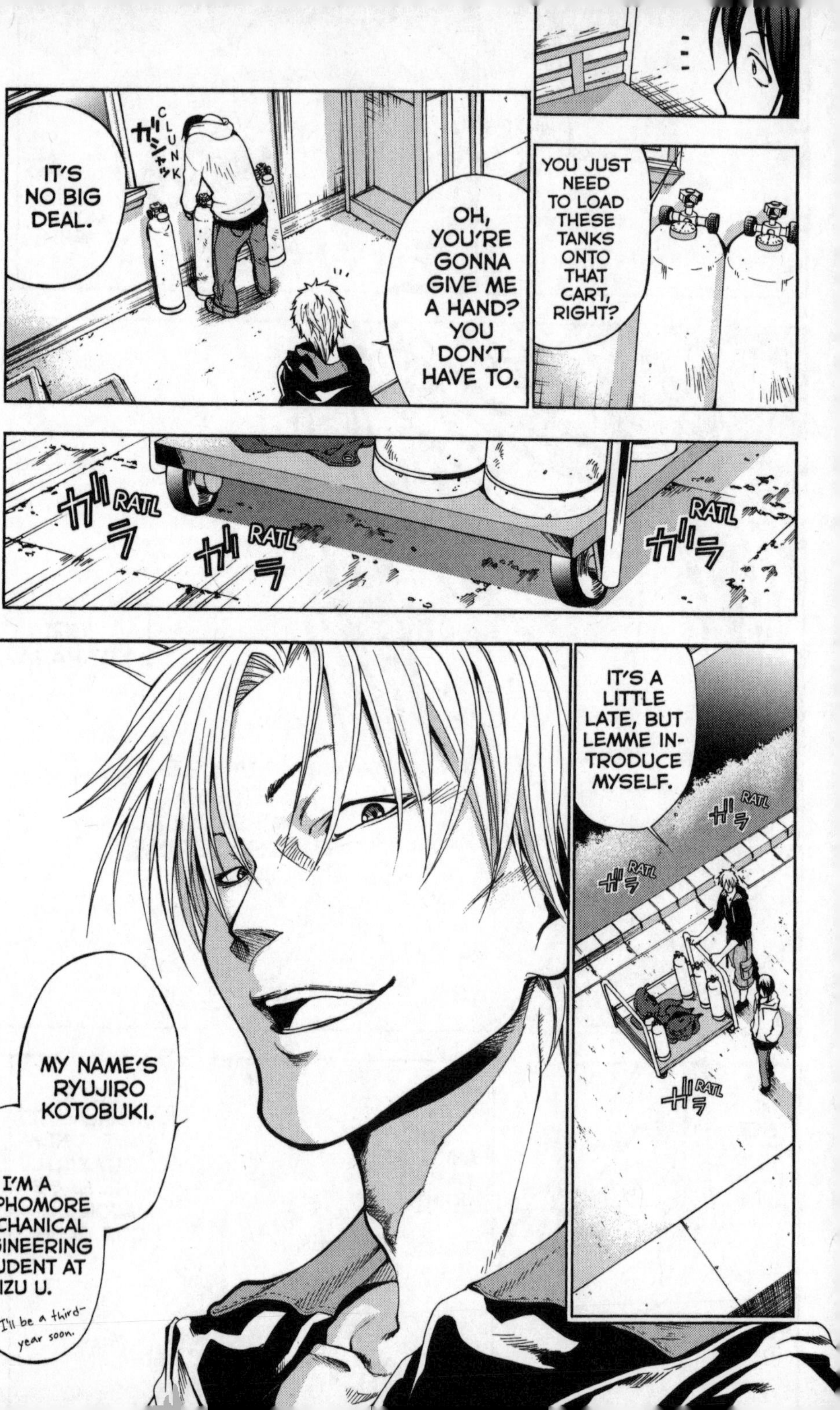
...
YOU JUST NEED TO LOAD THESE TANKS ONTO THAT CART, RIGHT?
OH, YOU'RE GONNA GIVE ME A HAND? YOU DON'T HAVE TO.
ガシャッ CLUNK
IT'S NO BIG DEAL.
ガラ RATL
ガラ RATL
ガラ RATL
IT'S A LITTLE LATE, BUT LEMME INTRODUCE MYSELF.
ガラ RATL
ガラ RATL
ガラ RATL
MY NAME'S RYUJIRO KOTOBUKI.
I'M A SOPHOMORE MECHANICAL ENGINEERING STUDENT AT IZU U.
I'll be a third-year soon.

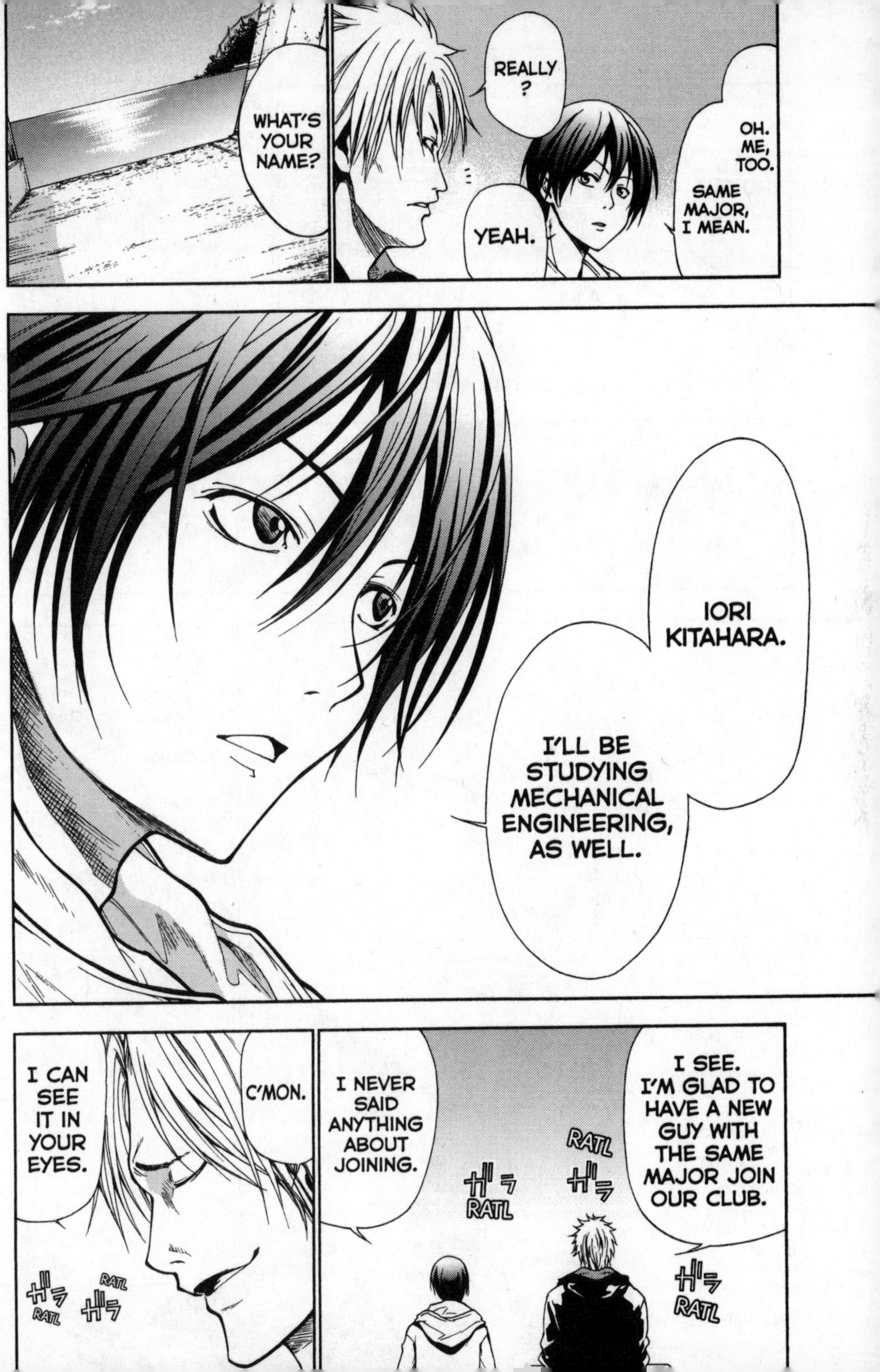
OH. ME, TOO. SAME MAJOR, I MEAN.
REALLY?
YEAH.
WHAT'S YOUR NAME?
IORI KITAHARA.
I'LL BE STUDYING MECHANICAL ENGINEERING, AS WELL.
I SEE. I'M GLAD TO HAVE A NEW GUY WITH THE SAME MAJOR JOIN OUR CLUB.
ガラ RATL
ガラ RATL
ガラ RATL
I NEVER SAID ANYTHING ABOUT JOINING.
C'MON.
I CAN SEE IT IN YOUR EYES.
ガラ RATL
ガラ RATL

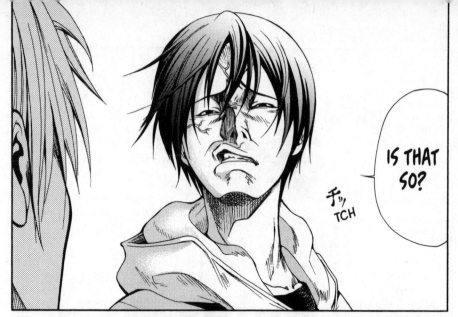

IS THAT SO?

チッ
TCH

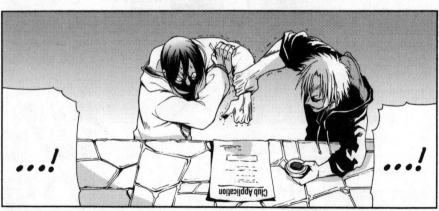

...!

...!

Club Application

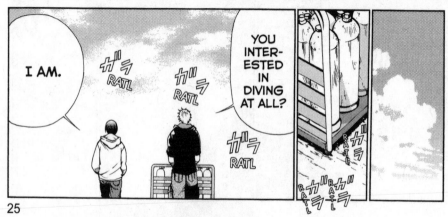

I AM.

ガラ
RATL

ガラ
RATL

YOU INTER-ESTED IN DIVING AT ALL?

ガラ
RATL

ガラ
RATL

ガラガラガラ
RATL RATL RATL

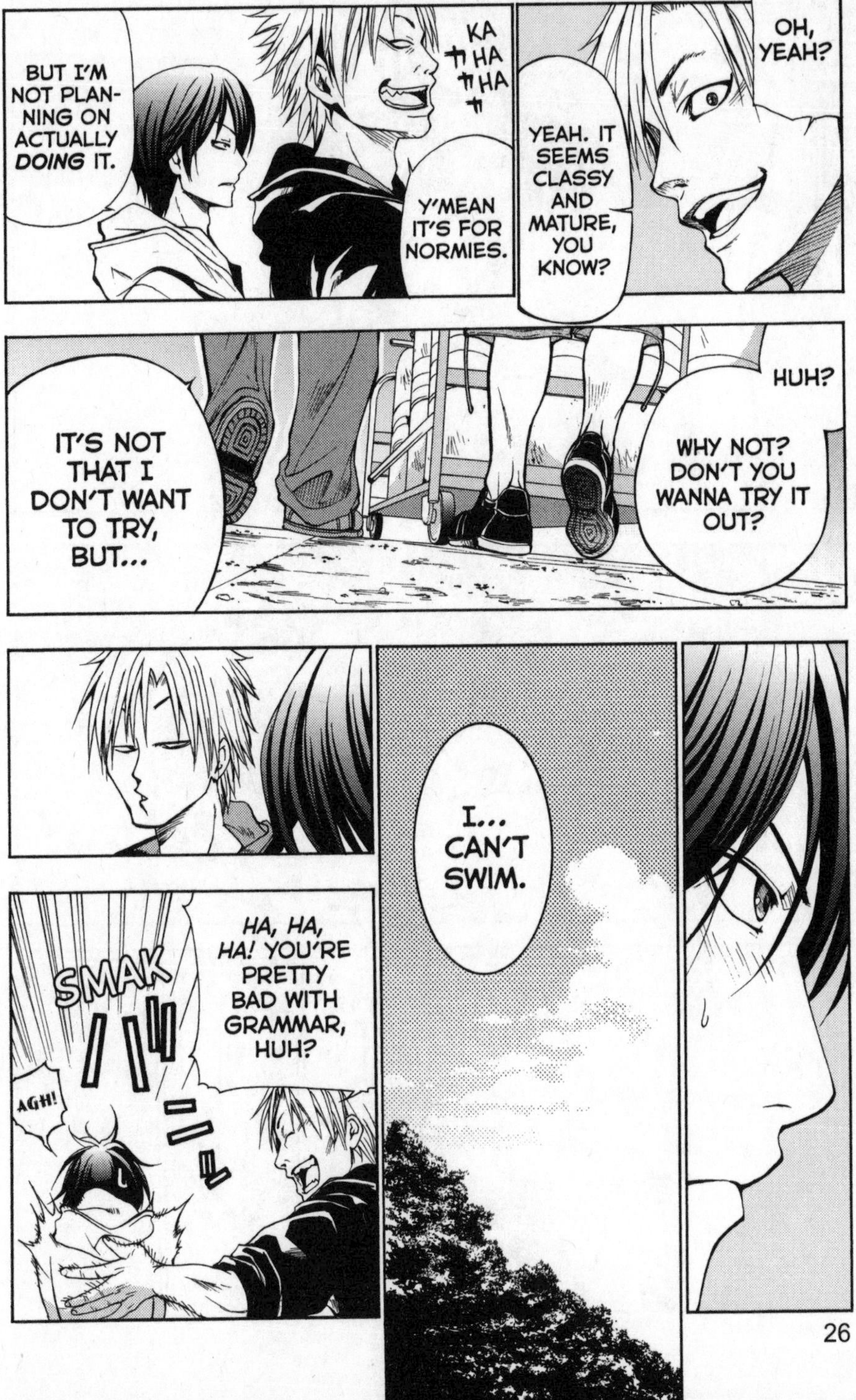
OH, YEAH?
YEAH. IT SEEMS CLASSY AND MATURE, YOU KNOW?
KA HA HA
Y'MEAN IT'S FOR NORMIES.
BUT I'M NOT PLANNING ON ACTUALLY *DOING* IT.
HUH?
WHY NOT? DON'T YOU WANNA TRY IT OUT?
IT'S NOT THAT I DON'T WANT TO TRY, BUT...
I... CAN'T SWIM.
HA, HA, HA! YOU'RE PRETTY BAD WITH GRAMMAR, HUH?
SMAK
AGH!

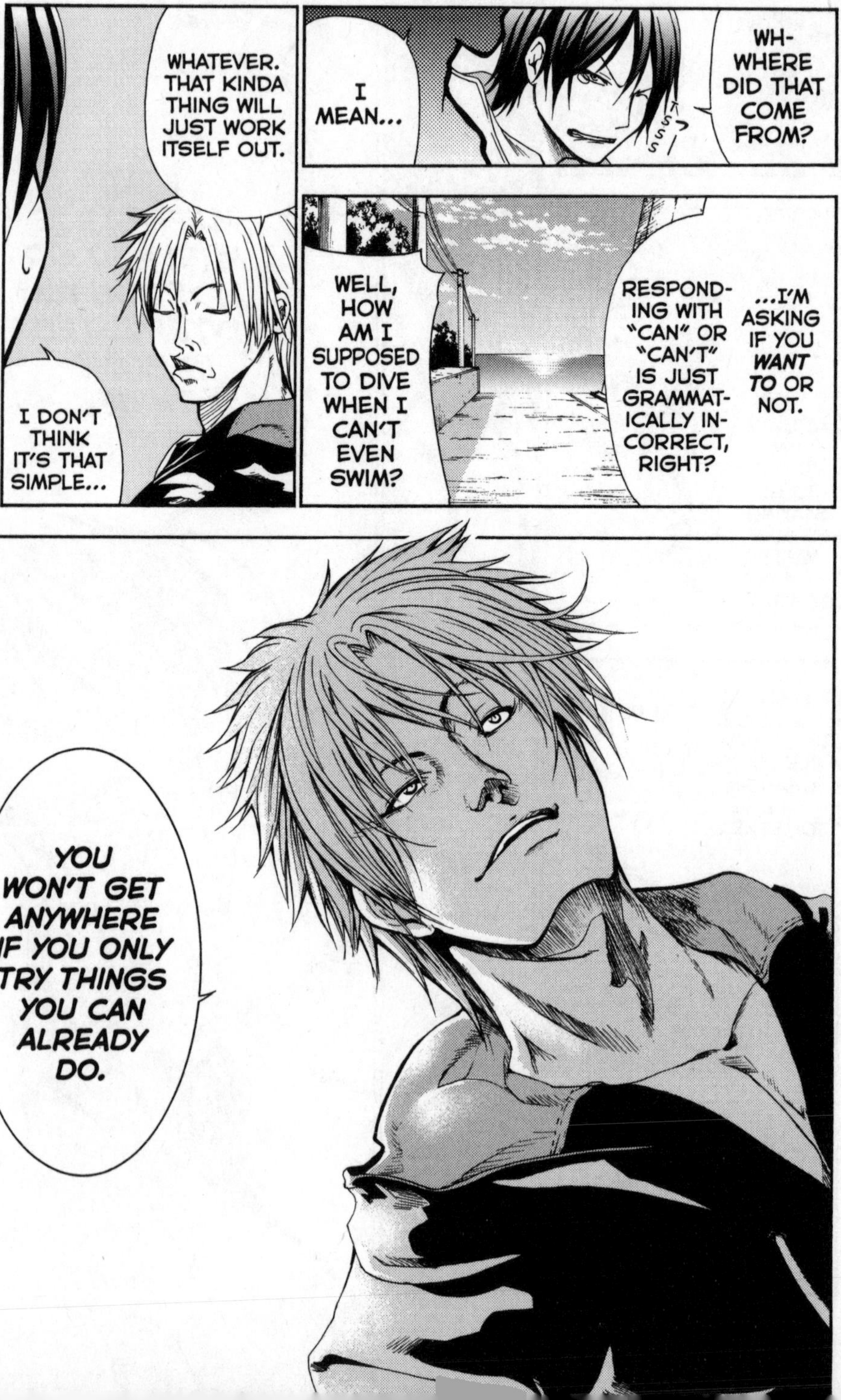
WH- WHERE DID THAT COME FROM?
TSSS
I MEAN...
...I'M ASKING IF YOU *WANT TO* OR NOT.
RESPONDING WITH "CAN" OR "CAN'T" IS JUST GRAMMATICALLY INCORRECT, RIGHT?
WELL, HOW AM I SUPPOSED TO DIVE WHEN I CAN'T EVEN SWIM?
WHATEVER. THAT KINDA THING WILL JUST WORK ITSELF OUT.
I DON'T THINK IT'S THAT SIMPLE...
YOU WON'T GET ANYWHERE IF YOU ONLY TRY THINGS YOU CAN ALREADY DO.

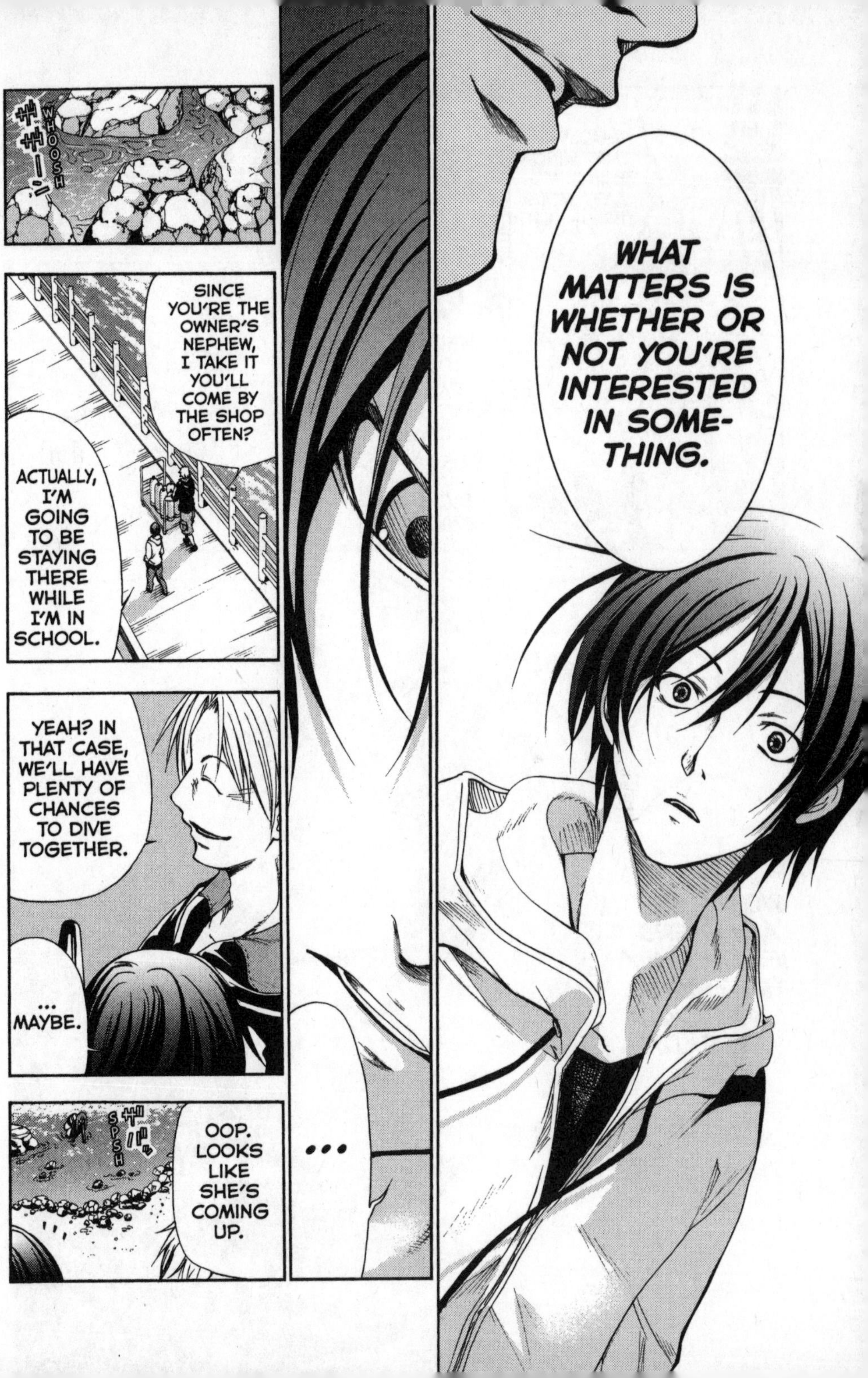
WHAT MATTERS IS WHETHER OR NOT YOU'RE INTERESTED IN SOME-THING.
...
WHOOSH
SINCE YOU'RE THE OWNER'S NEPHEW, I TAKE IT YOU'LL COME BY THE SHOP OFTEN?
ACTUALLY, I'M GOING TO BE STAYING THERE WHILE I'M IN SCHOOL.
YEAH? IN THAT CASE, WE'LL HAVE PLENTY OF CHANCES TO DIVE TOGETHER.
... MAYBE.
SPSH
OOP. LOOKS LIKE SHE'S COMING UP.

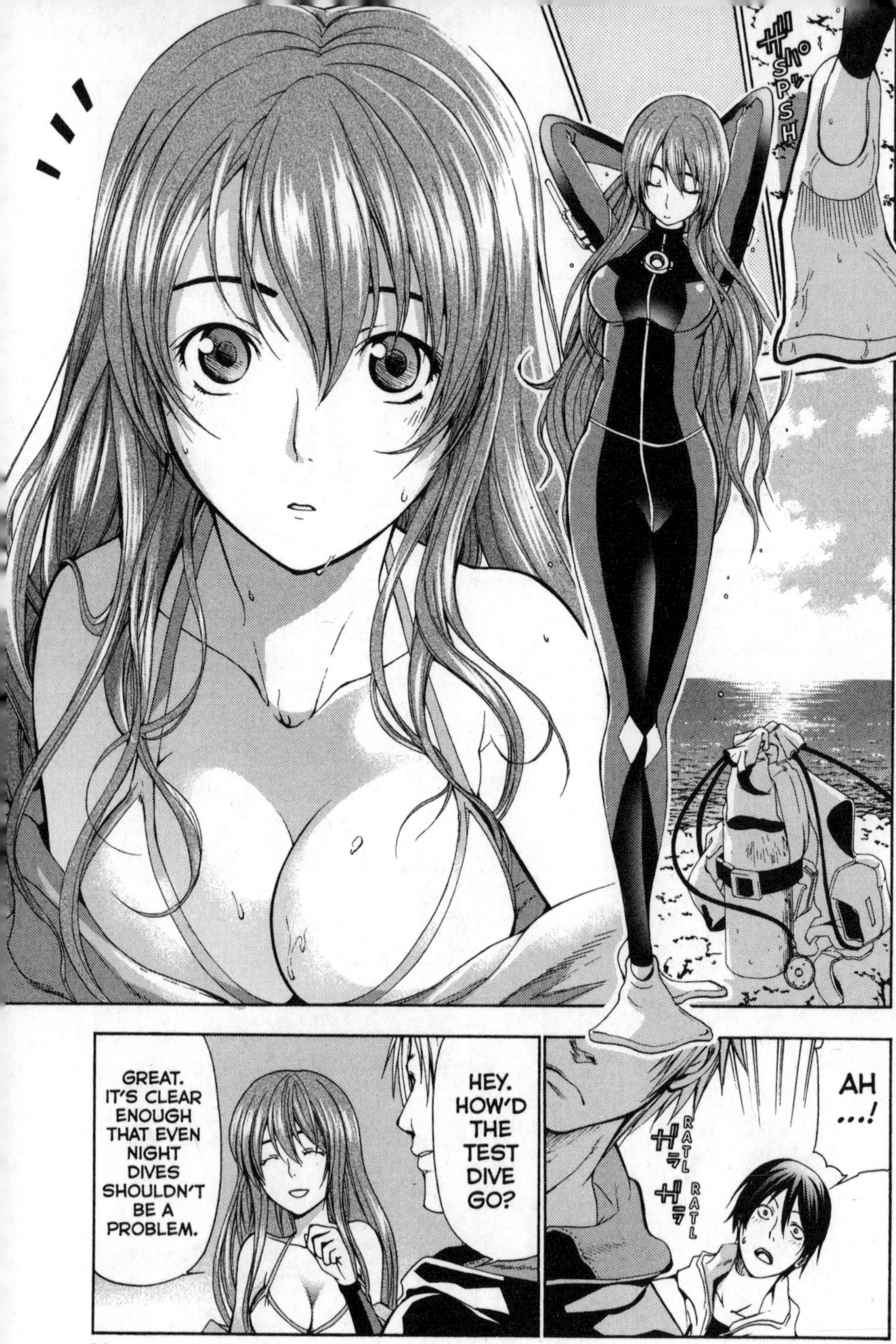
SPSH
AH ...!
RATL
RATL
HEY. HOW'D THE TEST DIVE GO?
GREAT. IT'S CLEAR ENOUGH THAT EVEN NIGHT DIVES SHOULDN'T BE A PROBLEM.

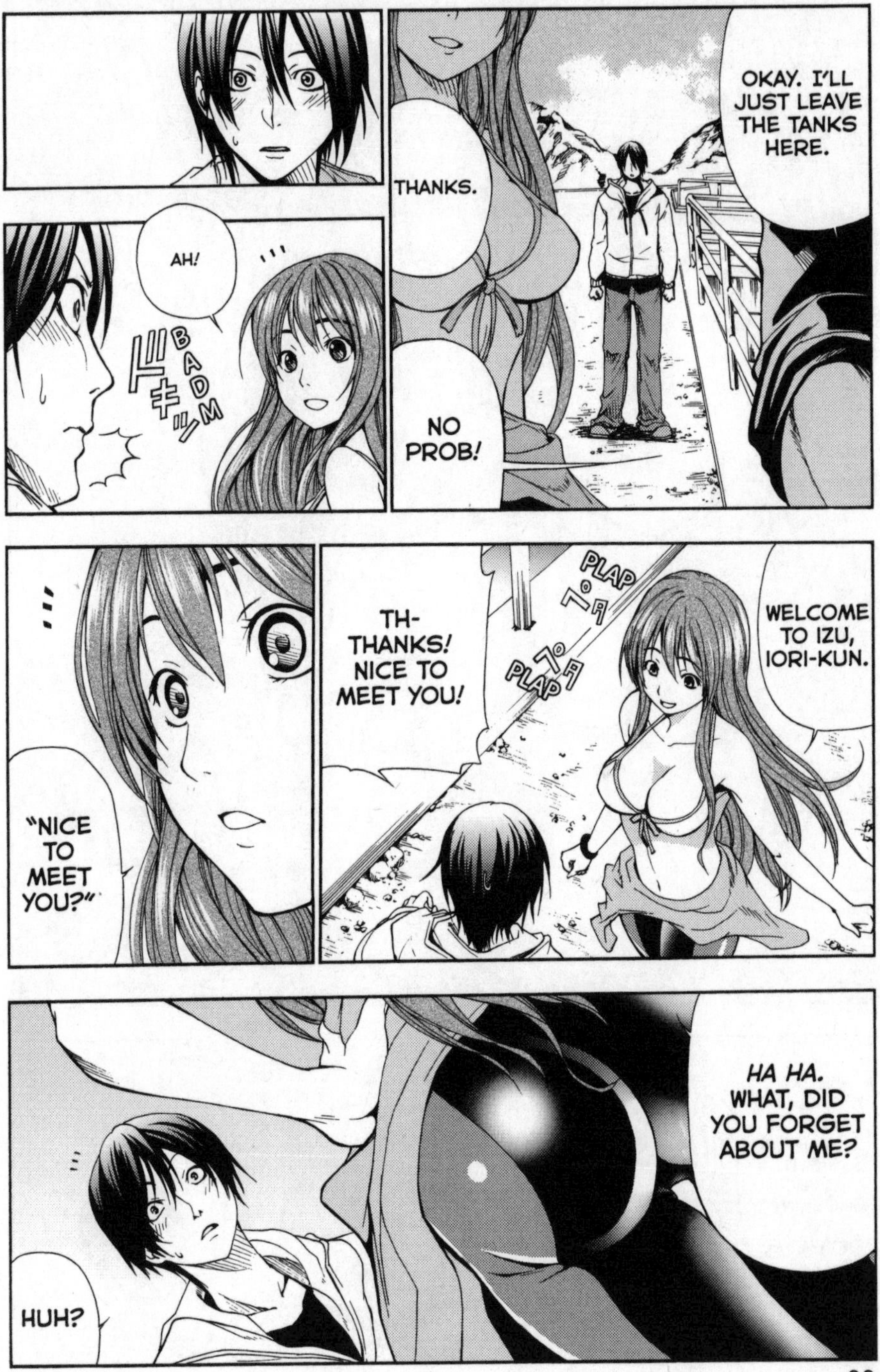
OKAY. I'LL JUST LEAVE THE TANKS HERE.
THANKS.
NO PROB!
AH!
BADM
ドキッ
WELCOME TO IZU, IORI-KUN.
PLAP
ペタ
PLAP
ペタ
TH- THANKS! NICE TO MEET YOU!
"NICE TO MEET YOU?"
HA HA. WHAT, DID YOU FORGET ABOUT ME?
HUH?

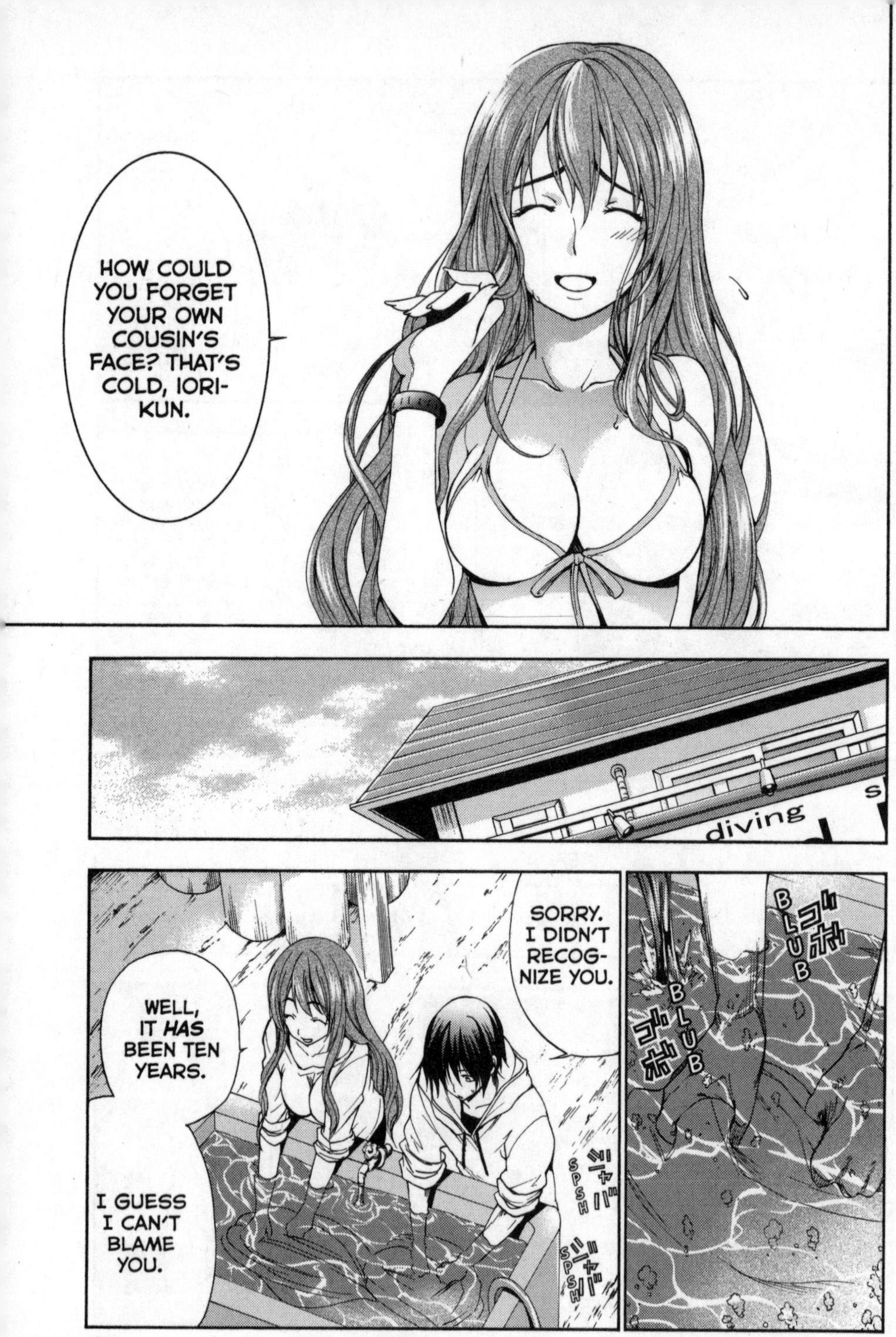
HOW COULD YOU FORGET YOUR OWN COUSIN'S FACE? THAT'S COLD, IORI-KUN.
diving
BLUB
ゴボ
BLUB
ゴボ
SORRY. I DIDN'T RECOG-NIZE YOU.
WELL, IT *HAS* BEEN TEN YEARS.
SPSH
SPSH
I GUESS I CAN'T BLAME YOU.

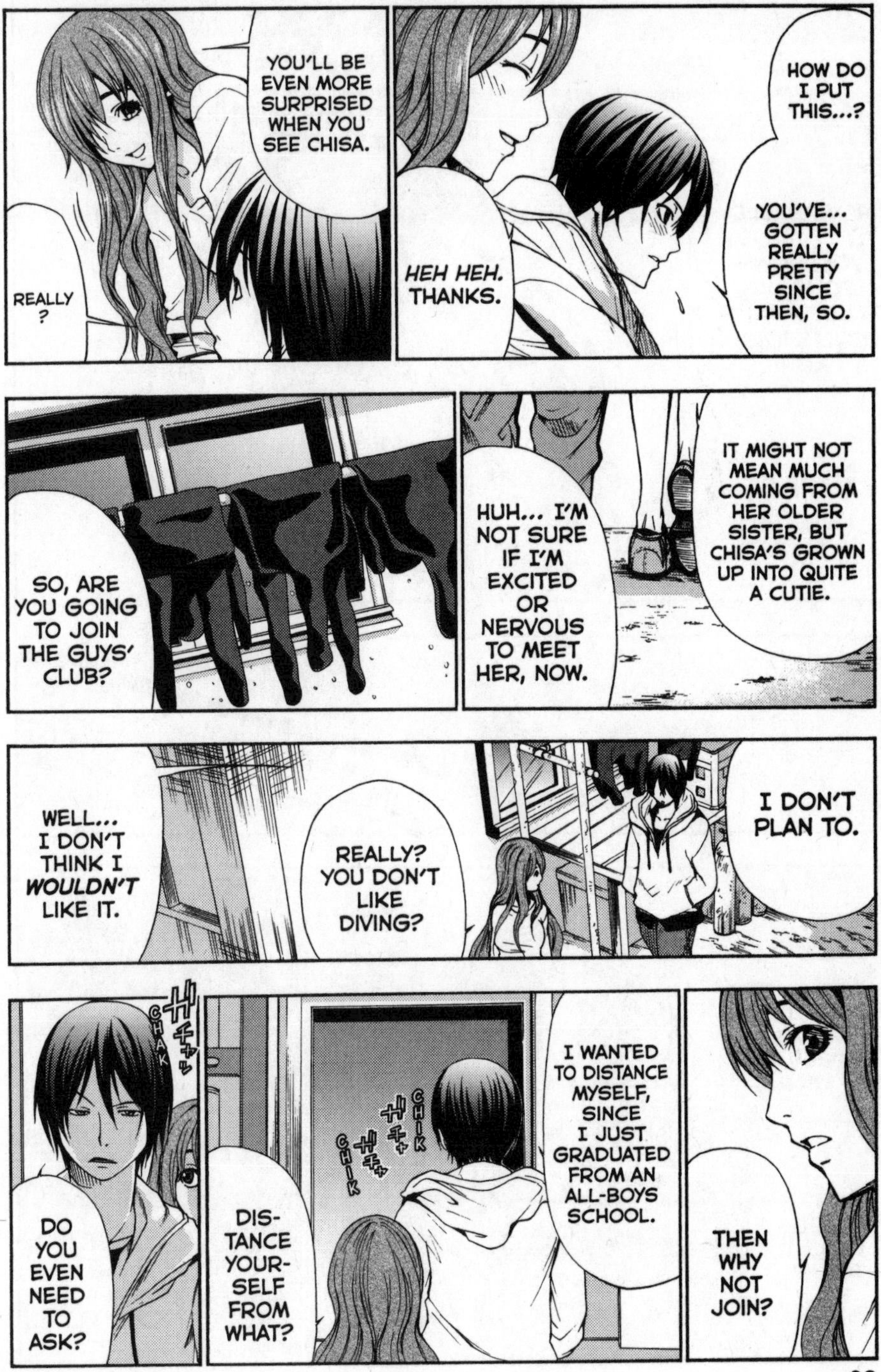
HOW DO I PUT THIS...?
YOU'VE... GOTTEN REALLY PRETTY SINCE THEN, SO.
HEH HEH. THANKS.
YOU'LL BE EVEN MORE SURPRISED WHEN YOU SEE CHISA.
REALLY?
IT MIGHT NOT MEAN MUCH COMING FROM HER OLDER SISTER, BUT CHISA'S GROWN UP INTO QUITE A CUTIE.
HUH... I'M NOT SURE IF I'M EXCITED OR NERVOUS TO MEET HER, NOW.
SO, ARE YOU GOING TO JOIN THE GUYS' CLUB?
I DON'T PLAN TO.
REALLY? YOU DON'T LIKE DIVING?
WELL... I DON'T THINK I WOULDN'T LIKE IT.
THEN WHY NOT JOIN?
I WANTED TO DISTANCE MYSELF, SINCE I JUST GRADUATED FROM AN ALL-BOYS SCHOOL.
CHIK
CHIK
DIS-TANCE YOUR-SELF FROM WHAT?
CHAK
DO YOU EVEN NEED TO ASK?

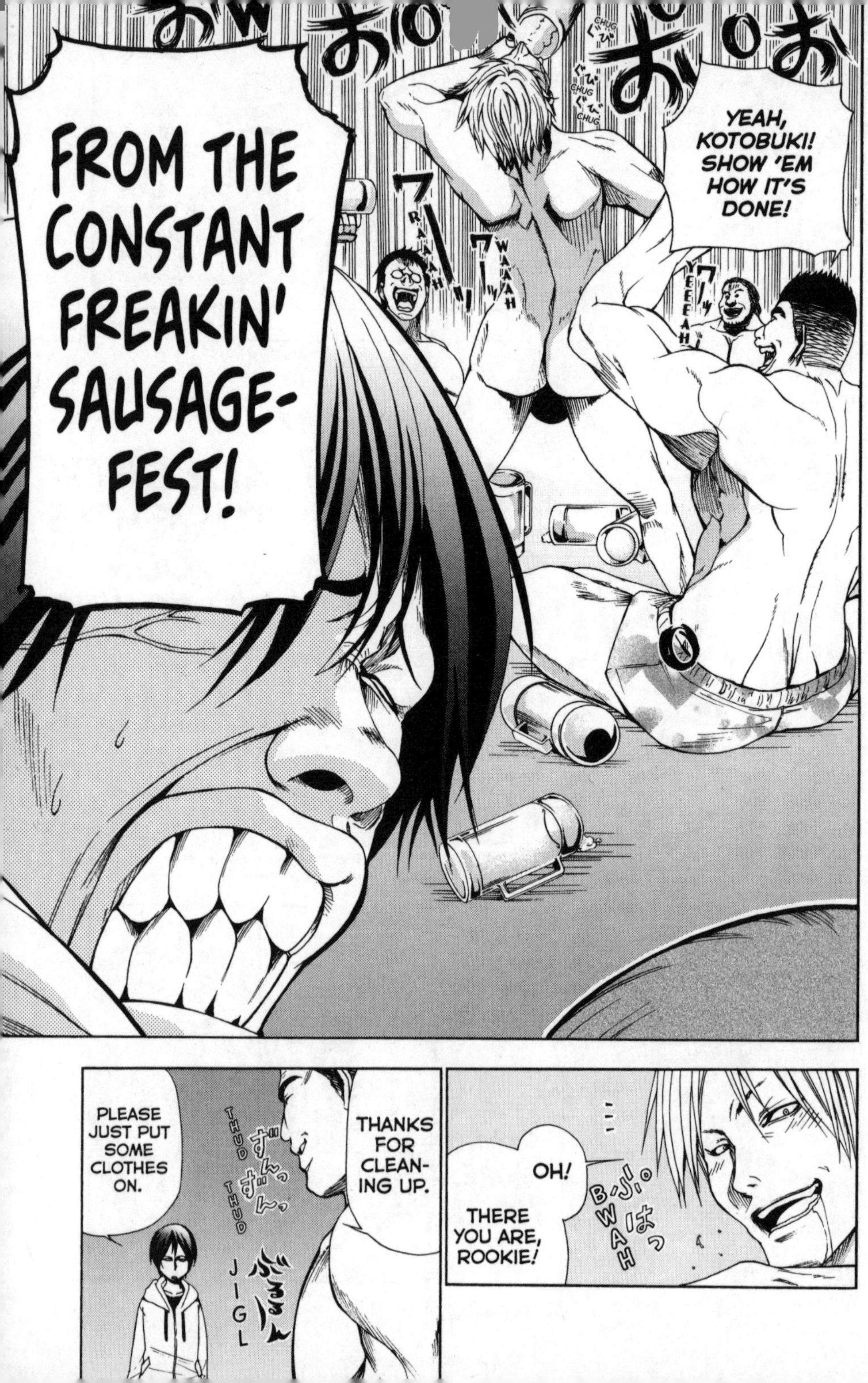
YEAH, KOTOBUKI! SHOW 'EM HOW IT'S DONE!
CHUG CHUG CHUG
YEEEAH!
WAAAH
RAAAAH
FROM THE CONSTANT FREAKIN' SAUSAGE-FEST!
...
OH!
BWAH
THERE YOU ARE, ROOKIE!
THANKS FOR CLEANING UP.
THUD THUD
JIGL
PLEASE JUST PUT SOME CLOTHES ON.

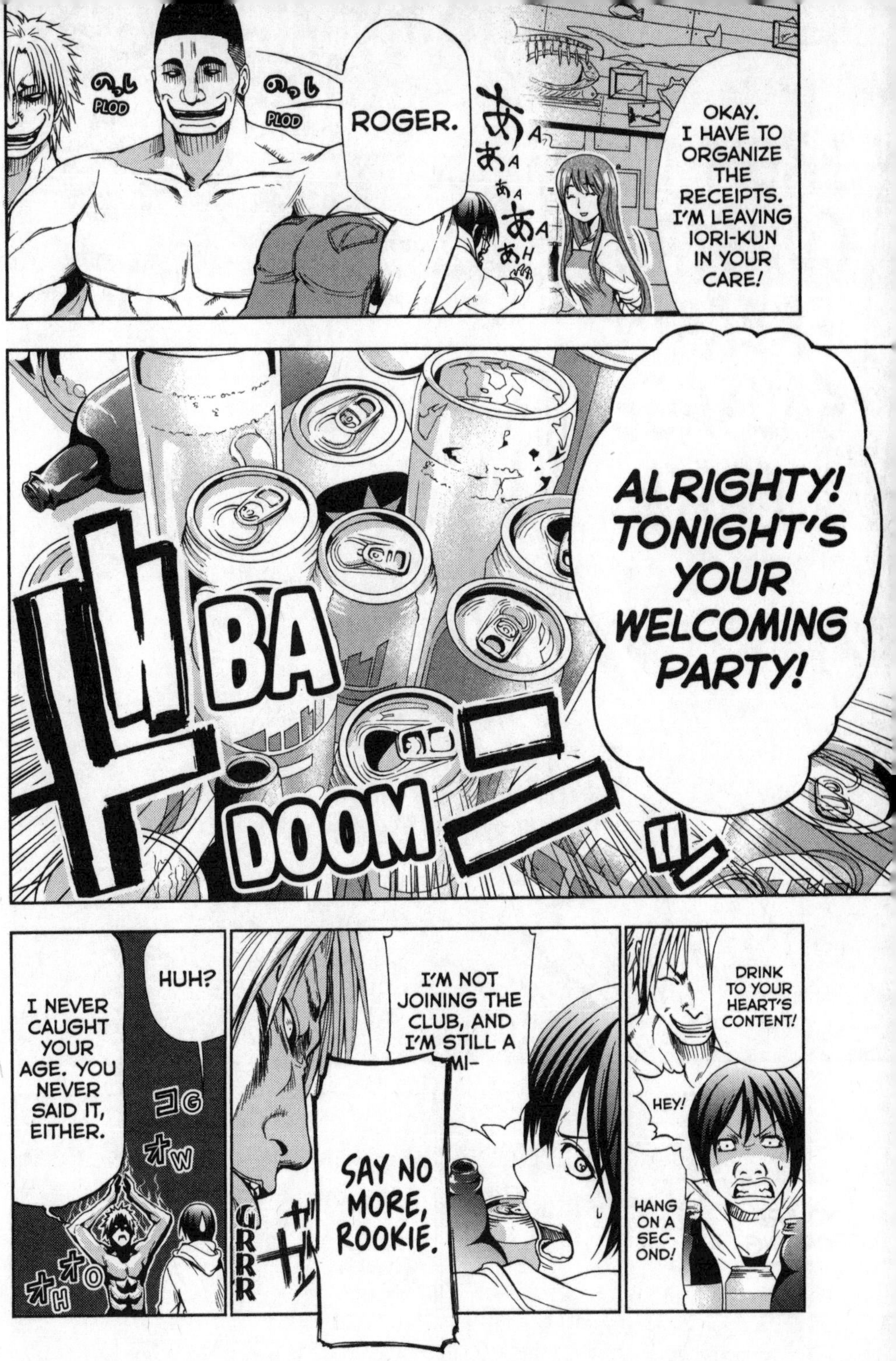
OKAY. I HAVE TO ORGANIZE THE RECEIPTS. I'M LEAVING IORI-KUN IN YOUR CARE!
あA あA あA あA あH
ROGER.
のっし PLOD
のっし PLOD
ALRIGHTY! TONIGHT'S YOUR WELCOMING PARTY!
BA
DOOM
DRINK TO YOUR HEART'S CONTENT!
HEY!
HANG ON A SEC-OND!
I'M NOT JOINING THE CLUB, AND I'M STILL A MI-
SAY NO MORE, ROOKIE.
GRRR
HUH?
I NEVER CAUGHT YOUR AGE. YOU NEVER SAID IT, EITHER.
ゴG
オW
オO
オH

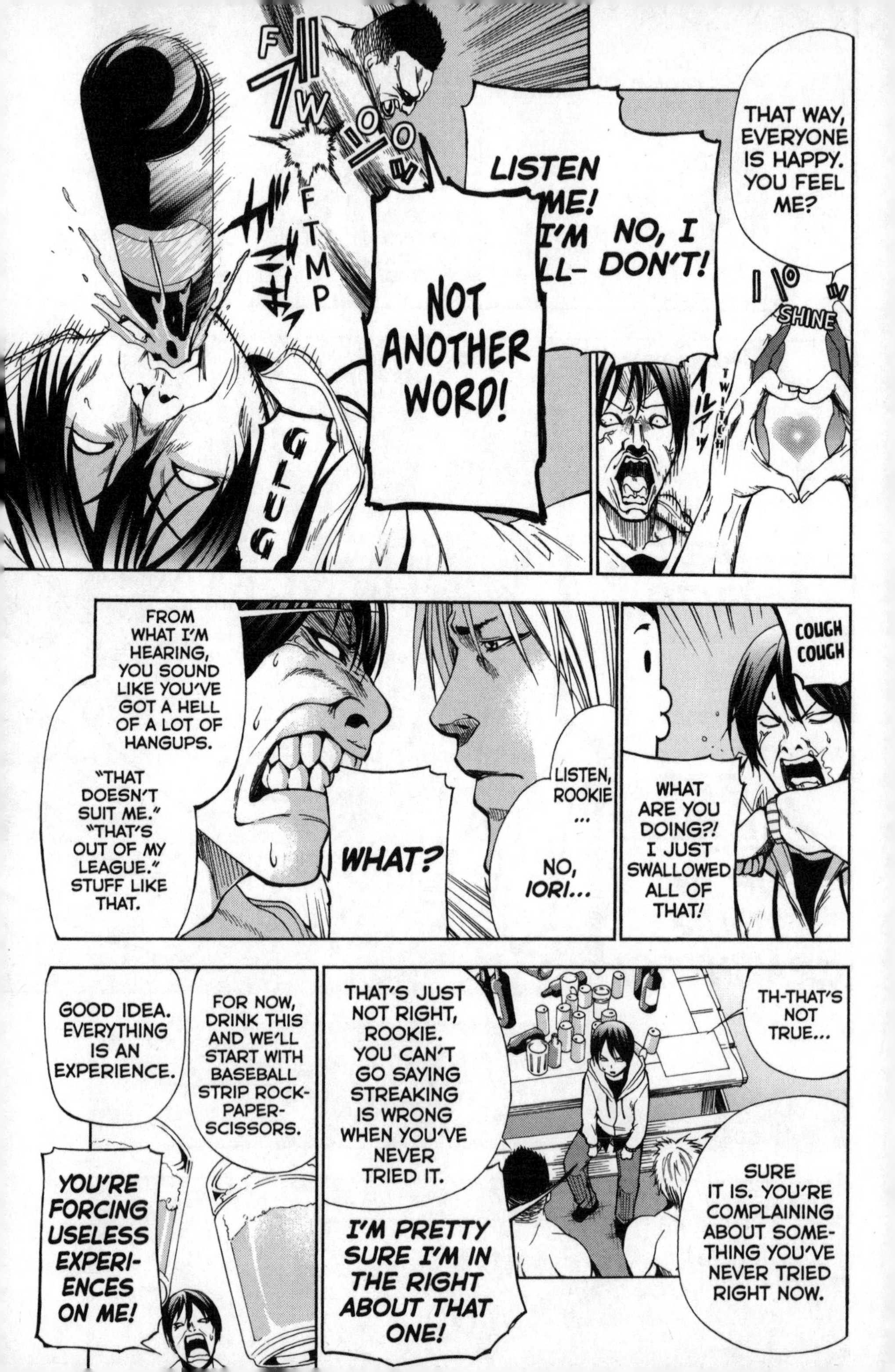
THAT WAY, EVERYONE IS HAPPY. YOU FEEL ME?
SHINE
TWITCH
NO, I DON'T!
LISTEN ME! I'M LL-
NOT ANOTHER WORD!
FTMP
GLUG
COUGH COUGH
WHAT ARE YOU DOING?! I JUST SWALLOWED ALL OF THAT!
LISTEN, ROOKIE ...
NO, IORI...
WHAT?
FROM WHAT I'M HEARING, YOU SOUND LIKE YOU'VE GOT A HELL OF A LOT OF HANGUPS.
"THAT DOESN'T SUIT ME." "THAT'S OUT OF MY LEAGUE." STUFF LIKE THAT.
TH-THAT'S NOT TRUE...
SURE IT IS. YOU'RE COMPLAINING ABOUT SOME-THING YOU'VE NEVER TRIED RIGHT NOW.
THAT'S JUST NOT RIGHT, ROOKIE. YOU CAN'T GO SAYING STREAKING IS WRONG WHEN YOU'VE NEVER TRIED IT.
I'M PRETTY SURE I'M IN THE RIGHT ABOUT THAT ONE!
FOR NOW, DRINK THIS AND WE'LL START WITH BASEBALL STRIP ROCK-PAPER-SCISSORS.
GOOD IDEA. EVERYTHING IS AN EXPERIENCE.
YOU'RE FORCING USELESS EXPERI-ENCES ON ME!

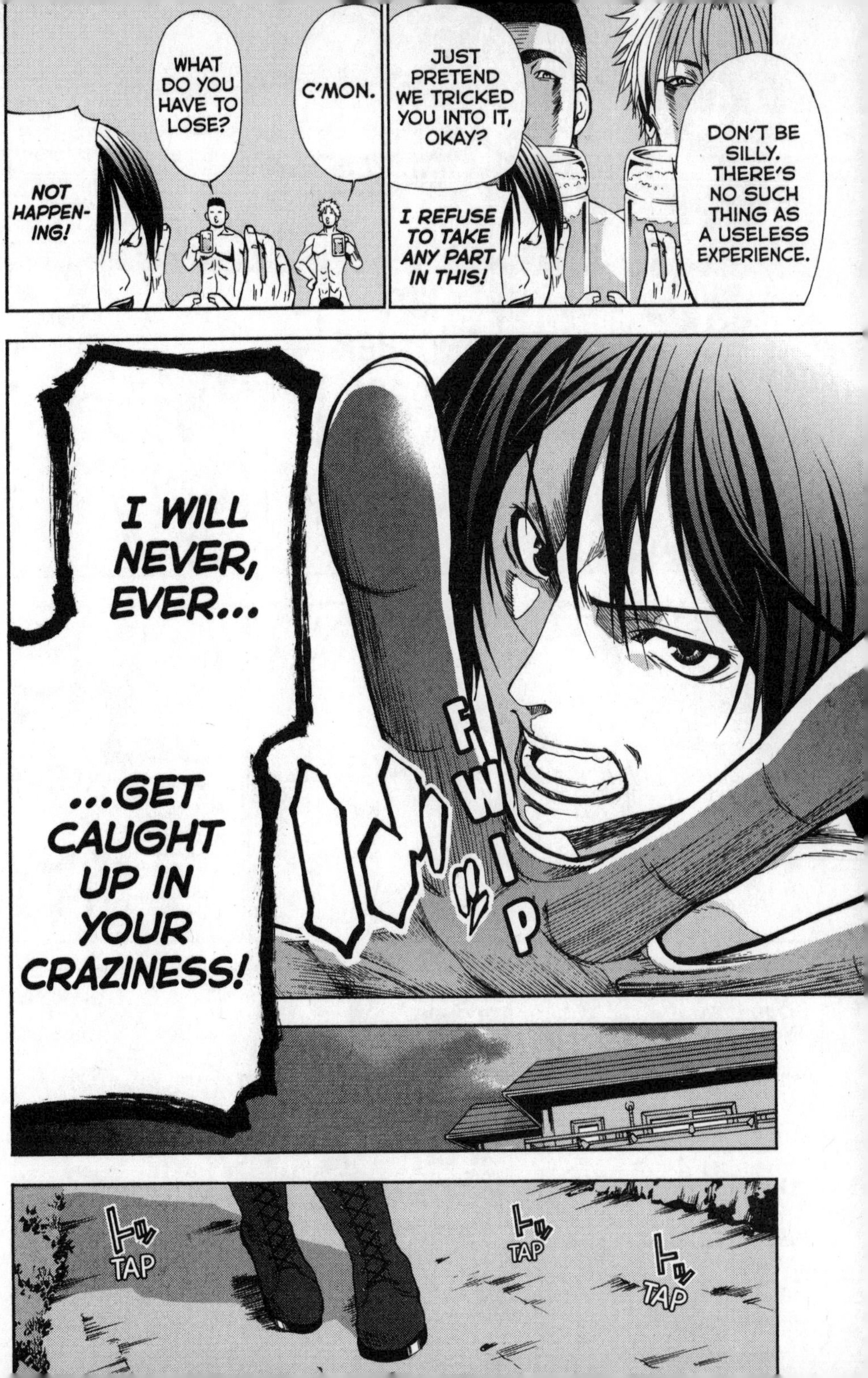
DON'T BE SILLY. THERE'S NO SUCH THING AS A USELESS EXPERIENCE.
JUST PRETEND WE TRICKED YOU INTO IT, OKAY?
I REFUSE TO TAKE ANY PART IN THIS!
C'MON.
WHAT DO YOU HAVE TO LOSE?
NOT HAPPEN-ING!
FWIP
I WILL NEVER, EVER...
...GET CAUGHT UP IN YOUR CRAZINESS!
トッ TAP
トッ TAP
トッ TAP

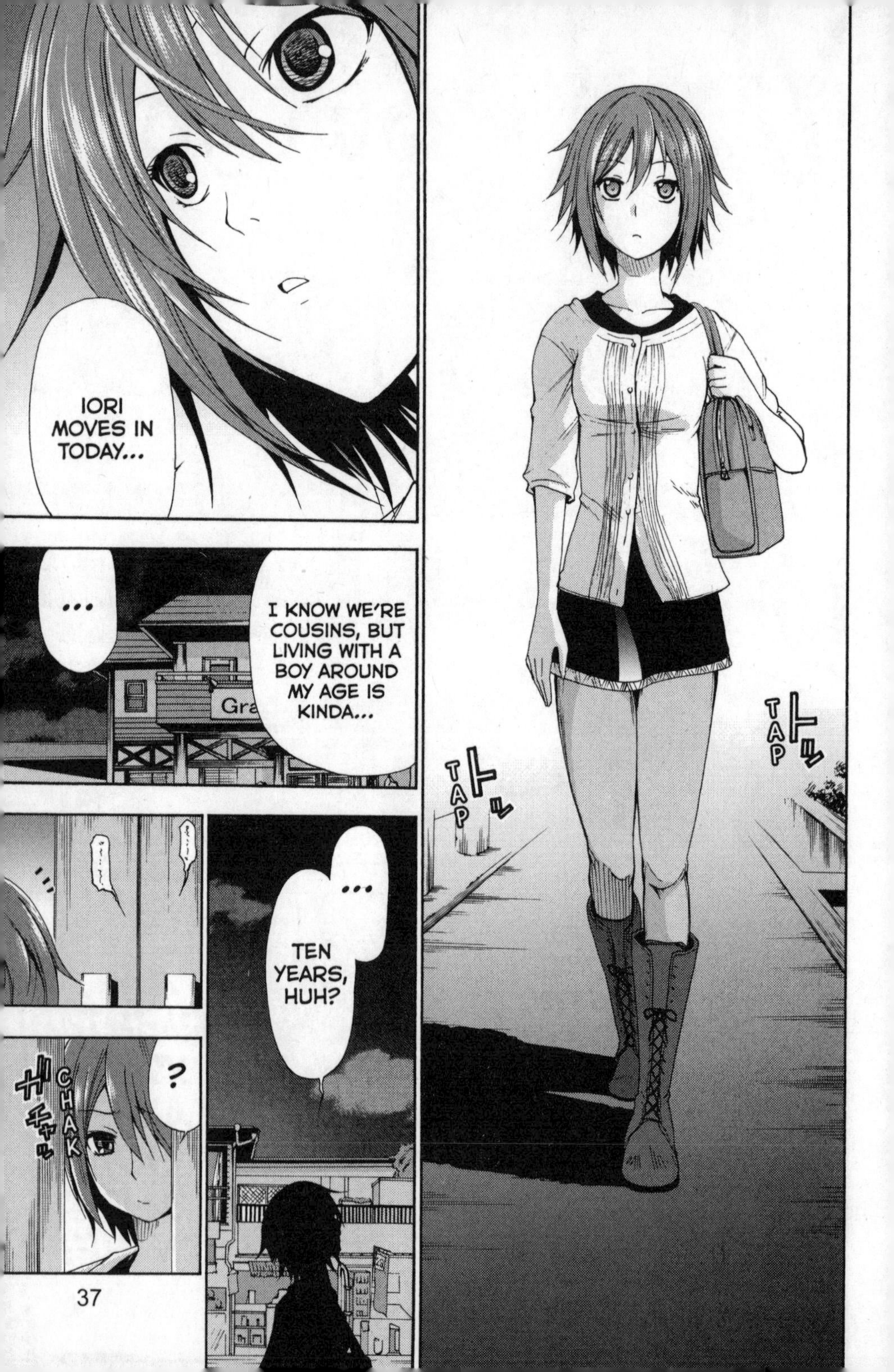
TAP
TAP
IORI MOVES IN TODAY...
I KNOW WE'RE COUSINS, BUT LIVING WITH A BOY AROUND MY AGE IS KINDA...
...
...
TEN YEARS, HUH?
?
CHAK

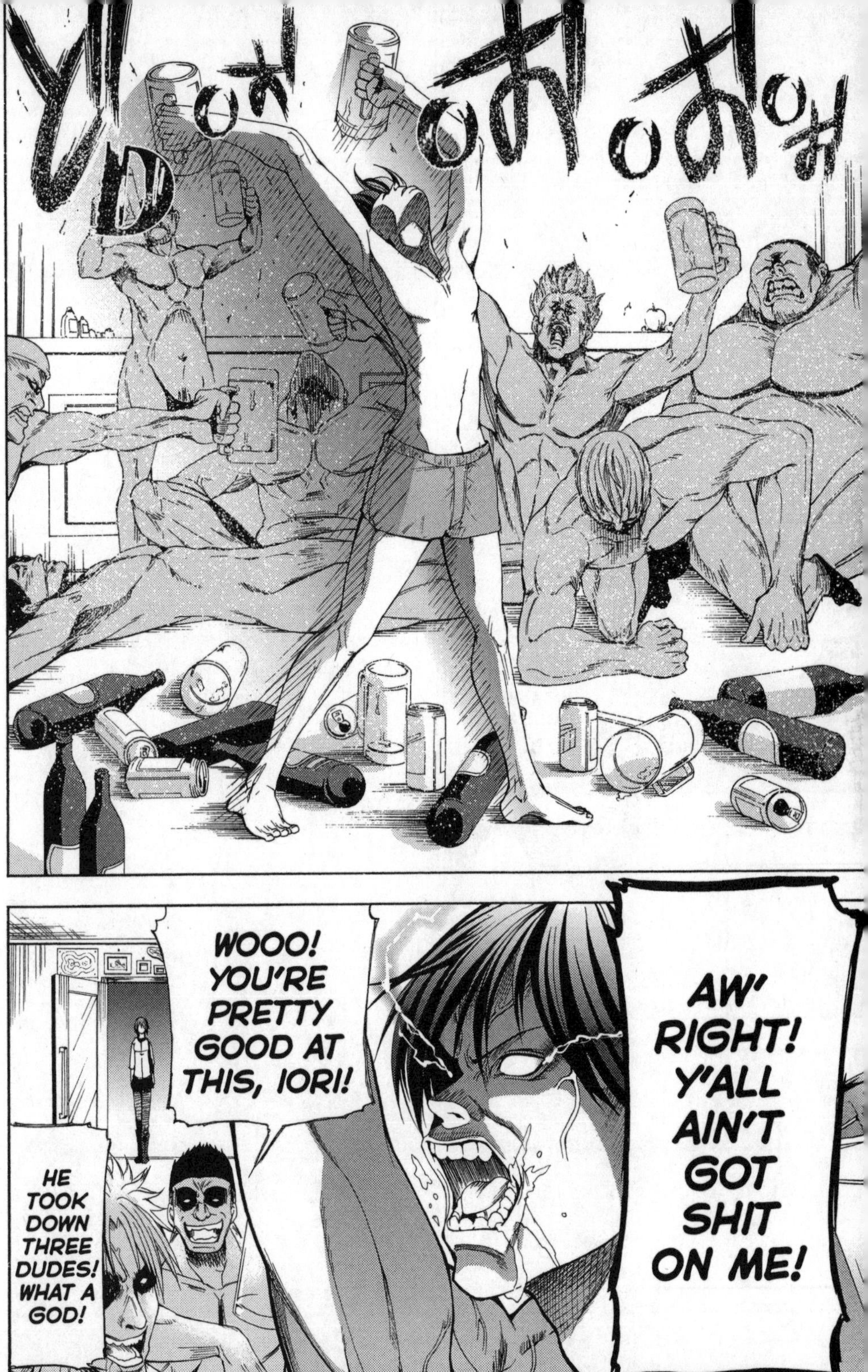
AW' RIGHT! Y'ALL AIN'T GOT SHIT ON ME!
WOOO! YOU'RE PRETTY GOOD AT THIS, IORI!
HE TOOK DOWN THREE DUDES! WHAT A GOD!

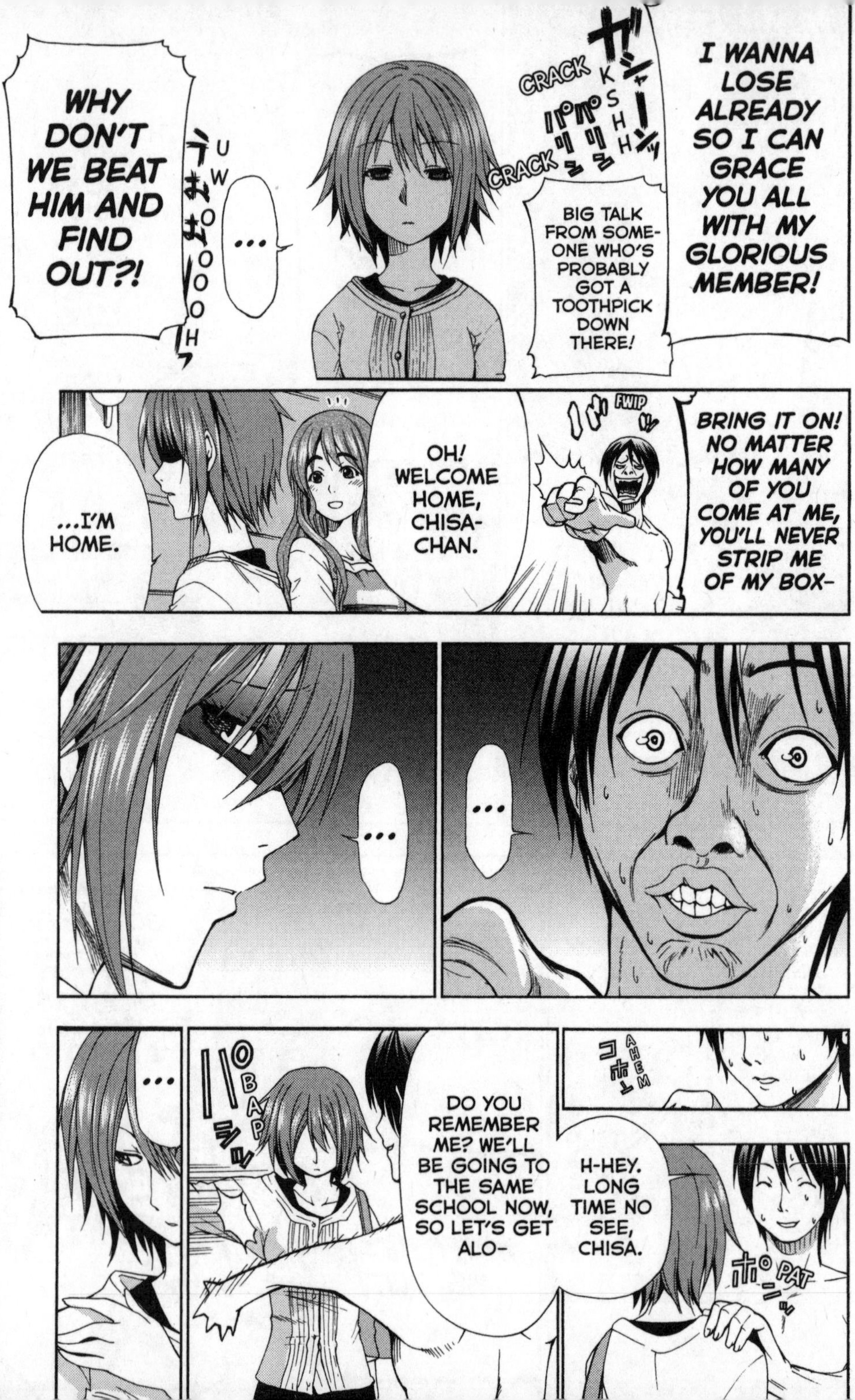
I WANNA LOSE ALREADY SO I CAN GRACE YOU ALL WITH MY GLORIOUS MEMBER!
CRACK
KSHH
CRACK
BIG TALK FROM SOME-ONE WHO'S PROBABLY GOT A TOOTHPICK DOWN THERE!
...
UWOOOOOH
WHY DON'T WE BEAT HIM AND FIND OUT?!
BRING IT ON! NO MATTER HOW MANY OF YOU COME AT ME, YOU'LL NEVER STRIP ME OF MY BOX-
FWIP
OH! WELCOME HOME, CHISA-CHAN.
...I'M HOME.
...
...
AHEM
H-HEY. LONG TIME NO SEE, CHISA.
PAT
DO YOU REMEMBER ME? WE'LL BE GOING TO THE SAME SCHOOL NOW, SO LET'S GET ALO-
OBAP
...

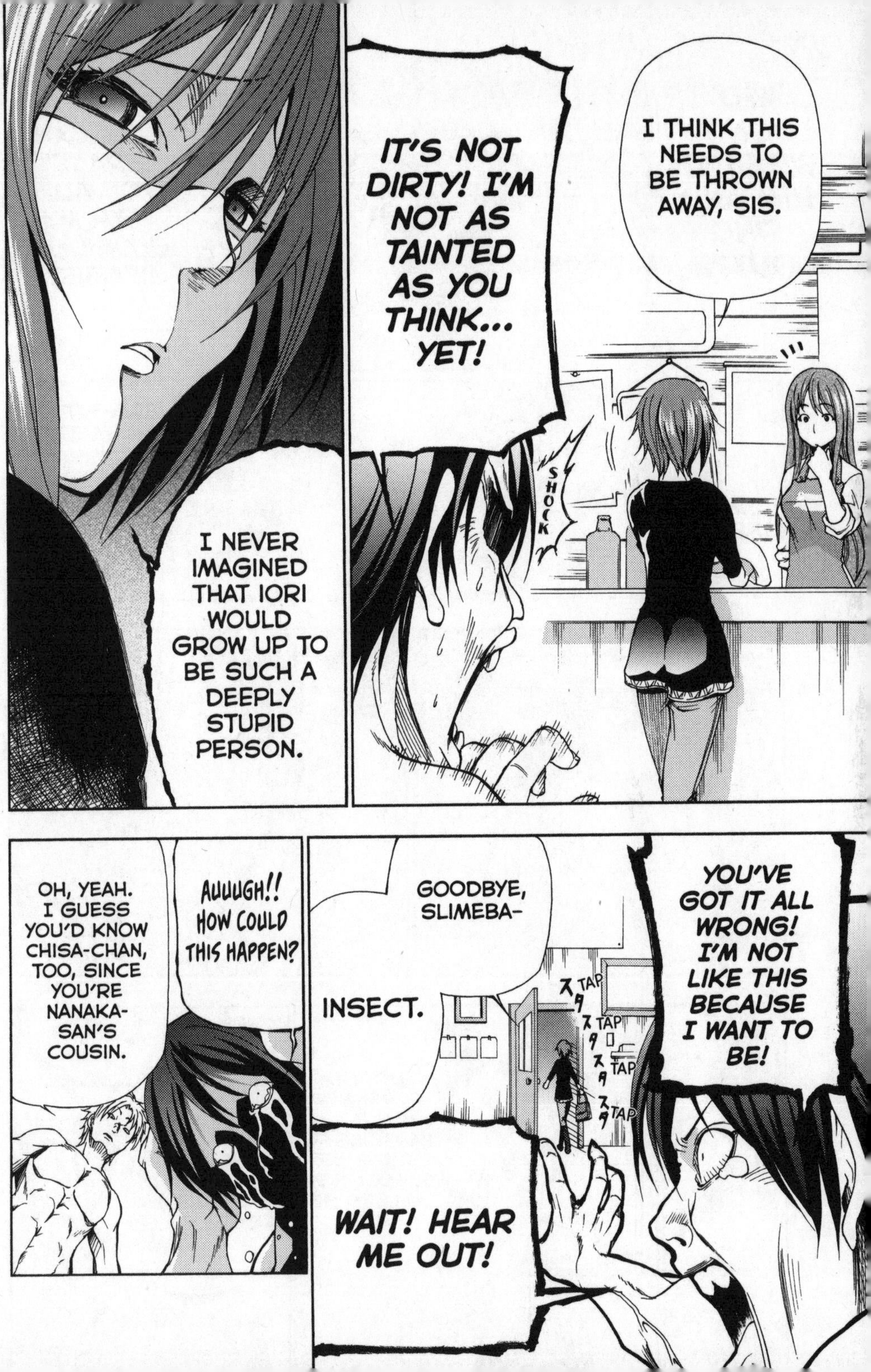
I THINK THIS NEEDS TO BE THROWN AWAY, SIS.
SHOCK
IT'S NOT DIRTY! I'M NOT AS TAINTED AS YOU THINK... YET!
I NEVER IMAGINED THAT IORI WOULD GROW UP TO BE SUCH A DEEPLY STUPID PERSON.
YOU'VE GOT IT ALL WRONG! I'M NOT LIKE THIS BECAUSE I WANT TO BE!
GOODBYE, SLIMEBA-
INSECT.
TAP
TAP
TAP
TAP
WAIT! HEAR ME OUT!
AUUUGH!! HOW COULD THIS HAPPEN?
OH, YEAH. I GUESS YOU'D KNOW CHISA-CHAN, TOO, SINCE YOU'RE NANAKA-SAN'S COUSIN.

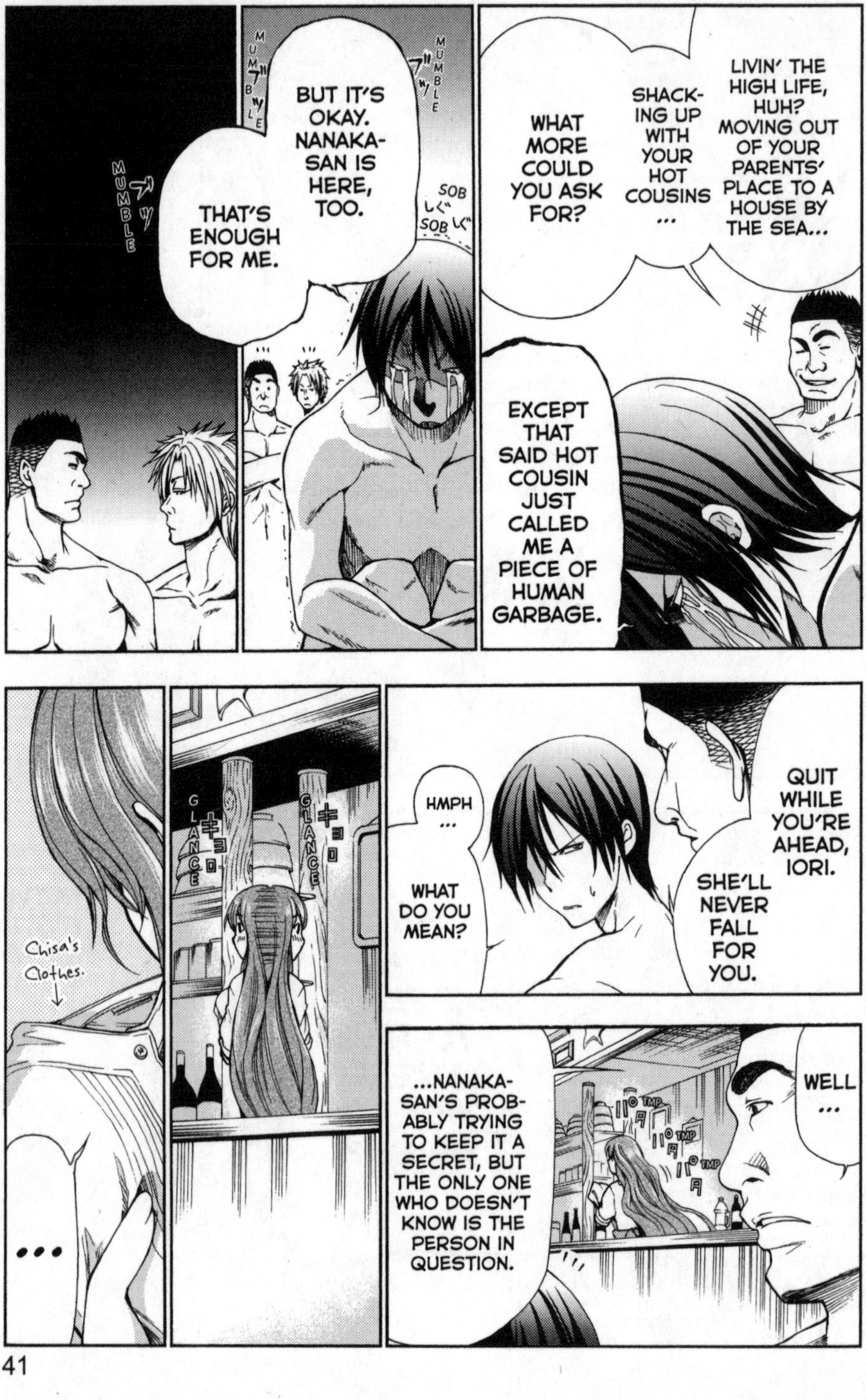
LIVIN' THE HIGH LIFE, HUH? MOVING OUT OF YOUR PARENTS' PLACE TO A HOUSE BY THE SEA...
SHACKING UP WITH YOUR HOT COUSINS...
WHAT MORE COULD YOU ASK FOR?
EXCEPT THAT SAID HOT COUSIN JUST CALLED ME A PIECE OF HUMAN GARBAGE.
MUMBLE
MUMBLE
BUT IT'S OKAY. NANAKA-SAN IS HERE, TOO.
SOB SOB
THAT'S ENOUGH FOR ME.
MUMBLE
QUIT WHILE YOU'RE AHEAD, IORI.
SHE'LL NEVER FALL FOR YOU.
HMPH...
WHAT DO YOU MEAN?
WELL...
...NANAKA-SAN'S PROBABLY TRYING TO KEEP IT A SECRET, BUT THE ONLY ONE WHO DOESN'T KNOW IS THE PERSON IN QUESTION.
TMP TMP TMP
GLANCE
GLANCE
Chisa's Clothes.
...

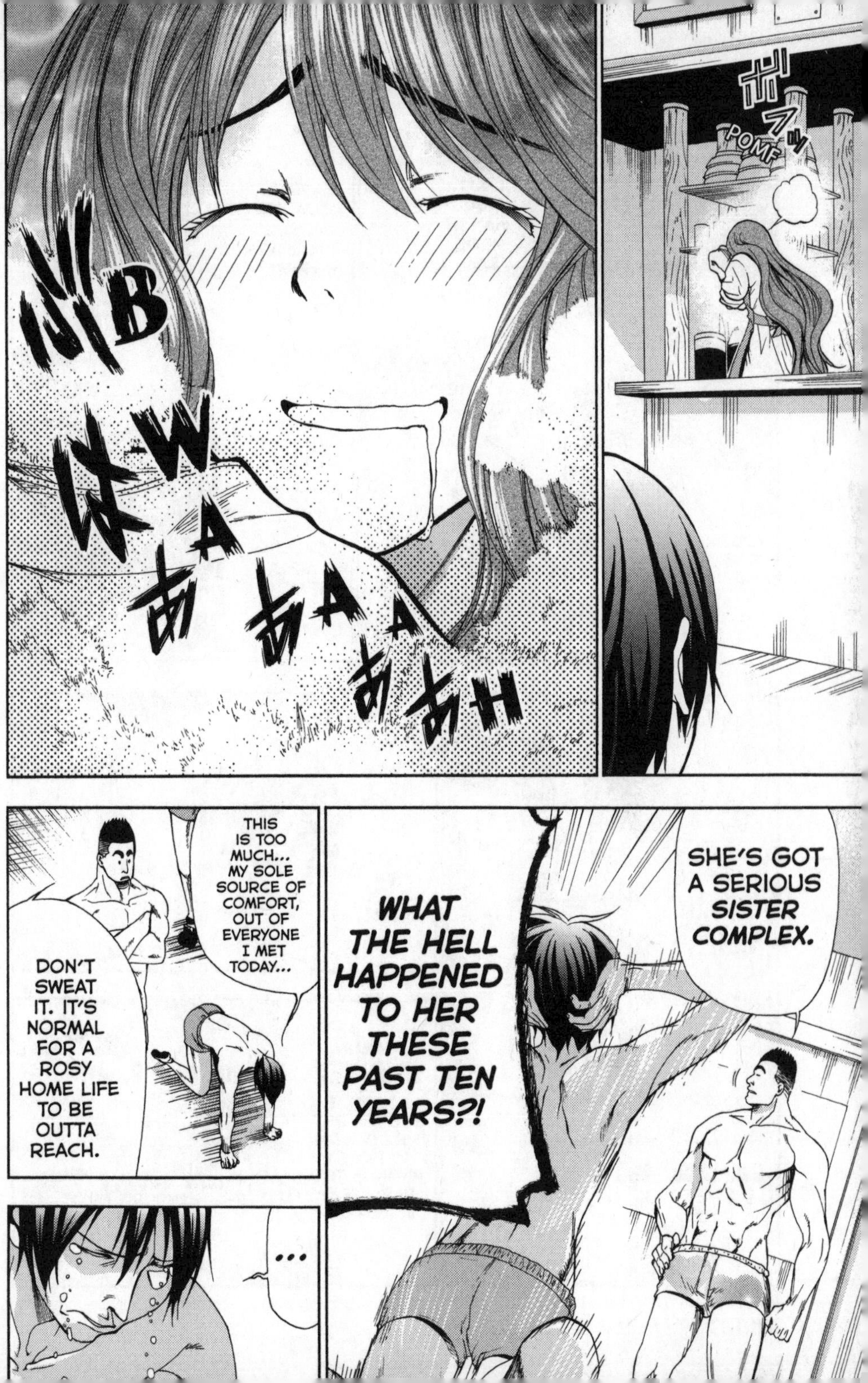

ポフッ
POMF
BWAAAH
SHE'S GOT A SERIOUS SISTER COMPLEX.
WHAT THE HELL HAPPENED TO HER THESE PAST TEN YEARS?!
THIS IS TOO MUCH... MY SOLE SOURCE OF COMFORT, OUT OF EVERYONE I MET TODAY...
DON'T SWEAT IT. IT'S NORMAL FOR A ROSY HOME LIFE TO BE OUTTA REACH.
...

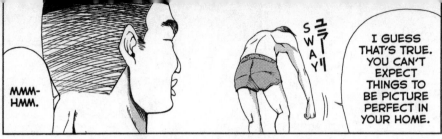

I GUESS THAT'S TRUE. YOU CAN'T EXPECT THINGS TO BE PICTURE PERFECT IN YOUR HOME.
SWAY
MMM-HMM.
IN THAT CASE, I'LL PUT ALL MY EFFORT INTO HAVING THE BEST COLLEGE LIFE POSSIBLE! I'M GOING TO MEET CUTE GIRLS, FALL IN LOVE, AND ENJOY THE PINNACLE OF MY YOUTH WITH GOOD FRIENDS!
OOH. SOMEONE'S GETTIN' FIRED UP.
BUT OF COURSE! I'M FINALLY A COLLEGE STUDENT! MARK MY WORDS, I'M GOING TO HAVE THE BEST CAMPUS LIFE. LIKE SOMETHING STRAIGHT OUT OF TV!
I SEE. WELL, ENOUGH NON-SENSE. LET'S DRINK.
Here.
DID YOU JUST CALL MY AMBITIONS "NON-SENSE?"
WHAT'S THAT? YOU WANT ME TO TELL YOU WHICH CLASSES ARE THE EASIEST?
I AM IN YOUR CARE, SENPAI.
YOU'RE SURE EASY TO UNDER-STAND. I LIKE THAT.
WHISH

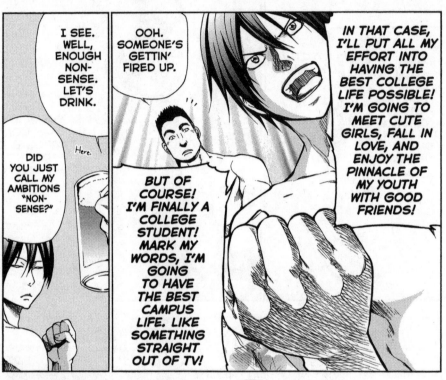

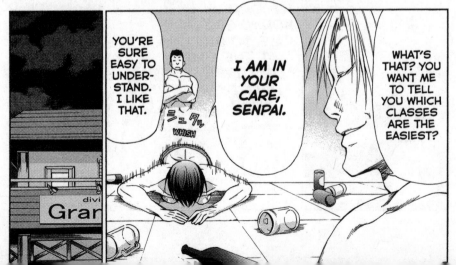

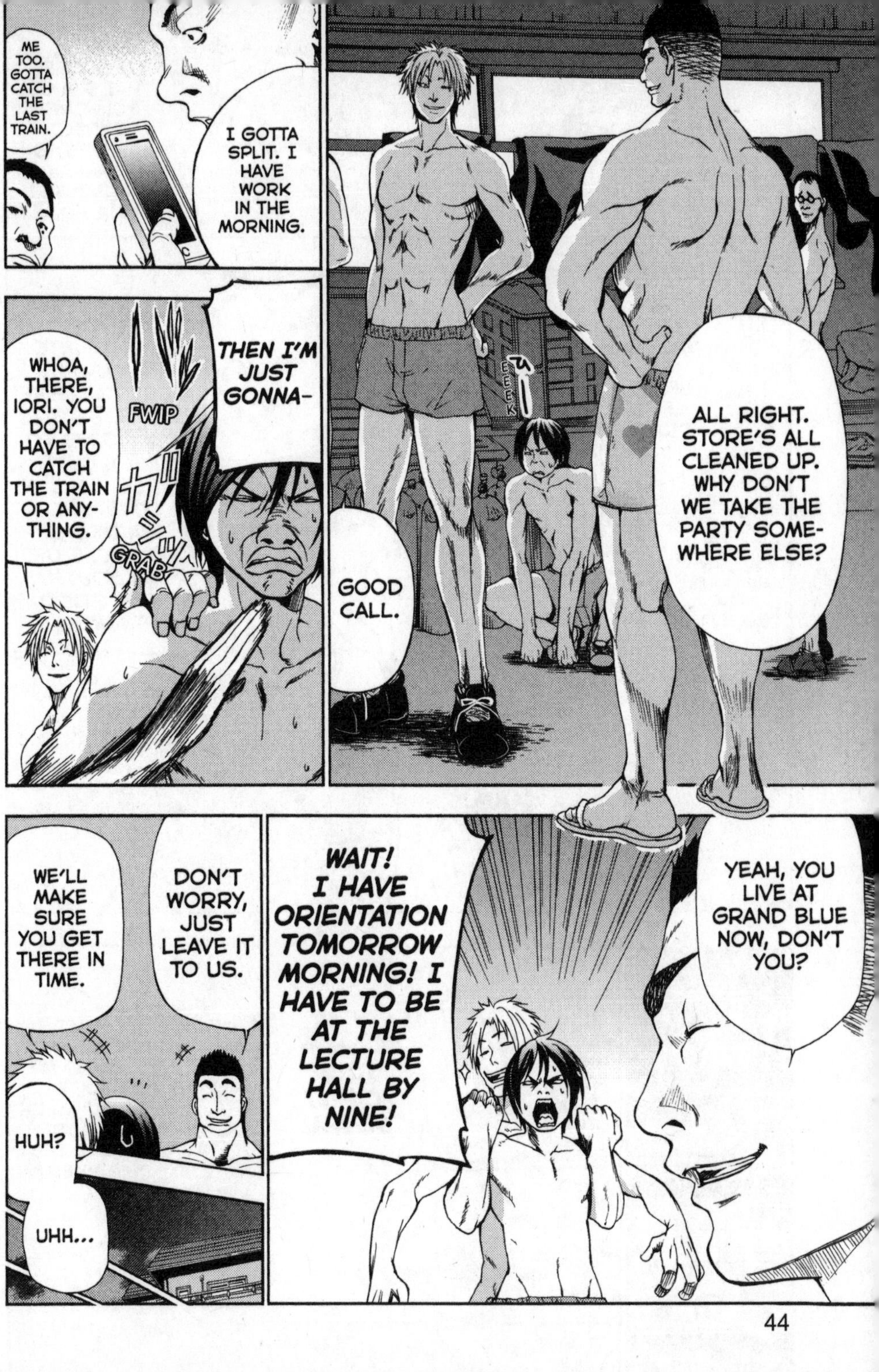
ALL RIGHT. STORE'S ALL CLEANED UP. WHY DON'T WE TAKE THE PARTY SOMEWHERE ELSE?
EEEK
GOOD CALL.
I GOTTA SPLIT. I HAVE WORK IN THE MORNING.
ME TOO. GOTTA CATCH THE LAST TRAIN.
THEN I'M JUST GONNA-
FWIP
GRAB
WHOA, THERE, IORI. YOU DON'T HAVE TO CATCH THE TRAIN OR ANYTHING.
YEAH, YOU LIVE AT GRAND BLUE NOW, DON'T YOU?
WAIT! I HAVE ORIENTATION TOMORROW MORNING! I HAVE TO BE AT THE LECTURE HALL BY NINE!
DON'T WORRY, JUST LEAVE IT TO US.
WE'LL MAKE SURE YOU GET THERE IN TIME.
HUH?
UHH...

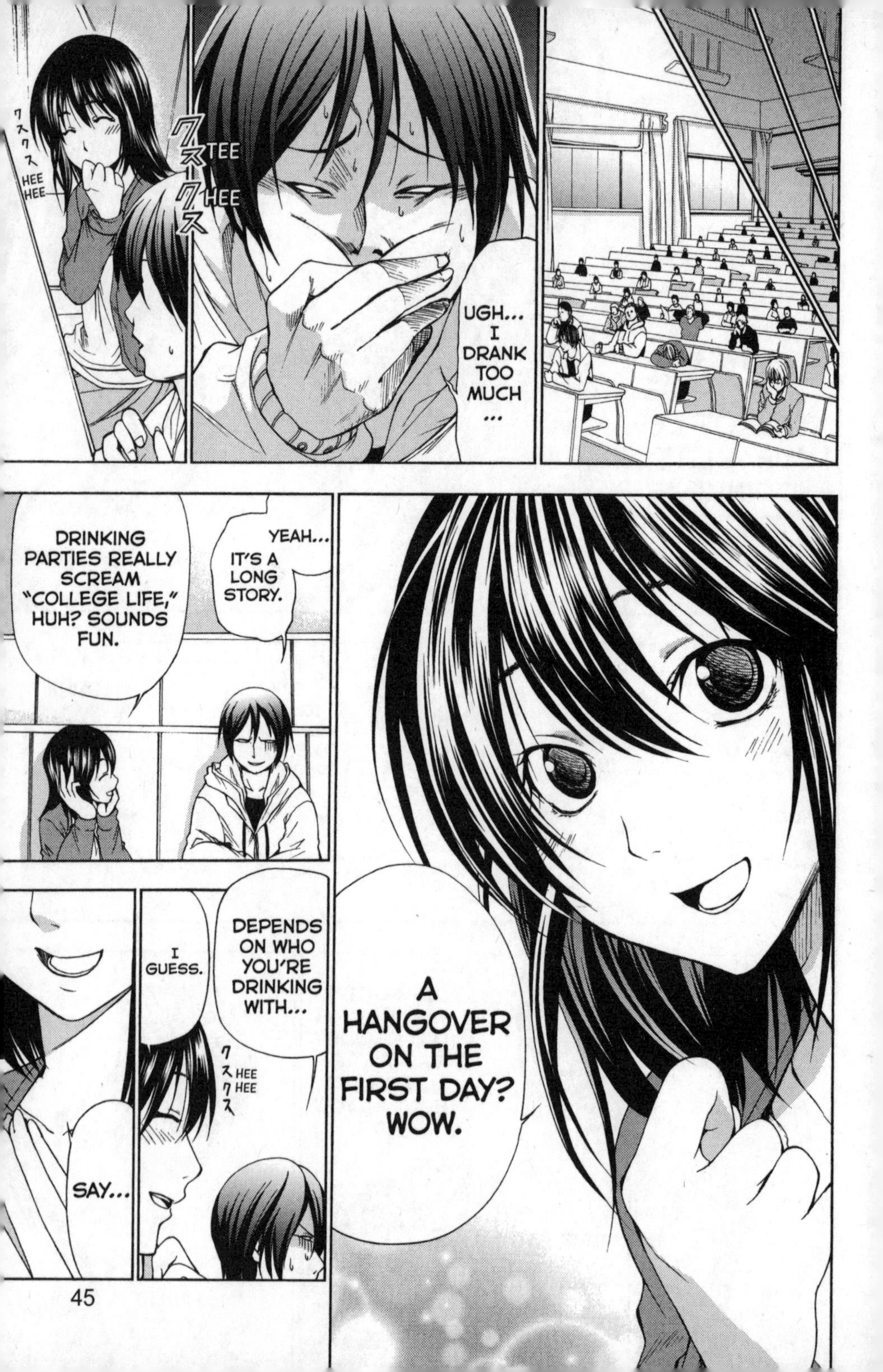
クスクス
TEE HEE
UGH... I DRANK TOO MUCH...
クスクス
HEE HEE
A HANGOVER ON THE FIRST DAY? WOW.
YEAH... IT'S A LONG STORY.
DRINKING PARTIES REALLY SCREAM "COLLEGE LIFE," HUH? SOUNDS FUN.
DEPENDS ON WHO YOU'RE DRINKING WITH...
クスクス
HEE HEE
I GUESS.
SAY...

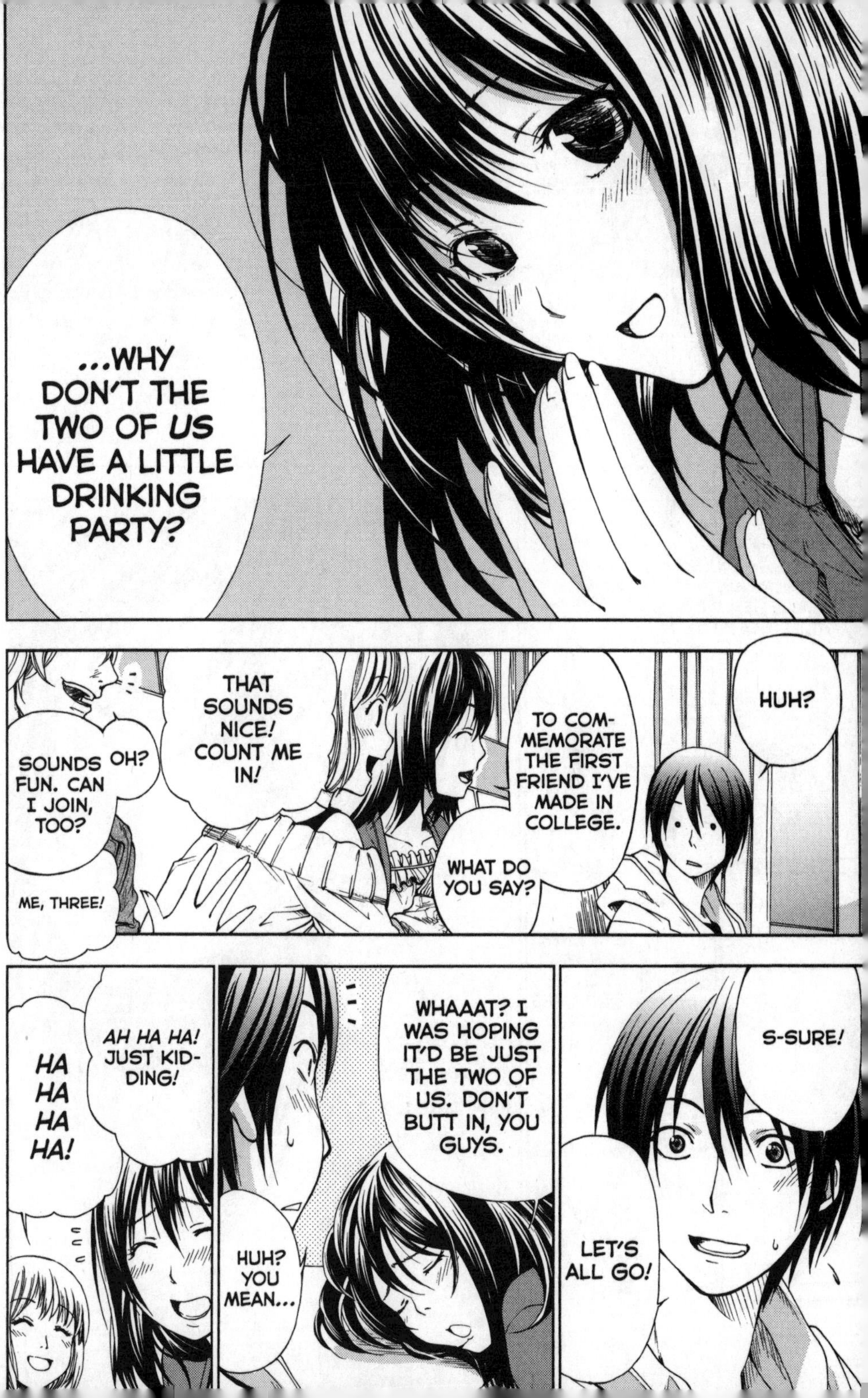
...WHY DON'T THE TWO OF *US* HAVE A LITTLE DRINKING PARTY?
HUH?
TO COMMEMORATE THE FIRST FRIEND I'VE MADE IN COLLEGE.
WHAT DO YOU SAY?
THAT SOUNDS NICE! COUNT ME IN!
OH?
SOUNDS FUN. CAN I JOIN, TOO?
ME, THREE!
S-SURE!
LET'S ALL GO!
WHAAAT? I WAS HOPING IT'D BE JUST THE TWO OF US. DON'T BUTT IN, YOU GUYS.
HUH? YOU MEAN...
AH HA HA! JUST KIDDING!
HA HA HA HA!

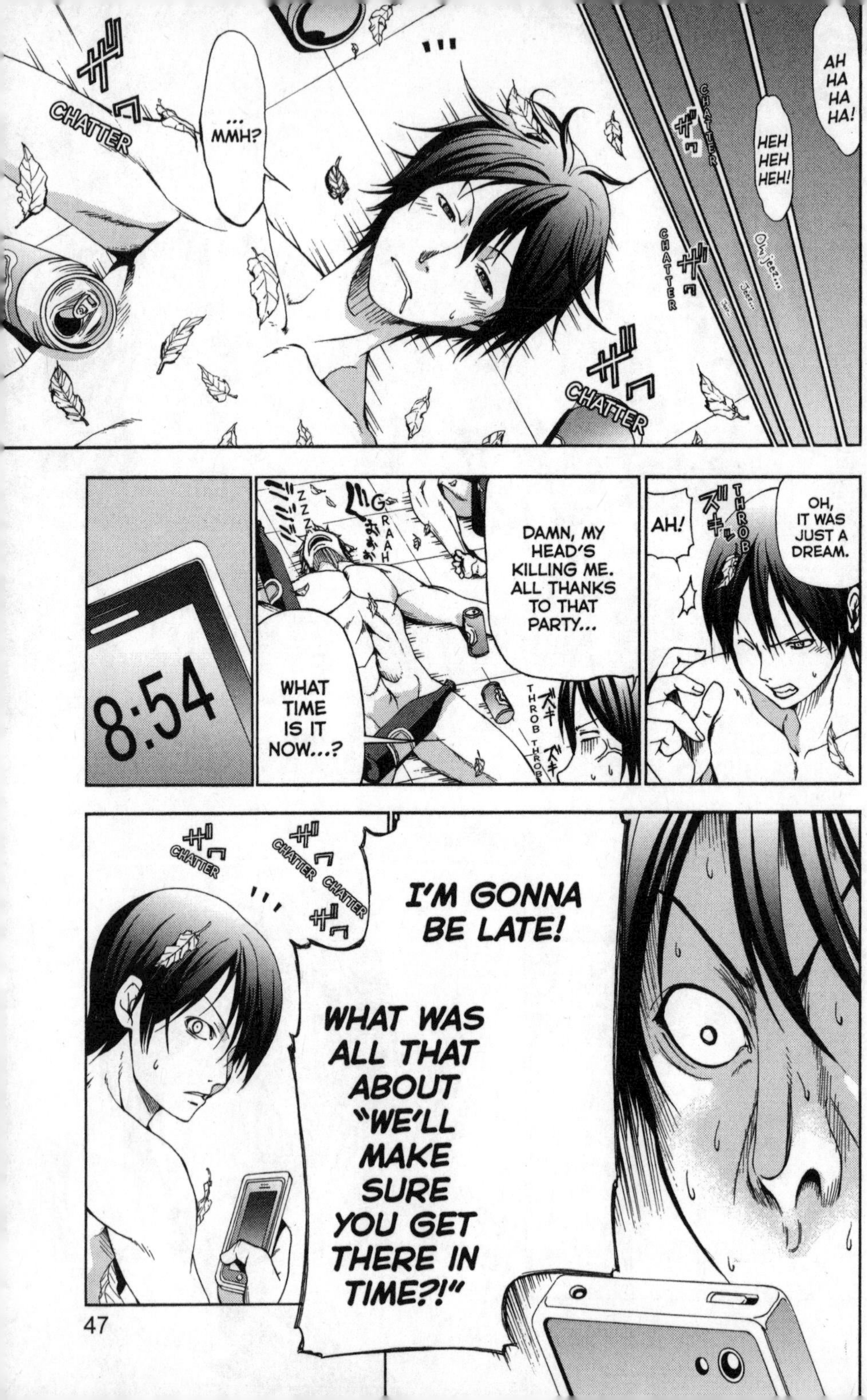

AH HA HA HA!
HEH HEH HEH!
CHATTER
Oh jeez...
Jeez...
CHATTER
...
... MMH?
CHATTER
CHATTER
OH, IT WAS JUST A DREAM.
THROB
AH!
DAMN, MY HEAD'S KILLING ME. ALL THANKS TO THAT PARTY...
GRAAH
Z Z Z
THROB THROB
WHAT TIME IS IT NOW...?
8:54
I'M GONNA BE LATE!
WHAT WAS ALL THAT ABOUT "WE'LL MAKE SURE YOU GET THERE IN TIME?!"
CHATTER
CHATTER
CHATTER
...

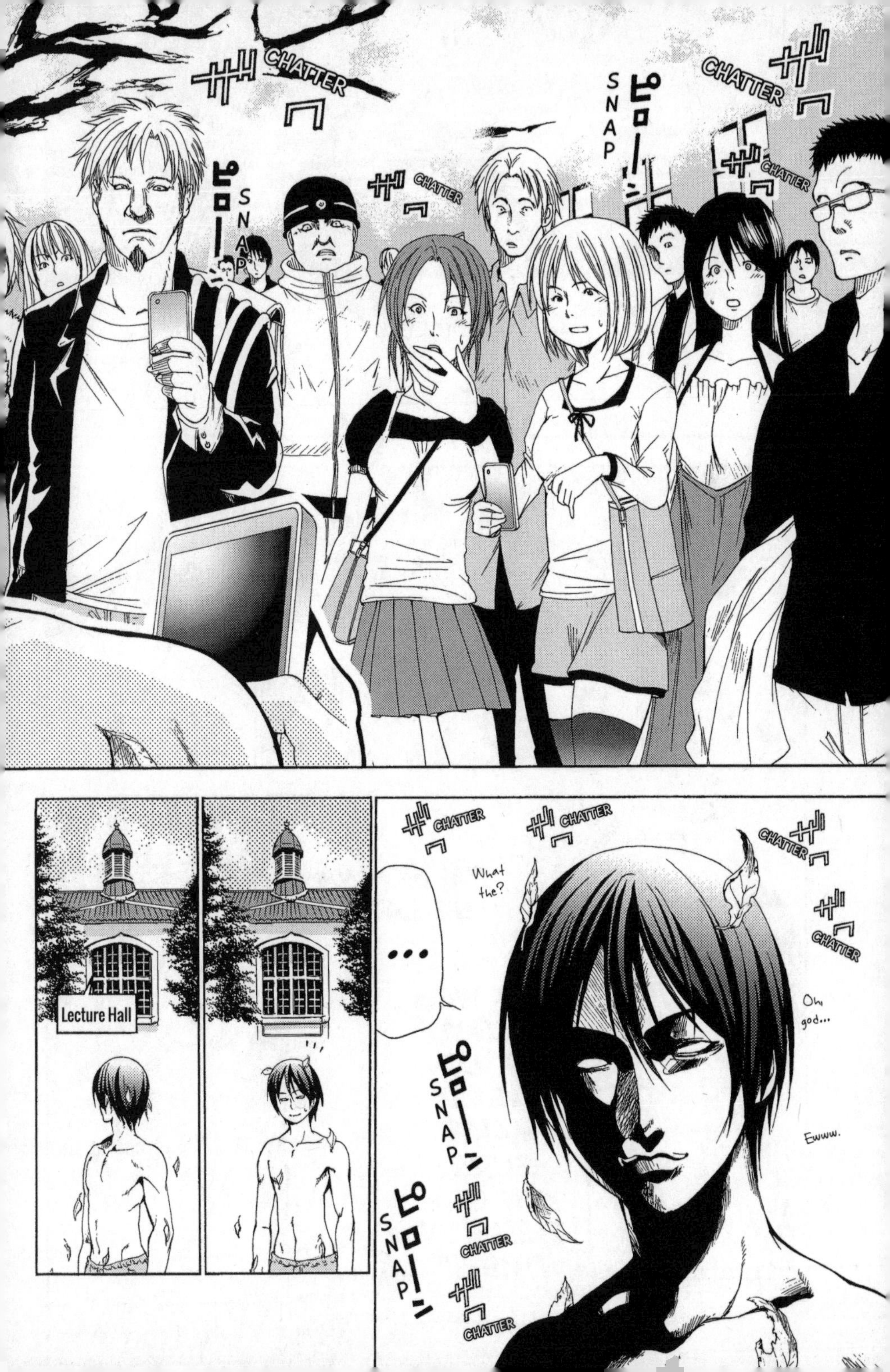
CHATTER
SNAP
CHATTER
CHATTER
CHATTER
SNAP
CHATTER
CHATTER
CHATTER
CHATTER
What the?
...
Oh god...
Ewww.
SNAP
SNAP
CHATTER
CHATTER
Lecture Hall

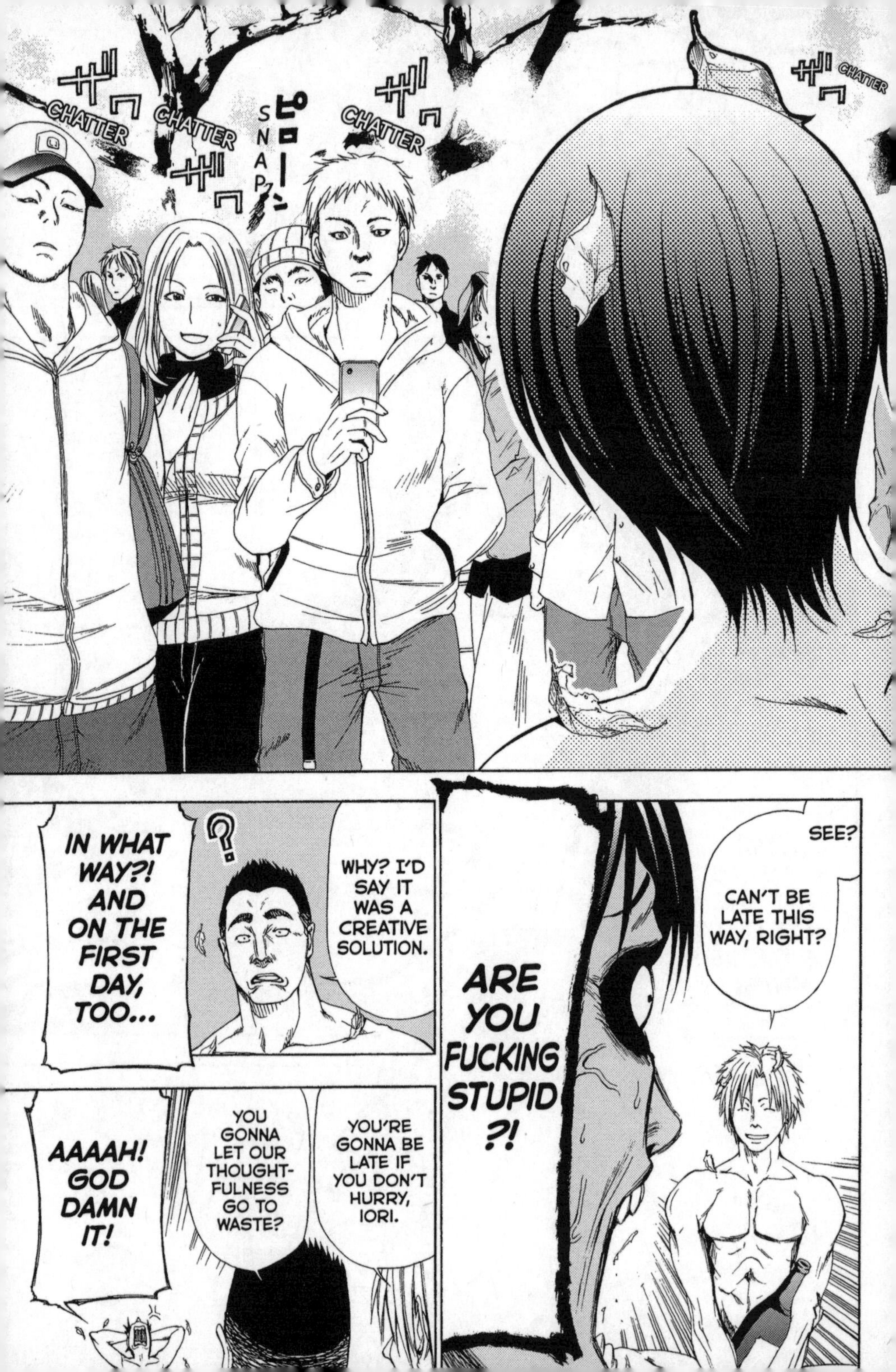

CHATTER
CHATTER
SNAP
CHATTER
CHATTER
SEE?
CAN'T BE LATE THIS WAY, RIGHT?
ARE YOU FUCKING STUPID?!
?
WHY? I'D SAY IT WAS A CREATIVE SOLUTION.
IN WHAT WAY?! AND ON THE FIRST DAY, TOO...
YOU'RE GONNA BE LATE IF YOU DON'T HURRY, IORI.
YOU GONNA LET OUR THOUGHTFULNESS GO TO WASTE?
AAAAH! GOD DAMN IT!

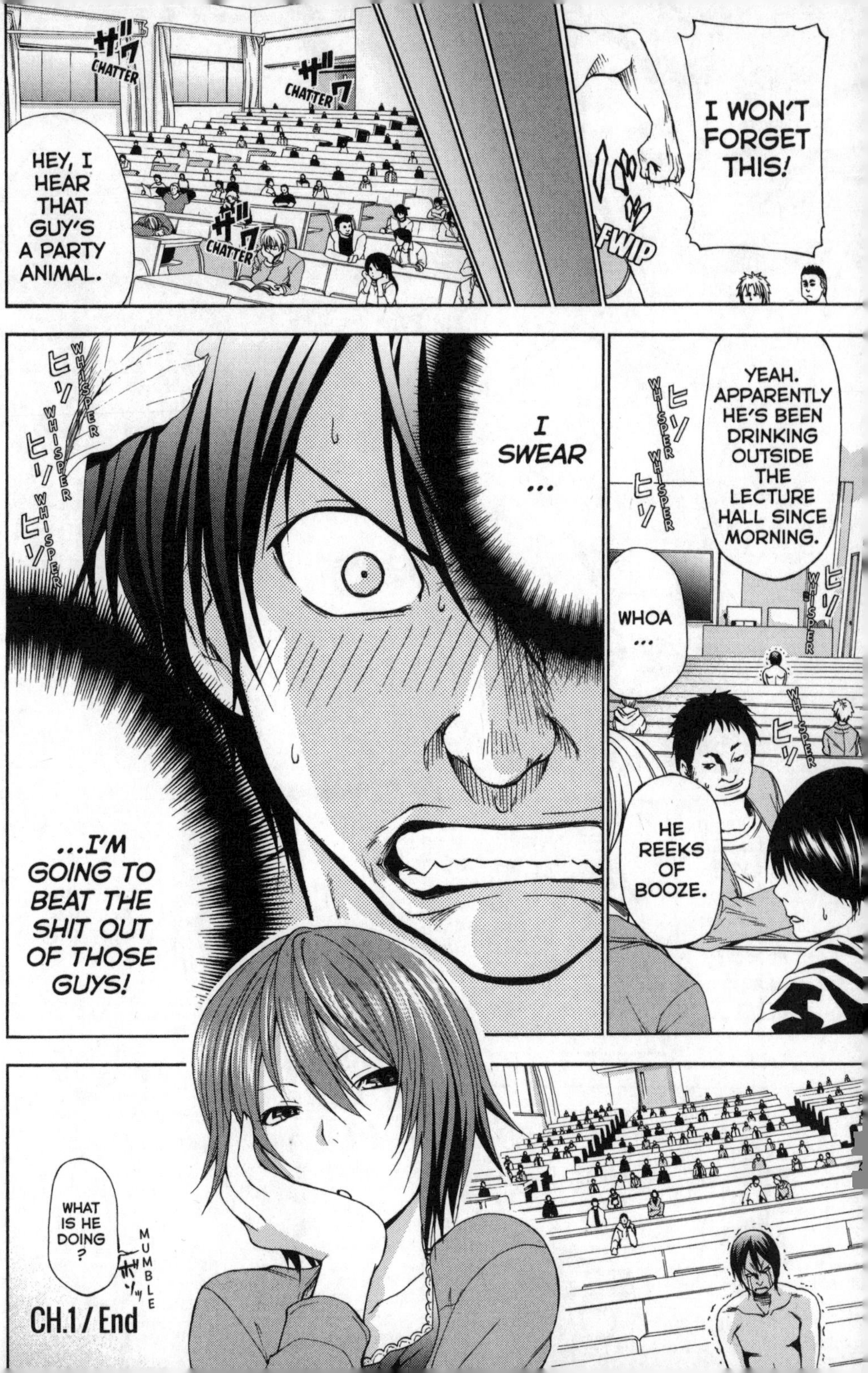

I WON'T FORGET THIS!
FWIP
ザワ CHATTER
ザワ CHATTER
ザワ CHATTER
HEY, I HEAR THAT GUY'S A PARTY ANIMAL.
YEAH. APPARENTLY HE'S BEEN DRINKING OUTSIDE THE LECTURE HALL SINCE MORNING.
ヒソ WHISPER
ヒソ WHISPER
WHOA ...
HE REEKS OF BOOZE.
I SWEAR ...
ヒソ WHISPER
ヒソ WHISPER
ヒソ WHISPER
...I'M GOING TO BEAT THE SHIT OUT OF THOSE GUYS!
WHAT IS HE DOING?
ボソッ MUMBLE
CH.1 / End

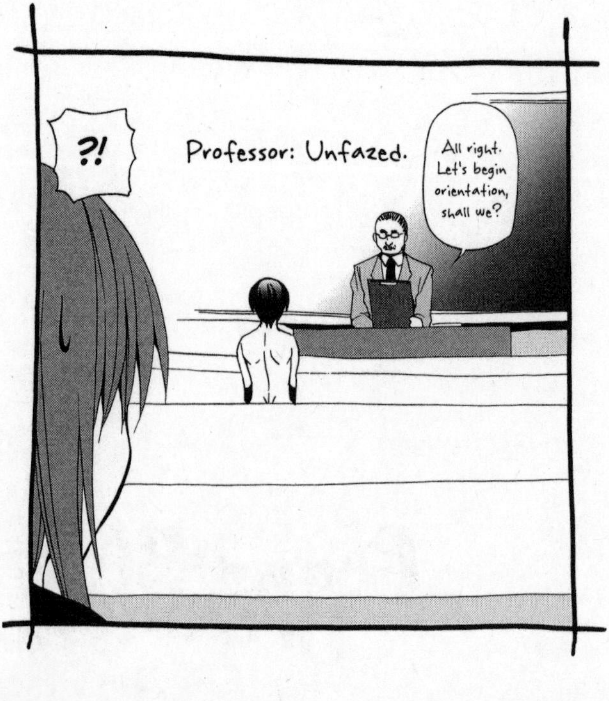
All right. Let's begin orientation, shall we?
Professor: Unfazed.
?!

Grand Blue
Dreaming

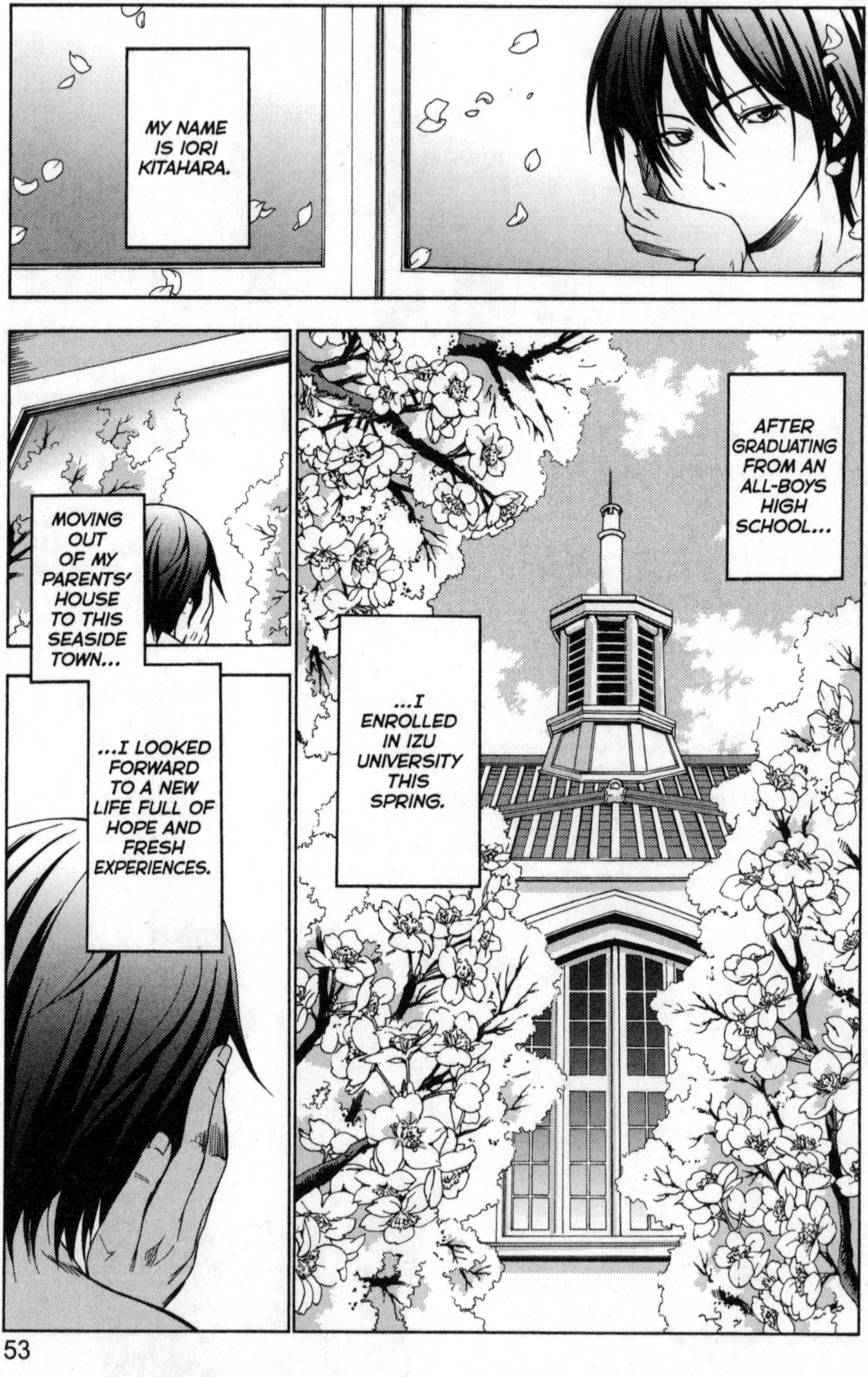
MY NAME IS IORI KITAHARA.
AFTER GRADUATING FROM AN ALL-BOYS HIGH SCHOOL...
...I ENROLLED IN IZU UNIVERSITY THIS SPRING.
MOVING OUT OF MY PARENTS' HOUSE TO THIS SEASIDE TOWN...
...I LOOKED FORWARD TO A NEW LIFE FULL OF HOPE AND FRESH EXPERIENCES.

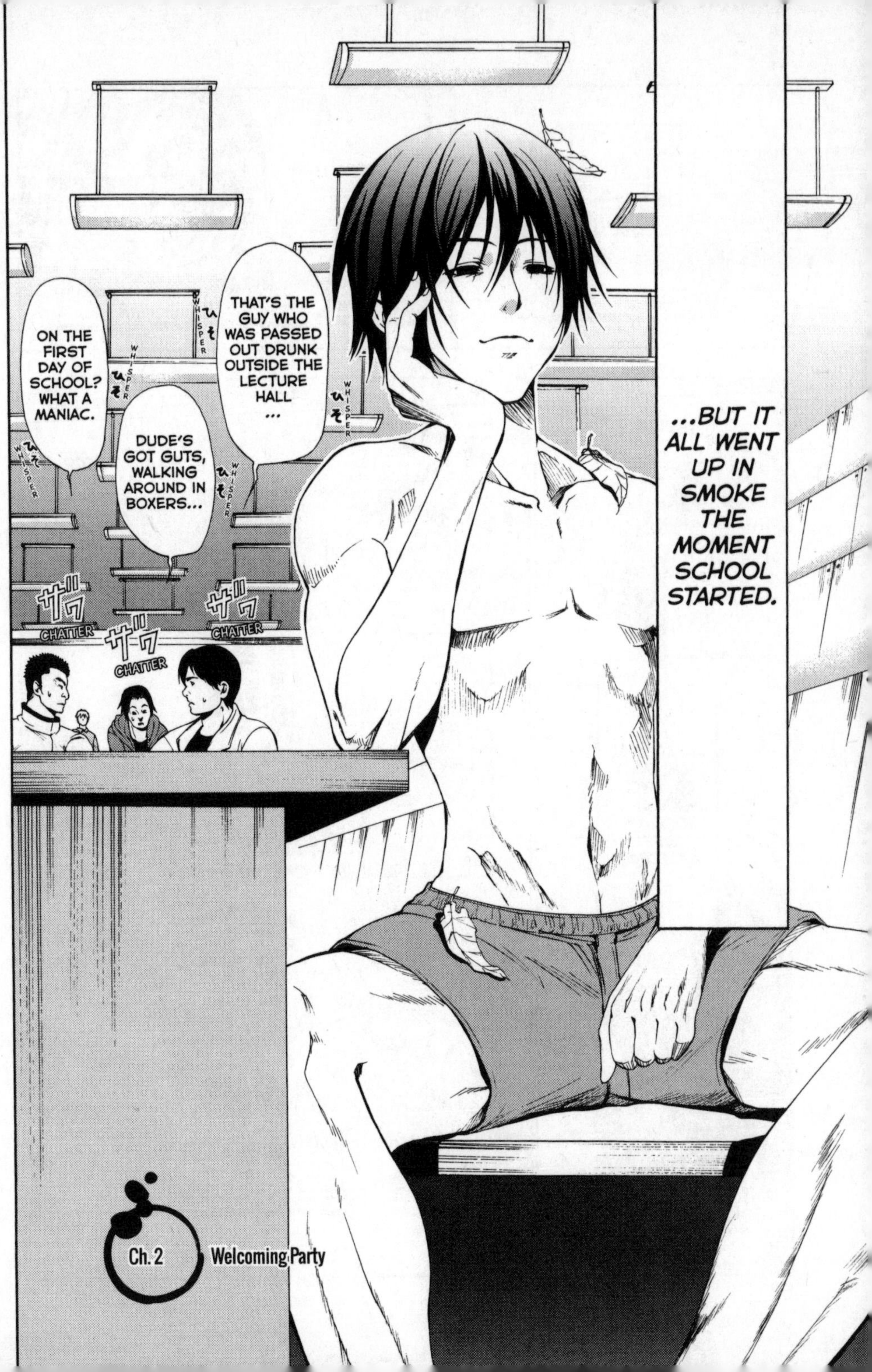
...BUT IT ALL WENT UP IN SMOKE THE MOMENT SCHOOL STARTED.
WHISPER
THAT'S THE GUY WHO WAS PASSED OUT DRUNK OUTSIDE THE LECTURE HALL ...
WHISPER
WHISPER
DUDE'S GOT GUTS, WALKING AROUND IN BOXERS...
WHISPER
ON THE FIRST DAY OF SCHOOL? WHAT A MANIAC.
WHISPER
CHATTER
CHATTER
CHATTER
Ch. 2
Welcoming Party

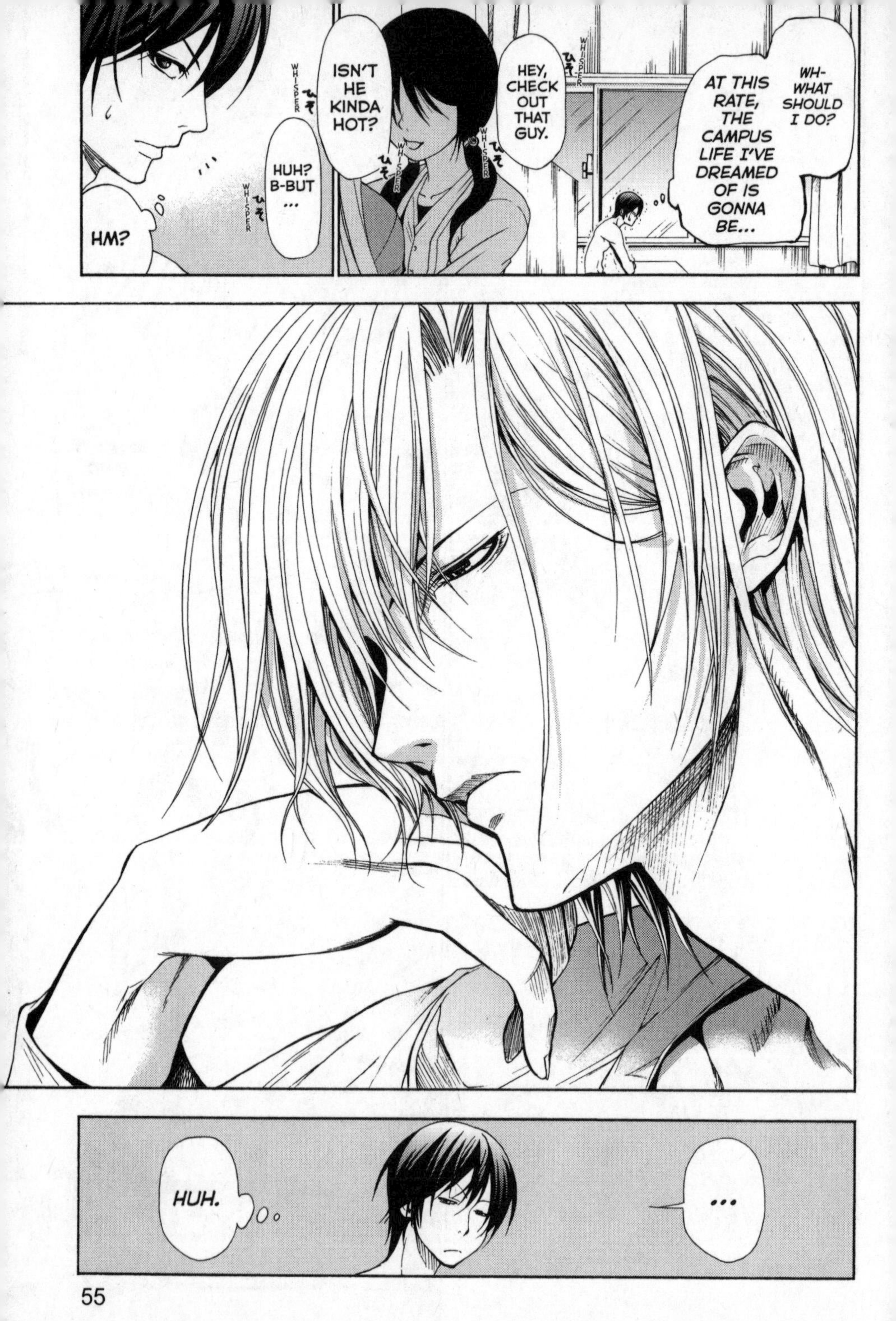
WH- WHAT SHOULD I DO?
AT THIS RATE, THE CAMPUS LIFE I'VE DREAMED OF IS GONNA BE...
WHISPER
HEY, CHECK OUT THAT GUY.
WHISPER
ISN'T HE KINDA HOT?
WHISPER
HUH? B-BUT ...
WHISPER
HM?
...
HUH.

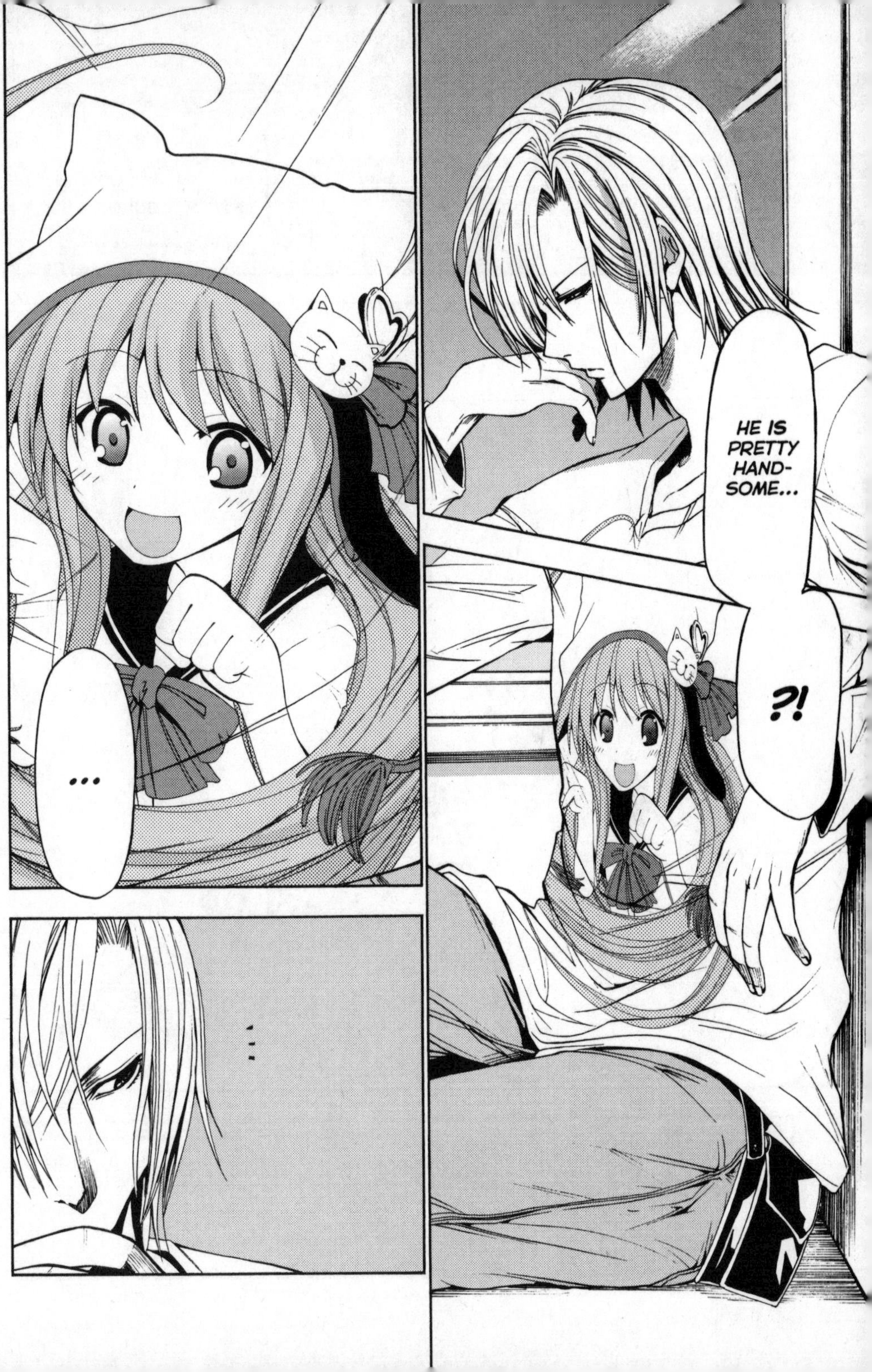
HE IS PRETTY HAND-SOME...
...
?!
...

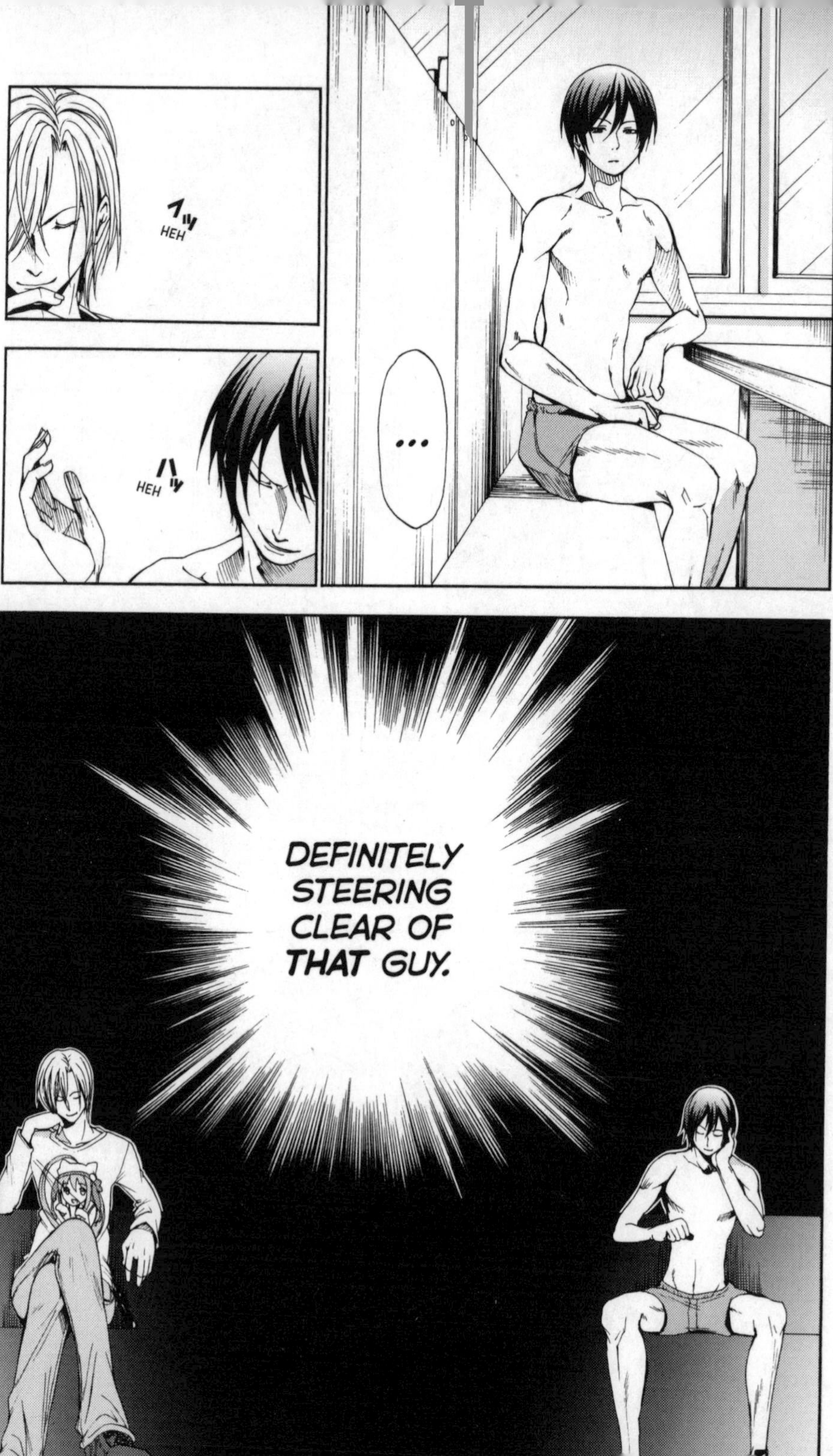
...
ヘッ
HEH
ハッ
HEH
DEFINITELY STEERING CLEAR OF THAT GUY.

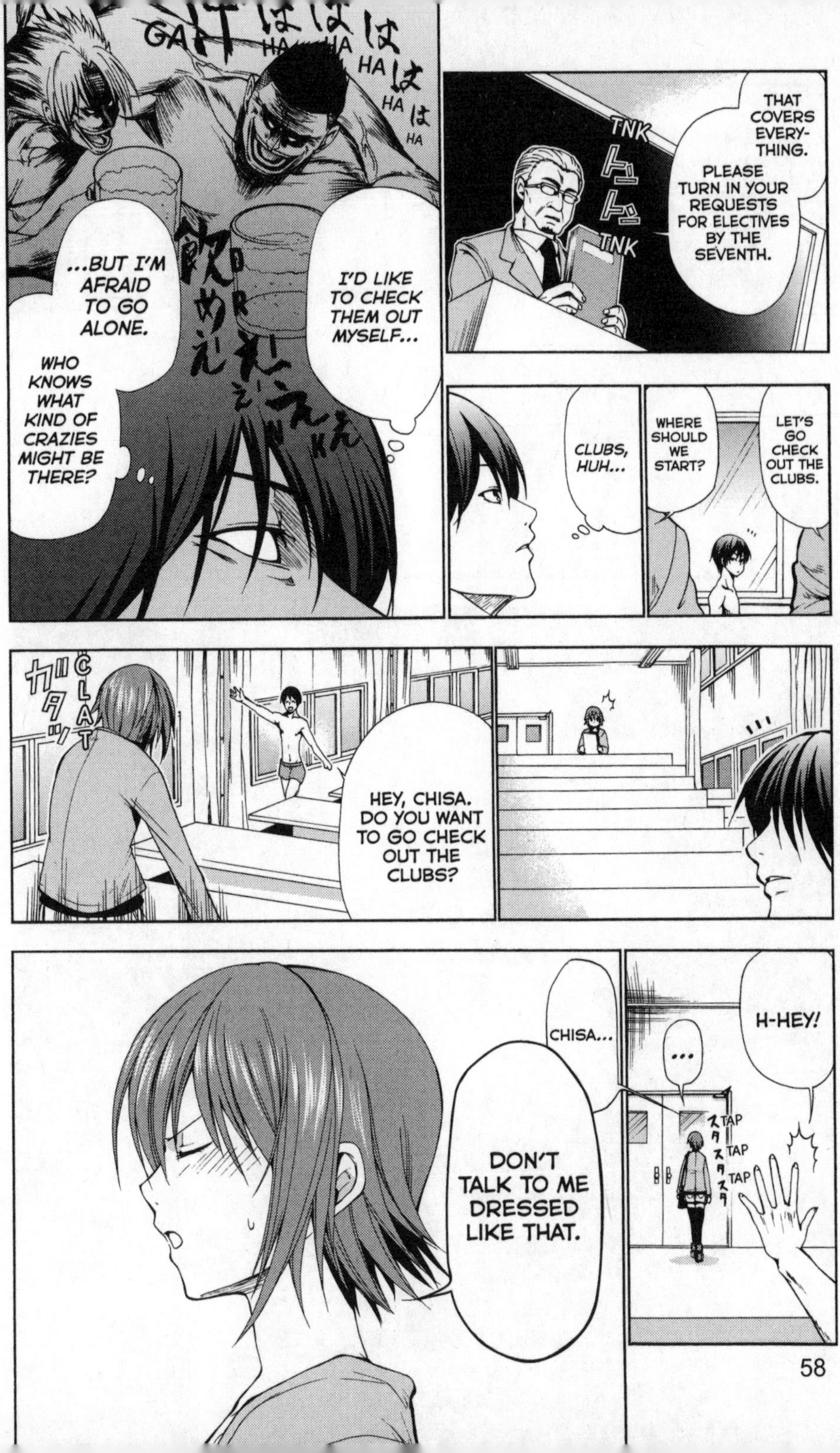
TNK TNK
THAT COVERS EVERY-THING.
PLEASE TURN IN YOUR REQUESTS FOR ELECTIVES BY THE SEVENTH.
LET'S GO CHECK OUT THE CLUBS.
WHERE SHOULD WE START?
CLUBS, HUH...
GAT
HA HA HA HA
DRINK
I'D LIKE TO CHECK THEM OUT MYSELF...
...BUT I'M AFRAID TO GO ALONE.
WHO KNOWS WHAT KIND OF CRAZIES MIGHT BE THERE?
CLAT
HEY, CHISA. DO YOU WANT TO GO CHECK OUT THE CLUBS?
H-HEY!
TAP TAP TAP
...
CHISA...
DON'T TALK TO ME DRESSED LIKE THAT.

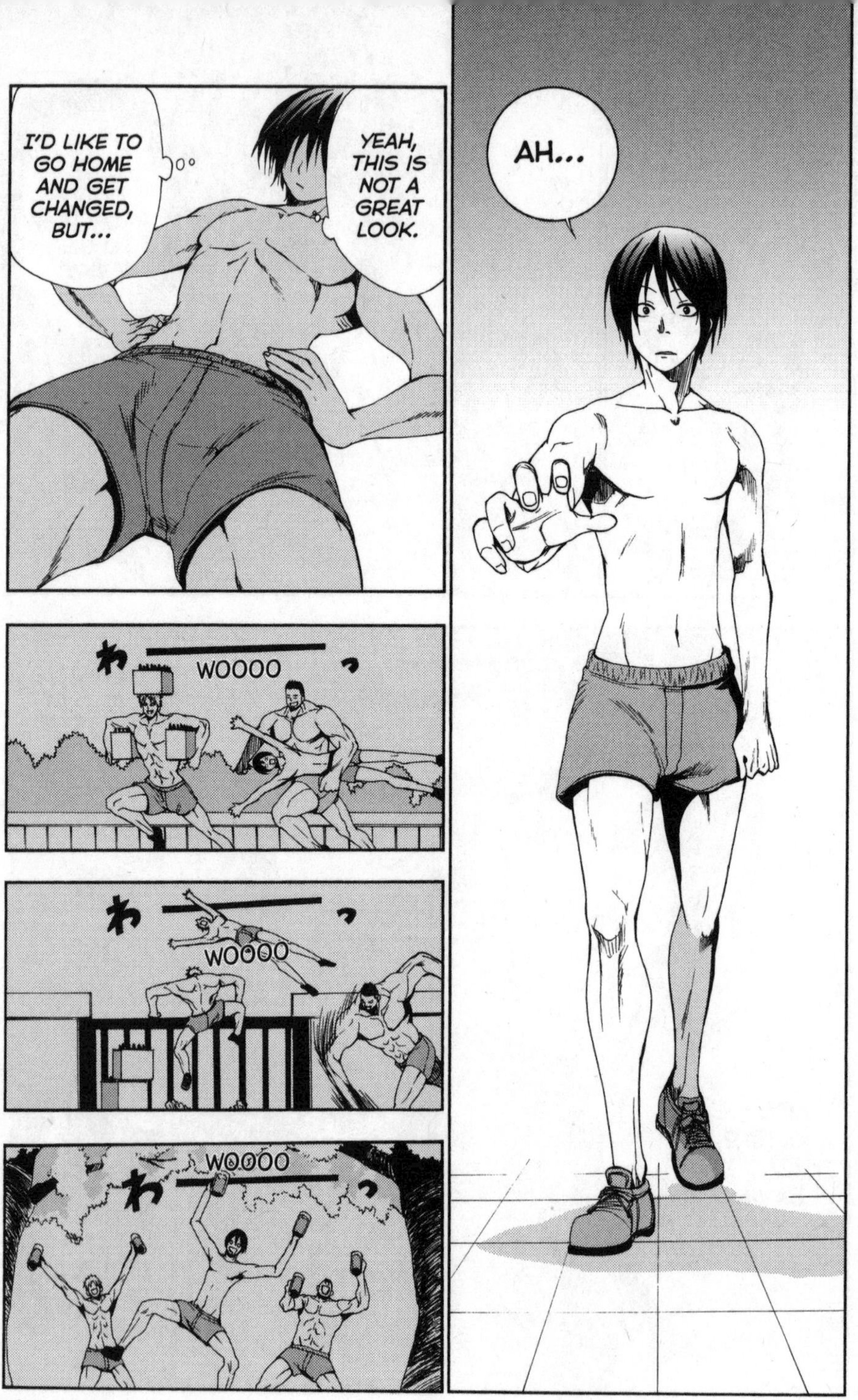
AH...
YEAH, THIS IS NOT A GREAT LOOK.
I'D LIKE TO GO HOME AND GET CHANGED, BUT...
わーっ
WOOOO
わーっ
WOOOO
わーっ
WOOOO

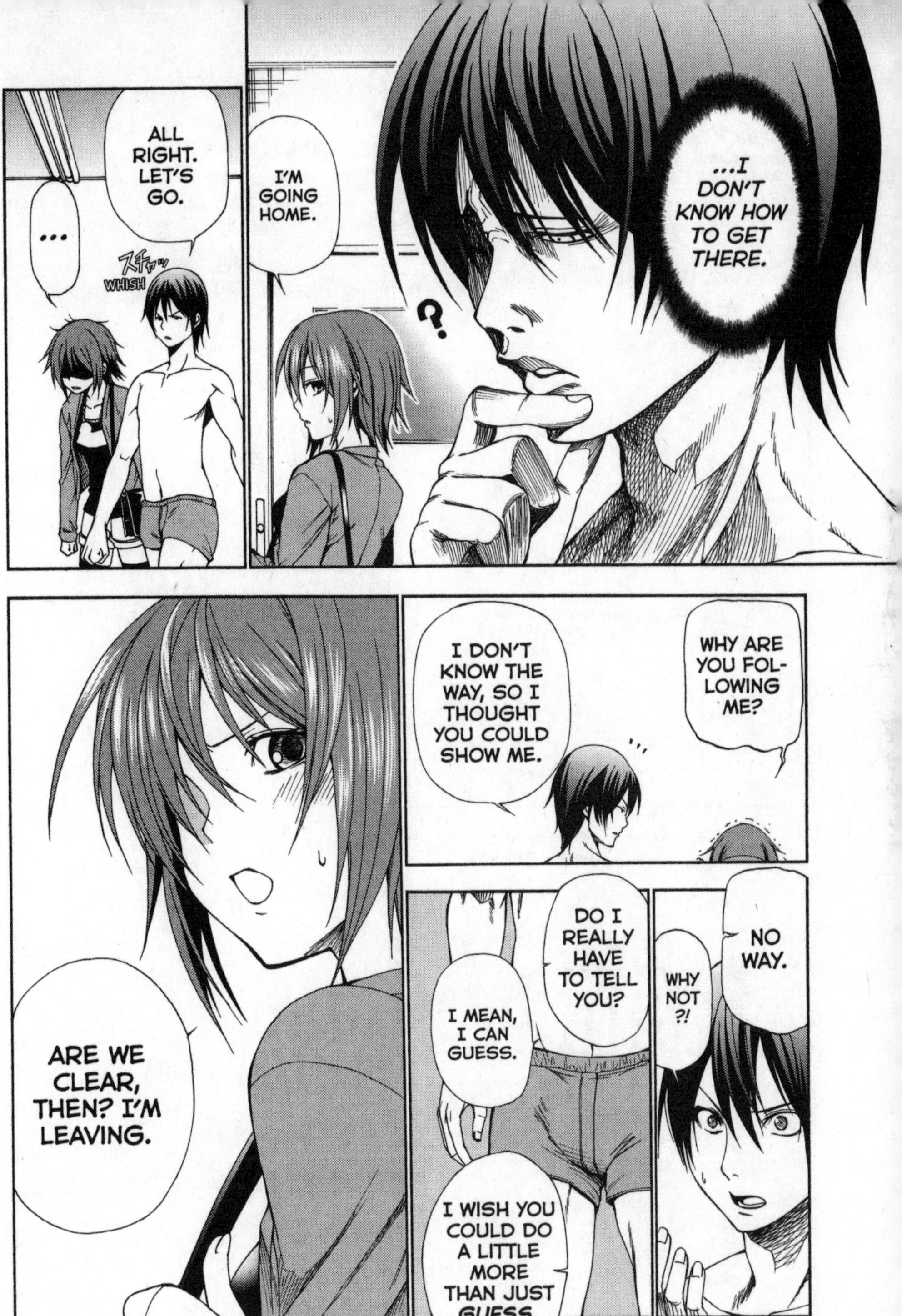
...I DON'T KNOW HOW TO GET THERE.
?
I'M GOING HOME.
ALL RIGHT. LET'S GO.
...
スチャッ
WHISH
WHY ARE YOU FOL-LOWING ME?
I DON'T KNOW THE WAY, SO I THOUGHT YOU COULD SHOW ME.
NO WAY.
WHY NOT?!
DO I REALLY HAVE TO TELL YOU?
I MEAN, I CAN GUESS.
I WISH YOU COULD DO A LITTLE MORE THAN JUST *GUESS.*
ARE WE CLEAR, THEN? I'M LEAVING.

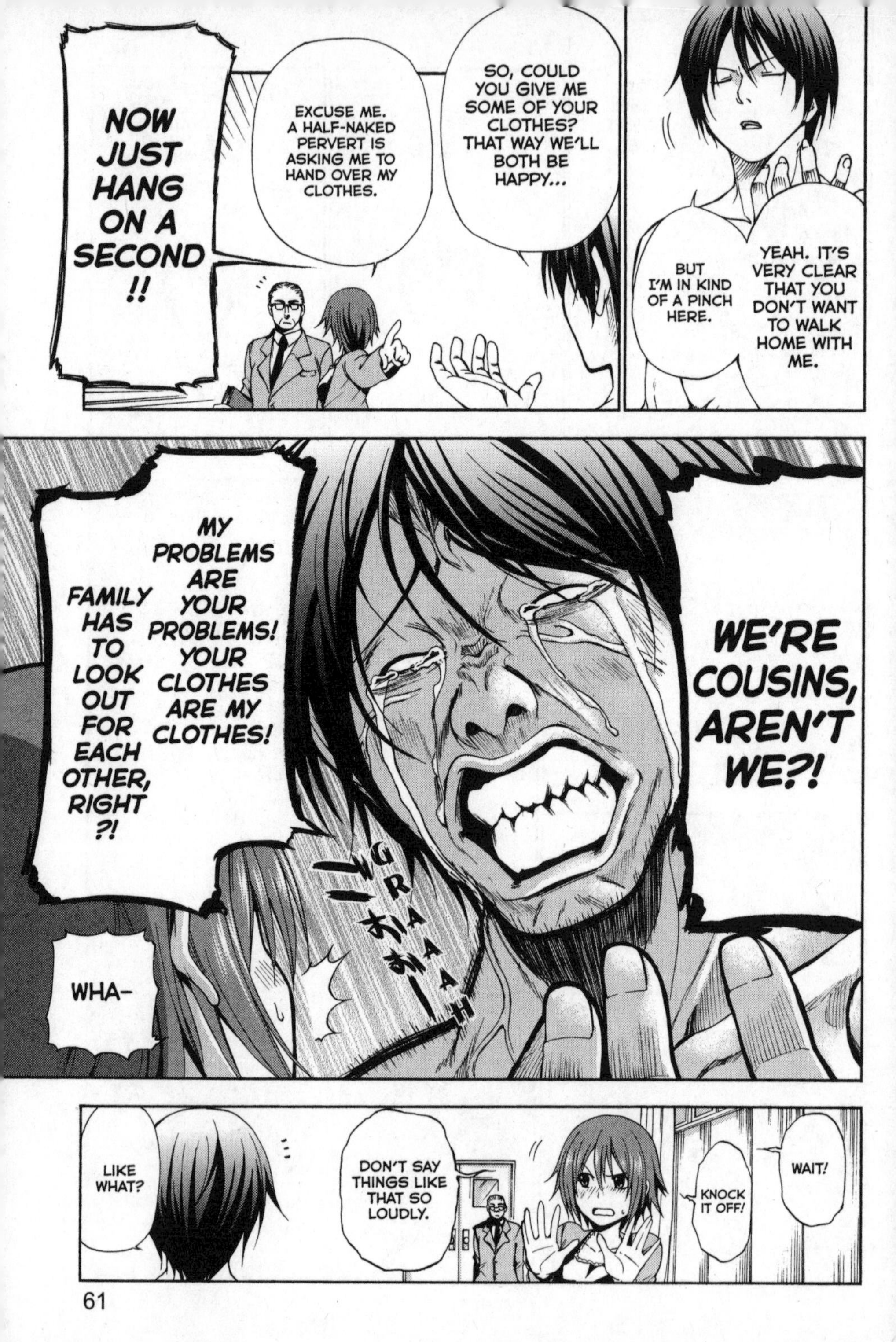
YEAH. IT'S VERY CLEAR THAT YOU DON'T WANT TO WALK HOME WITH ME.
BUT I'M IN KIND OF A PINCH HERE.
SO, COULD YOU GIVE ME SOME OF YOUR CLOTHES? THAT WAY WE'LL BOTH BE HAPPY...
EXCUSE ME. A HALF-NAKED PERVERT IS ASKING ME TO HAND OVER MY CLOTHES.
NOW JUST HANG ON A SECOND!!
WE'RE COUSINS, AREN'T WE?!
MY PROBLEMS ARE YOUR PROBLEMS! YOUR CLOTHES ARE MY CLOTHES!
FAMILY HAS TO LOOK OUT FOR EACH OTHER, RIGHT?!
GRAAAAH
WHA-
WAIT!
KNOCK IT OFF!
DON'T SAY THINGS LIKE THAT SO LOUDLY.
LIKE WHAT?

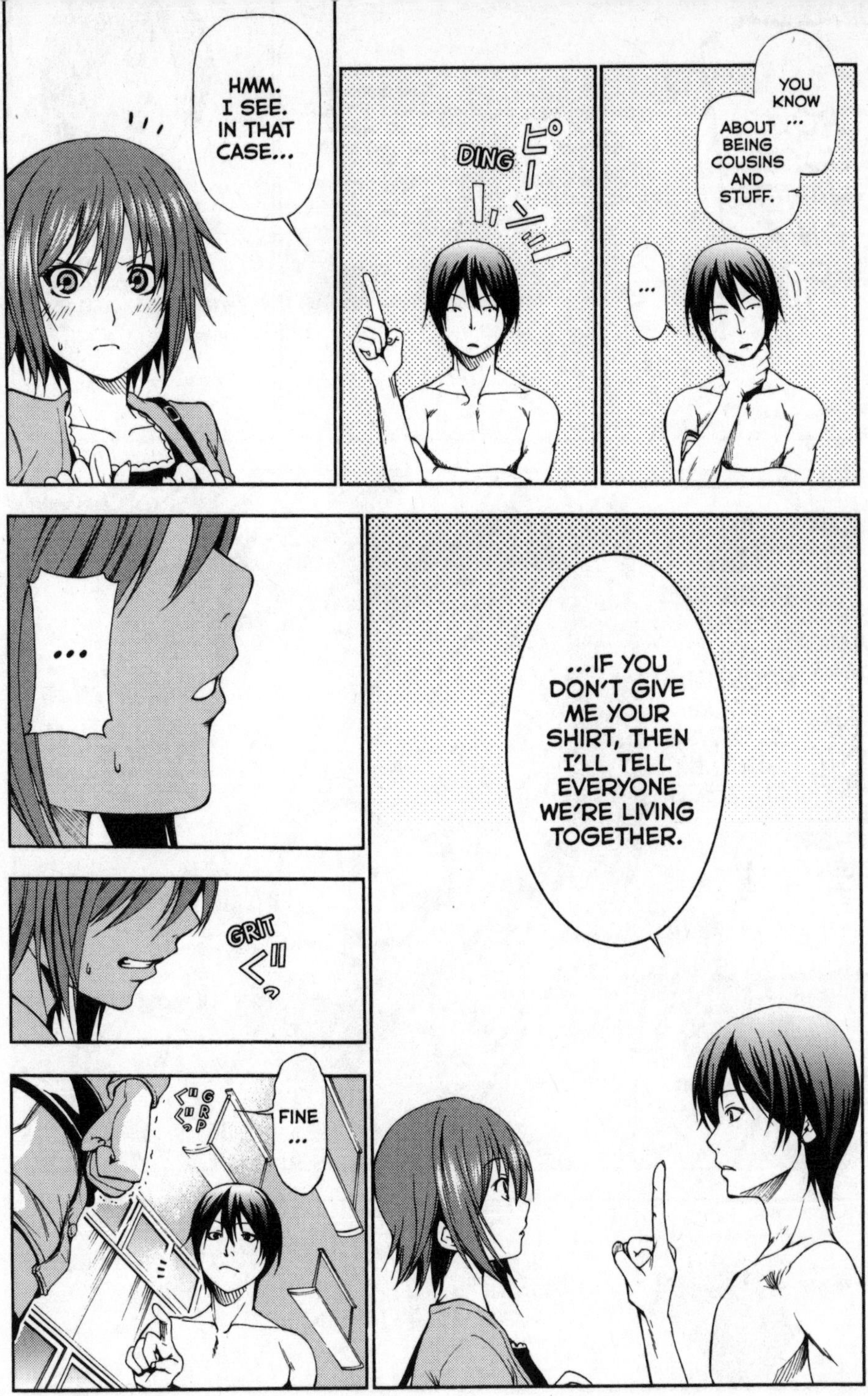
YOU KNOW ... ABOUT BEING COUSINS AND STUFF.
...
DING
ピーン
HMM. I SEE. IN THAT CASE...
...IF YOU DON'T GIVE ME YOUR SHIRT, THEN I'LL TELL EVERYONE WE'RE LIVING TOGETHER.
...
GRIT
ぐっ
FINE ...
GRP

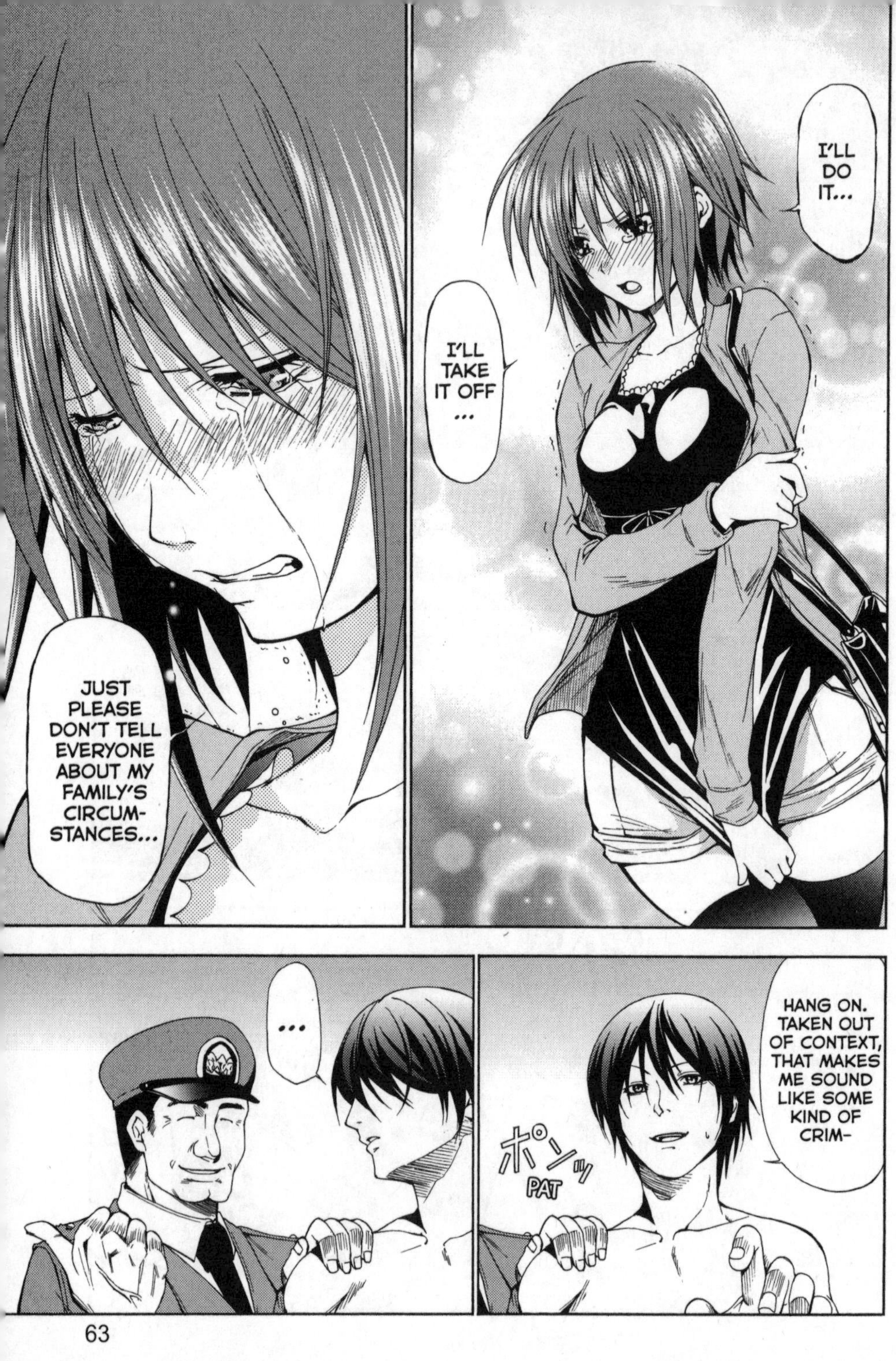
I'LL DO IT...
I'LL TAKE IT OFF ...
JUST PLEASE DON'T TELL EVERYONE ABOUT MY FAMILY'S CIRCUM-STANCES...
HANG ON. TAKEN OUT OF CONTEXT, THAT MAKES ME SOUND LIKE SOME KIND OF CRIM-
ポンッ
PAT
...

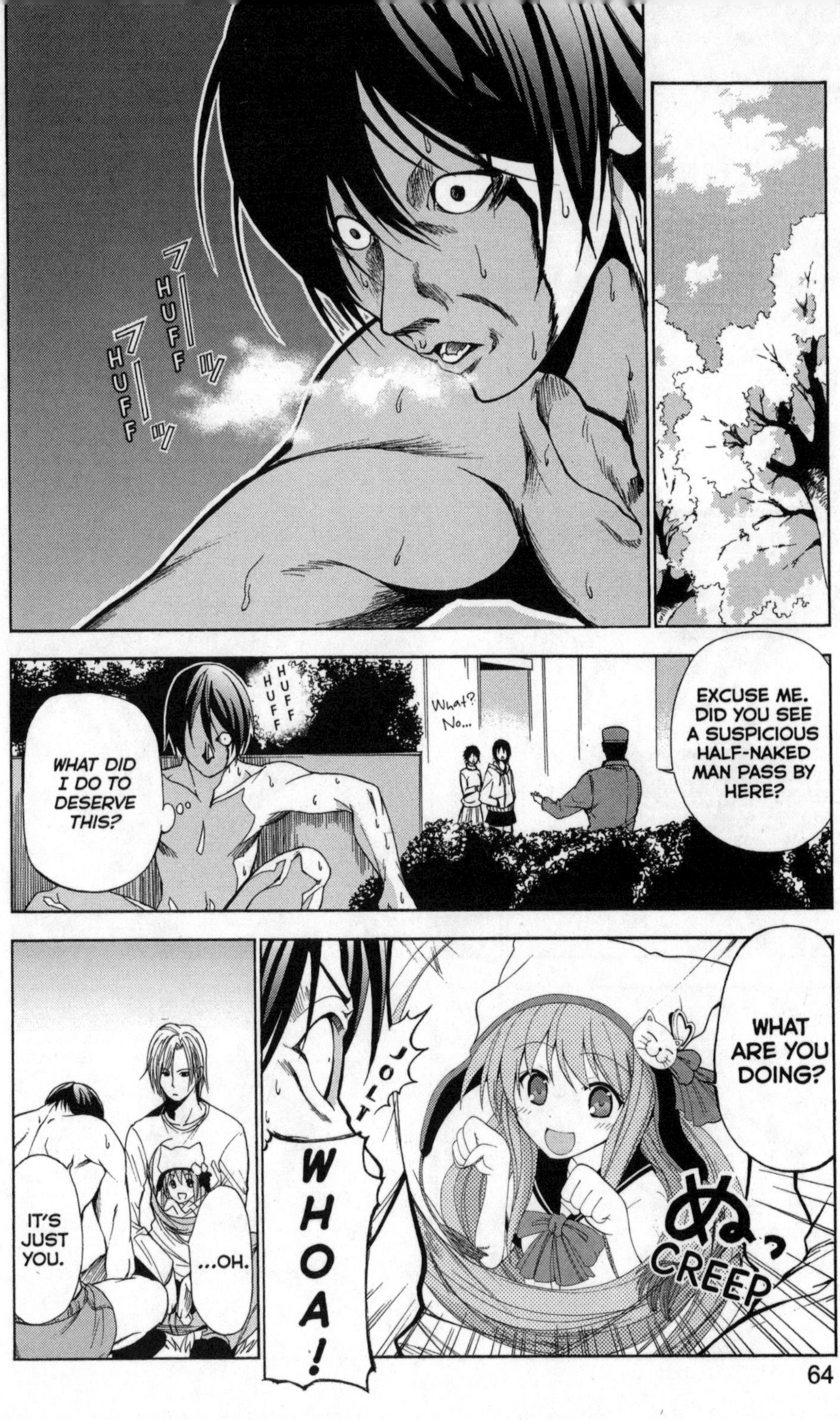
フーッ
HUFF
フーッ
HUFF
EXCUSE ME. DID YOU SEE A SUSPICIOUS HALF-NAKED MAN PASS BY HERE?
What? No...
HUFF HUFF
WHAT DID I DO TO DESERVE THIS?
WHAT ARE YOU DOING?
ぬっ
CREEP
JOLT
WHOA!
...OH.
IT'S JUST YOU.

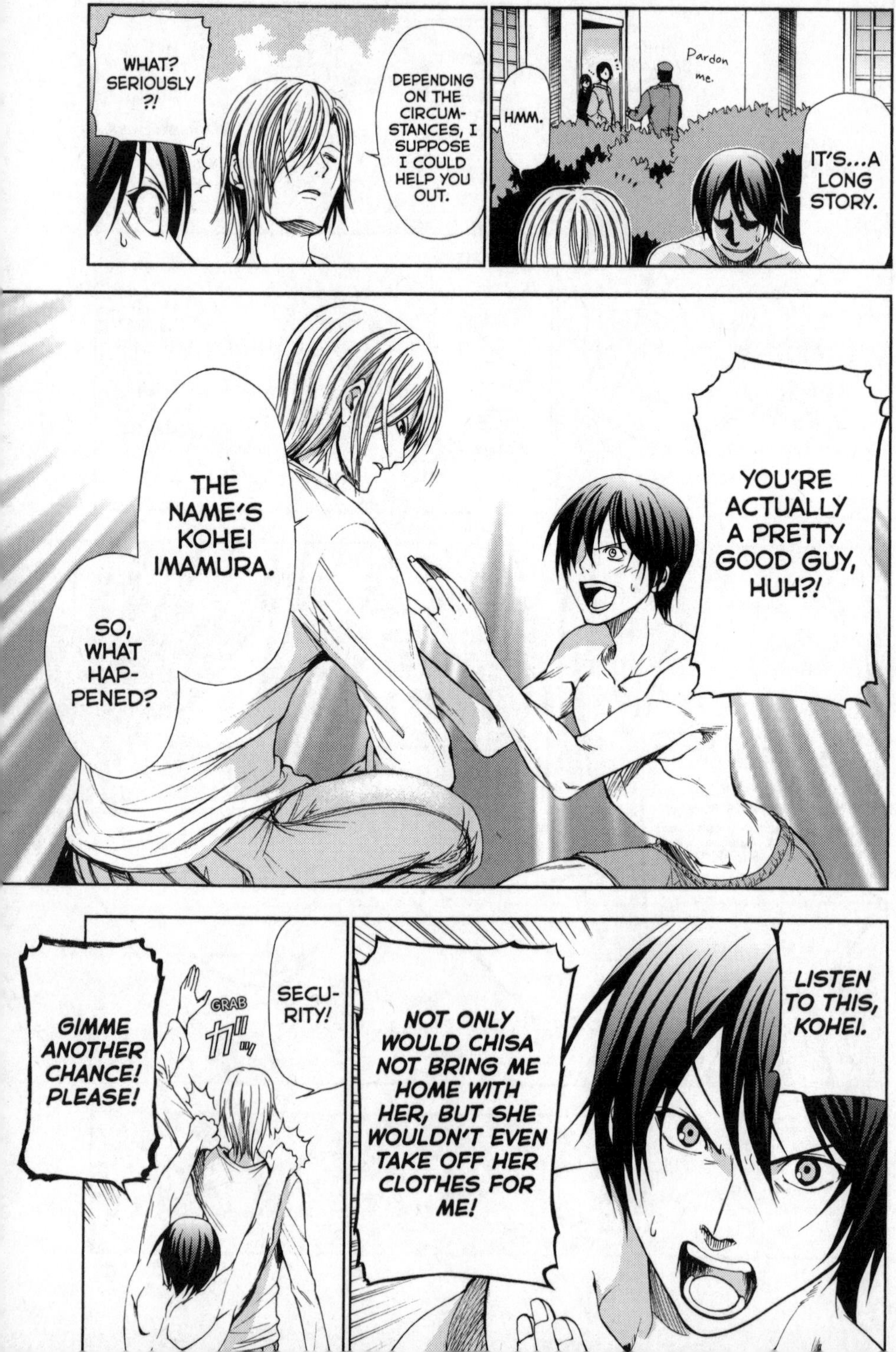
IT'S...A LONG STORY.
HMM.
Pardon me.
DEPENDING ON THE CIRCUM-STANCES, I SUPPOSE I COULD HELP YOU OUT.
WHAT? SERIOUSLY ?!
YOU'RE ACTUALLY A PRETTY GOOD GUY, HUH?!
THE NAME'S KOHEI IMAMURA.
SO, WHAT HAP-PENED?
LISTEN TO THIS, KOHEI.
NOT ONLY WOULD CHISA NOT BRING ME HOME WITH HER, BUT SHE WOULDN'T EVEN TAKE OFF HER CLOTHES FOR ME!
SECU-RITY!
GRAB
GIMME ANOTHER CHANCE! PLEASE!

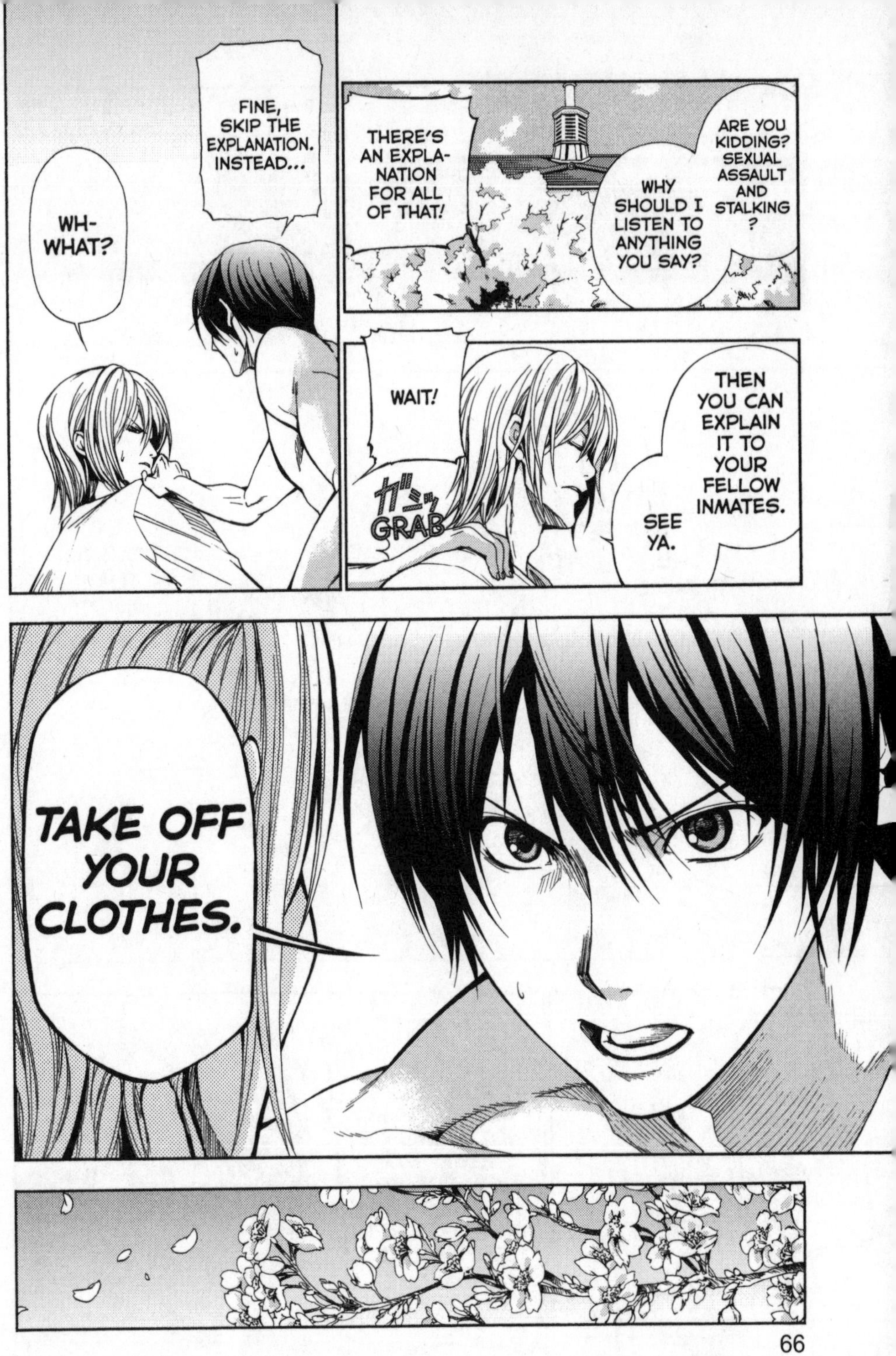
ARE YOU KIDDING? SEXUAL ASSAULT AND STALKING?
WHY SHOULD I LISTEN TO ANYTHING YOU SAY?
THERE'S AN EXPLANATION FOR ALL OF THAT!
THEN YOU CAN EXPLAIN IT TO YOUR FELLOW INMATES.
SEE YA.
WAIT!
ガシッ GRAB
FINE, SKIP THE EXPLANATION. INSTEAD...
WH-WHAT?
TAKE OFF YOUR CLOTHES.

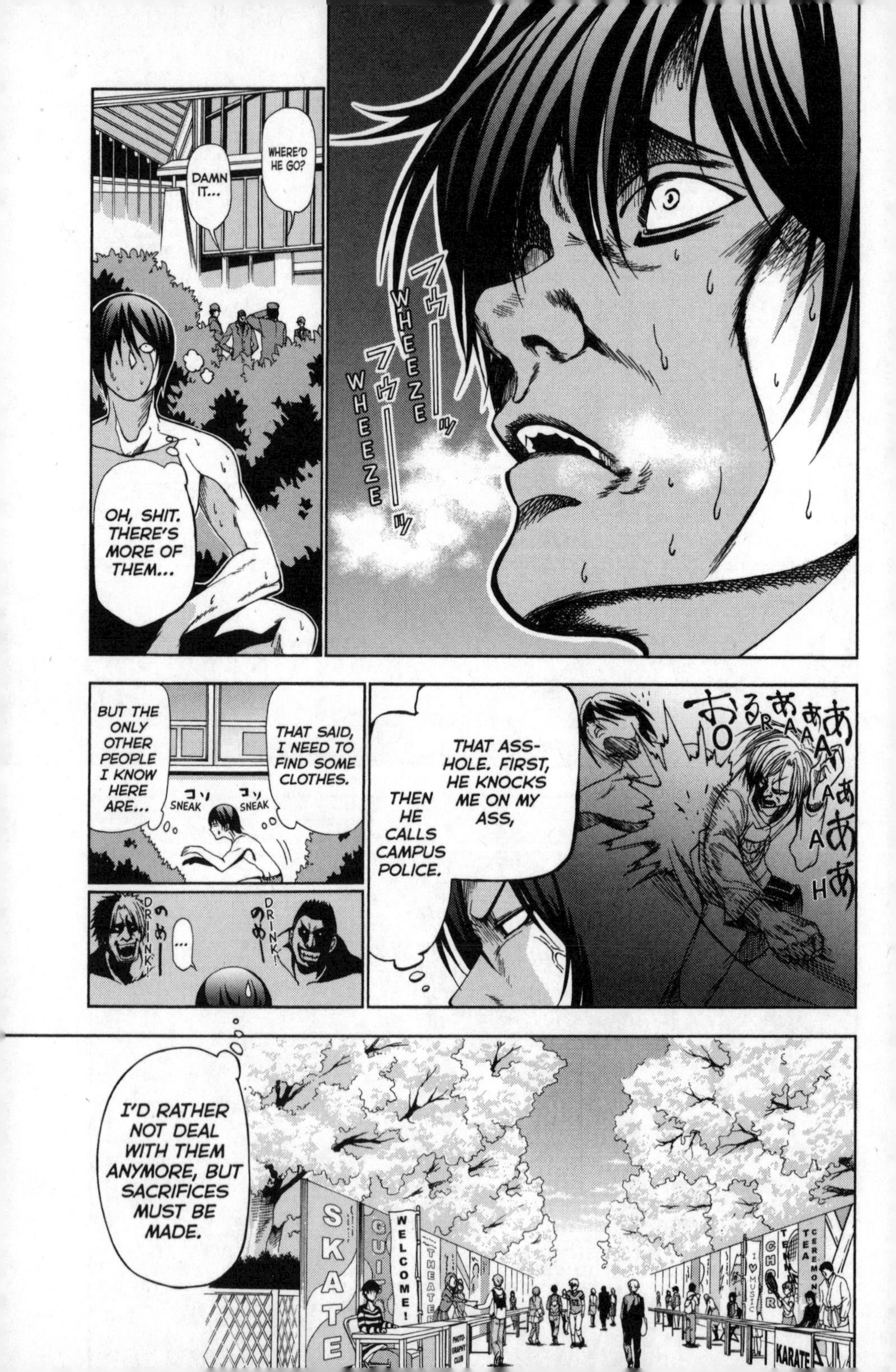

フゥーッ
WHEEZE
フゥーッ
WHEEZE
WHERE'D HE GO?
DAMN IT...
OH, SHIT. THERE'S MORE OF THEM...
おるあああ
ORAAAAAH
THAT ASS-HOLE. FIRST, HE KNOCKS ME ON MY ASS,
THEN HE CALLS CAMPUS POLICE.
THAT SAID, I NEED TO FIND SOME CLOTHES.
コソ
SNEAK
コソ
SNEAK
BUT THE ONLY OTHER PEOPLE I KNOW HERE ARE...
のめー
DRINK!
...
のめー
DRINK!
I'D RATHER NOT DEAL WITH THEM ANYMORE, BUT SACRIFICES MUST BE MADE.
TEA CEREMONY
KARATE
I ♥ MUSIC
THEATER
WELCOME!
PHOTO-GRAPHY CLUB
SKATE

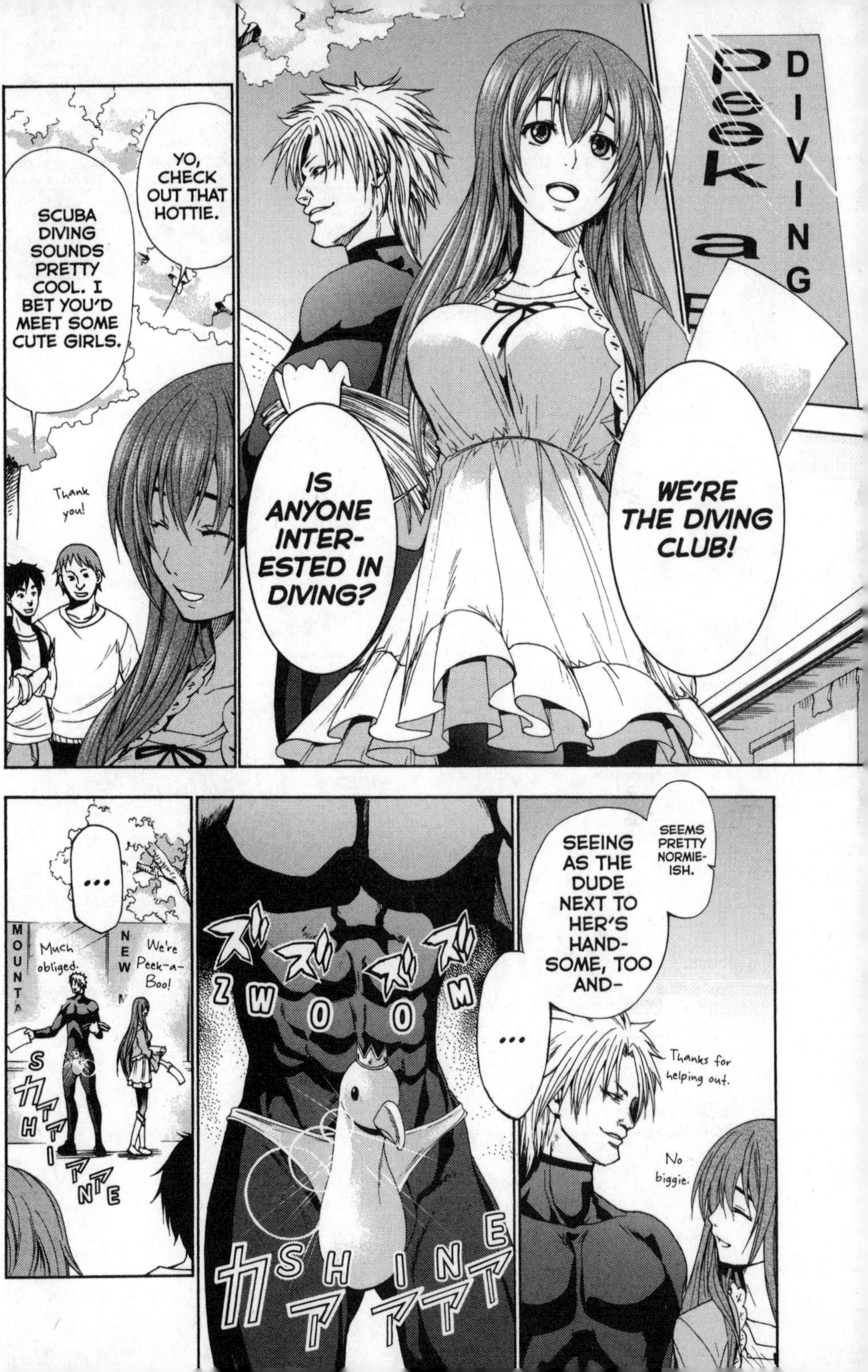
DIVING
Peek a
WE'RE THE DIVING CLUB!
IS ANYONE INTER-ESTED IN DIVING?
YO, CHECK OUT THAT HOTTIE.
SCUBA DIVING SOUNDS PRETTY COOL. I BET YOU'D MEET SOME CUTE GIRLS.
Thank you!
SEEMS PRETTY NORMIE-ISH.
SEEING AS THE DUDE NEXT TO HER'S HAND-SOME, TOO AND-
...
Thanks for helping out.
No biggie.
ZWOOM
SHINE
...
We're Peek-a-Boo!
Much obliged.
MOUNTA
NEW M
SHINE

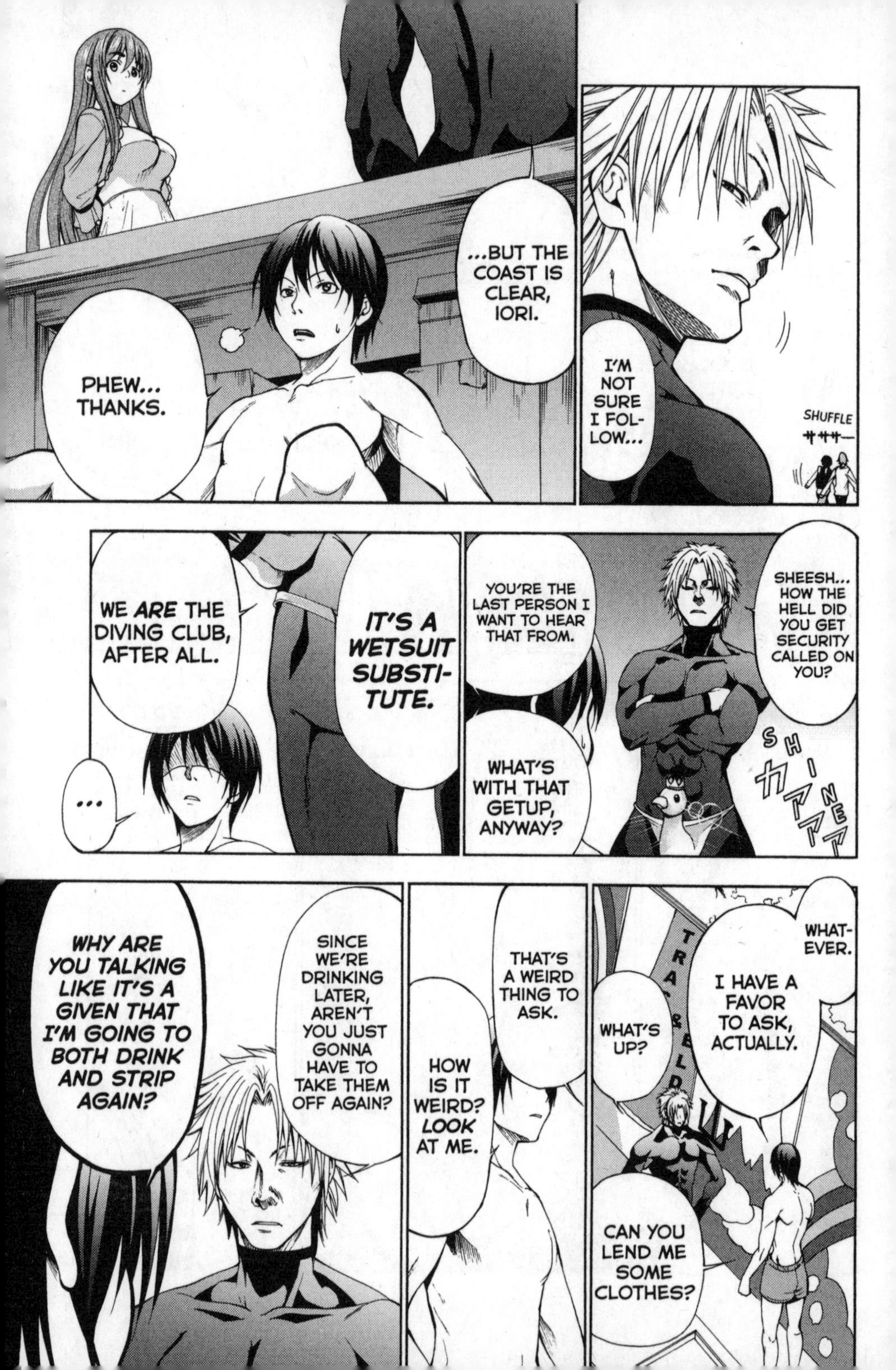
I'M NOT SURE I FOLLOW...
SHUFFLE
...BUT THE COAST IS CLEAR, IORI.
PHEW... THANKS.
SHEESH... HOW THE HELL DID YOU GET SECURITY CALLED ON YOU?
YOU'RE THE LAST PERSON I WANT TO HEAR THAT FROM.
WHAT'S WITH THAT GETUP, ANYWAY?
SHINE
IT'S A WETSUIT SUBSTITUTE.
WE ARE THE DIVING CLUB, AFTER ALL.
...
WHATEVER.
I HAVE A FAVOR TO ASK, ACTUALLY.
WHAT'S UP?
CAN YOU LEND ME SOME CLOTHES?
THAT'S A WEIRD THING TO ASK.
HOW IS IT WEIRD? LOOK AT ME.
SINCE WE'RE DRINKING LATER, AREN'T YOU JUST GONNA HAVE TO TAKE THEM OFF AGAIN?
WHY ARE YOU TALKING LIKE IT'S A GIVEN THAT I'M GOING TO BOTH DRINK AND STRIP AGAIN?

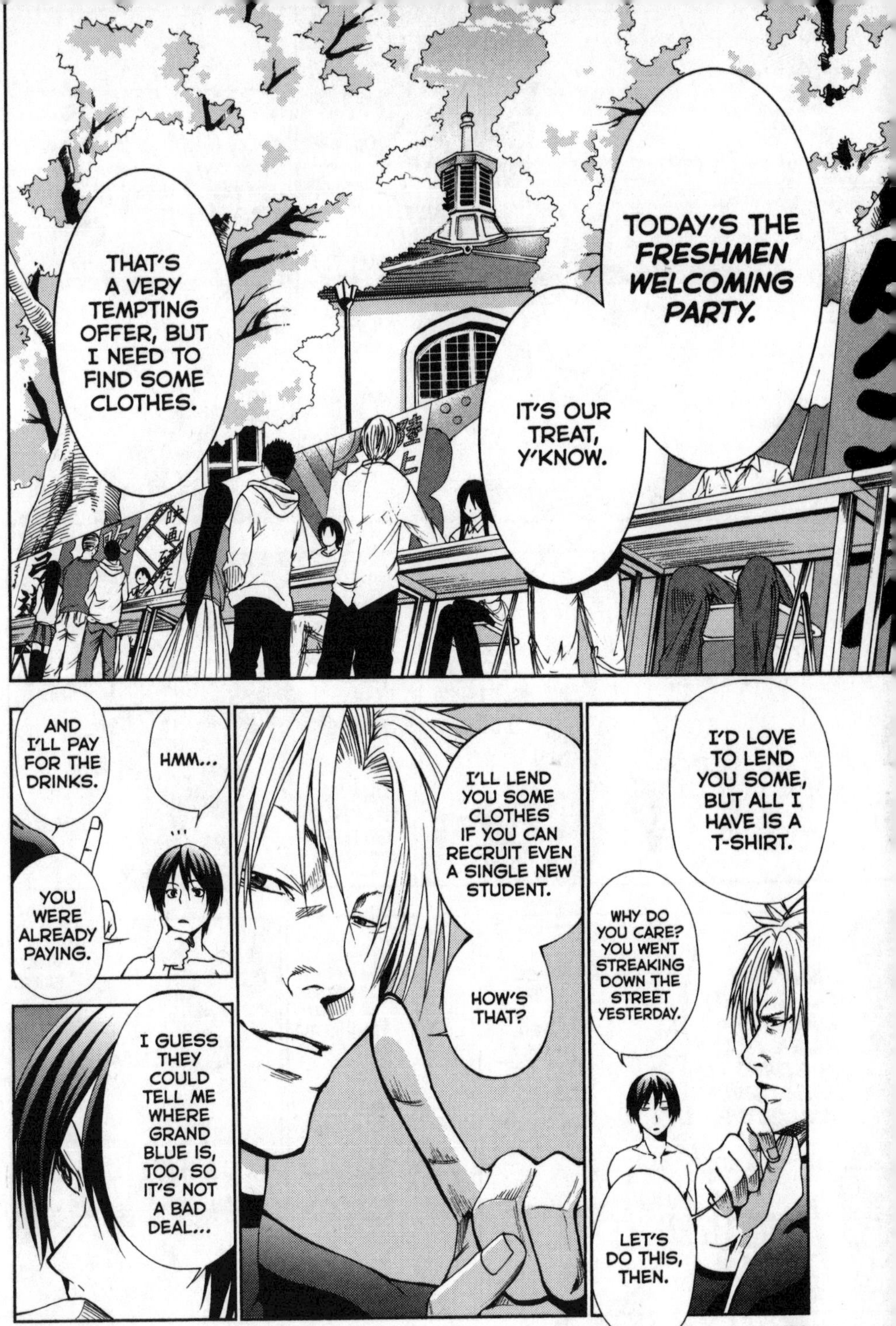
TODAY'S THE *FRESHMEN WELCOMING PARTY.*
IT'S OUR TREAT, Y'KNOW.
THAT'S A VERY TEMPTING OFFER, BUT I NEED TO FIND SOME CLOTHES.
I'D LOVE TO LEND YOU SOME, BUT ALL I HAVE IS A T-SHIRT.
WHY DO YOU CARE? YOU WENT STREAKING DOWN THE STREET YESTERDAY.
LET'S DO THIS, THEN.
I'LL LEND YOU SOME CLOTHES IF YOU CAN RECRUIT EVEN A SINGLE NEW STUDENT.
HOW'S THAT?
HMM...
AND I'LL PAY FOR THE DRINKS.
...
YOU WERE ALREADY PAYING.
I GUESS THEY COULD TELL ME WHERE GRAND BLUE IS, TOO, SO IT'S NOT A BAD DEAL...

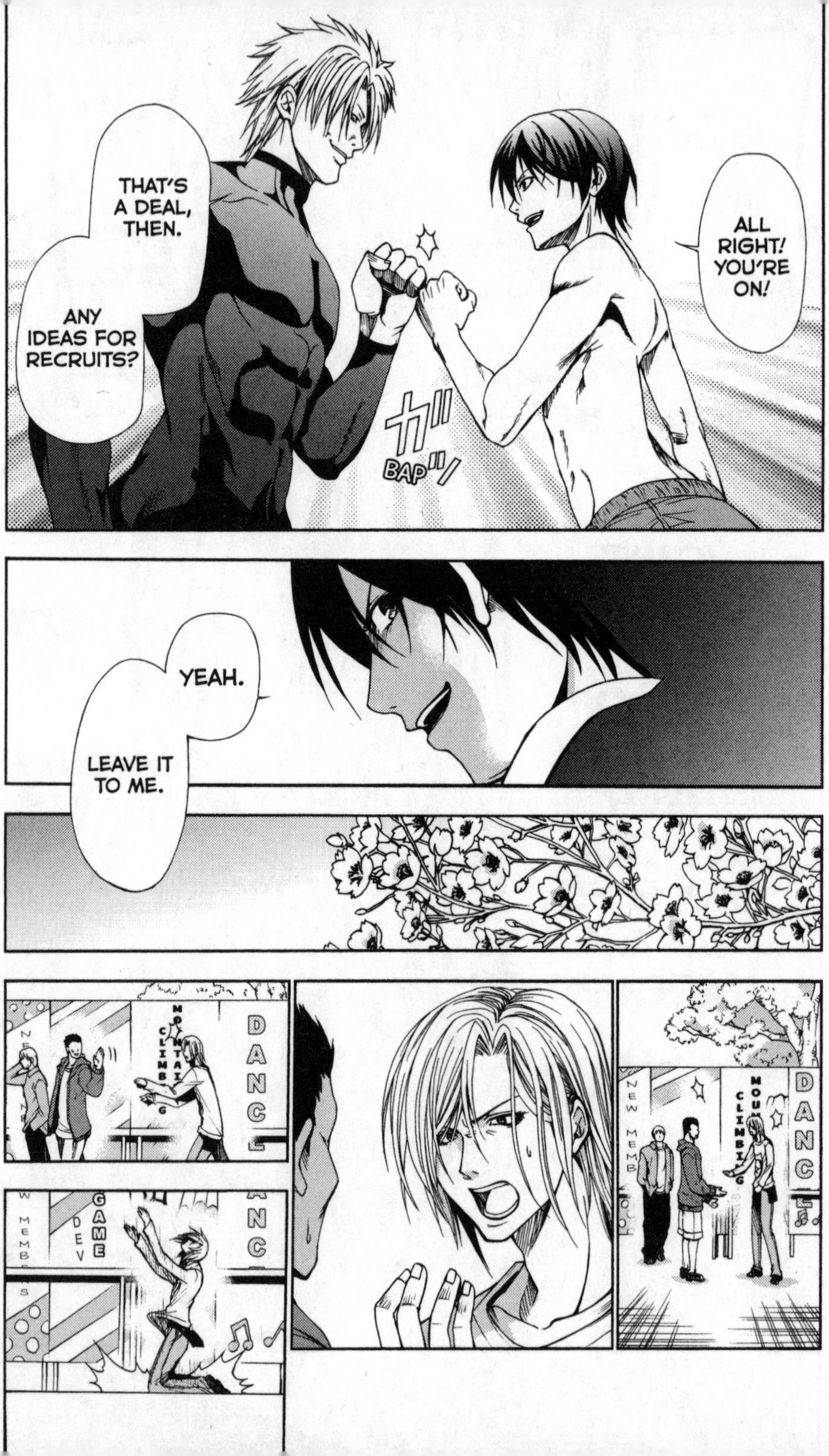
ALL RIGHT! YOU'RE ON!
THAT'S A DEAL, THEN.
ANY IDEAS FOR RECRUITS?
BAP
YEAH.
LEAVE IT TO ME.
NEW MEMB
DANC
NEW MEMBERS
GAME DEV

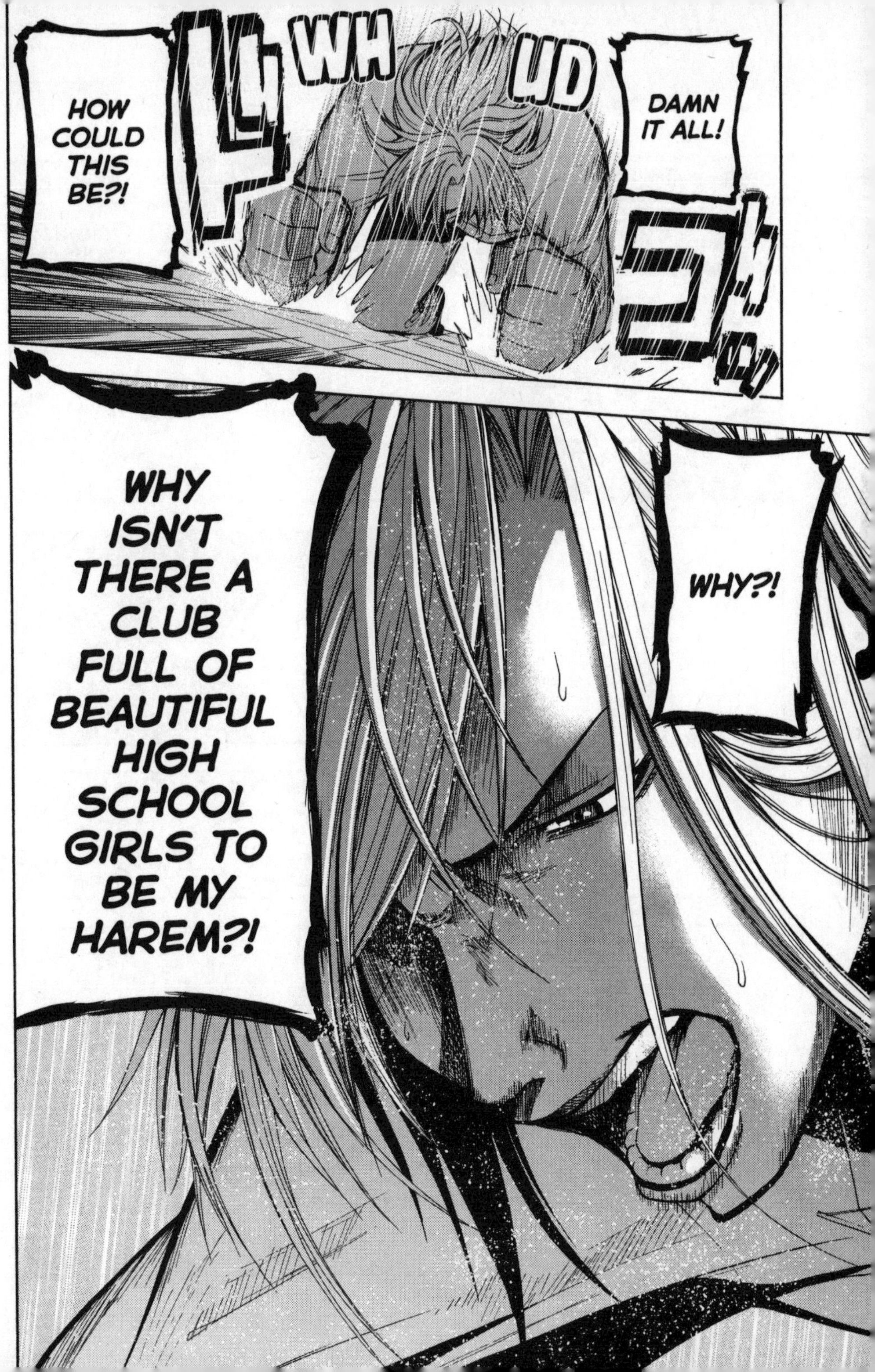
DAMN IT ALL!
WH UD
HOW COULD THIS BE?!
WHY?!
WHY ISN'T THERE A CLUB FULL OF BEAUTIFUL HIGH SCHOOL GIRLS TO BE MY HAREM?!

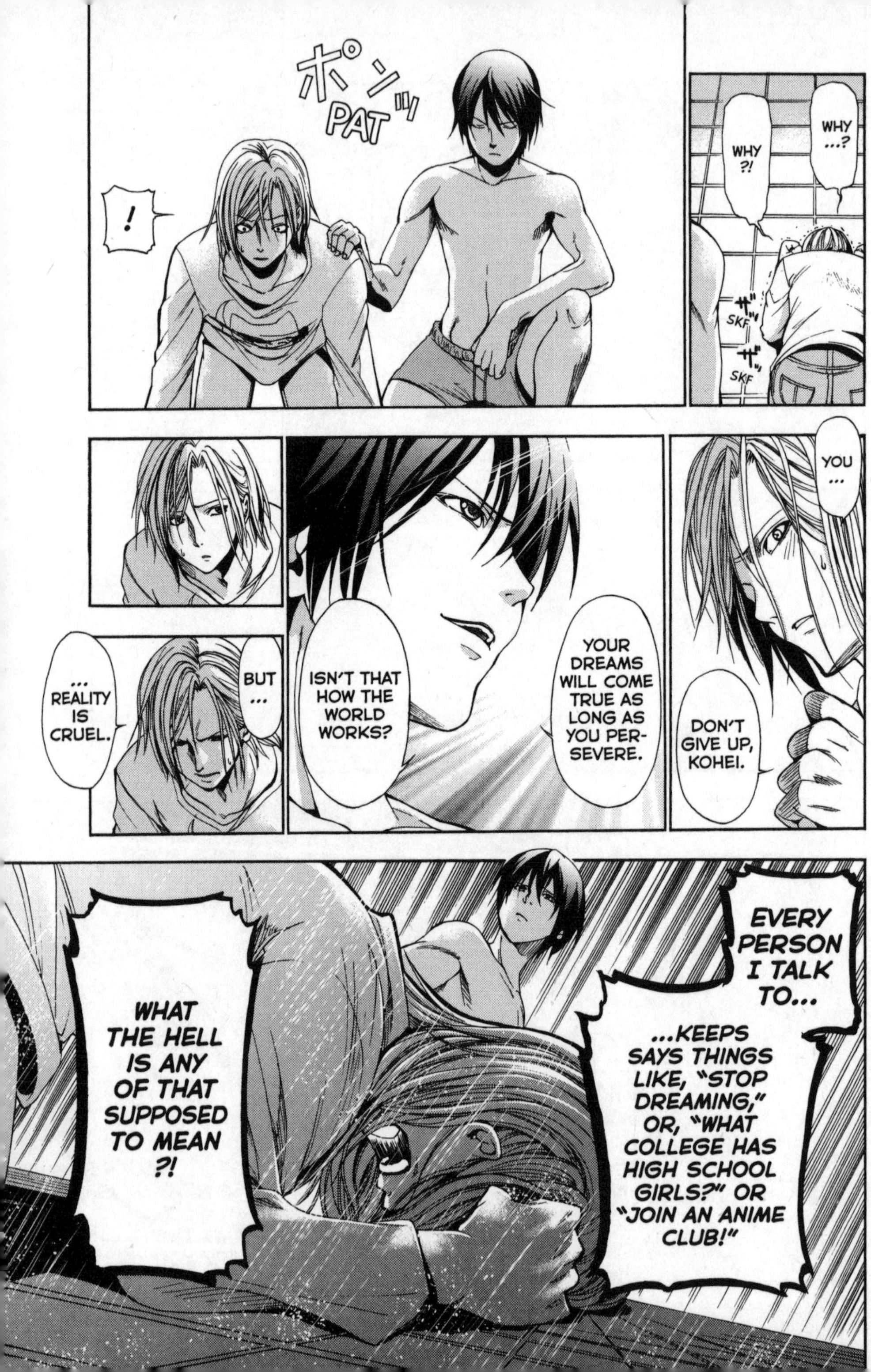
WHY ...?
WHY ?!
ザッ SKF
ザッ SKF
ポンッ PAT
!
YOU ...
DON'T GIVE UP, KOHEI.
YOUR DREAMS WILL COME TRUE AS LONG AS YOU PER-SEVERE.
ISN'T THAT HOW THE WORLD WORKS?
BUT ...
... REALITY IS CRUEL.
EVERY PERSON I TALK TO...
...KEEPS SAYS THINGS LIKE, "STOP DREAMING," OR, "WHAT COLLEGE HAS HIGH SCHOOL GIRLS?" OR "JOIN AN ANIME CLUB!"
WHAT THE HELL IS ANY OF THAT SUPPOSED TO MEAN ?!

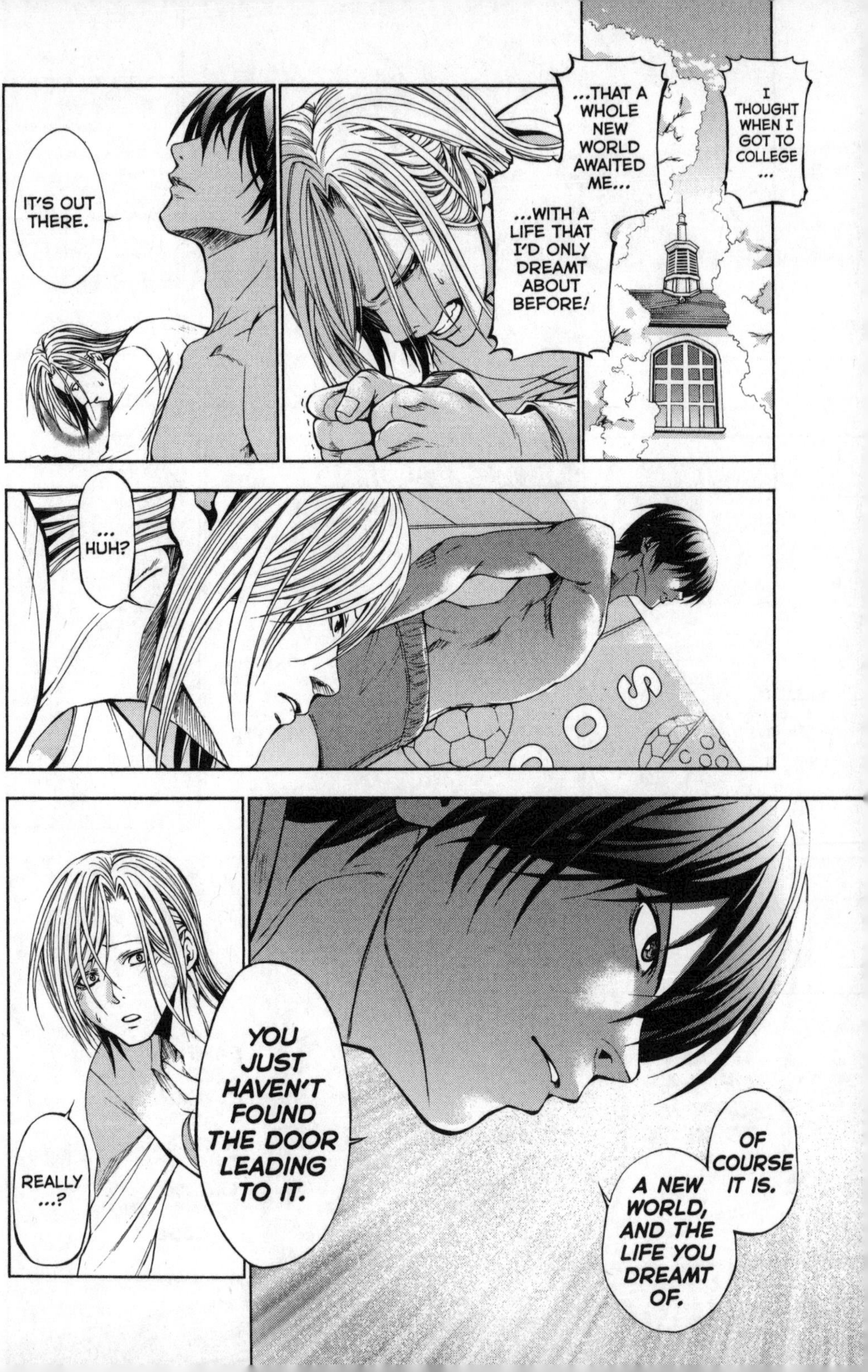
I THOUGHT WHEN I GOT TO COLLEGE...
...THAT A WHOLE NEW WORLD AWAITED ME...
...WITH A LIFE THAT I'D ONLY DREAMT ABOUT BEFORE!
IT'S OUT THERE.
...HUH?
OF COURSE IT IS.
A NEW WORLD, AND THE LIFE YOU DREAMT OF.
YOU JUST HAVEN'T FOUND THE DOOR LEADING TO IT.
REALLY...?

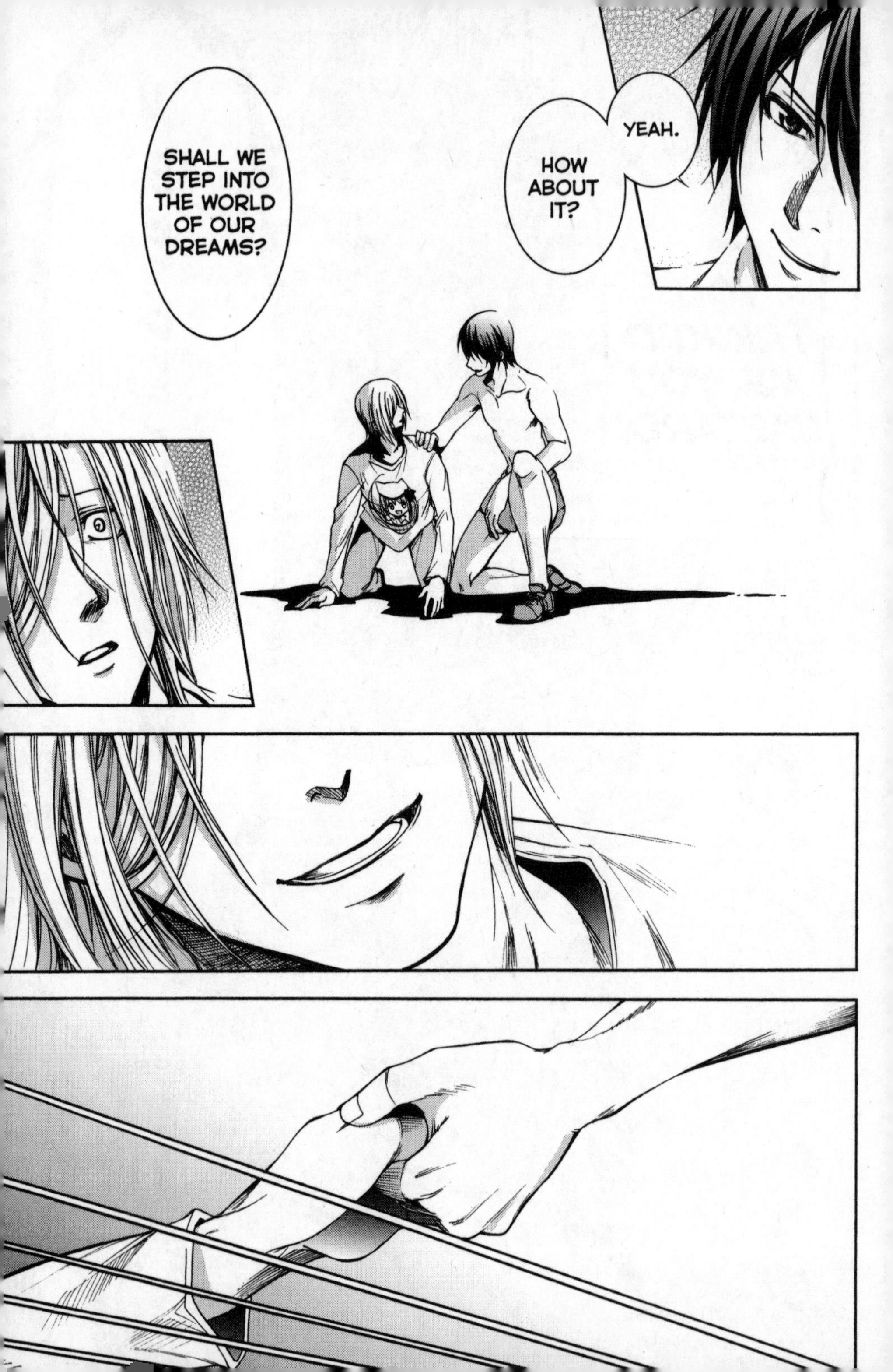
YEAH.
HOW ABOUT IT?
SHALL WE STEP INTO THE WORLD OF OUR DREAMS?

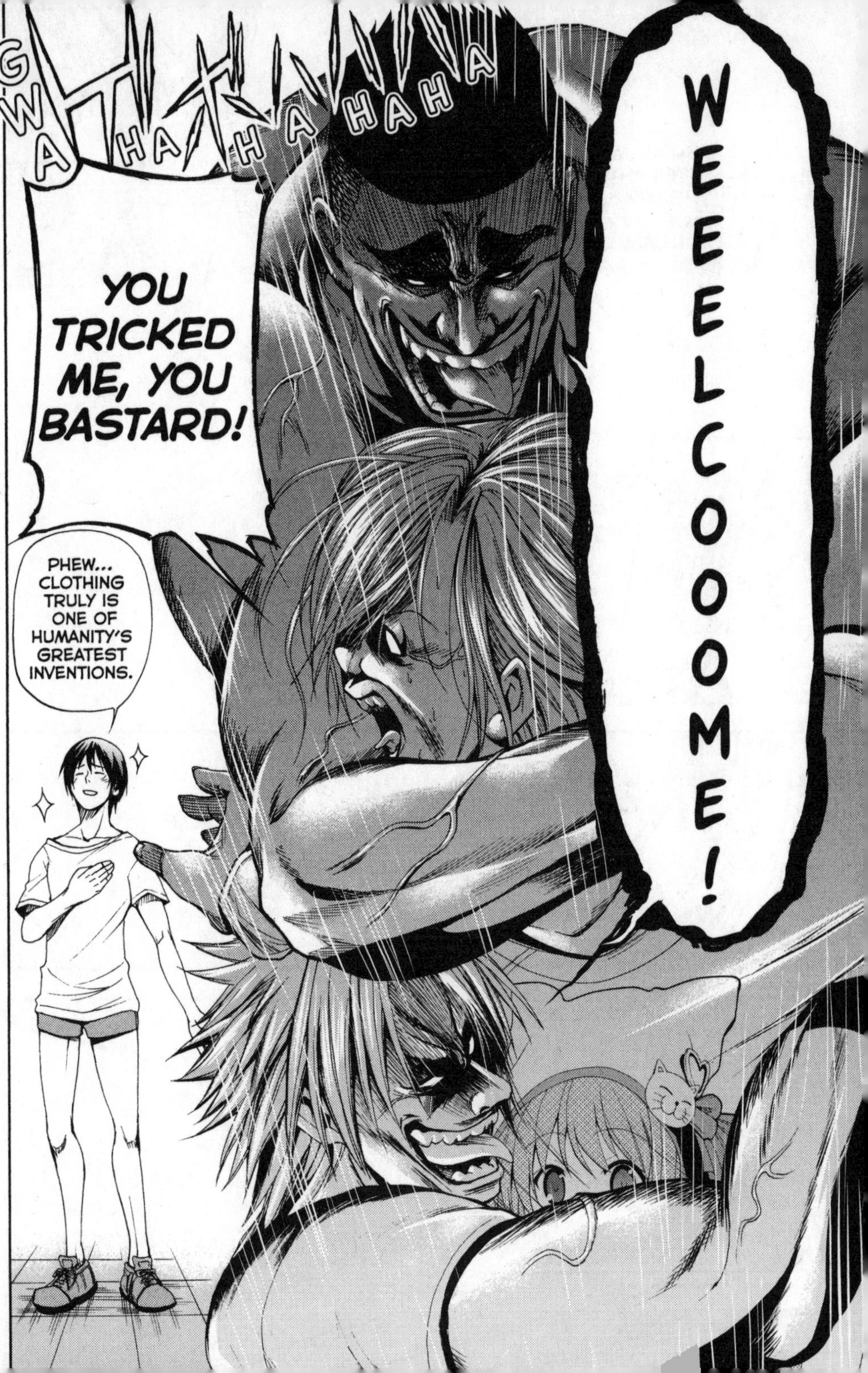
WEEELCOOOME!
GWAHAHAHAHA
YOU TRICKED ME, YOU BASTARD!
PHEW... CLOTHING TRULY IS ONE OF HUMANITY'S GREATEST INVENTIONS.

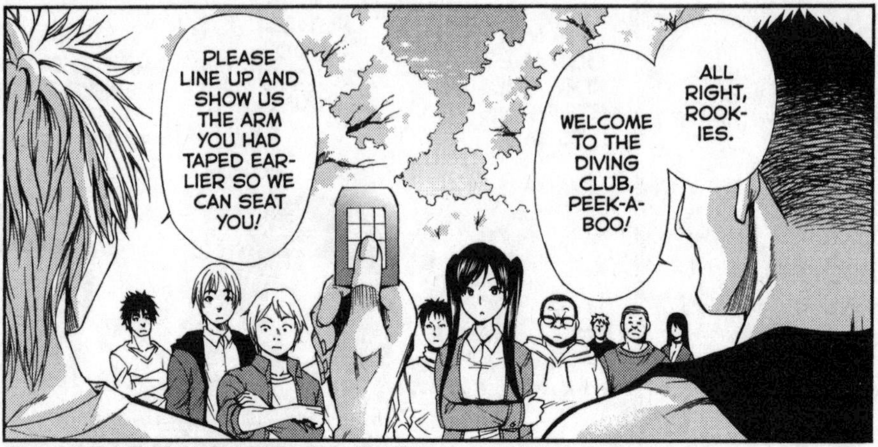
ALL RIGHT, ROOKIES.
WELCOME TO THE DIVING CLUB, PEEK-A-BOO!
PLEASE LINE UP AND SHOW US THE ARM YOU HAD TAPED EARLIER SO WE CAN SEAT YOU!

*TO PROMOTE SAFE DRINKING, THEY'RE USING PATCH TESTS TO MEASURE ALCOHOL TOLERANCE.

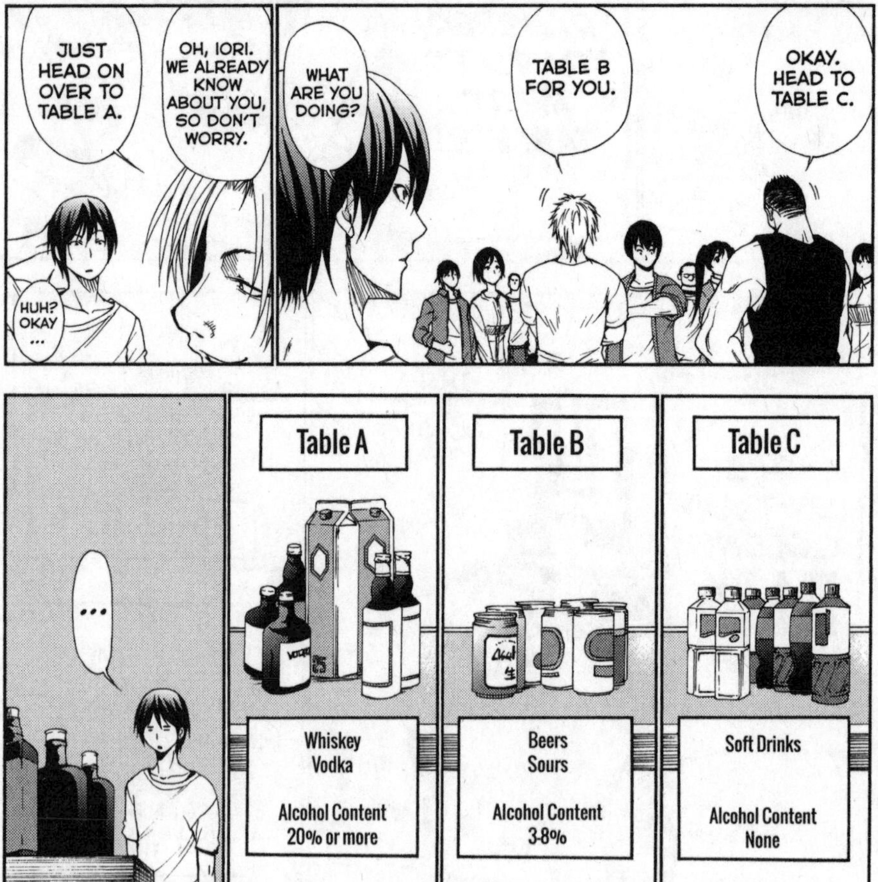
OKAY. HEAD TO TABLE C.
TABLE B FOR YOU.
WHAT ARE YOU DOING?
OH, IORI. WE ALREADY KNOW ABOUT YOU, SO DON'T WORRY.
JUST HEAD ON OVER TO TABLE A.
HUH? OKAY ...
Table C
Soft Drinks
Alcohol Content None
Table B
Beers Sours
Alcohol Content 3-8%
Table A
Whiskey Vodka
Alcohol Content 20% or more
...

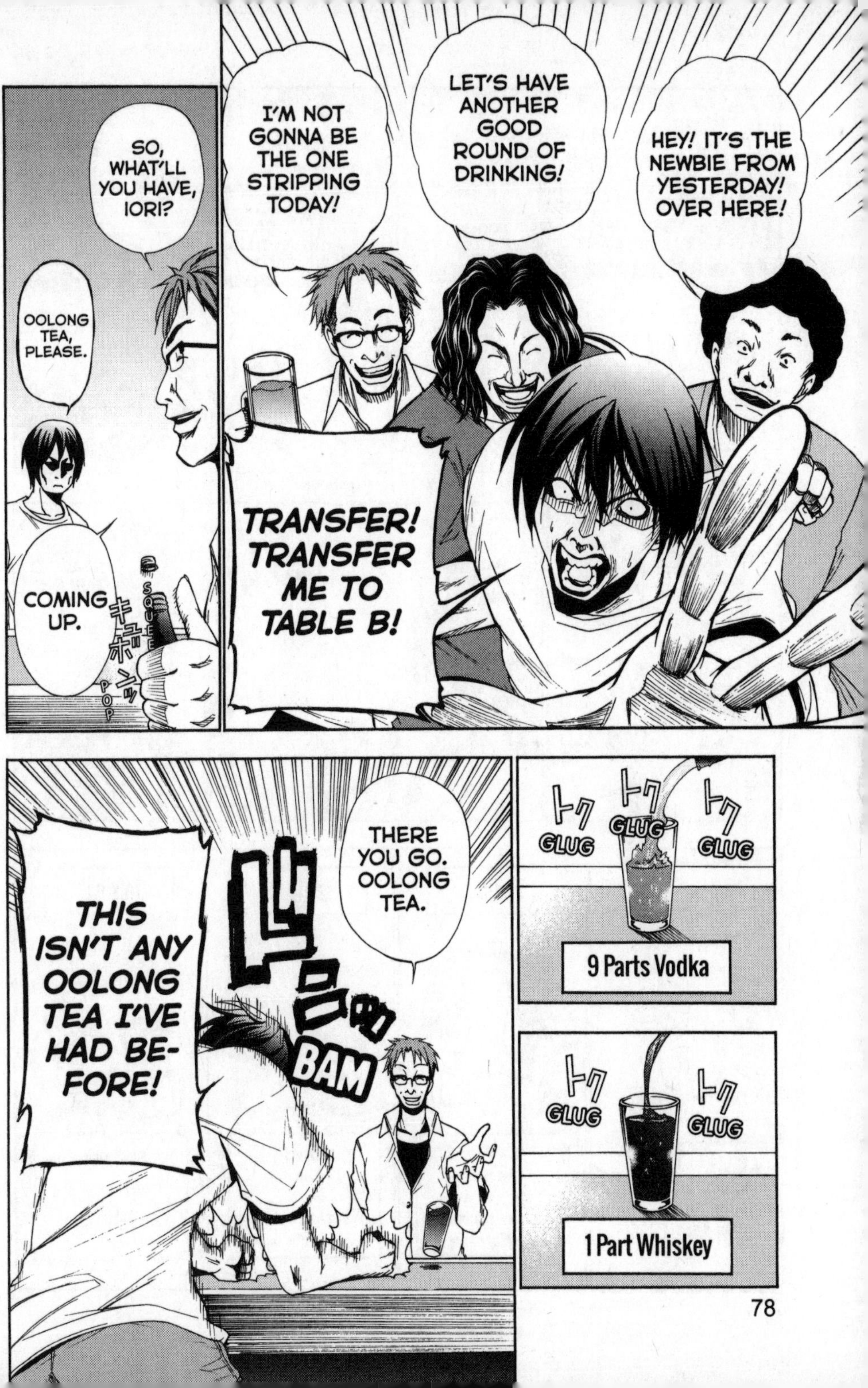
HEY! IT'S THE NEWBIE FROM YESTERDAY! OVER HERE!
LET'S HAVE ANOTHER GOOD ROUND OF DRINKING!
I'M NOT GONNA BE THE ONE STRIPPING TODAY!
TRANSFER! TRANSFER ME TO TABLE B!
SO, WHAT'LL YOU HAVE, IORI?
OOLONG TEA, PLEASE.
COMING UP.
キュ SQUEE
ポン POP
トク GLUG
トク GLUG
トク GLUG
9 Parts Vodka
トク GLUG
トク GLUG
1 Part Whiskey
THERE YOU GO. OOLONG TEA.
ドン BAM
THIS ISN'T ANY OOLONG TEA I'VE HAD BE-FORE!

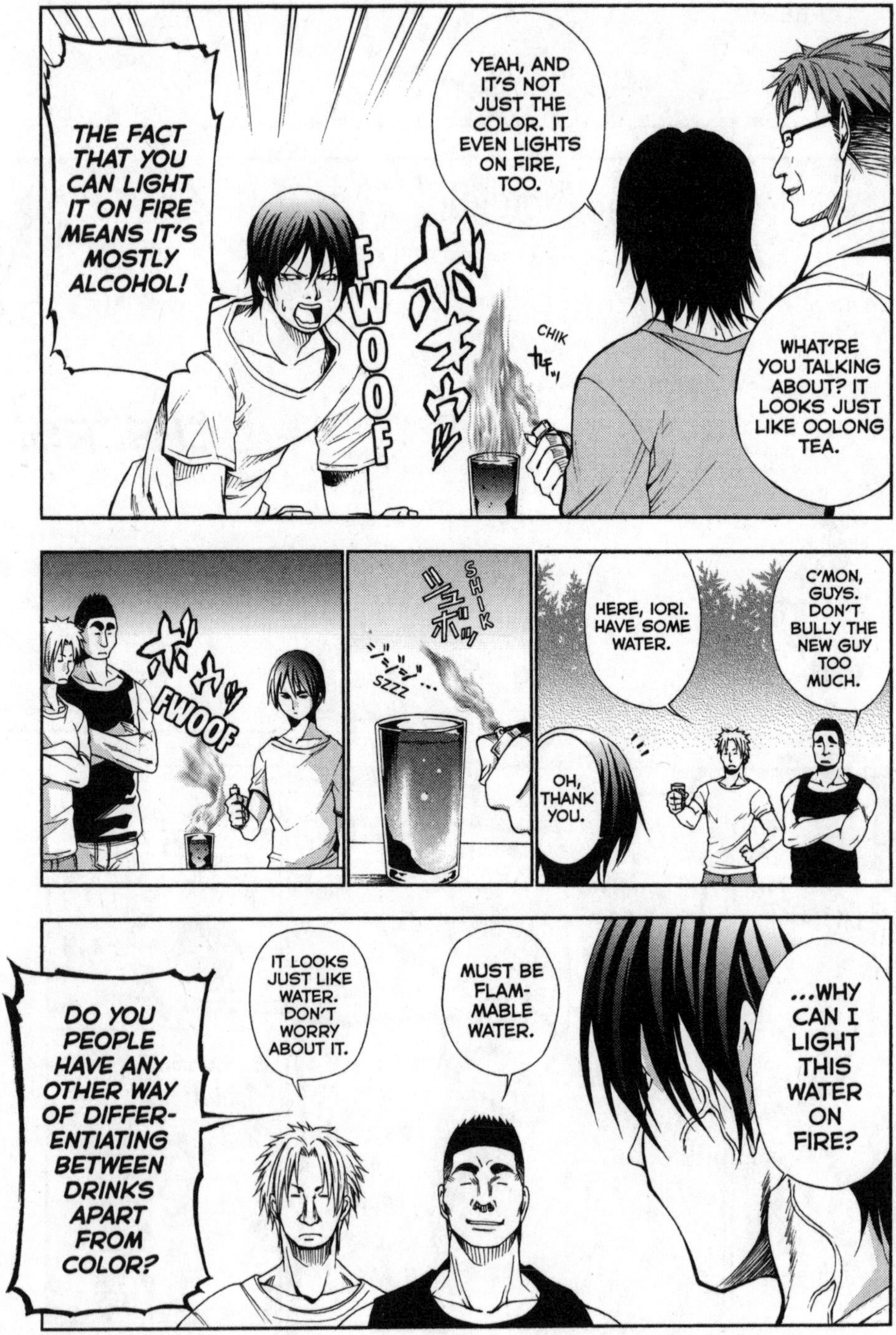
WHAT'RE YOU TALKING ABOUT? IT LOOKS JUST LIKE OOLONG TEA.
YEAH, AND IT'S NOT JUST THE COLOR. IT EVEN LIGHTS ON FIRE, TOO.
CHIK
FWOOF
THE FACT THAT YOU CAN LIGHT IT ON FIRE MEANS IT'S MOSTLY ALCOHOL!
C'MON, GUYS. DON'T BULLY THE NEW GUY TOO MUCH.
HERE, IORI. HAVE SOME WATER.
OH, THANK YOU.
SHIK
SZZZ...
FWOOF
...WHY CAN I LIGHT THIS WATER ON FIRE?
MUST BE FLAM-MABLE WATER.
IT LOOKS JUST LIKE WATER. DON'T WORRY ABOUT IT.
DO YOU PEOPLE HAVE ANY OTHER WAY OF DIFFER-ENTIATING BETWEEN DRINKS APART FROM COLOR?

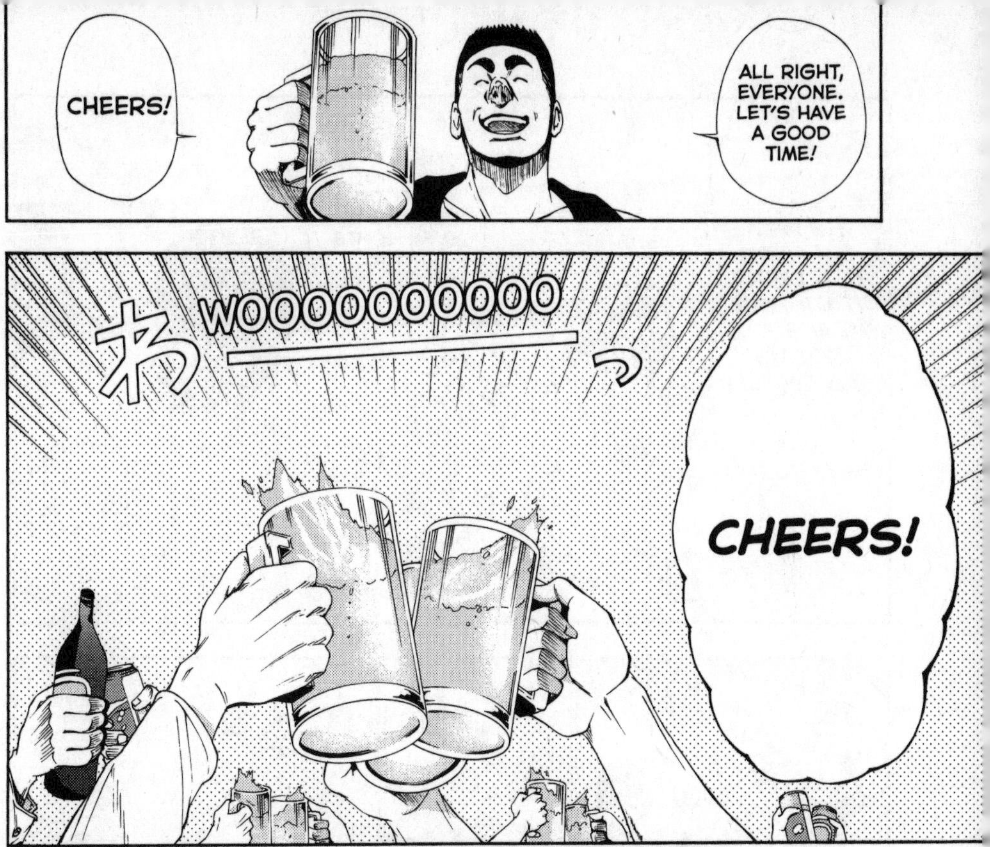

ALL RIGHT, EVERYONE. LET'S HAVE A GOOD TIME!
CHEERS!
わ WOOOOOOOOOOO っ
CHEERS!

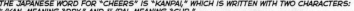

*THE JAPANESE WORD FOR "CHEERS" IS "KANPAI," WHICH IS WRITTEN WITH TWO CHARACTERS: 乾/KAN, MEANING "DRY," AND 杯/PAI, MEANING "CUP."

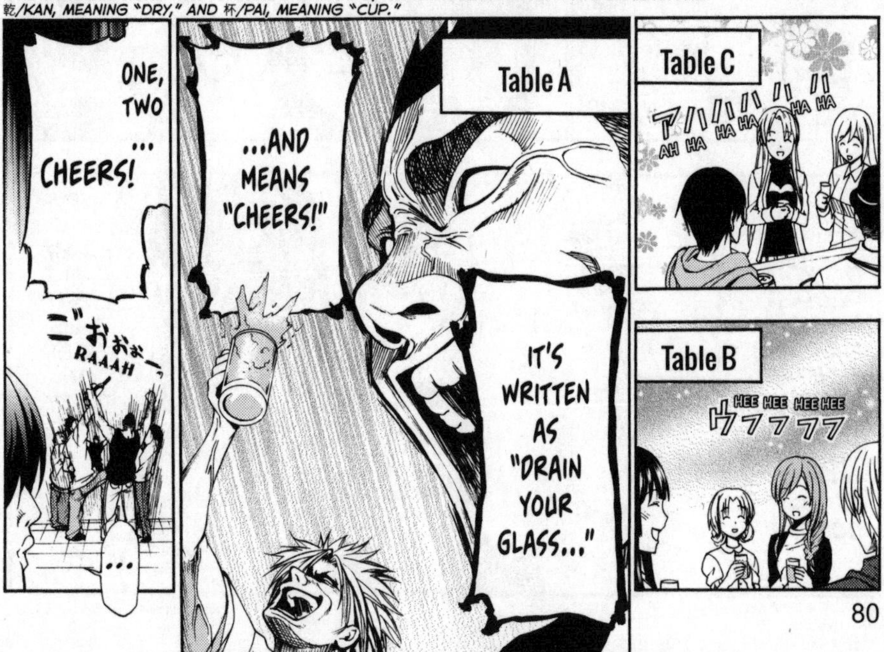

Table C
アハハハハハ AH HA HA HA HA HA
Table B
ウフフフフ HEE HEE HEE HEE
Table A
IT'S WRITTEN AS "DRAIN YOUR GLASS..."
...AND MEANS "CHEERS!"
ONE, TWO ... CHEERS!
ごおぉー RAAAH
...

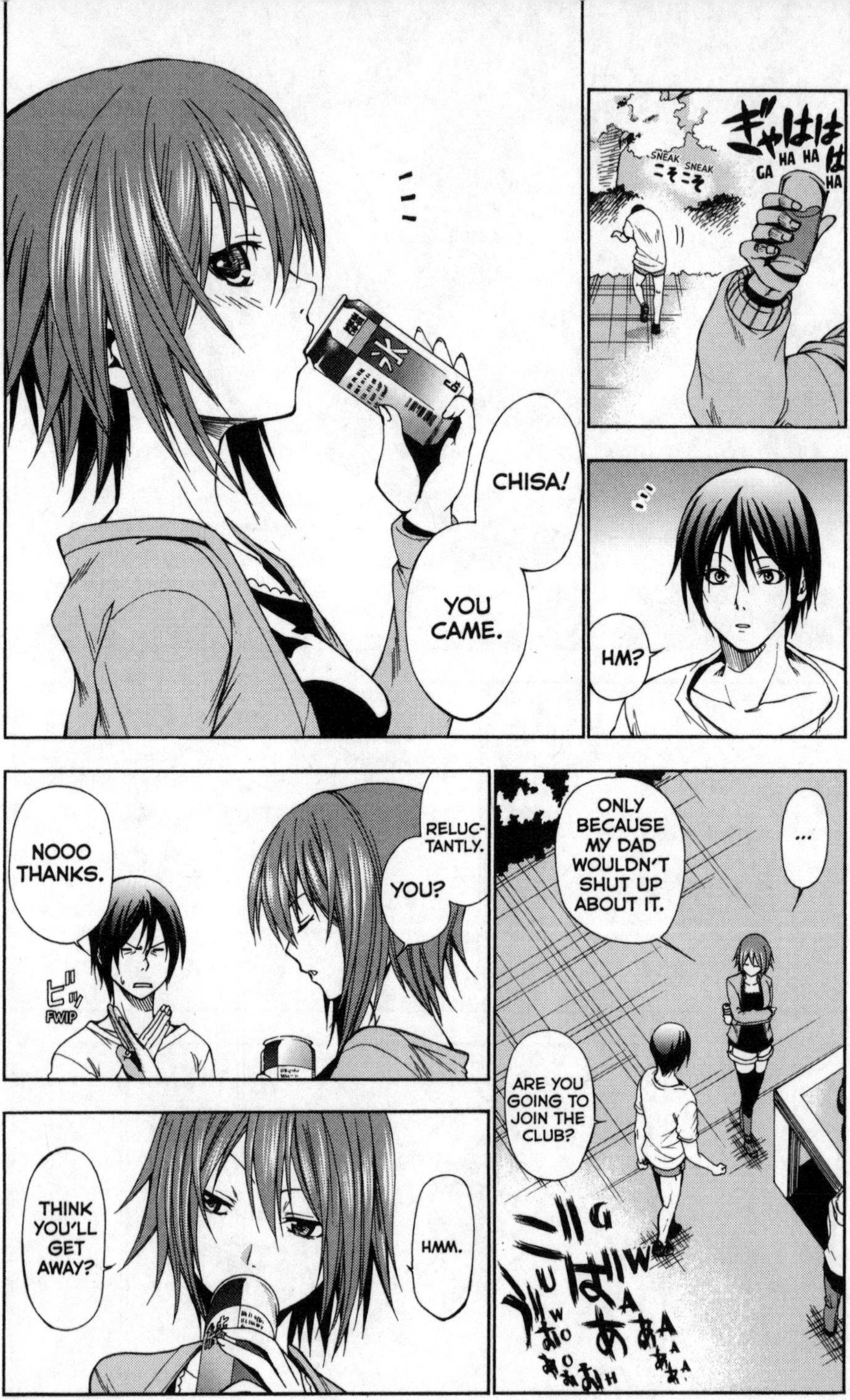
ぎゃははは
GA HA HA HA
SNEAK SNEAK
こそこそ
...
HM?
...
CHISA!
YOU CAME.
...
ONLY BECAUSE MY DAD WOULDN'T SHUT UP ABOUT IT.
ARE YOU GOING TO JOIN THE CLUB?
RELUC-TANTLY.
YOU?
NOOO THANKS.
ビッ
FWIP
HMM.
THINK YOU'LL GET AWAY?

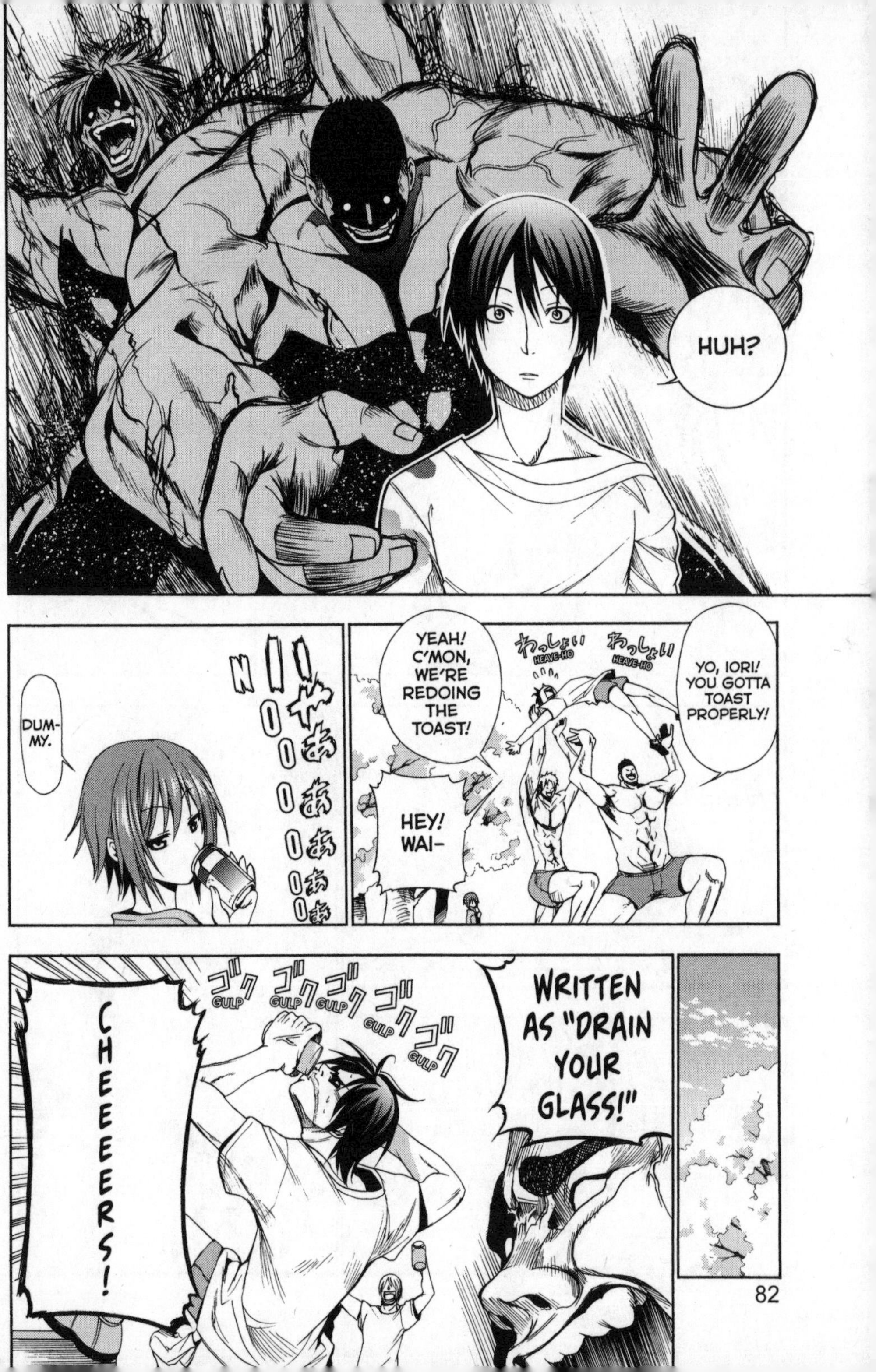
HUH?
YO, IORI! YOU GOTTA TOAST PROPERLY!
わっしょい HEAVE-HO
わっしょい HEAVE-HO
YEAH! C'MON, WE'RE REDOING THE TOAST!
HEY! WAI-
いやあああああ NOOOOOO
DUM-MY.
WRITTEN AS "DRAIN YOUR GLASS!"
ゴクゴクゴクゴクゴク GULP GULP GULP GULP GULP
CHEEEERS!

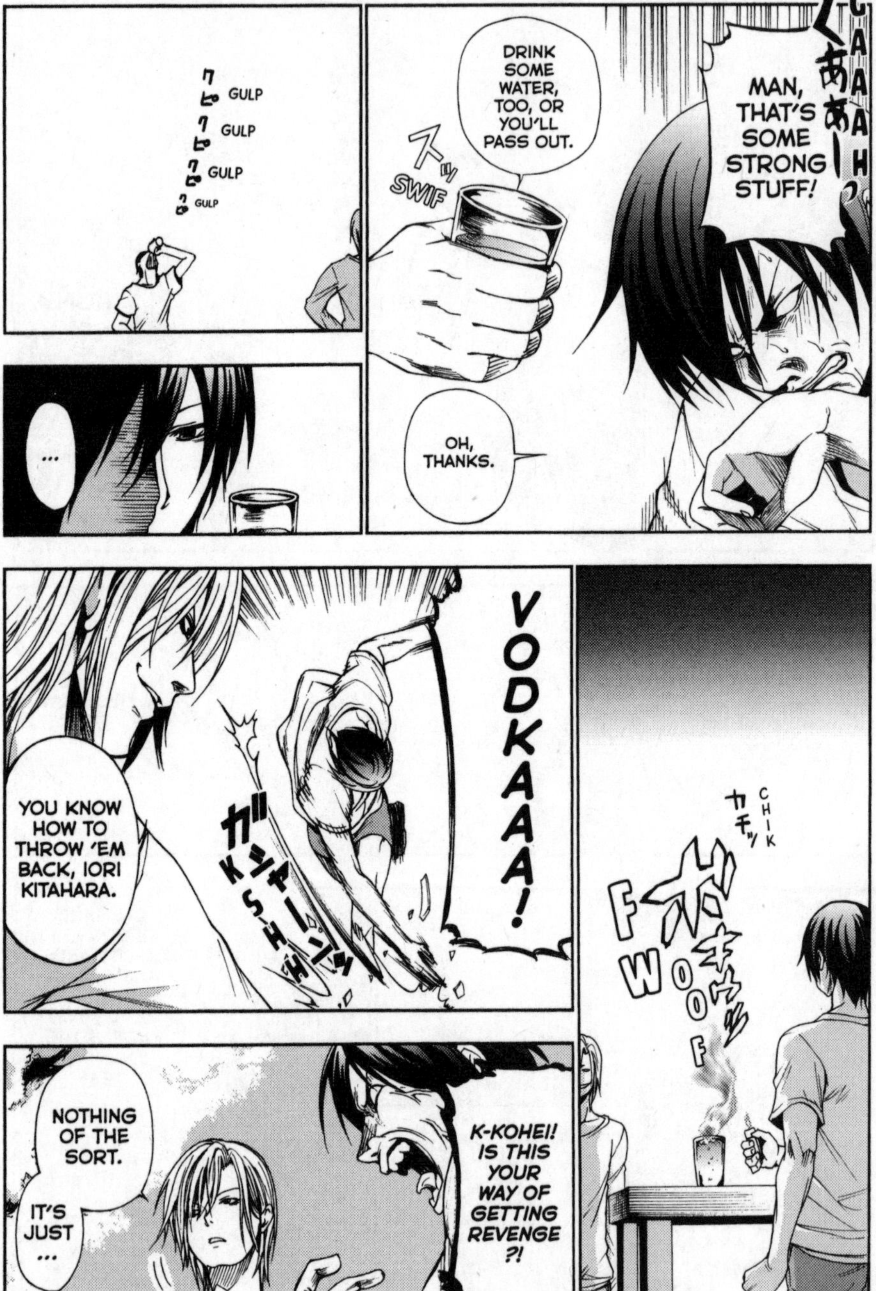
GAAAH,
MAN, THAT'S SOME STRONG STUFF!
SWIF
DRINK SOME WATER, TOO, OR YOU'LL PASS OUT.
OH, THANKS.
GULP
GULP
GULP
GULP
...
CHIK
FWOOF
VODKAAA!
KSHH
YOU KNOW HOW TO THROW 'EM BACK, IORI KITAHARA.
K-KOHEI! IS THIS YOUR WAY OF GETTING REVENGE?!
NOTHING OF THE SORT.
IT'S JUST ...

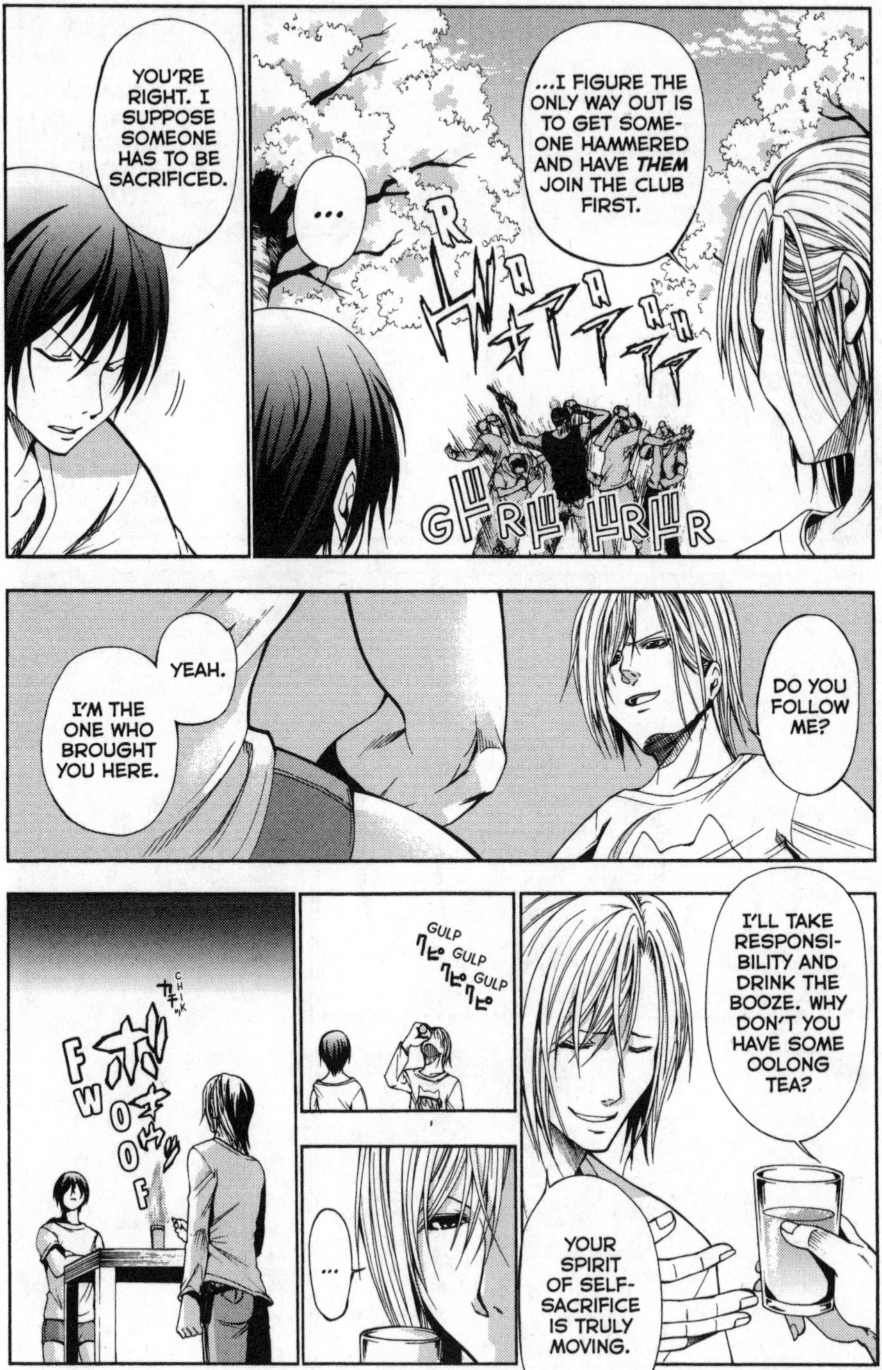
...I FIGURE THE ONLY WAY OUT IS TO GET SOME-ONE HAMMERED AND HAVE *THEM* JOIN THE CLUB FIRST.
...
RWAAAH
GRRR
YOU'RE RIGHT. I SUPPOSE SOMEONE HAS TO BE SACRIFICED.
DO YOU FOLLOW ME?
YEAH.
I'M THE ONE WHO BROUGHT YOU HERE.
I'LL TAKE RESPONSI-BILITY AND DRINK THE BOOZE. WHY DON'T YOU HAVE SOME OOLONG TEA?
YOUR SPIRIT OF SELF-SACRIFICE IS TRULY MOVING.
GULP GULP GULP
...
CHIK
FWOOOF

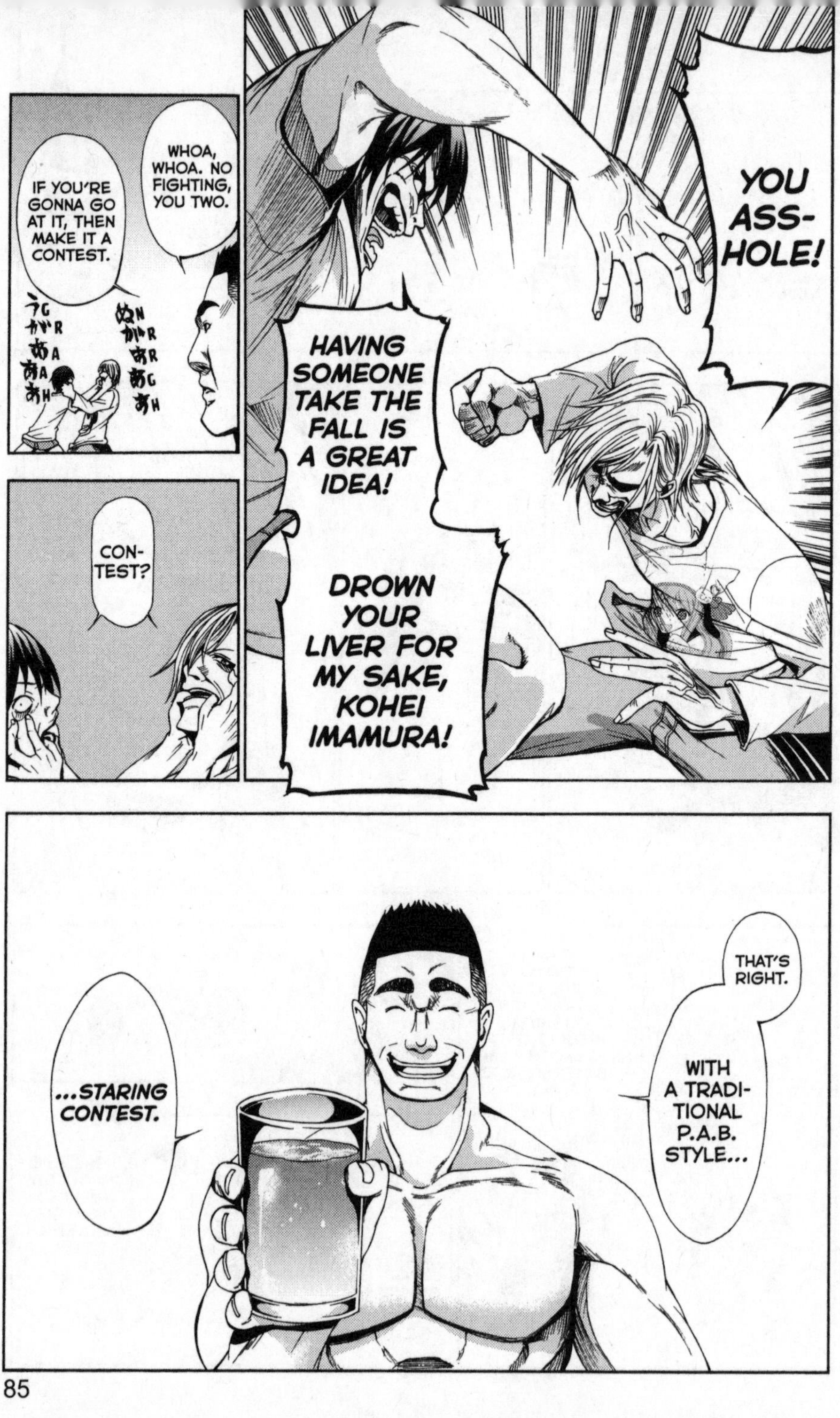
YOU ASS-HOLE!
HAVING SOMEONE TAKE THE FALL IS A GREAT IDEA!
DROWN YOUR LIVER FOR MY SAKE, KOHEI IMAMURA!
WHOA, WHOA. NO FIGHTING, YOU TWO.
IF YOU'RE GONNA GO AT IT, THEN MAKE IT A CONTEST.
ぬがあああ NRRGH
うがあああ GRAAH
CON-TEST?
THAT'S RIGHT.
WITH A TRADI-TIONAL P.A.B. STYLE...
...STARING CONTEST.

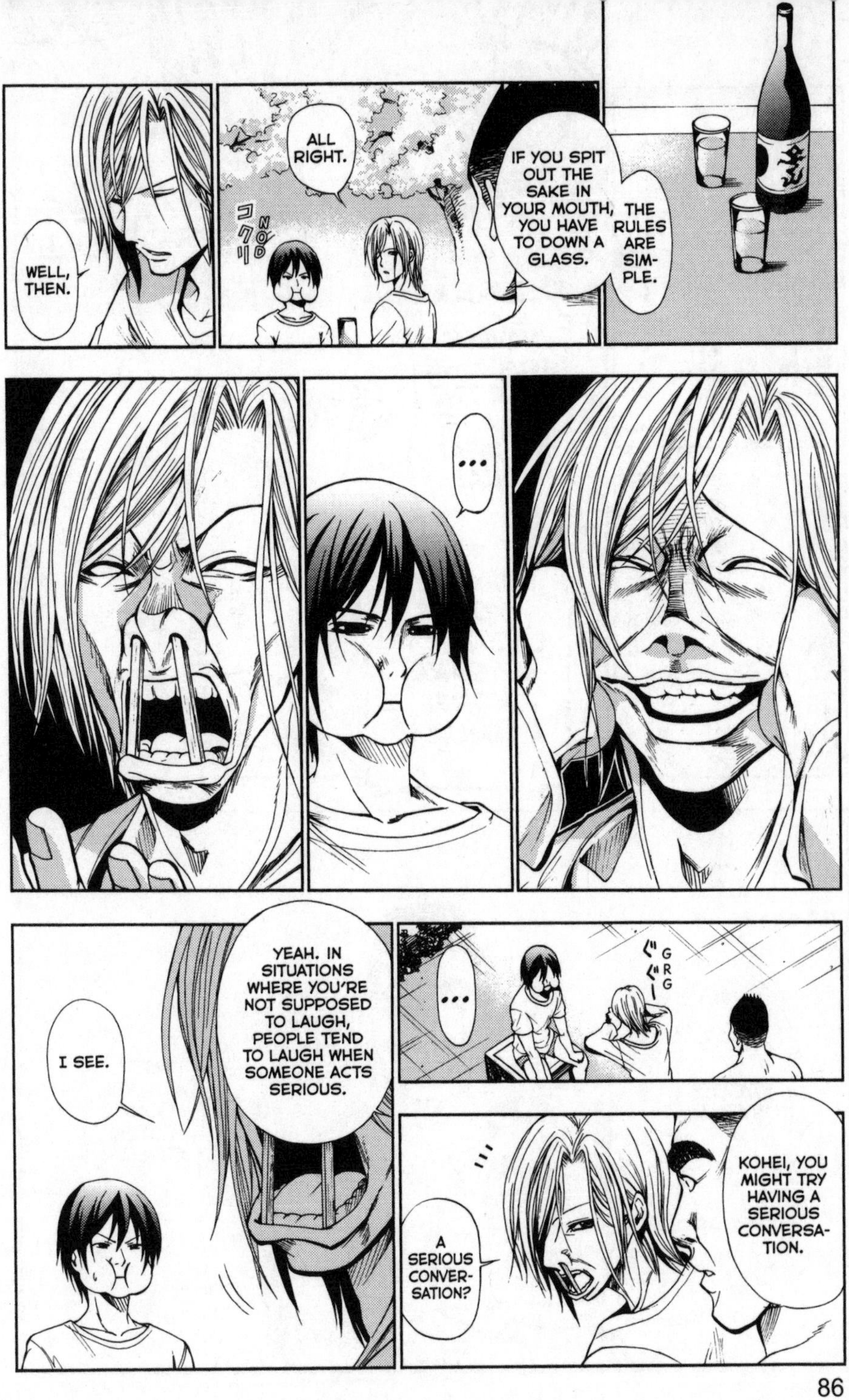
THE RULES ARE SIMPLE.
IF YOU SPIT OUT THE SAKE IN YOUR MOUTH, YOU HAVE TO DOWN A GLASS.
ALL RIGHT.
NOD
WELL, THEN.
...
GRG
...
KOHEI, YOU MIGHT TRY HAVING A SERIOUS CONVERSATION.
!!
A SERIOUS CONVERSATION?
YEAH. IN SITUATIONS WHERE YOU'RE NOT SUPPOSED TO LAUGH, PEOPLE TEND TO LAUGH WHEN SOMEONE ACTS SERIOUS.
I SEE.

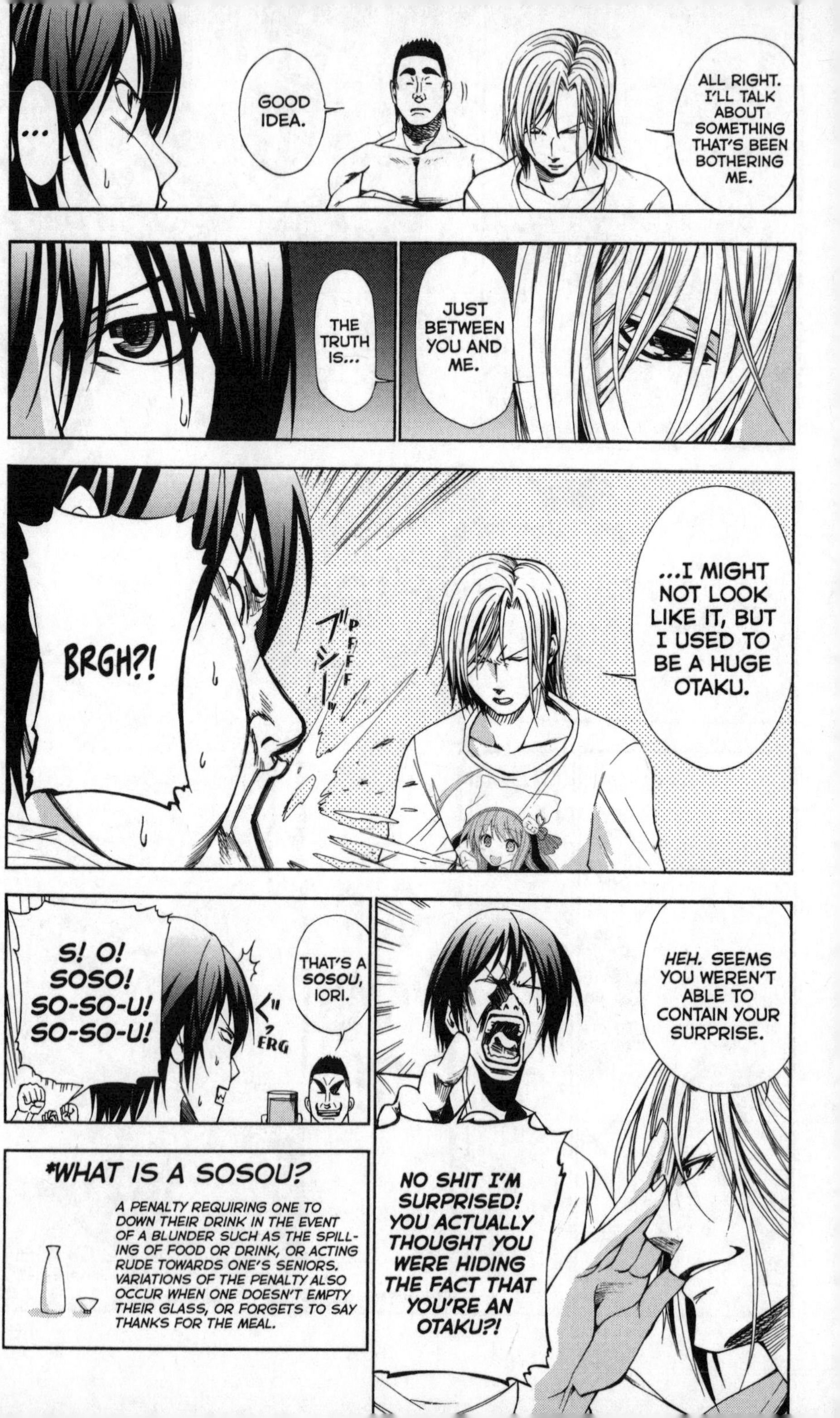
ALL RIGHT. I'LL TALK ABOUT SOMETHING THAT'S BEEN BOTHERING ME.
GOOD IDEA.
...
JUST BETWEEN YOU AND ME.
THE TRUTH IS...
...I MIGHT NOT LOOK LIKE IT, BUT I USED TO BE A HUGE OTAKU.
PFFFF
BRGH?!
HEH. SEEMS YOU WEREN'T ABLE TO CONTAIN YOUR SURPRISE.
NO SHIT I'M SURPRISED! YOU ACTUALLY THOUGHT YOU WERE HIDING THE FACT THAT YOU'RE AN OTAKU?!
THAT'S A SOSOU, IORI.
ERG
S! O! SOSO! SO-SO-U! SO-SO-U!
*WHAT IS A SOSOU?
A PENALTY REQUIRING ONE TO DOWN THEIR DRINK IN THE EVENT OF A BLUNDER SUCH AS THE SPILLING OF FOOD OR DRINK, OR ACTING RUDE TOWARDS ONE'S SENIORS. VARIATIONS OF THE PENALTY ALSO OCCUR WHEN ONE DOESN'T EMPTY THEIR GLASS, OR FORGETS TO SAY THANKS FOR THE MEAL.

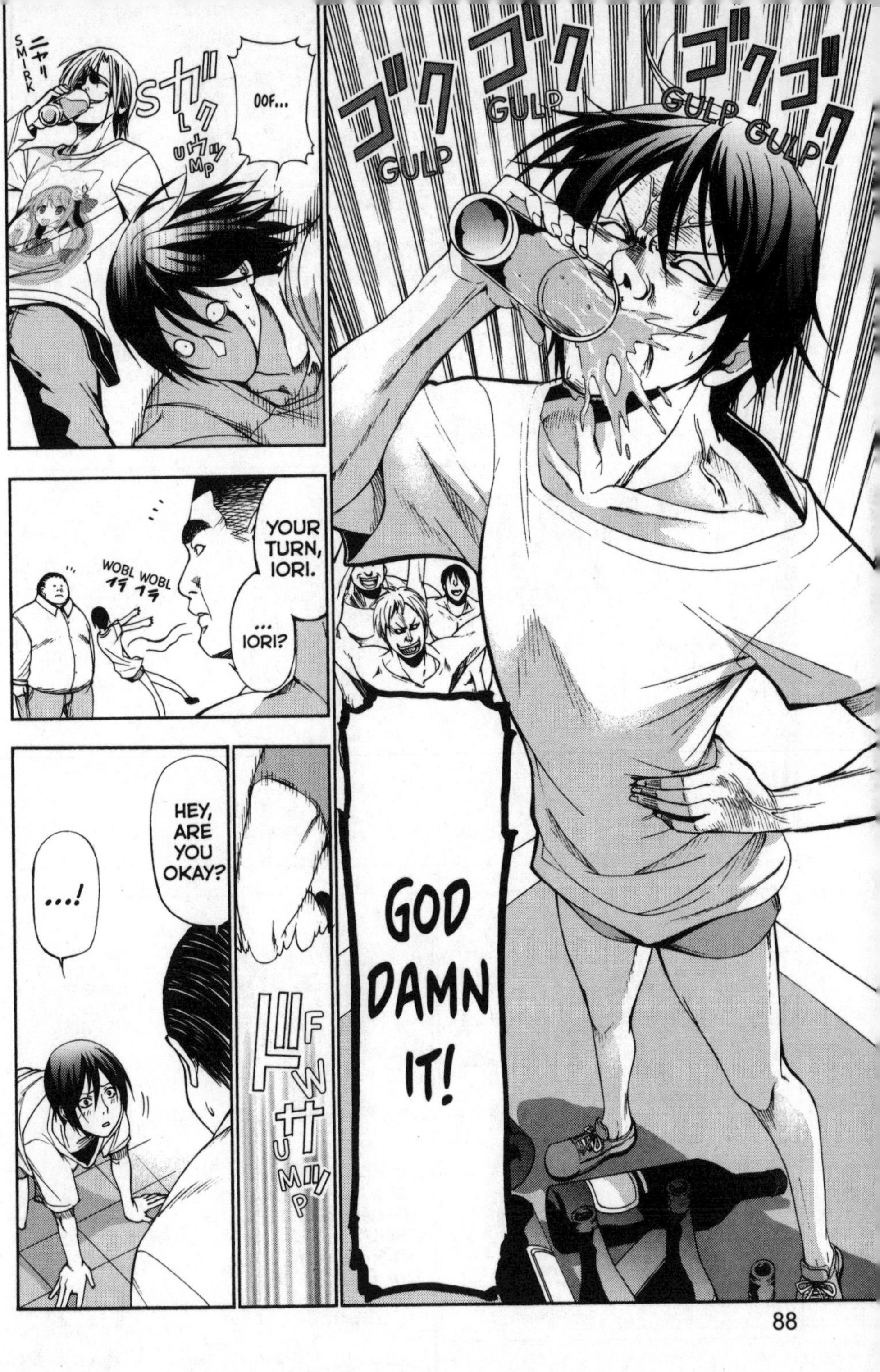
GULP
GULP
GULP GULP
GOD DAMN IT!
OOF...
SLUMP
SMIRK
YOUR TURN, IORI.
... IORI?
WOBL WOBL
FWUMP
HEY, ARE YOU OKAY?
...!

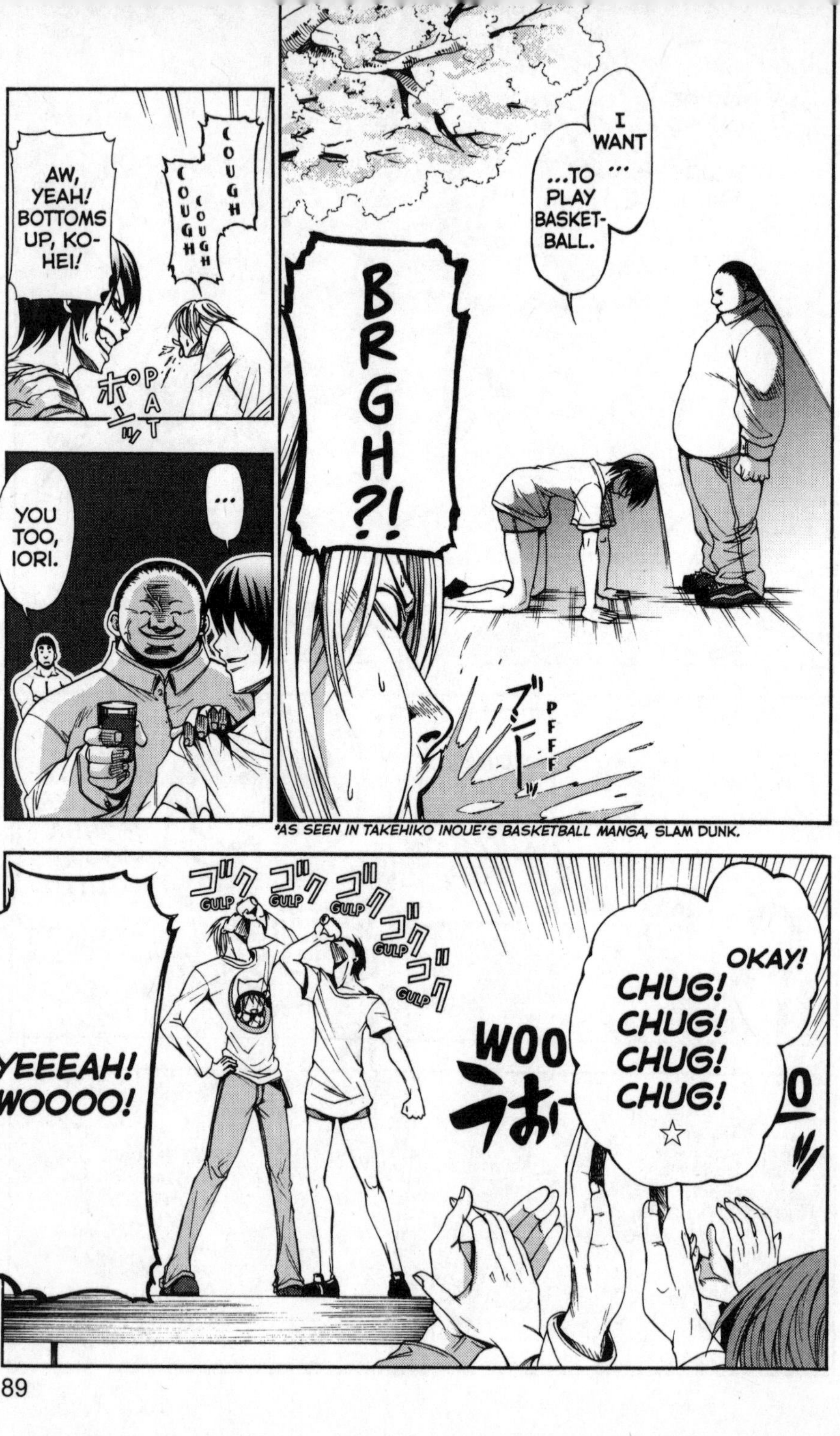
I WANT ...
...TO PLAY BASKET-BALL.
BRGH?!
PFFF
COUGH COUGH
COUGH COUGH
AW, YEAH! BOTTOMS UP, KO-HEI!
PAT
...
YOU TOO, IORI.
OKAY! CHUG! CHUG! CHUG! CHUG! ☆
WOO
O
GULP
GULP
GULP
GULP
GULP
YEEEAH! WOOOO!

*AS SEEN IN TAKEHIKO INOUE'S BASKETBALL MANGA, SLAM DUNK.

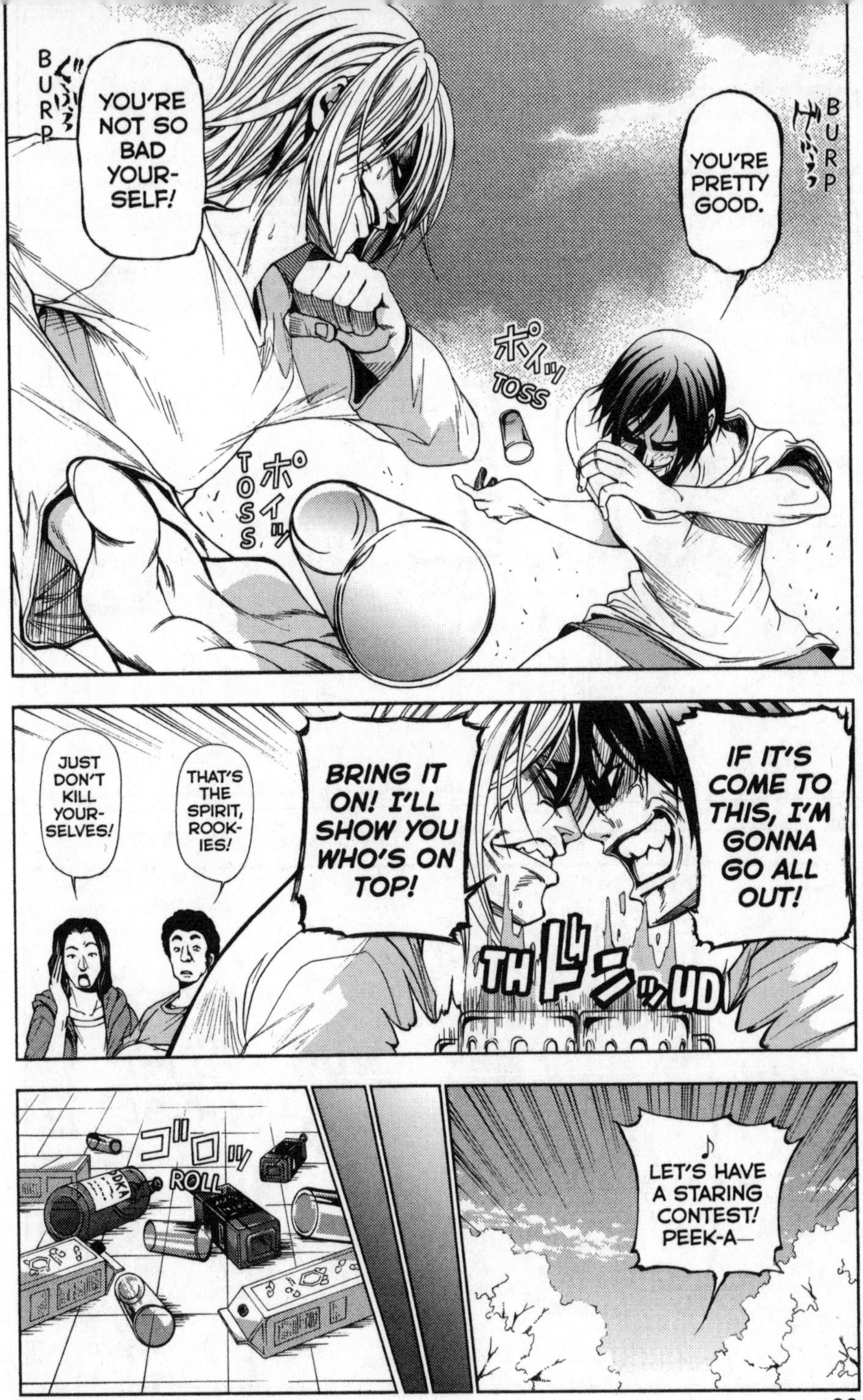
BURP
YOU'RE PRETTY GOOD.
BURP
YOU'RE NOT SO BAD YOUR-SELF!
TOSS
TOSS
IF IT'S COME TO THIS, I'M GONNA GO ALL OUT!
BRING IT ON! I'LL SHOW YOU WHO'S ON TOP!
THUD
THAT'S THE SPIRIT, ROOK-IES!
JUST DON'T KILL YOUR-SELVES!
♪ LET'S HAVE A STARING CONTEST! PEEK-A—
ROLL

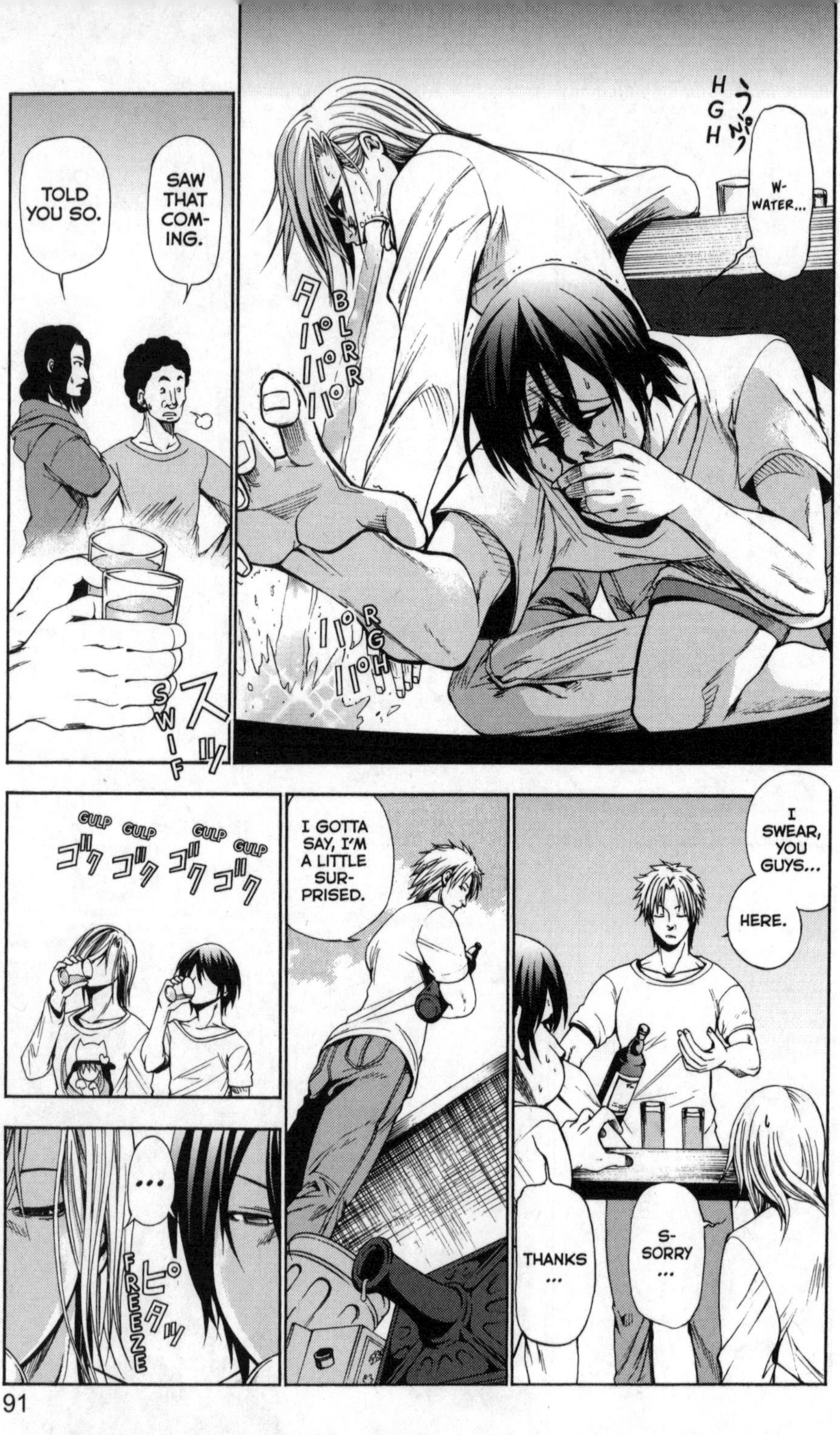
HGH
W-WATER...
BLRRR
ORGH
SAW THAT COMING.
TOLD YOU SO.
SWIF
I SWEAR, YOU GUYS...
HERE.
S-SORRY...
THANKS...
I GOTTA SAY, I'M A LITTLE SURPRISED.
GULP
GULP
GULP
GULP
...
FREEZE

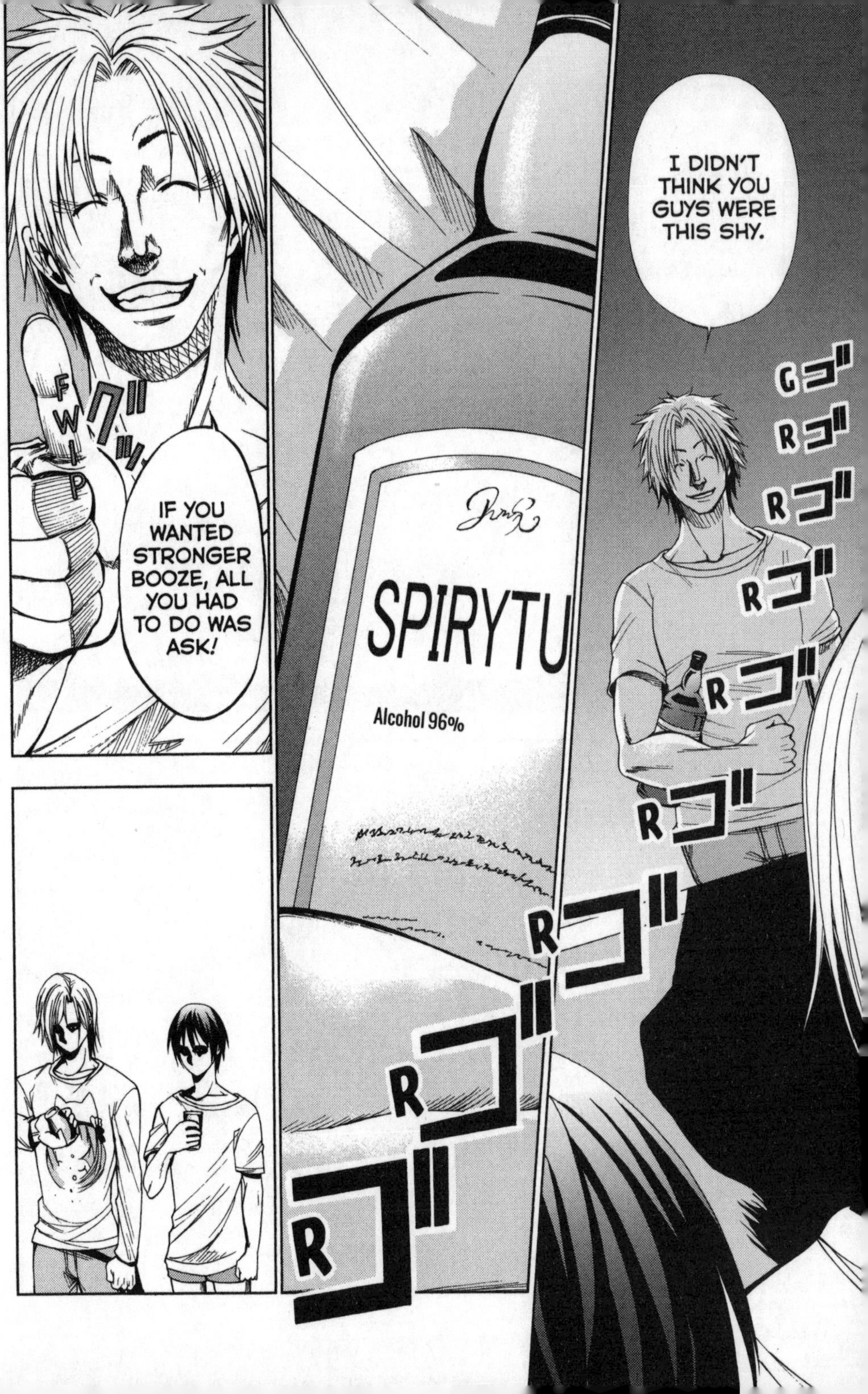
I DIDN'T THINK YOU GUYS WERE THIS SHY.
SPIRYTU
Alcohol 96%
GRRRRRRRR
FWIP
IF YOU WANTED STRONGER BOOZE, ALL YOU HAD TO DO WAS ASK!

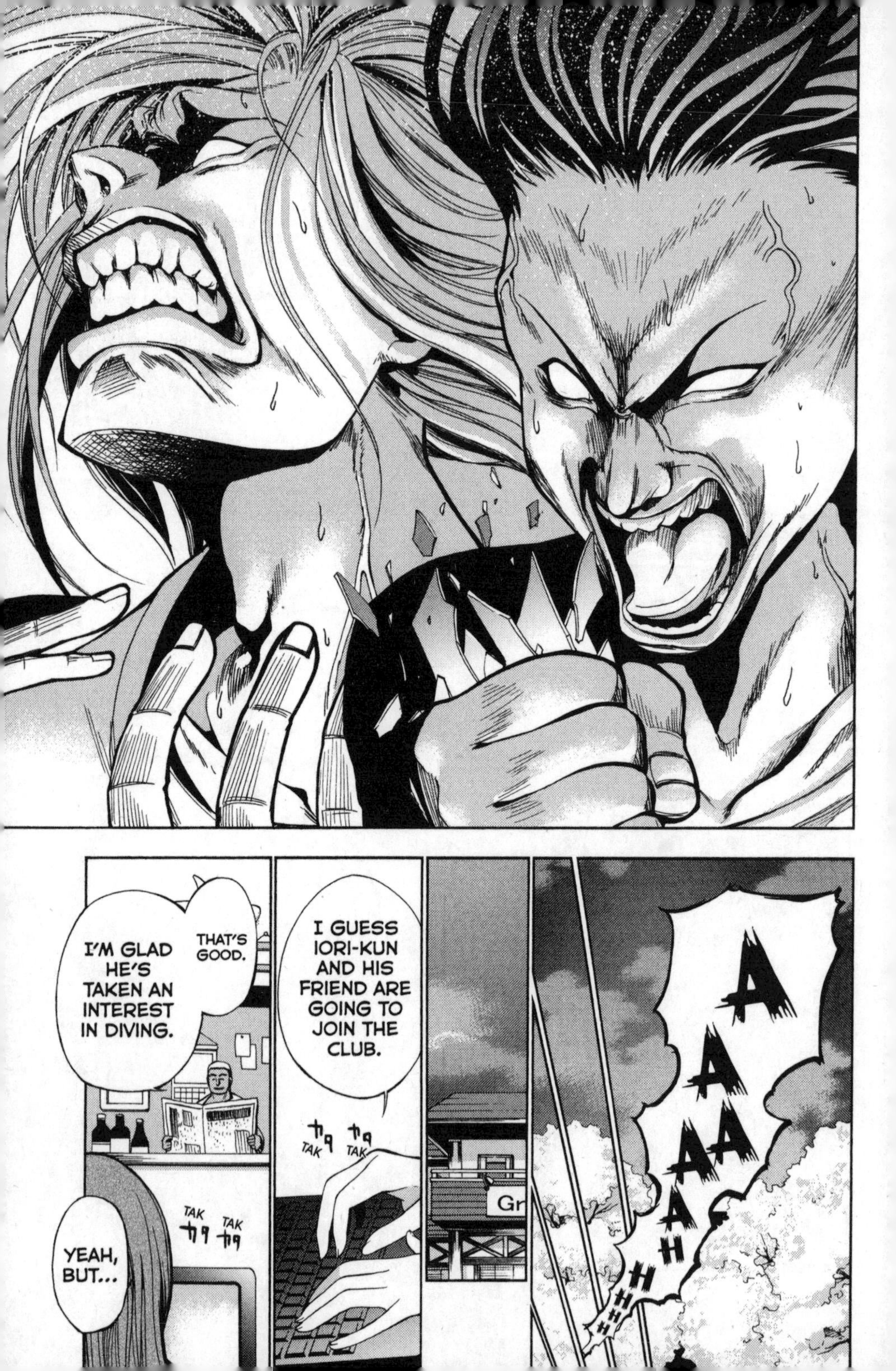
AAAAAAHHHHH
Gr
I GUESS IORI-KUN AND HIS FRIEND ARE GOING TO JOIN THE CLUB.
TAK TAK
THAT'S GOOD.
I'M GLAD HE'S TAKEN AN INTEREST IN DIVING.
TAK TAK
YEAH, BUT...

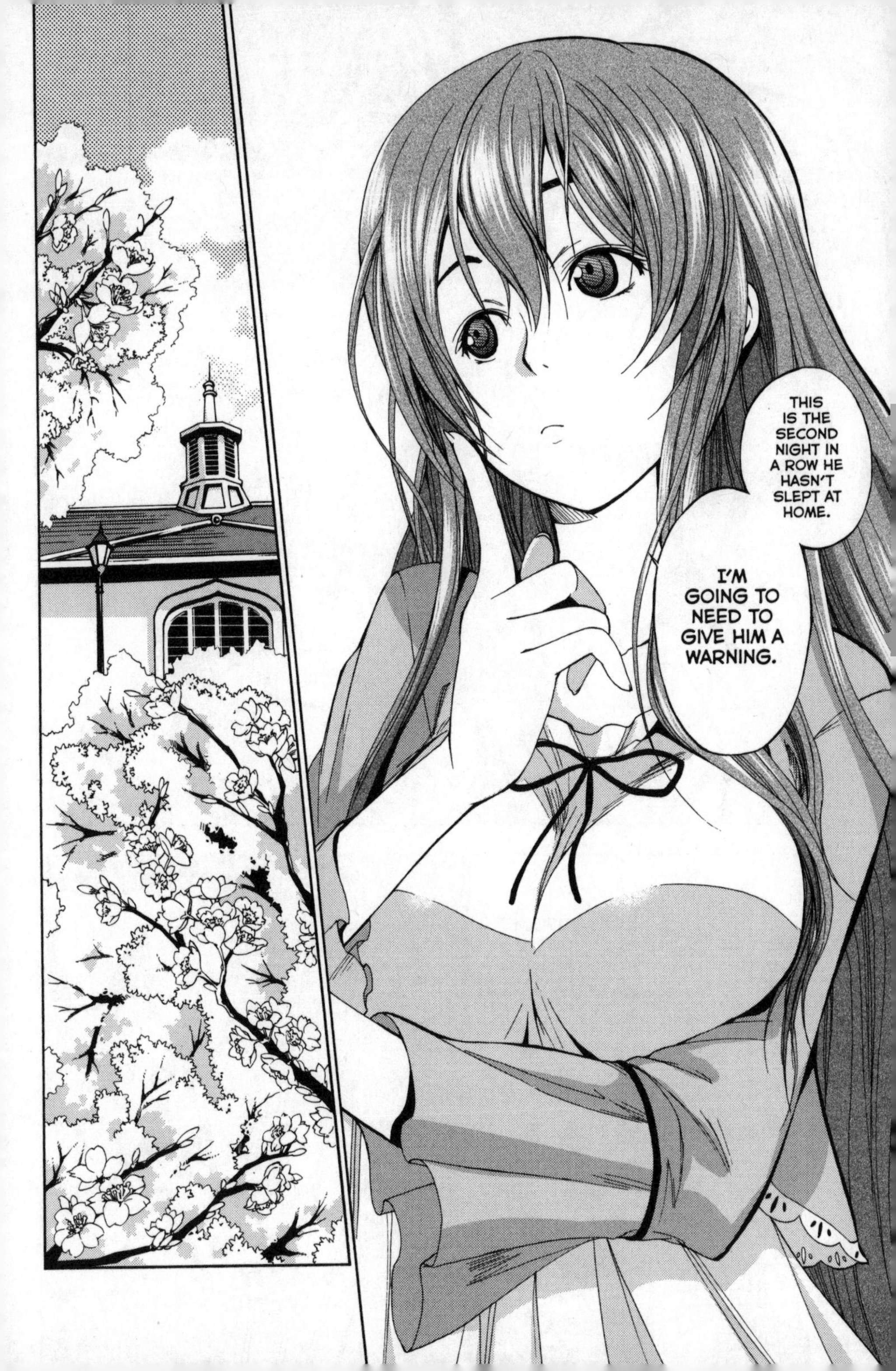
THIS IS THE SECOND NIGHT IN A ROW HE HASN'T SLEPT AT HOME.
I'M GOING TO NEED TO GIVE HIM A WARNING.

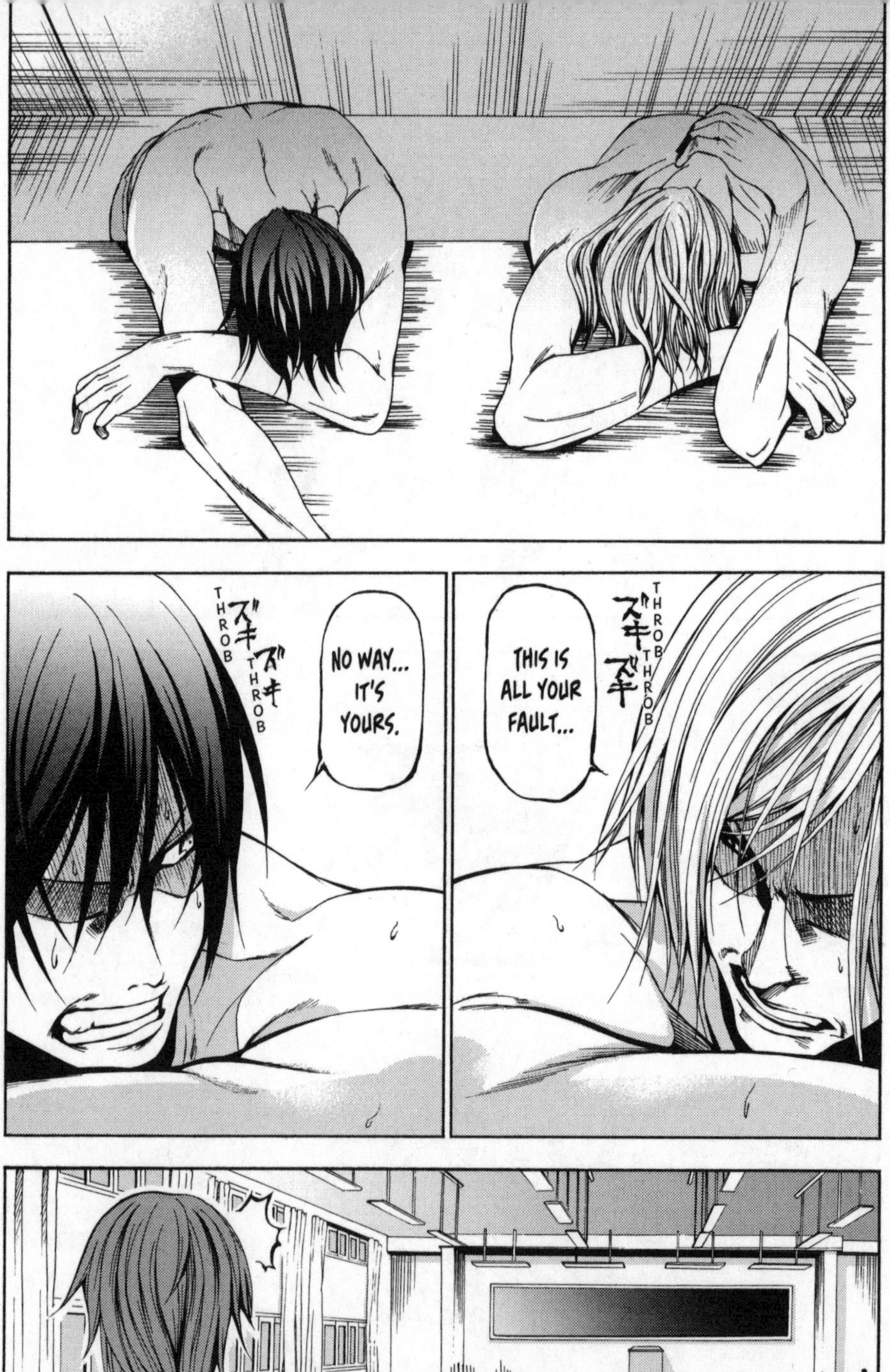
ズキ ズキ
THROB THROB
THIS IS ALL YOUR FAULT...
ズキ ズキ
THROB THROB
NO WAY... IT'S YOURS.

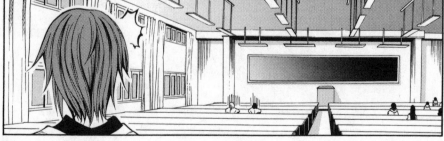

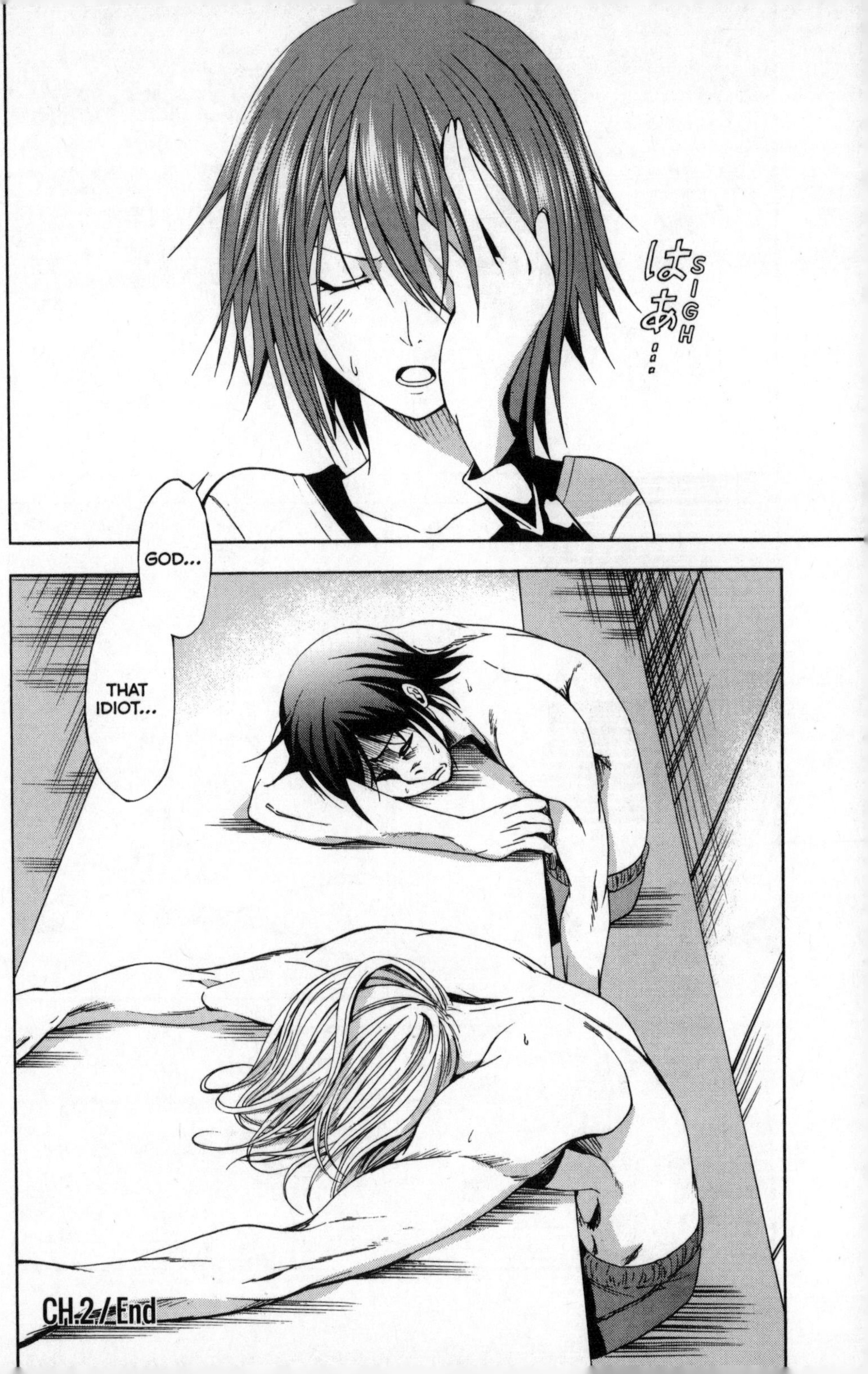
はあ…
SIGH
GOD...
THAT IDIOT...
CH.2 / End

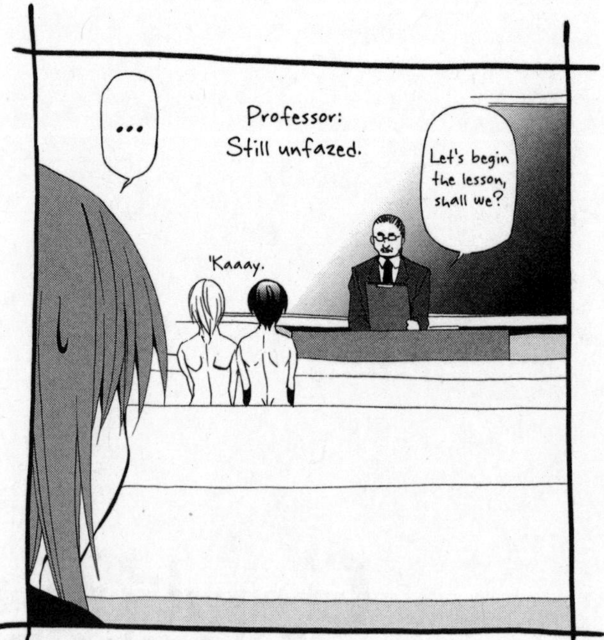
Let's begin the lesson, shall we?
Professor: Still unfazed.
...
'Kaaay.

Grand Blue Dreaming

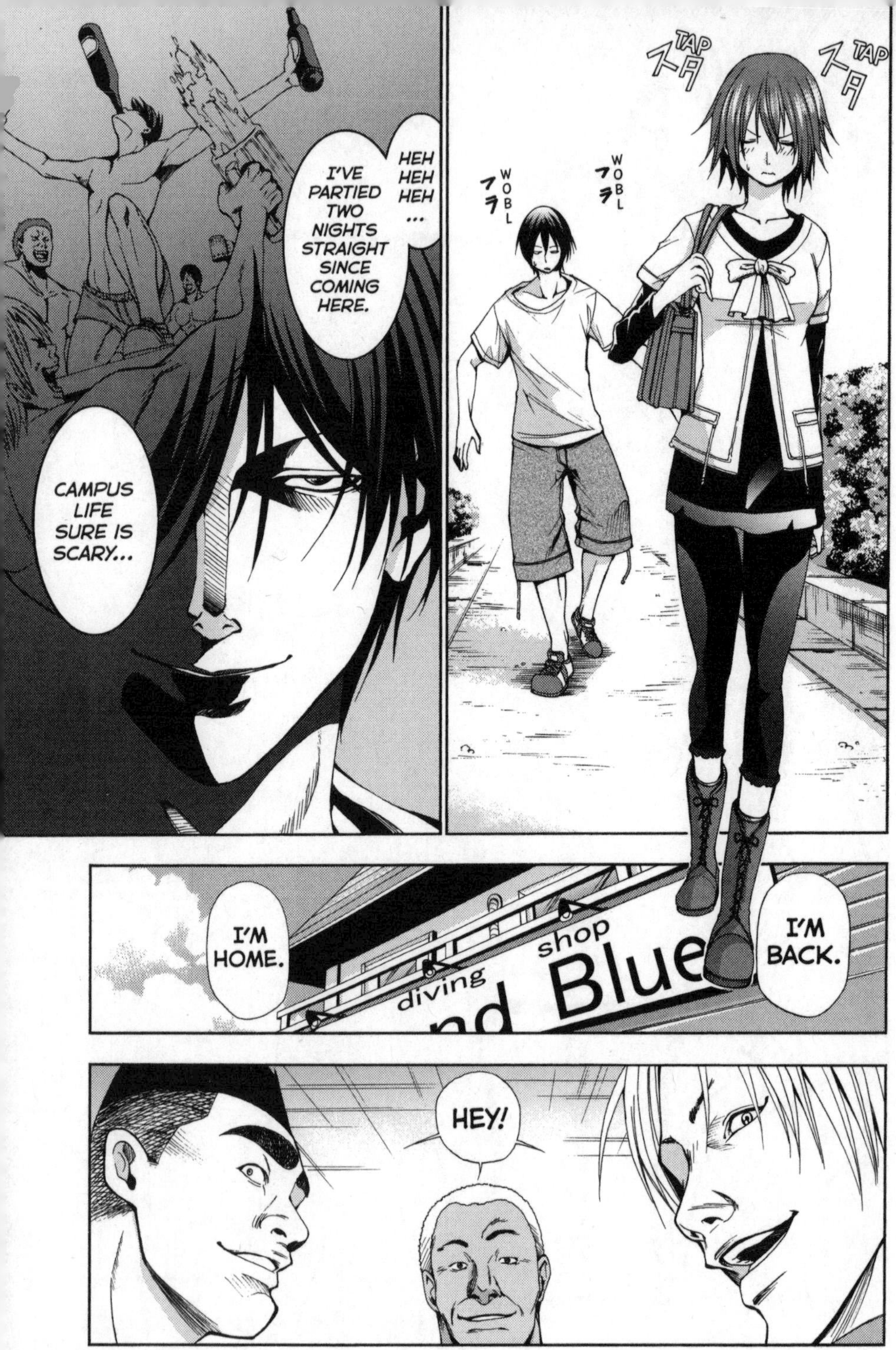
TAP
TAP
WOBL
WOBL
HEH HEH HEH ...
I'VE PARTIED TWO NIGHTS STRAIGHT SINCE COMING HERE.
CAMPUS LIFE SURE IS SCARY...
I'M BACK.
diving shop
nd Blue
I'M HOME.
HEY!

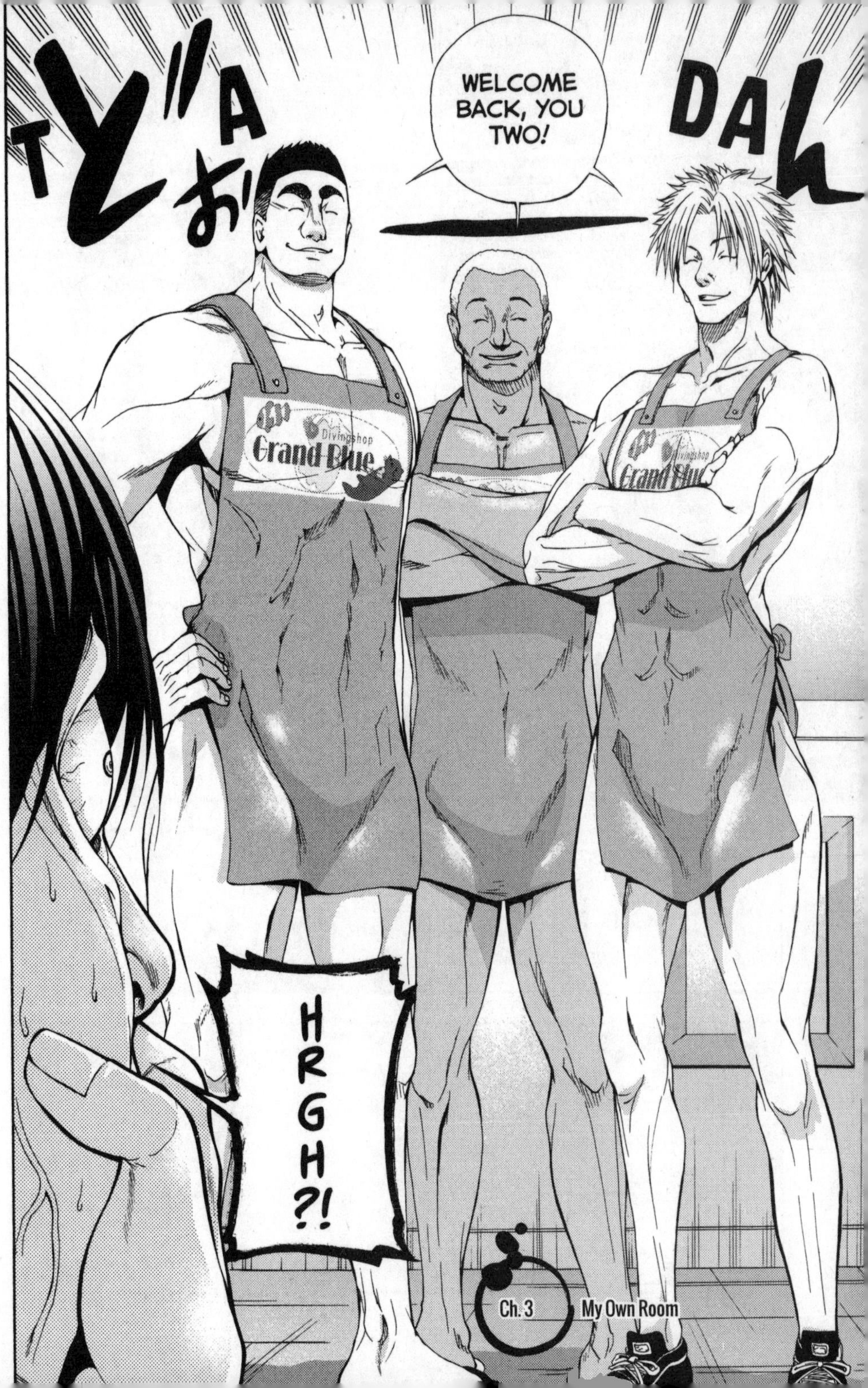
T どお A
DAh
WELCOME BACK, YOU TWO!
Divingshop Grand Blue
Divingshop Grand Blue
HRGH?!
Ch. 3 My Own Room

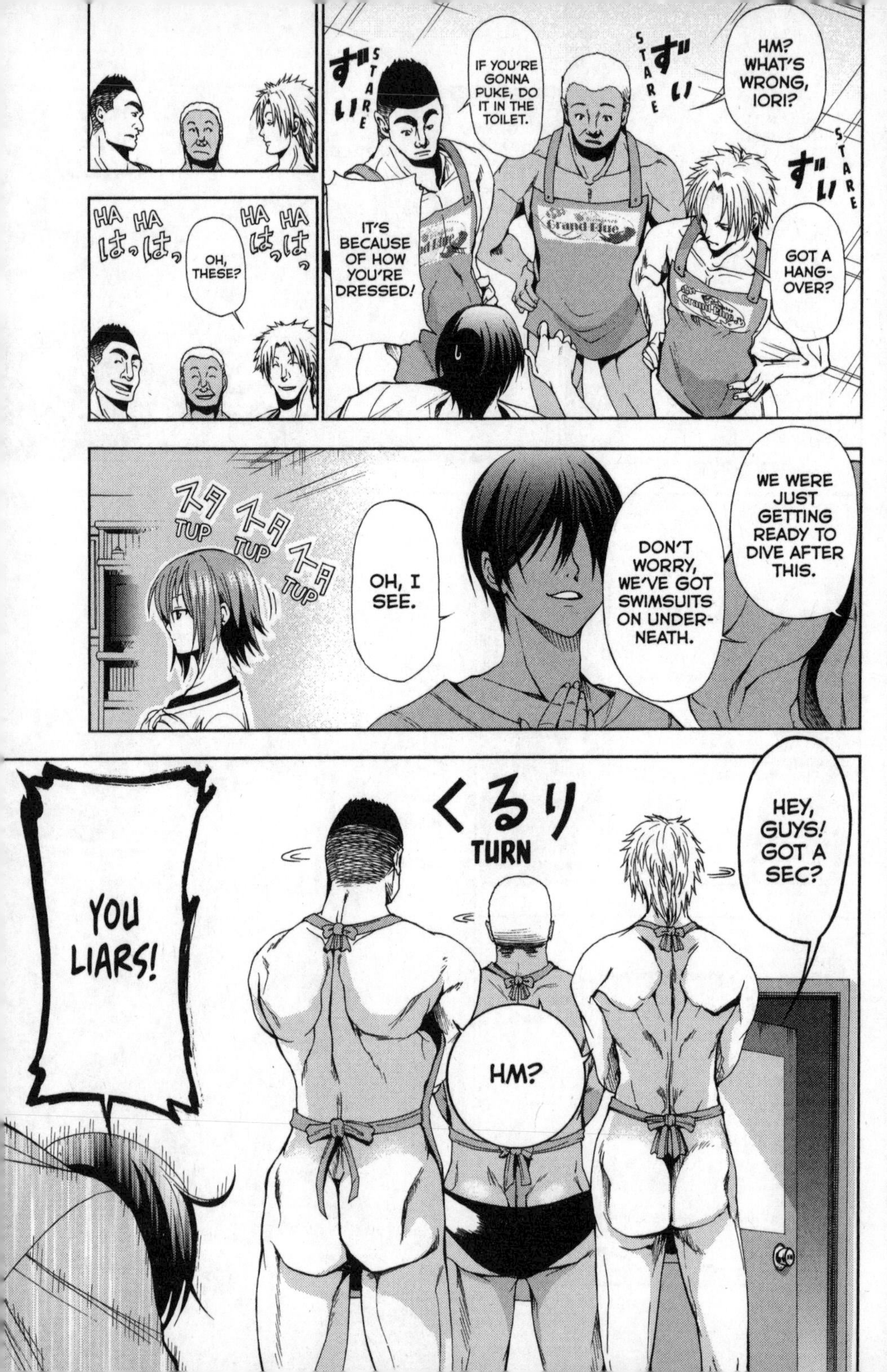

HM? WHAT'S WRONG, IORI?
ずい STARE
ずい STARE
GOT A HANG-OVER?
ずい STARE
IF YOU'RE GONNA PUKE, DO IT IN THE TOILET.
IT'S BECAUSE OF HOW YOU'RE DRESSED!
HA HA はっはっ
OH, THESE?
HA HA はっはっ
WE WERE JUST GETTING READY TO DIVE AFTER THIS.
DON'T WORRY, WE'VE GOT SWIMSUITS ON UNDER-NEATH.
OH, I SEE.
スタ TUP スタ TUP スタ TUP
HEY, GUYS! GOT A SEC?
くるり TURN
HM?
YOU LIARS!

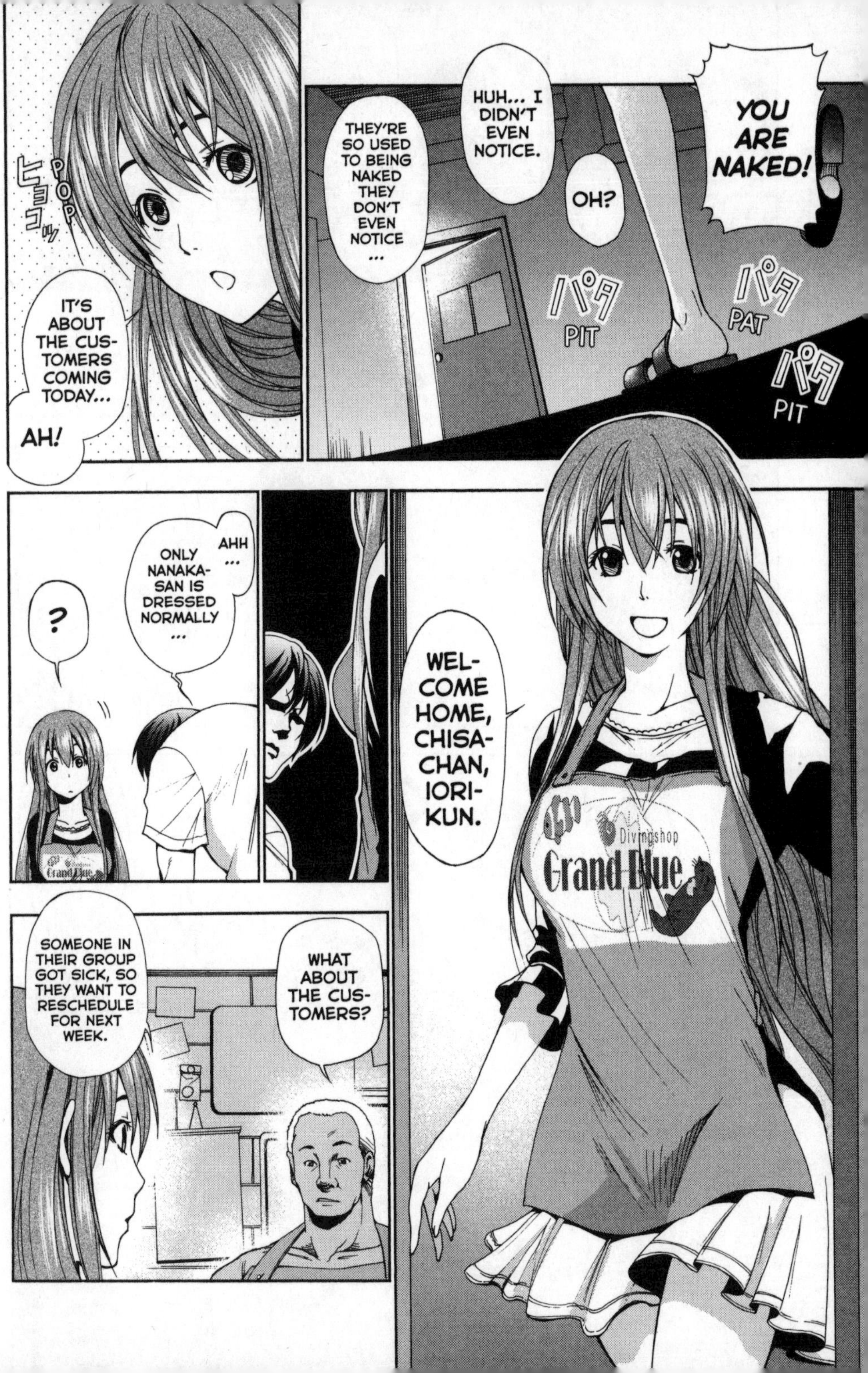
YOU ARE NAKED!
OH?
HUH... I DIDN'T EVEN NOTICE.
THEY'RE SO USED TO BEING NAKED THEY DON'T EVEN NOTICE ...
パタ PAT
パタ PIT
パタ PIT
ヒョコッ POP
IT'S ABOUT THE CUS-TOMERS COMING TODAY...
AH!
WEL-COME HOME, CHISA-CHAN, IORI-KUN.
Divingshop Grand Blue
AHH ... ONLY NANAKA-SAN IS DRESSED NORMALLY ...
?
WHAT ABOUT THE CUS-TOMERS?
SOMEONE IN THEIR GROUP GOT SICK, SO THEY WANT TO RESCHEDULE FOR NEXT WEEK.

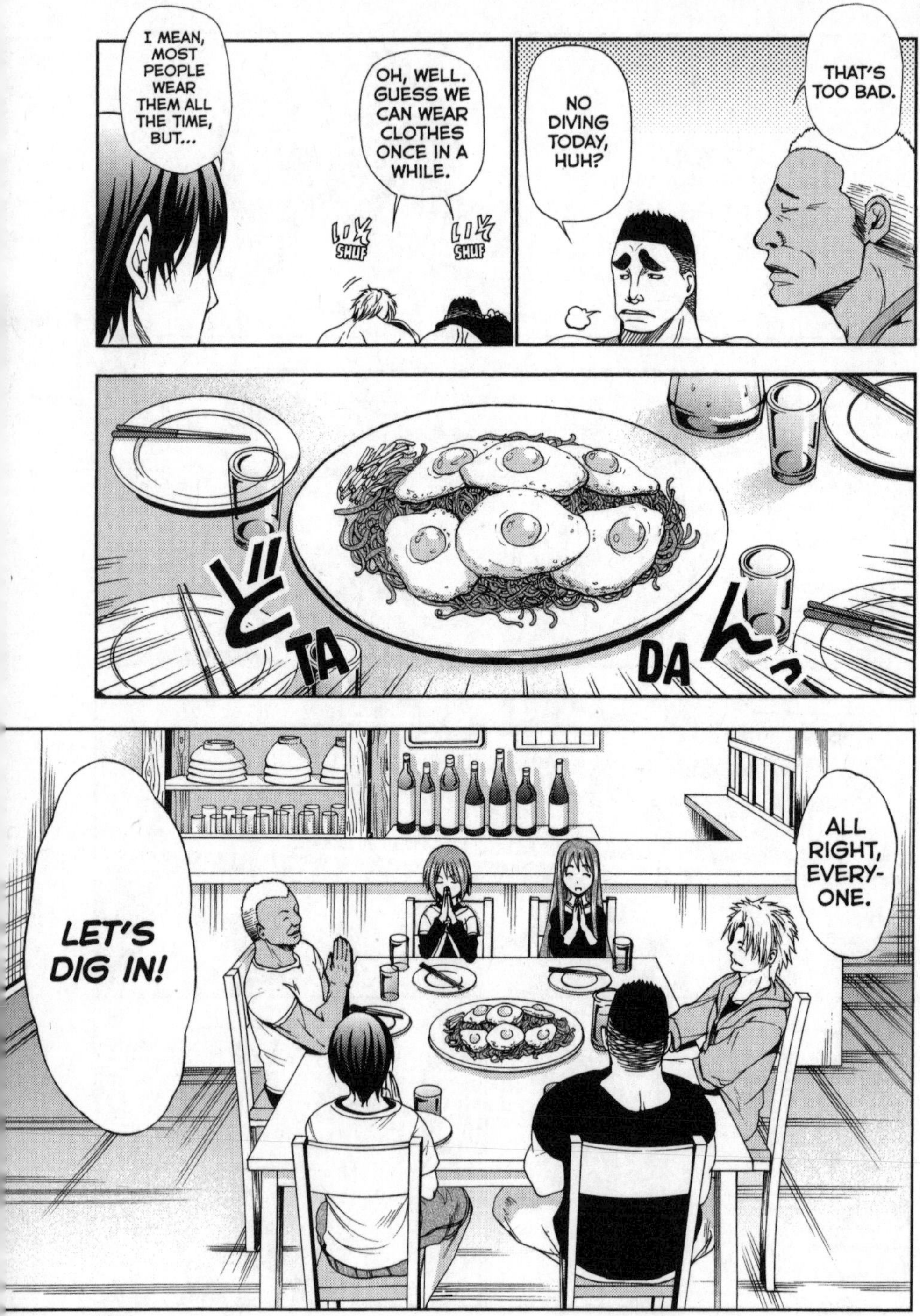
THAT'S TOO BAD.
NO DIVING TODAY, HUH?
OH, WELL. GUESS WE CAN WEAR CLOTHES ONCE IN A WHILE.
SHUF
SHUF
I MEAN, MOST PEOPLE WEAR THEM ALL THE TIME, BUT...
TA
DA
ALL RIGHT, EVERYONE.
LET'S DIG IN!

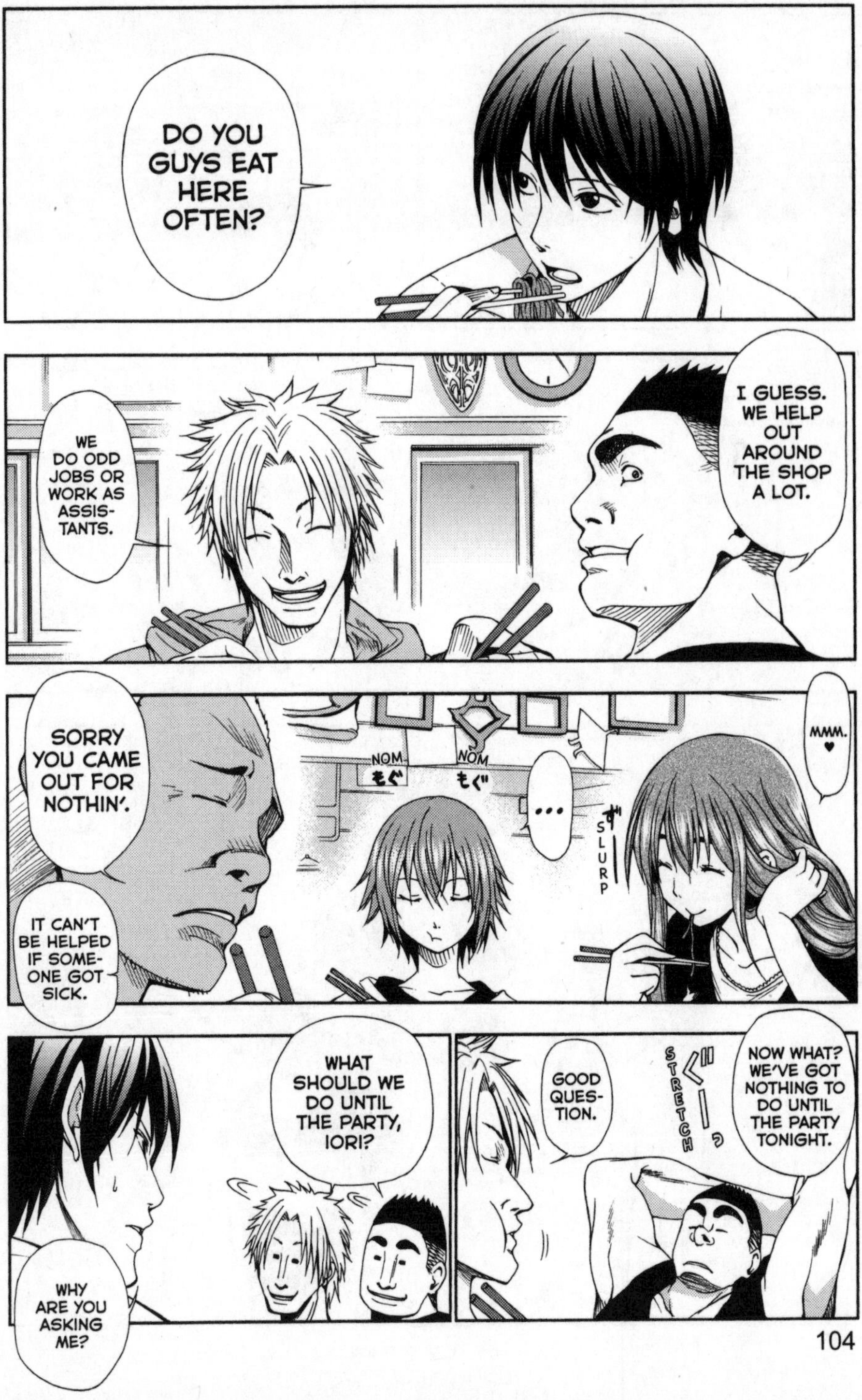
DO YOU GUYS EAT HERE OFTEN?
I GUESS. WE HELP OUT AROUND THE SHOP A LOT.
WE DO ODD JOBS OR WORK AS ASSIS-TANTS.
MMM. ♥
ず SLURP
...
NOM もぐ
NOM もぐ
SORRY YOU CAME OUT FOR NOTHIN'.
IT CAN'T BE HELPED IF SOME-ONE GOT SICK.
NOW WHAT? WE'VE GOT NOTHING TO DO UNTIL THE PARTY TONIGHT.
ぐーっ STRETCH
GOOD QUES-TION.
WHAT SHOULD WE DO UNTIL THE PARTY, IORI?
WHY ARE YOU ASKING ME?

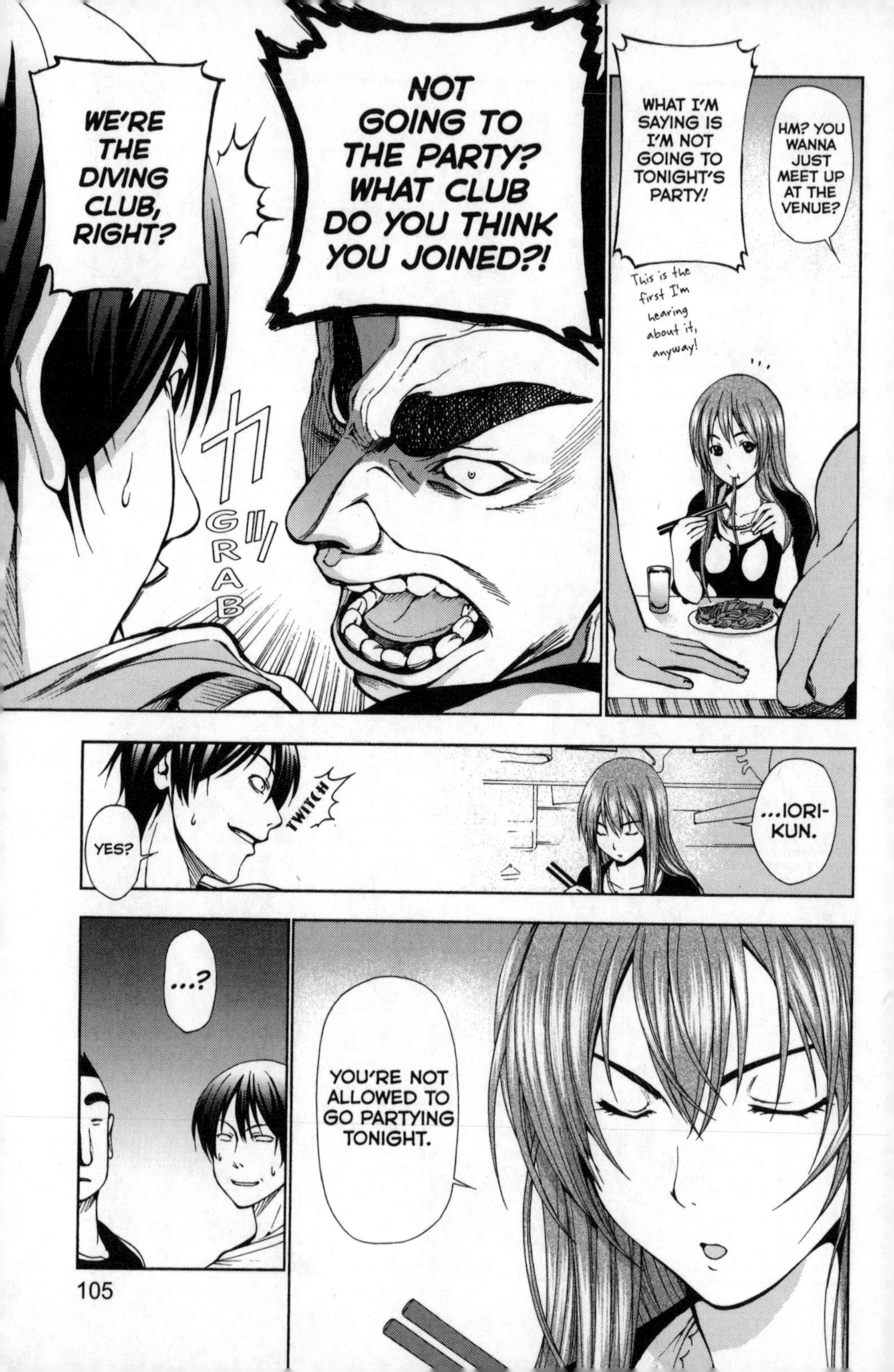
HM? YOU WANNA JUST MEET UP AT THE VENUE?
WHAT I'M SAYING IS I'M NOT GOING TO TONIGHT'S PARTY!
This is the first I'm hearing about it, anyway!
NOT GOING TO THE PARTY? WHAT CLUB DO YOU THINK YOU JOINED?!
WE'RE THE DIVING CLUB, RIGHT?
GRAB
...IORI-KUN.
TWITCH
YES?
YOU'RE NOT ALLOWED TO GO PARTYING TONIGHT.
...?

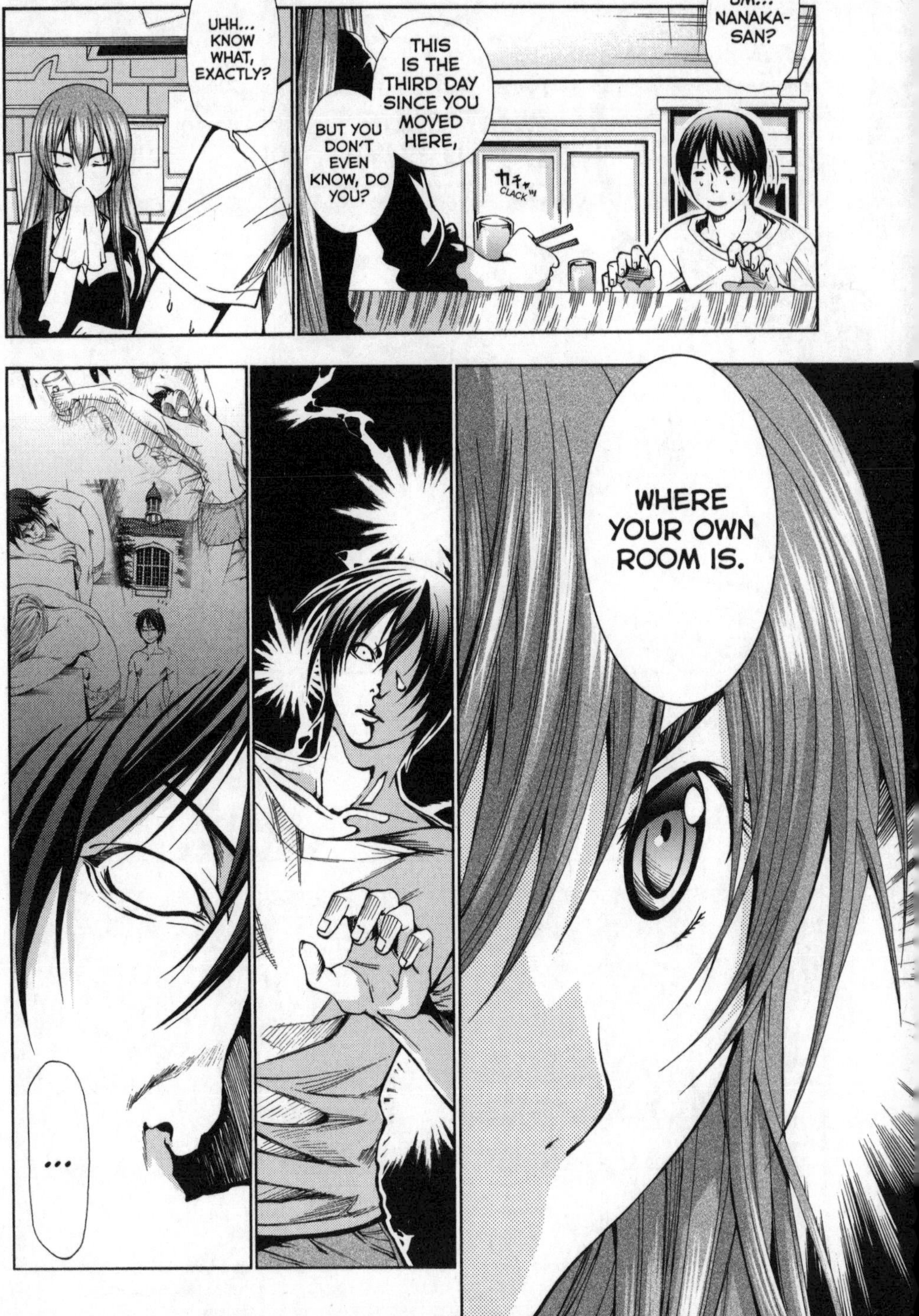
UM... NANAKA-SAN?
カチャ
CLACK
THIS IS THE THIRD DAY SINCE YOU MOVED HERE,
BUT YOU DON'T EVEN KNOW, DO YOU?
UHH... KNOW WHAT, EXACTLY?
WHERE YOUR OWN ROOM IS.
...

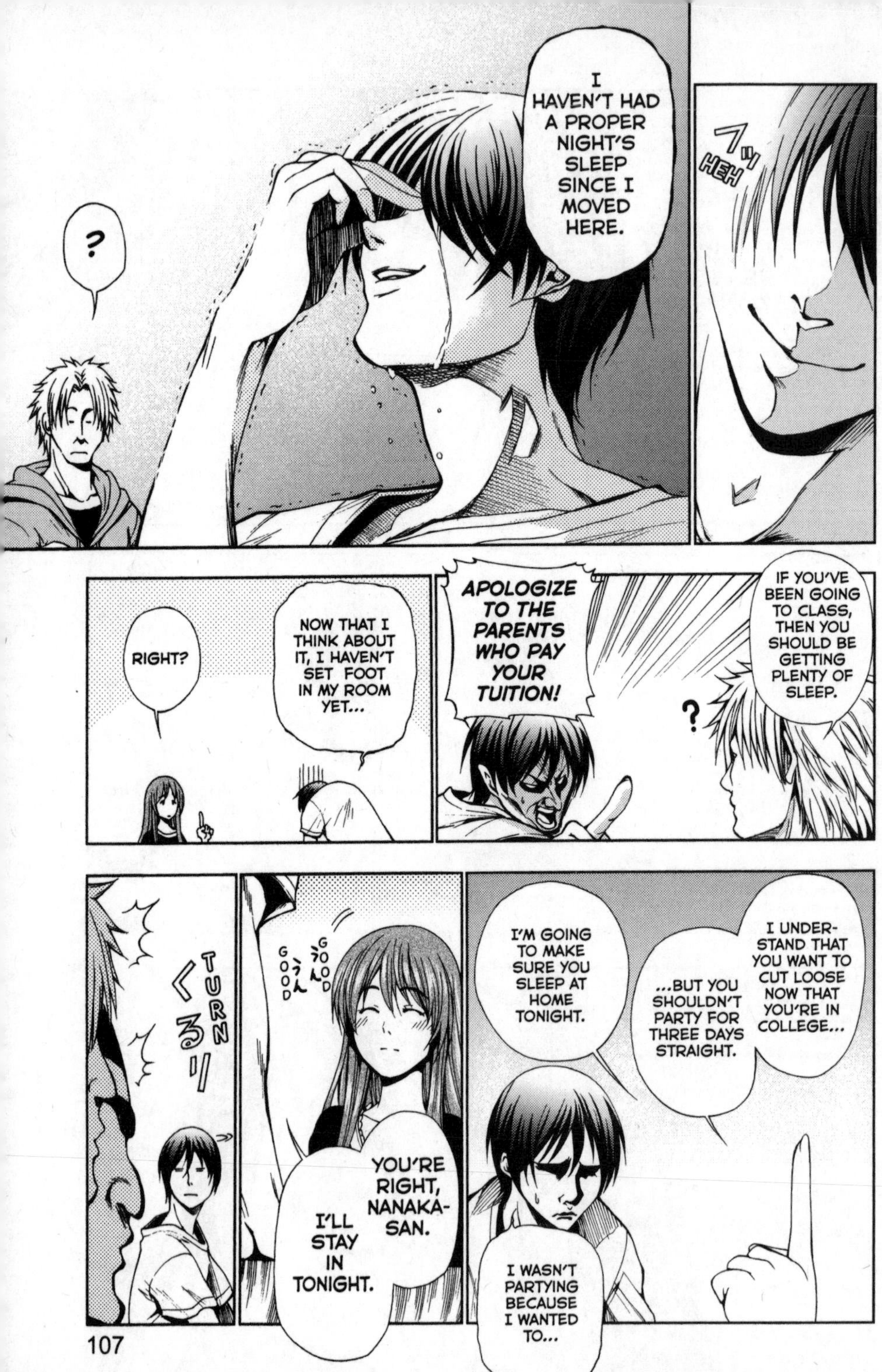

ヘッ HEH
I HAVEN'T HAD A PROPER NIGHT'S SLEEP SINCE I MOVED HERE.
?
IF YOU'VE BEEN GOING TO CLASS, THEN YOU SHOULD BE GETTING PLENTY OF SLEEP.
?
APOLOGIZE TO THE PARENTS WHO PAY YOUR TUITION!
NOW THAT I THINK ABOUT IT, I HAVEN'T SET FOOT IN MY ROOM YET...
RIGHT?
I UNDER-STAND THAT YOU WANT TO CUT LOOSE NOW THAT YOU'RE IN COLLEGE...
...BUT YOU SHOULDN'T PARTY FOR THREE DAYS STRAIGHT.
I'M GOING TO MAKE SURE YOU SLEEP AT HOME TONIGHT.
I WASN'T PARTYING BECAUSE I WANTED TO...
うん GOOD
うん GOOD
YOU'RE RIGHT, NANAKA-SAN.
I'LL STAY IN TONIGHT.
くるり TURN

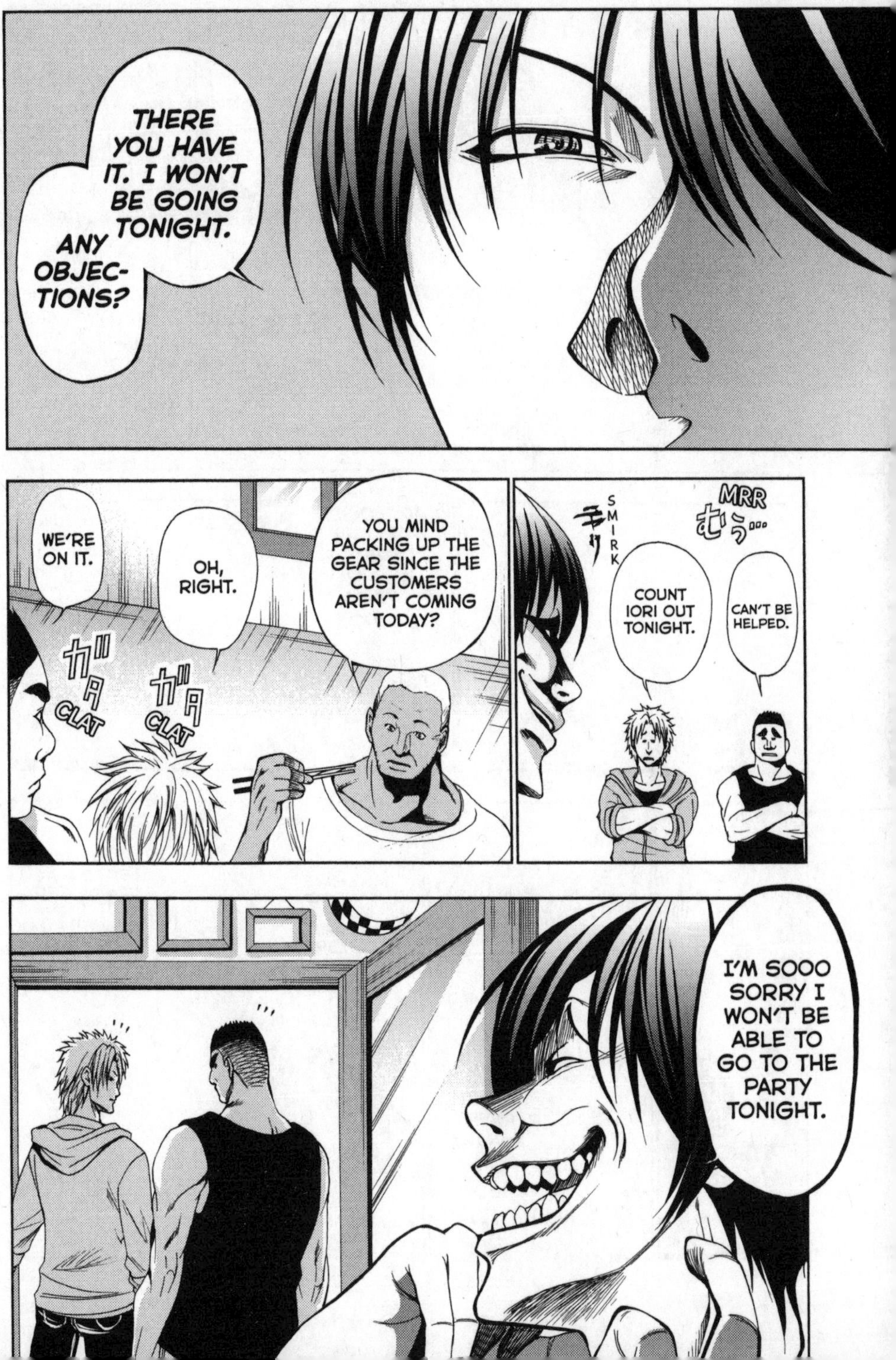
THERE YOU HAVE IT. I WON'T BE GOING TONIGHT.
ANY OBJECTIONS?
MRR
SMIRK
CAN'T BE HELPED.
COUNT IORI OUT TONIGHT.
YOU MIND PACKING UP THE GEAR SINCE THE CUSTOMERS AREN'T COMING TODAY?
OH, RIGHT.
WE'RE ON IT.
CLAT
CLAT
I'M SOOO SORRY I WON'T BE ABLE TO GO TO THE PARTY TONIGHT.

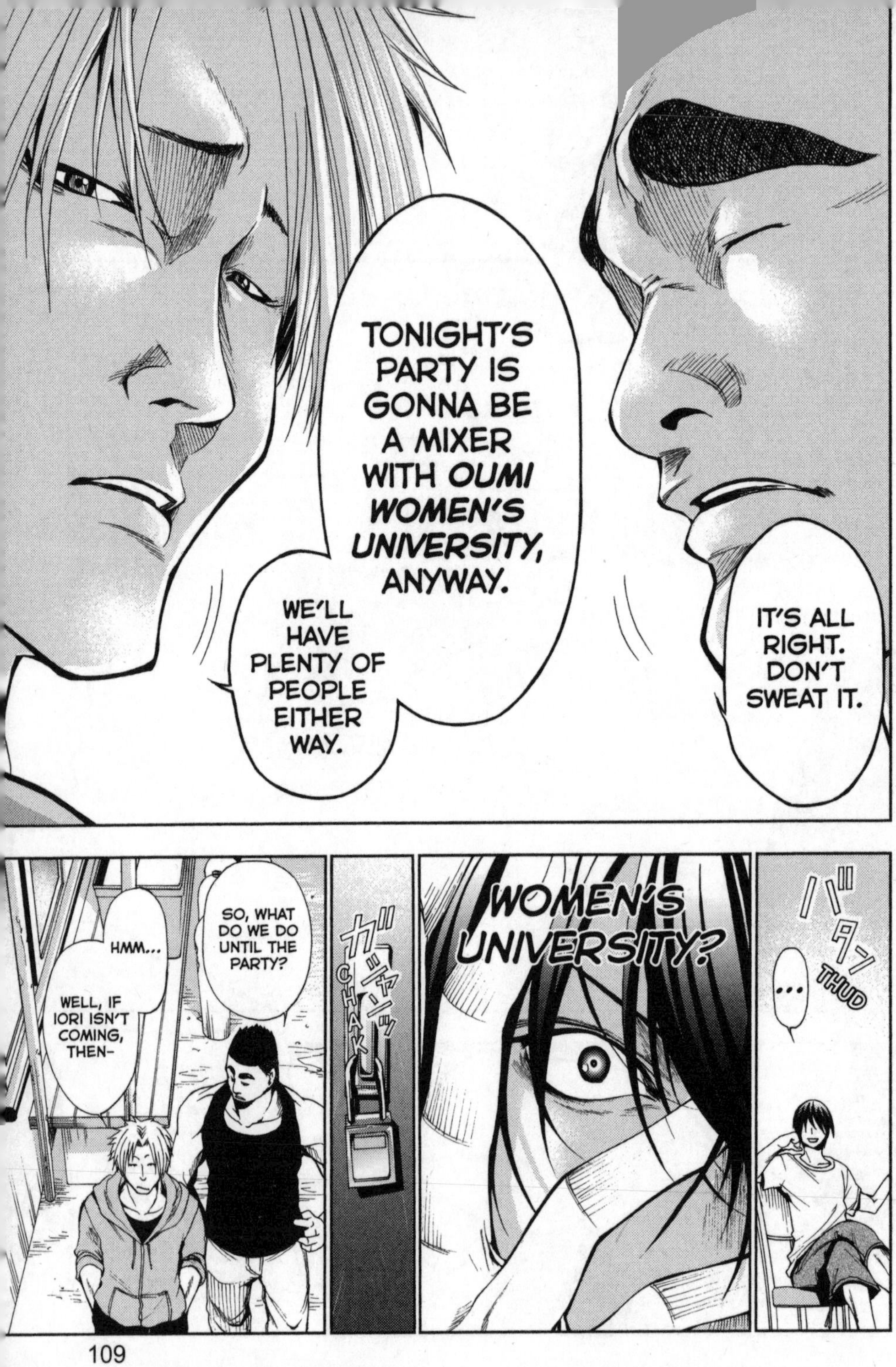
IT'S ALL RIGHT. DON'T SWEAT IT.
WE'LL HAVE PLENTY OF PEOPLE EITHER WAY.
TONIGHT'S PARTY IS GONNA BE A MIXER WITH *OUMI WOMEN'S UNIVERSITY*, ANYWAY.
バタン
THUD
...
WOMEN'S UNIVERSITY?
ガシャンッ
CHAK
SO, WHAT DO WE DO UNTIL THE PARTY?
HMM...
WELL, IF IORI ISN'T COMING, THEN-

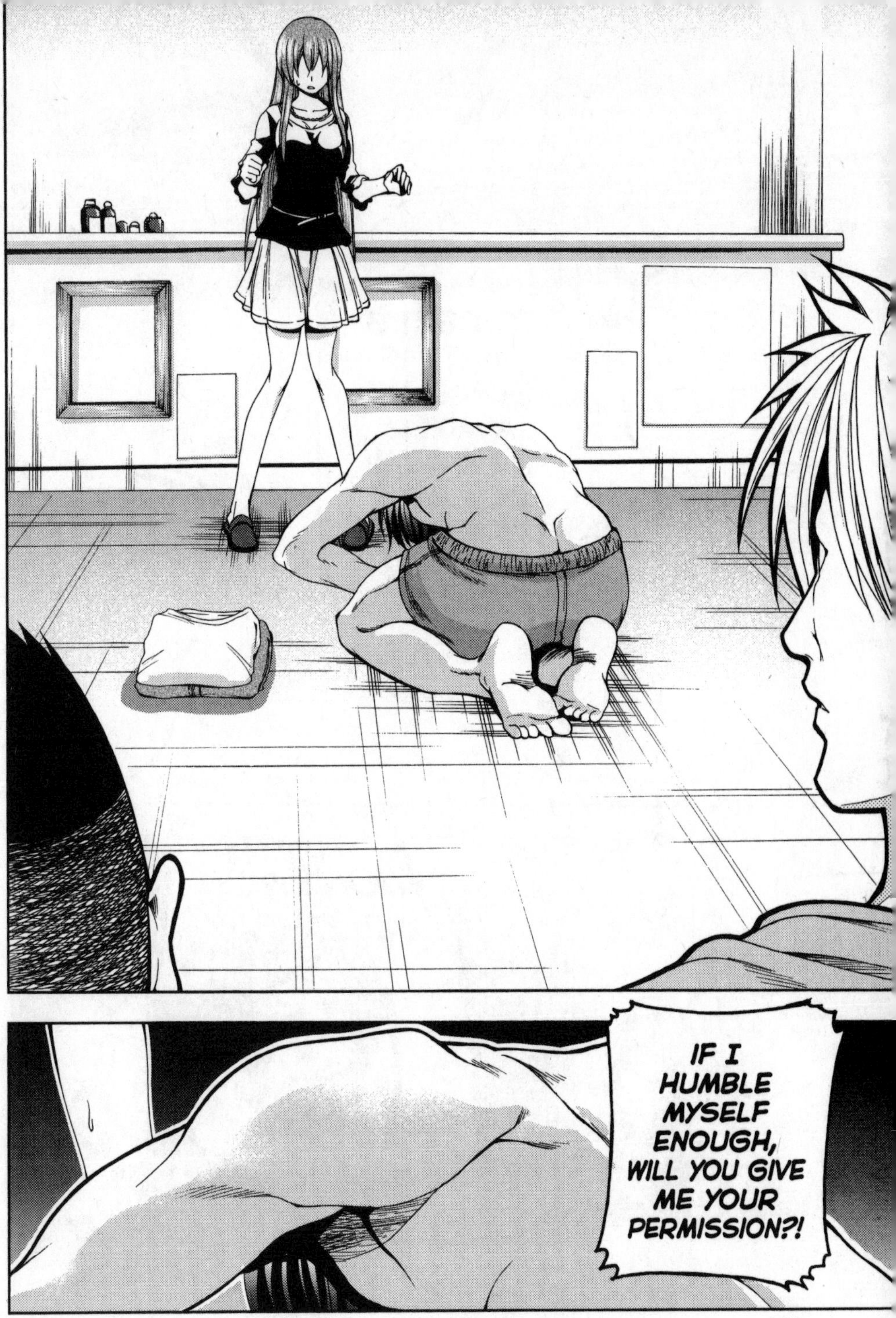
IF I HUMBLE MYSELF ENOUGH, WILL YOU GIVE ME YOUR PERMISSION?!

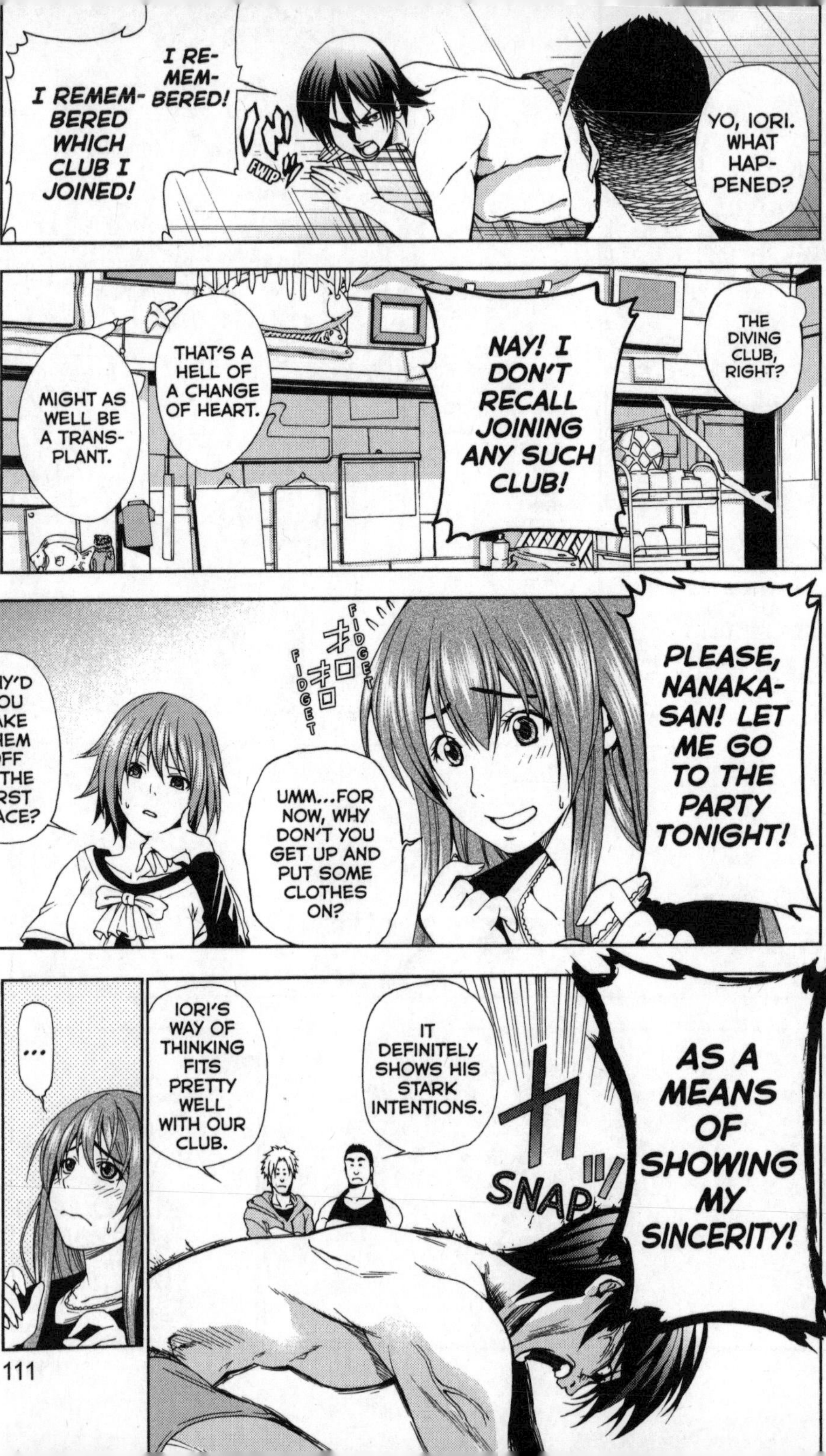
YO, IORI. WHAT HAP-PENED?
I RE-MEM-BERED!
I REMEM-BERED WHICH CLUB I JOINED!
FWIP
THE DIVING CLUB, RIGHT?
NAY! I DON'T RECALL JOINING ANY SUCH CLUB!
THAT'S A HELL OF A CHANGE OF HEART.
MIGHT AS WELL BE A TRANS-PLANT.
PLEASE, NANAKA-SAN! LET ME GO TO THE PARTY TONIGHT!
FIDGET
FIDGET
UMM...FOR NOW, WHY DON'T YOU GET UP AND PUT SOME CLOTHES ON?
WHY'D YOU TAKE THEM OFF IN THE FIRST PLACE?
AS A MEANS OF SHOWING MY SINCERITY!
SNAP!
IT DEFINITELY SHOWS HIS STARK INTENTIONS.
IORI'S WAY OF THINKING FITS PRETTY WELL WITH OUR CLUB.
...

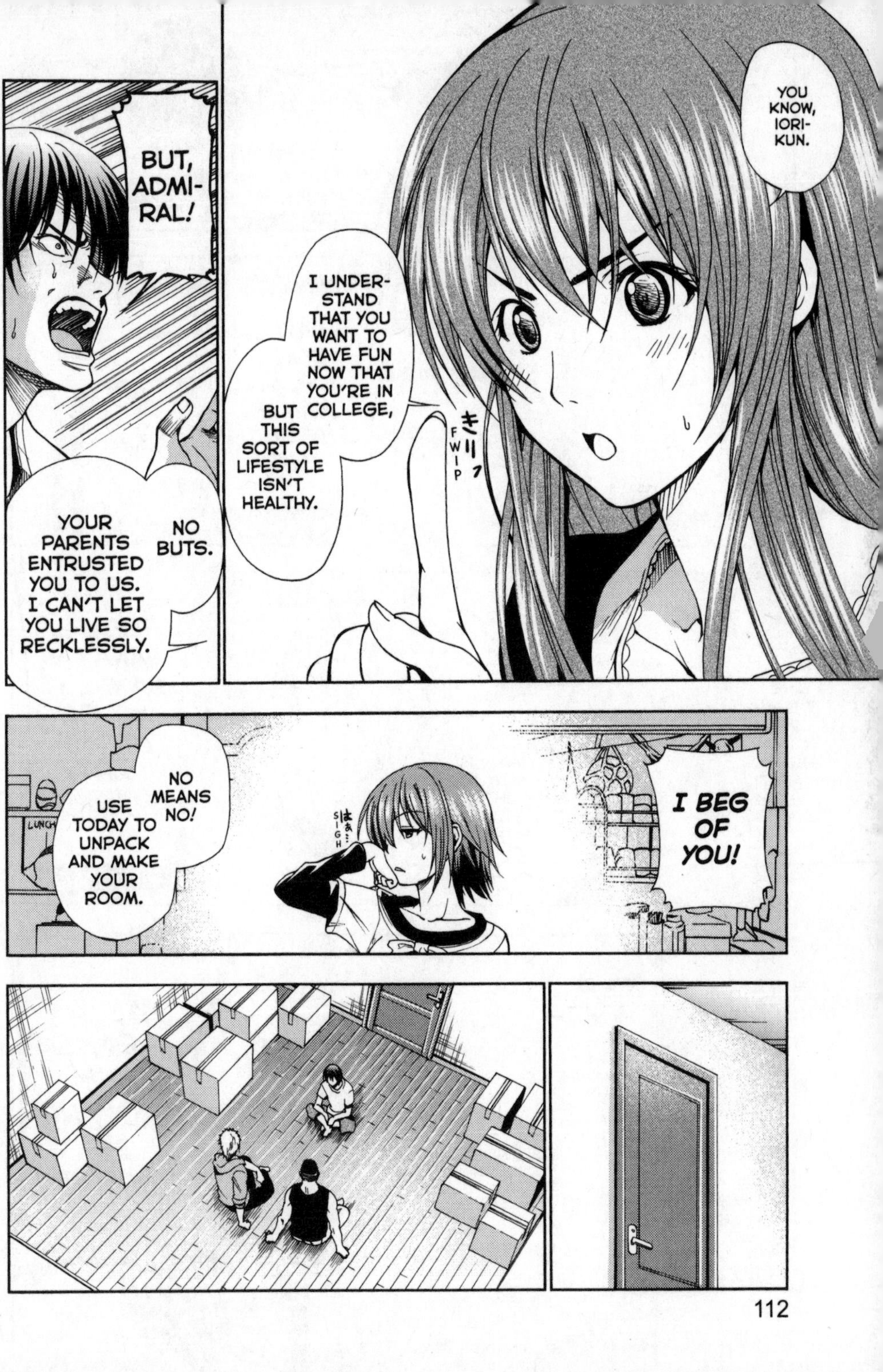
YOU KNOW, IORI-KUN.
I UNDERSTAND THAT YOU WANT TO HAVE FUN NOW THAT YOU'RE IN COLLEGE, BUT THIS SORT OF LIFESTYLE ISN'T HEALTHY.
FWIP
BUT, ADMIRAL!
NO BUTS.
YOUR PARENTS ENTRUSTED YOU TO US. I CAN'T LET YOU LIVE SO RECKLESSLY.
I BEG OF YOU!
SIGH
NO MEANS NO!
USE TODAY TO UNPACK AND MAKE YOUR ROOM.

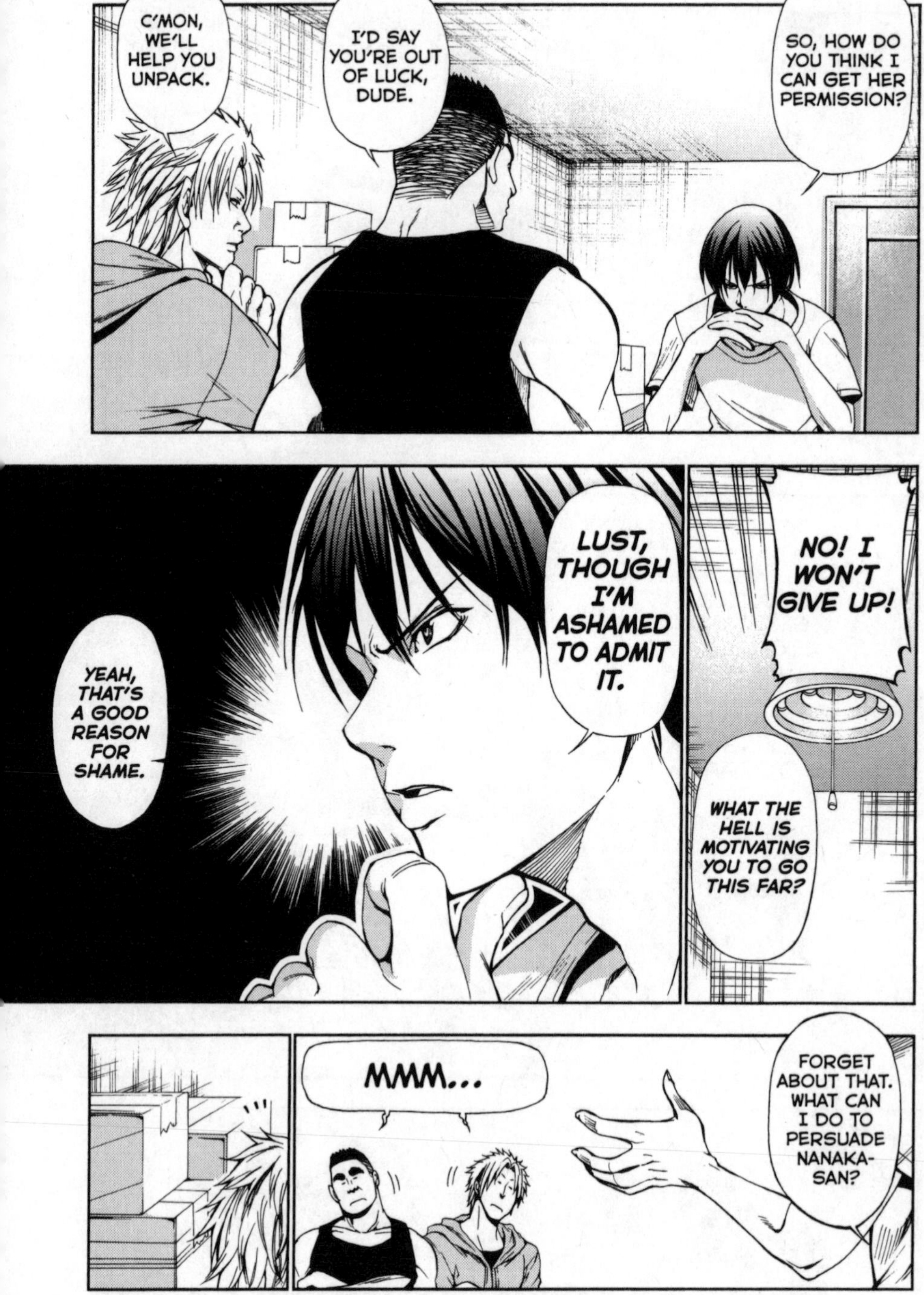
SO, HOW DO YOU THINK I CAN GET HER PERMISSION?
I'D SAY YOU'RE OUT OF LUCK, DUDE.
C'MON, WE'LL HELP YOU UNPACK.
NO! I WON'T GIVE UP!
WHAT THE HELL IS MOTIVATING YOU TO GO THIS FAR?
LUST, THOUGH I'M ASHAMED TO ADMIT IT.
YEAH, THAT'S A GOOD REASON FOR SHAME.
FORGET ABOUT THAT. WHAT CAN I DO TO PERSUADE NANAKA-SAN?
MMM...

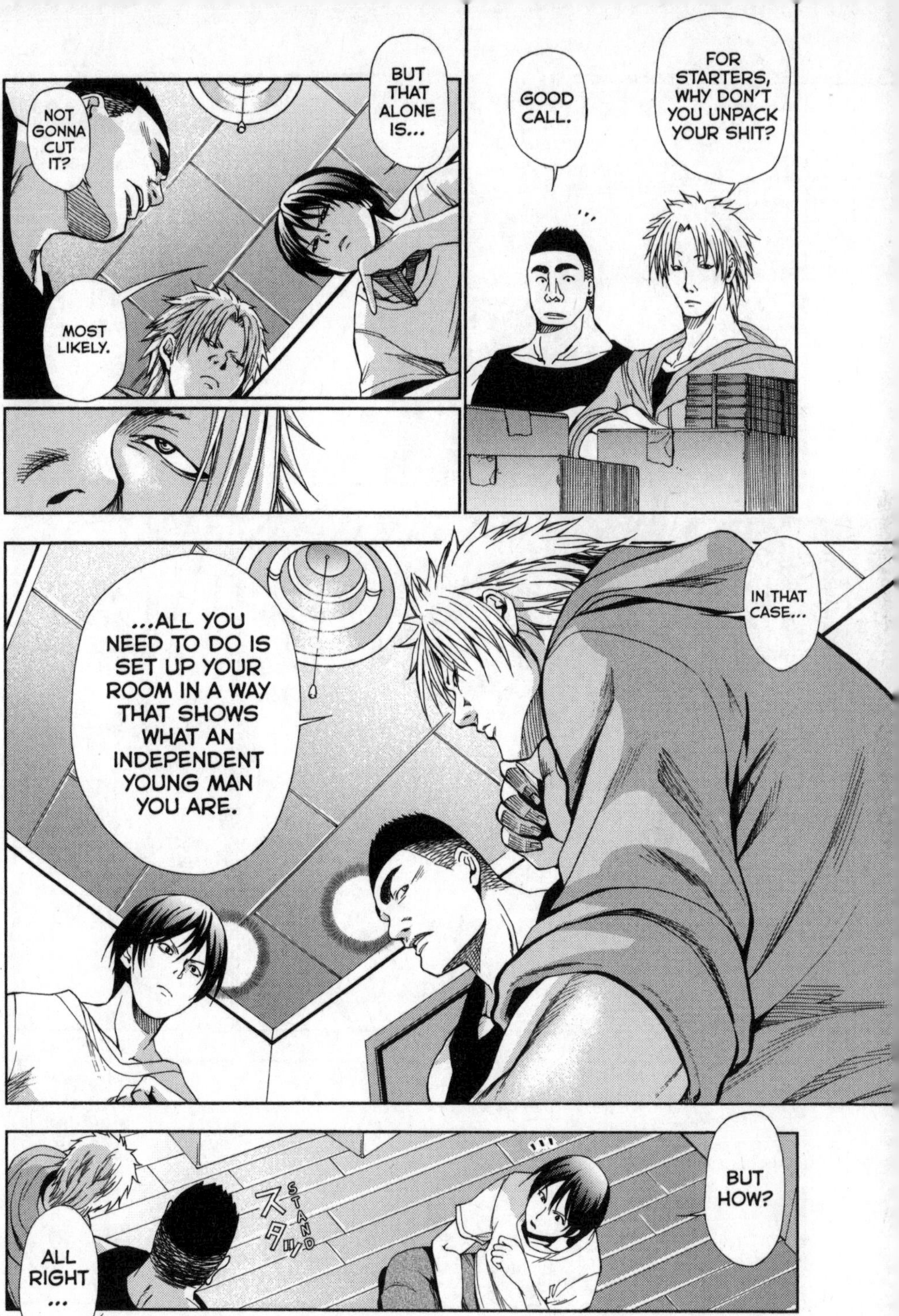
FOR STARTERS, WHY DON'T YOU UNPACK YOUR SHIT?
GOOD CALL.
BUT THAT ALONE IS...
NOT GONNA CUT IT?
MOST LIKELY.
IN THAT CASE...
...ALL YOU NEED TO DO IS SET UP YOUR ROOM IN A WAY THAT SHOWS WHAT AN INDEPENDENT YOUNG MAN YOU ARE.
BUT HOW?
STAND
ALL RIGHT ...

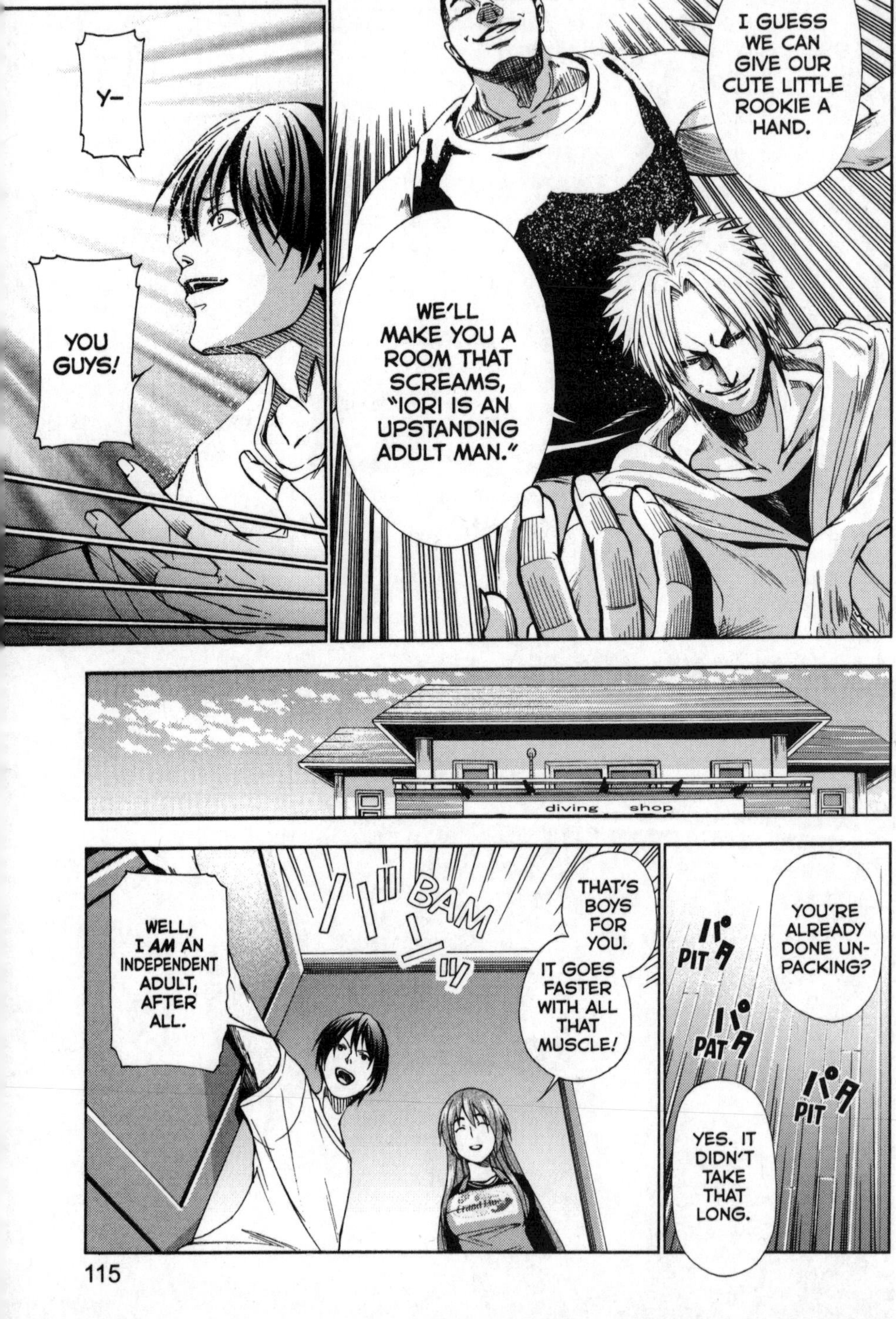
I GUESS WE CAN GIVE OUR CUTE LITTLE ROOKIE A HAND.
WE'LL MAKE YOU A ROOM THAT SCREAMS, "IORI IS AN UPSTANDING ADULT MAN."
Y-
YOU GUYS!
diving shop
YOU'RE ALREADY DONE UN-PACKING?
PIT
PAT
PIT
YES. IT DIDN'T TAKE THAT LONG.
THAT'S BOYS FOR YOU.
IT GOES FASTER WITH ALL THAT MUSCLE!
BAM
WELL, I *AM* AN INDEPENDENT ADULT, AFTER ALL.

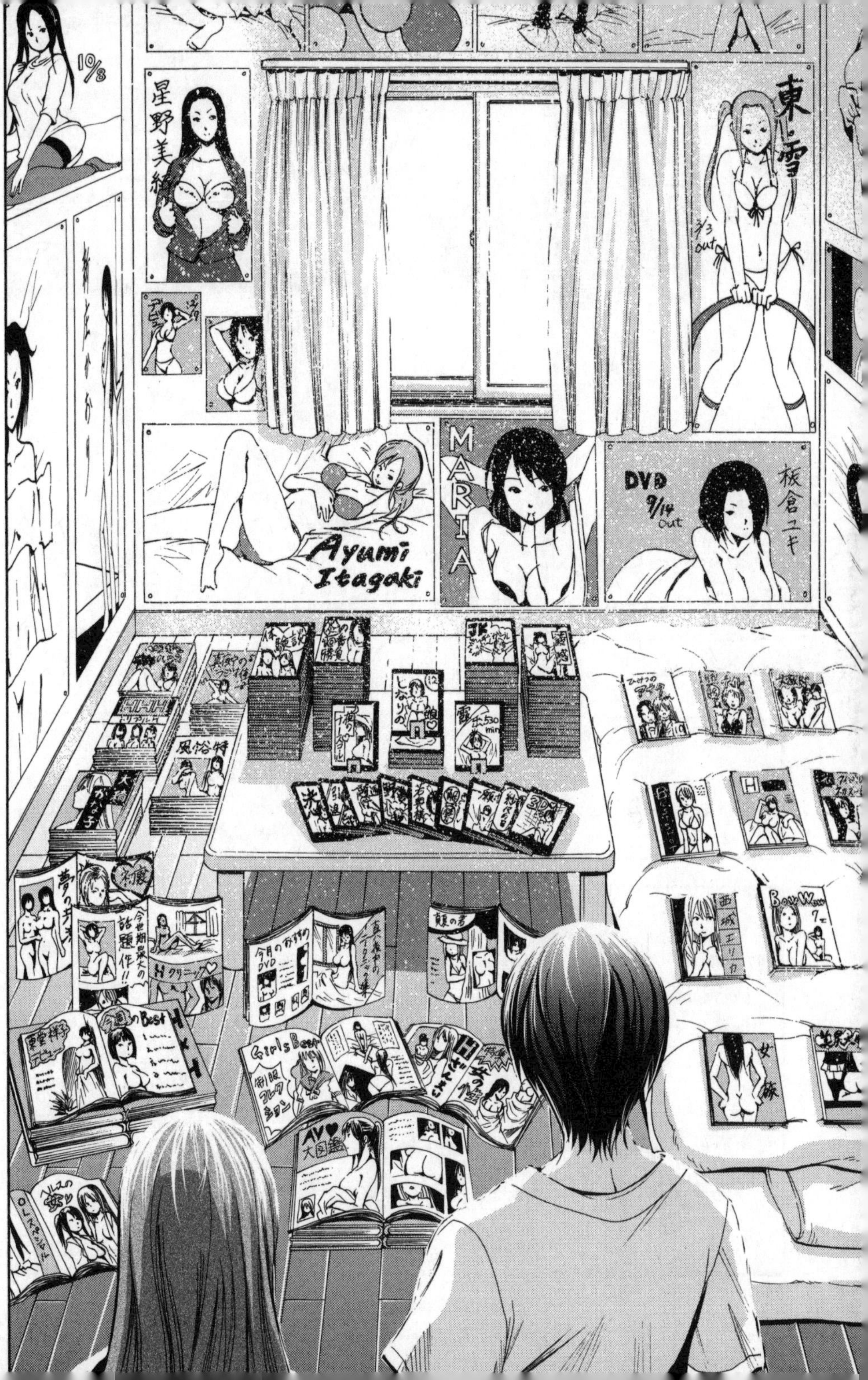
10/8
2/3 out
MARIA
Ayumi Itagaki
DVD 9/14 out
板倉ユキ
風俗特
今月のおすすめ DVD
今世紀最大の話題作!!
Hクリニック♡
今週のBest
Girls Best
制服コレクション
AV♡大図鑑
ヘルスの女♡
OLスペシャル
西城エリカ
Bow Wow
530min

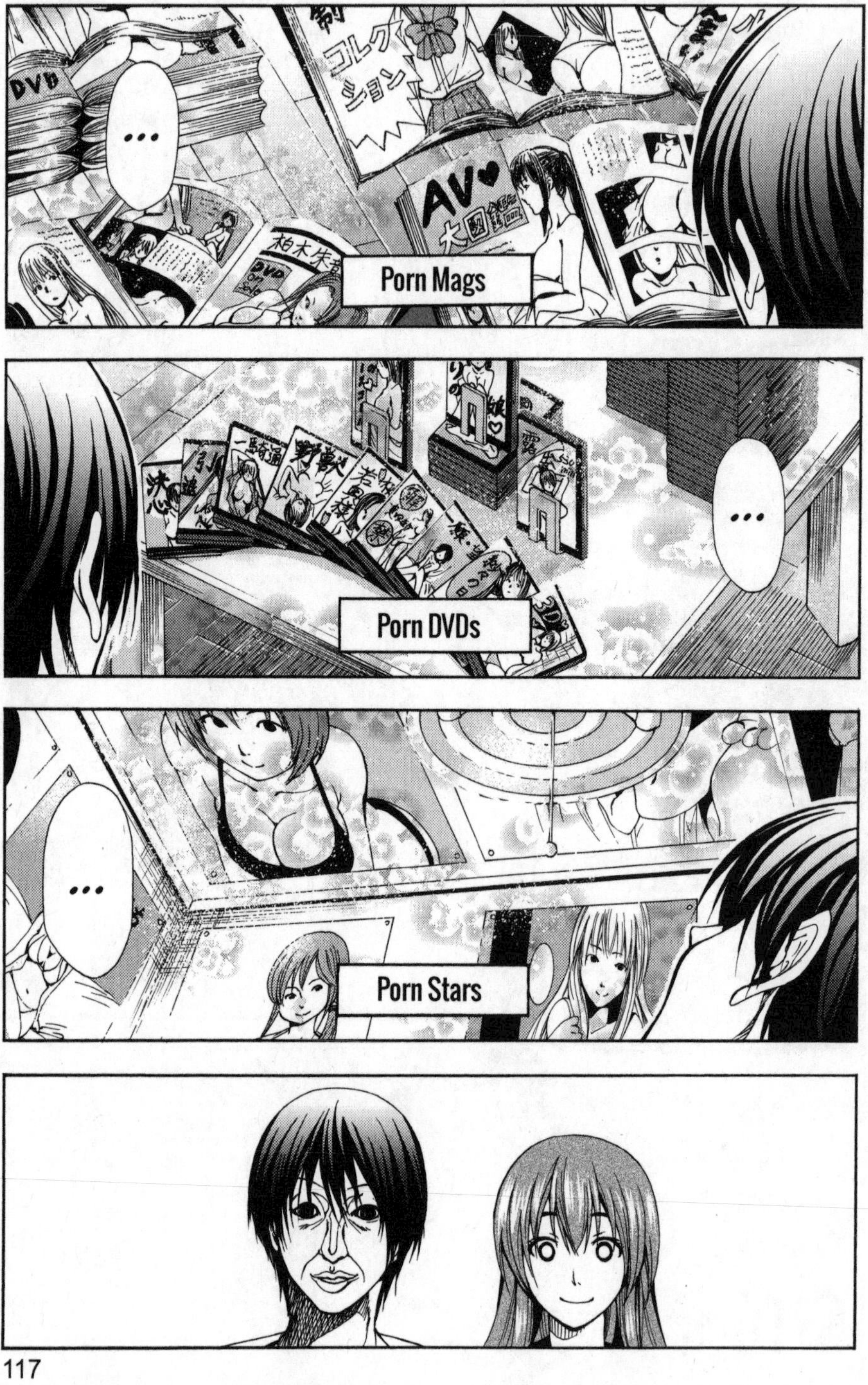

コレクション
AV
DVD
...
Porn Mags
...
Porn DVDs
...
Porn Stars

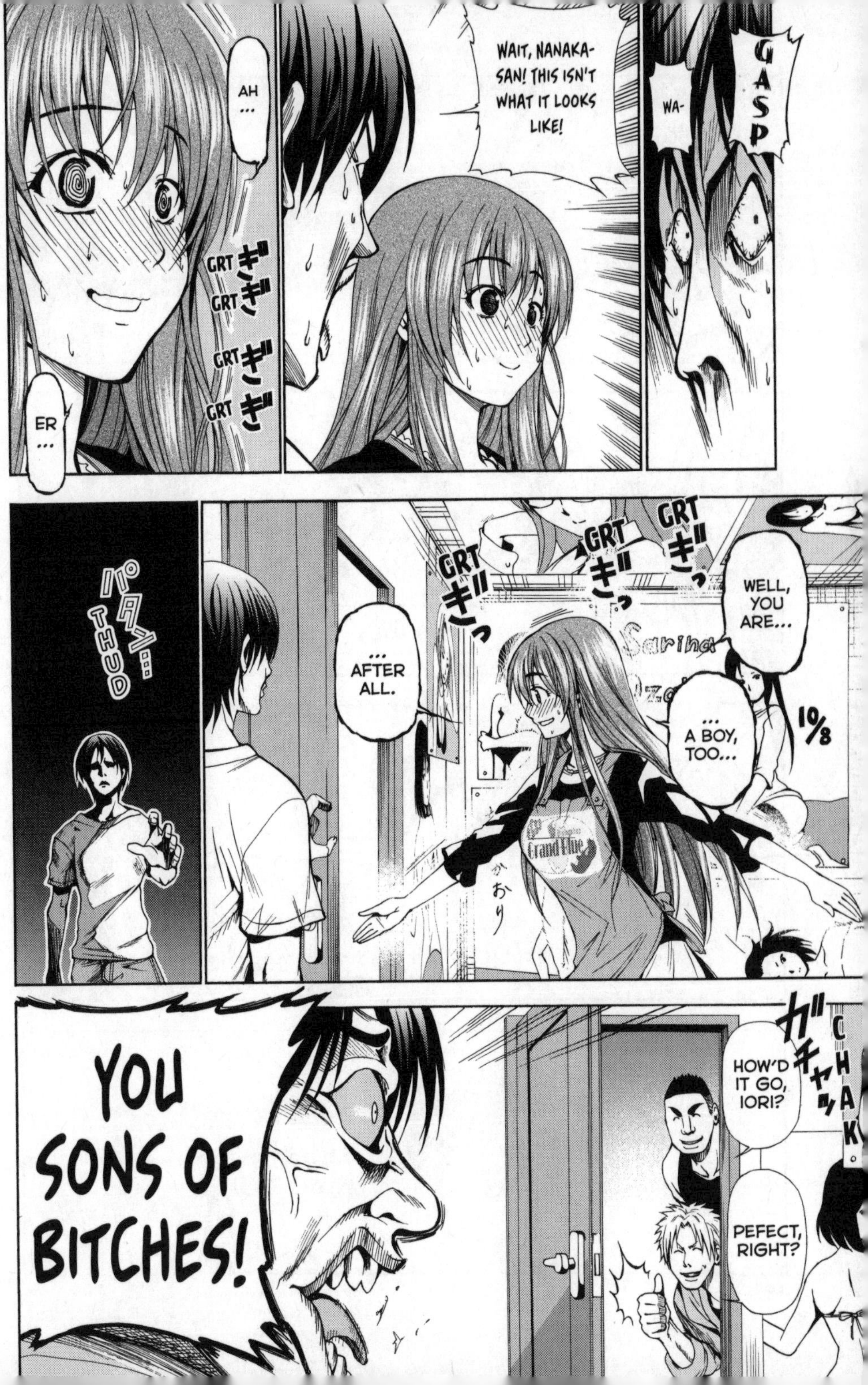
GASP
WA-
WAIT, NANAKA-SAN! THIS ISN'T WHAT IT LOOKS LIKE!
AH ...
GRT ぎ GRT ぎ GRT ぎ GRT ぎ
ER ...
GRT ぎっ GRT ぎっ GRT ぎっ
WELL, YOU ARE...
... A BOY, TOO...
10/8
Grand Blue
かおり
... AFTER ALL.
パタン... THUD
ガチャッ CHAK.
HOW'D IT GO, IORI?
PEFECT, RIGHT?
YOU SONS OF BITCHES!

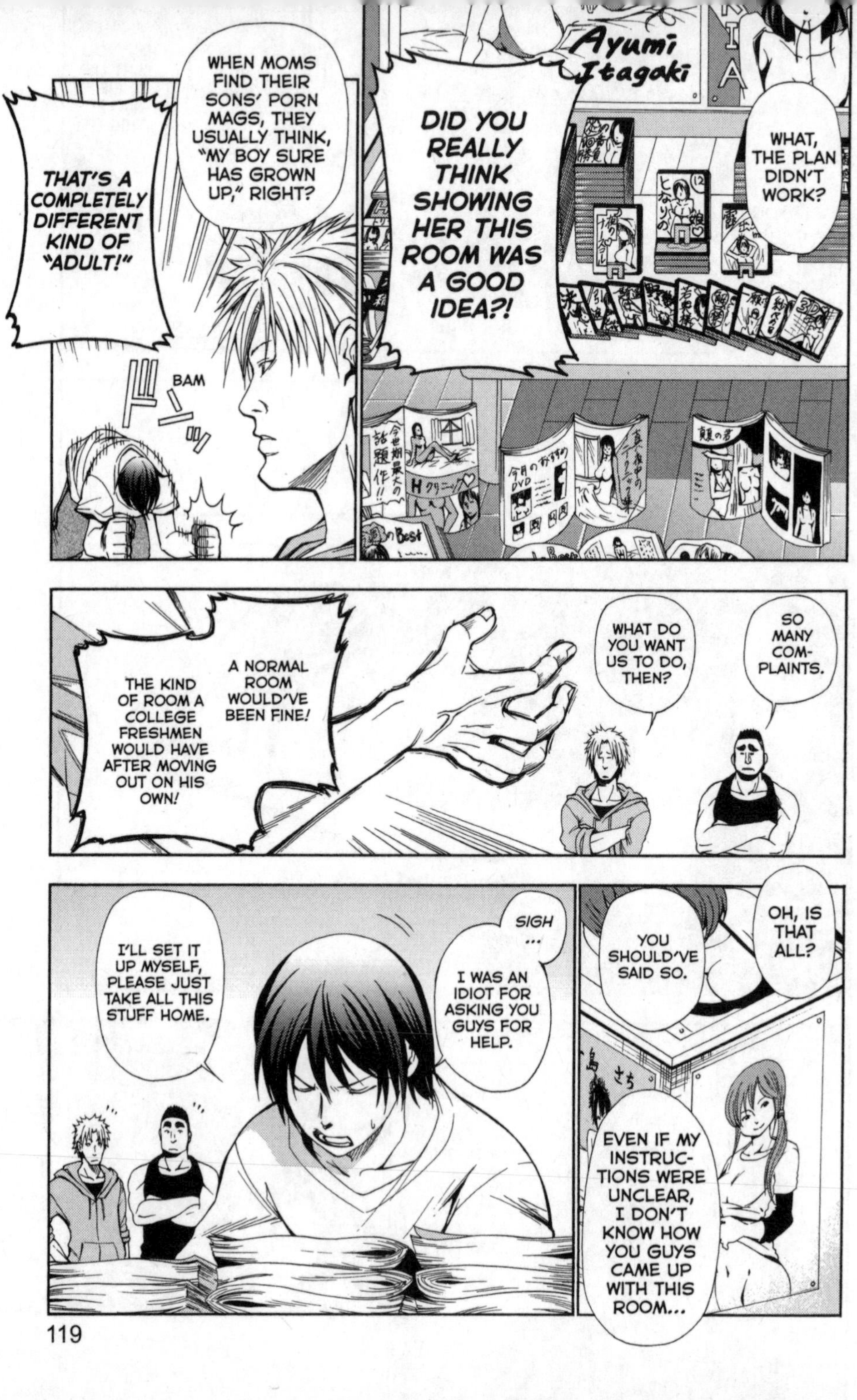
Ayumi Itagaki
WHAT, THE PLAN DIDN'T WORK?
DID YOU REALLY THINK SHOWING HER THIS ROOM WAS A GOOD IDEA?!
WHEN MOMS FIND THEIR SONS' PORN MAGS, THEY USUALLY THINK, "MY BOY SURE HAS GROWN UP," RIGHT?
THAT'S A COMPLETELY DIFFERENT KIND OF "ADULT!"
BAM
SO MANY COM-PLAINTS.
WHAT DO YOU WANT US TO DO, THEN?
A NORMAL ROOM WOULD'VE BEEN FINE!
THE KIND OF ROOM A COLLEGE FRESHMEN WOULD HAVE AFTER MOVING OUT ON HIS OWN!
OH, IS THAT ALL?
YOU SHOULD'VE SAID SO.
EVEN IF MY INSTRUC-TIONS WERE UNCLEAR, I DON'T KNOW HOW YOU GUYS CAME UP WITH THIS ROOM...
SIGH ...
I WAS AN IDIOT FOR ASKING YOU GUYS FOR HELP.
I'LL SET IT UP MYSELF, PLEASE JUST TAKE ALL THIS STUFF HOME.

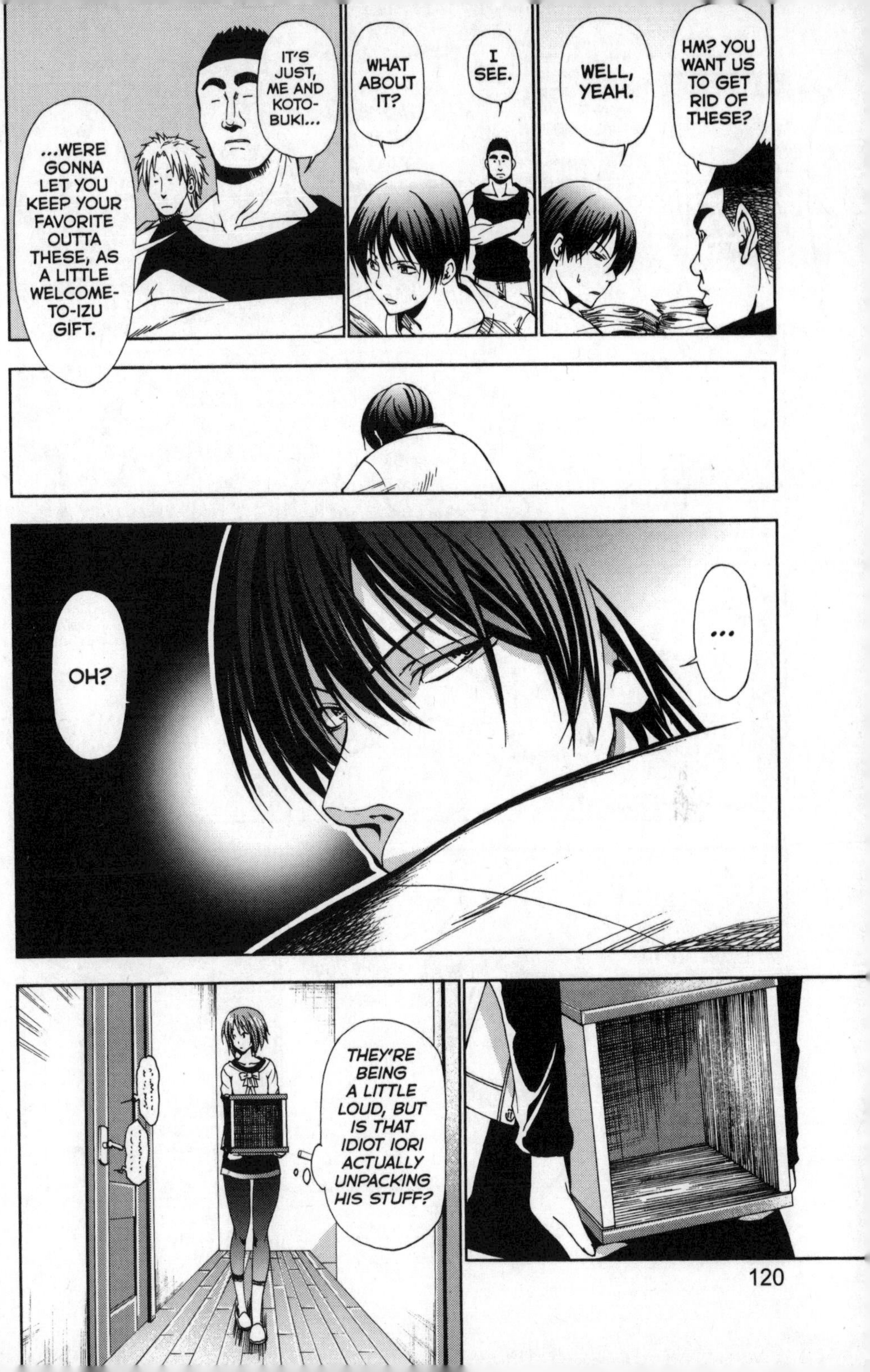
HM? YOU WANT US TO GET RID OF THESE?
WELL, YEAH.
I SEE.
WHAT ABOUT IT?
IT'S JUST, ME AND KOTO-BUKI...
...WERE GONNA LET YOU KEEP YOUR FAVORITE OUTTA THESE, AS A LITTLE WELCOME-TO-IZU GIFT.
...
OH?
THEY'RE BEING A LITTLE LOUD, BUT IS THAT IDIOT IORI ACTUALLY UNPACKING HIS STUFF?

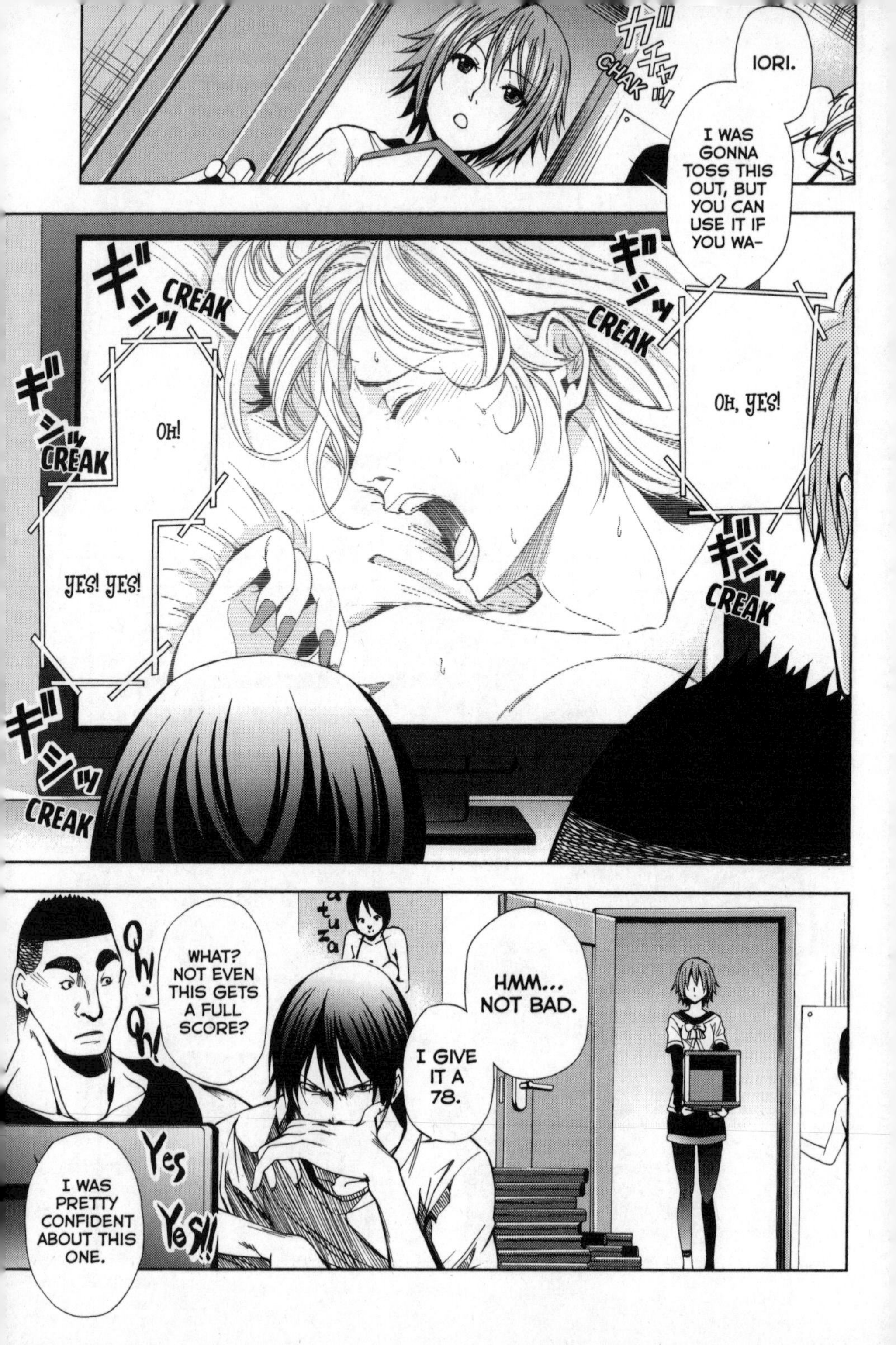
ガチャッ
CHAK
IORI.
I WAS GONNA TOSS THIS OUT, BUT YOU CAN USE IT IF YOU WA-
ギシッ
CREAK
OH, YES!
ギシッ
CREAK
ギシッ
CREAK
OH!
ギシッ
CREAK
YES! YES!
ギシッ
CREAK
HMM... NOT BAD.
I GIVE IT A 78.
WHAT? NOT EVEN THIS GETS A FULL SCORE?
Oh! Oh!
I WAS PRETTY CONFIDENT ABOUT THIS ONE.
Yes Yes!!

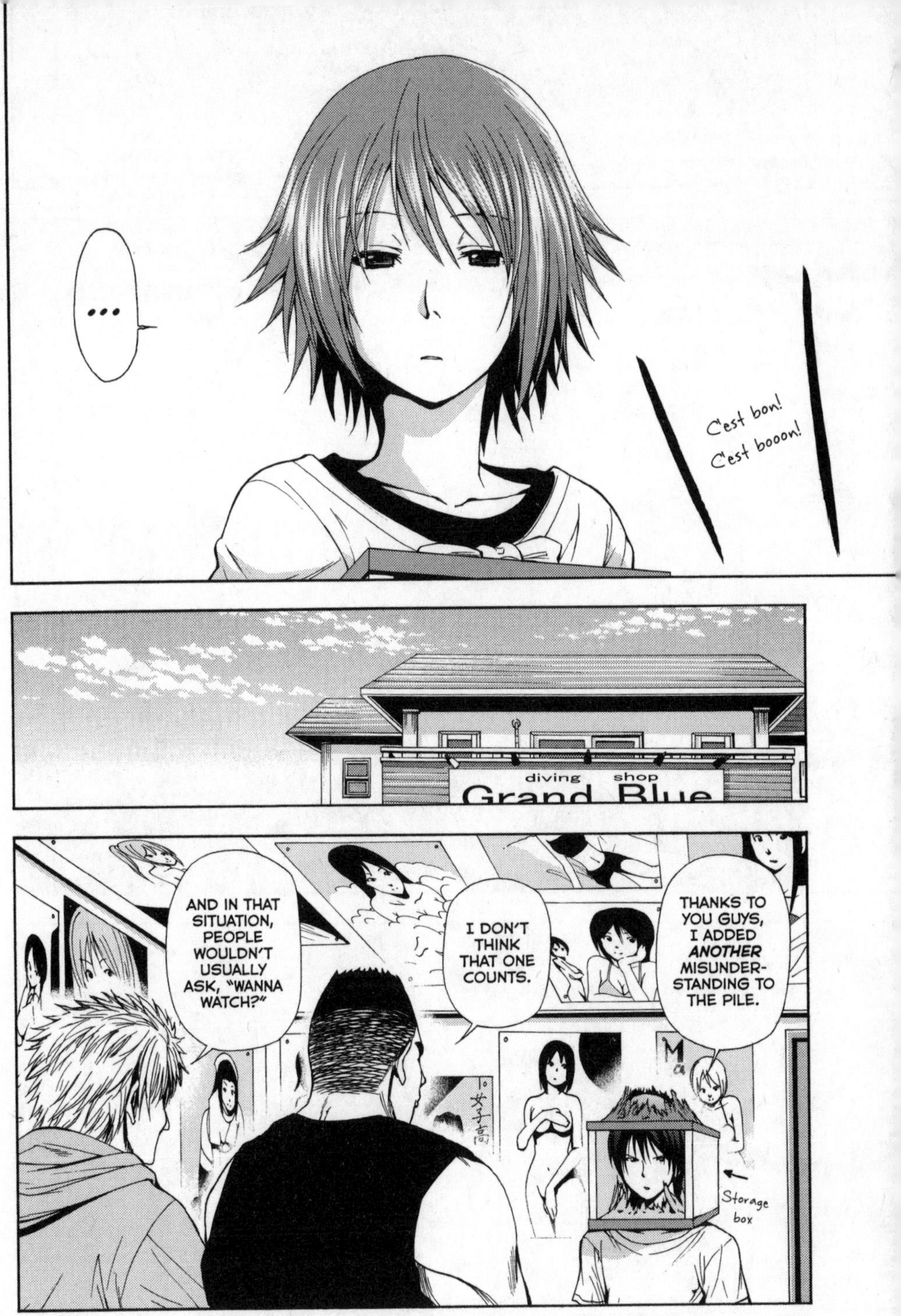
C'est bon! C'est booon!
...
diving shop
Grand Blue
THANKS TO YOU GUYS, I ADDED *ANOTHER* MISUNDER-STANDING TO THE PILE.
I DON'T THINK THAT ONE COUNTS.
AND IN THAT SITUATION, PEOPLE WOULDN'T USUALLY ASK, "WANNA WATCH?"
Storage box

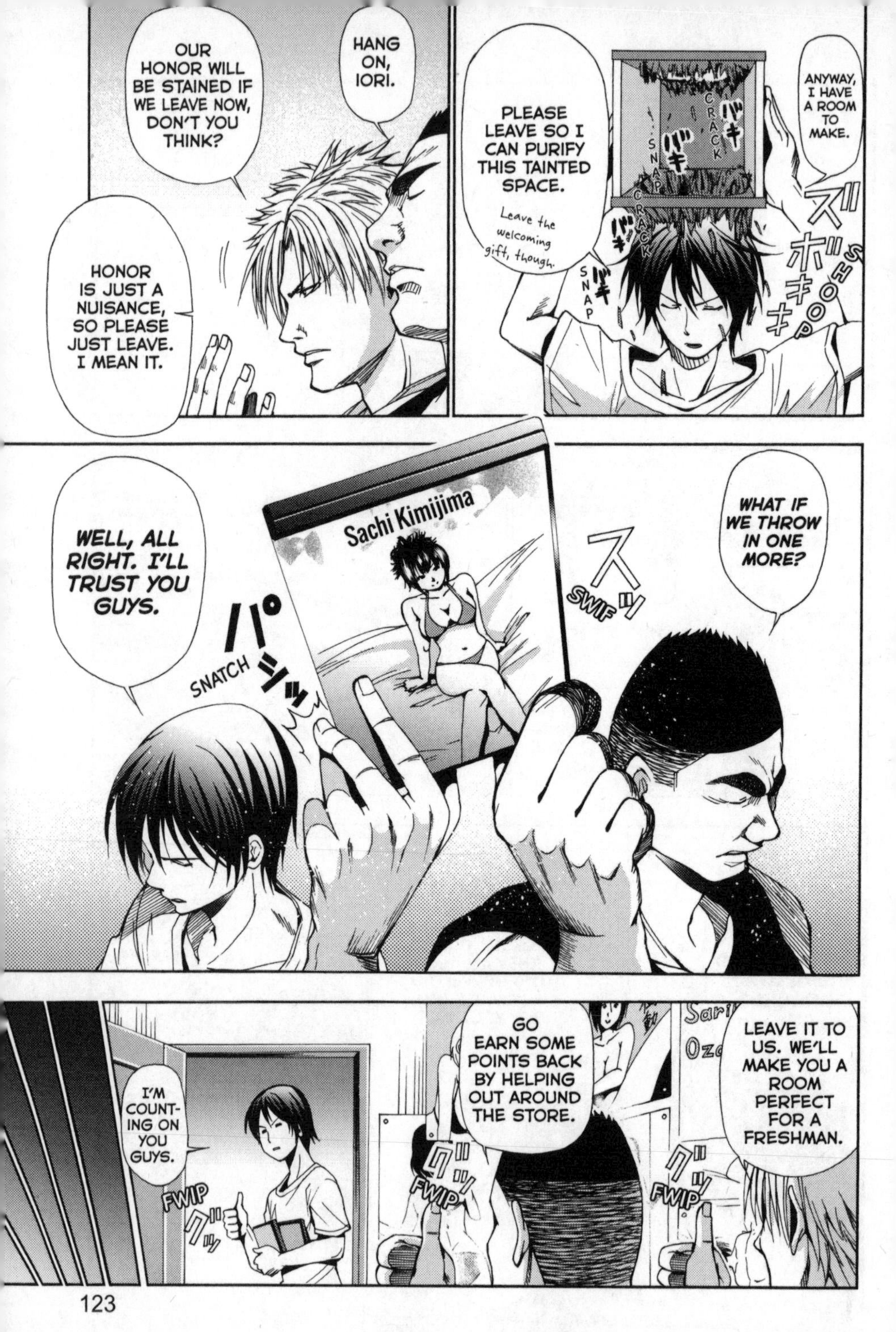
ANYWAY, I HAVE A ROOM TO MAKE.
SHOOP
CRACK
SNAP
CRACK
SNAP
PLEASE LEAVE SO I CAN PURIFY THIS TAINTED SPACE.
Leave the welcoming gift, though.
HANG ON, IORI.
OUR HONOR WILL BE STAINED IF WE LEAVE NOW, DON'T YOU THINK?
HONOR IS JUST A NUISANCE, SO PLEASE JUST LEAVE. I MEAN IT.
WHAT IF WE THROW IN ONE MORE?
SWIF
Sachi Kimijima
SNATCH
WELL, ALL RIGHT. I'LL TRUST YOU GUYS.
LEAVE IT TO US. WE'LL MAKE YOU A ROOM PERFECT FOR A FRESHMAN.
FWIP
GO EARN SOME POINTS BACK BY HELPING OUT AROUND THE STORE.
FWIP
I'M COUNTING ON YOU GUYS.
FWIP

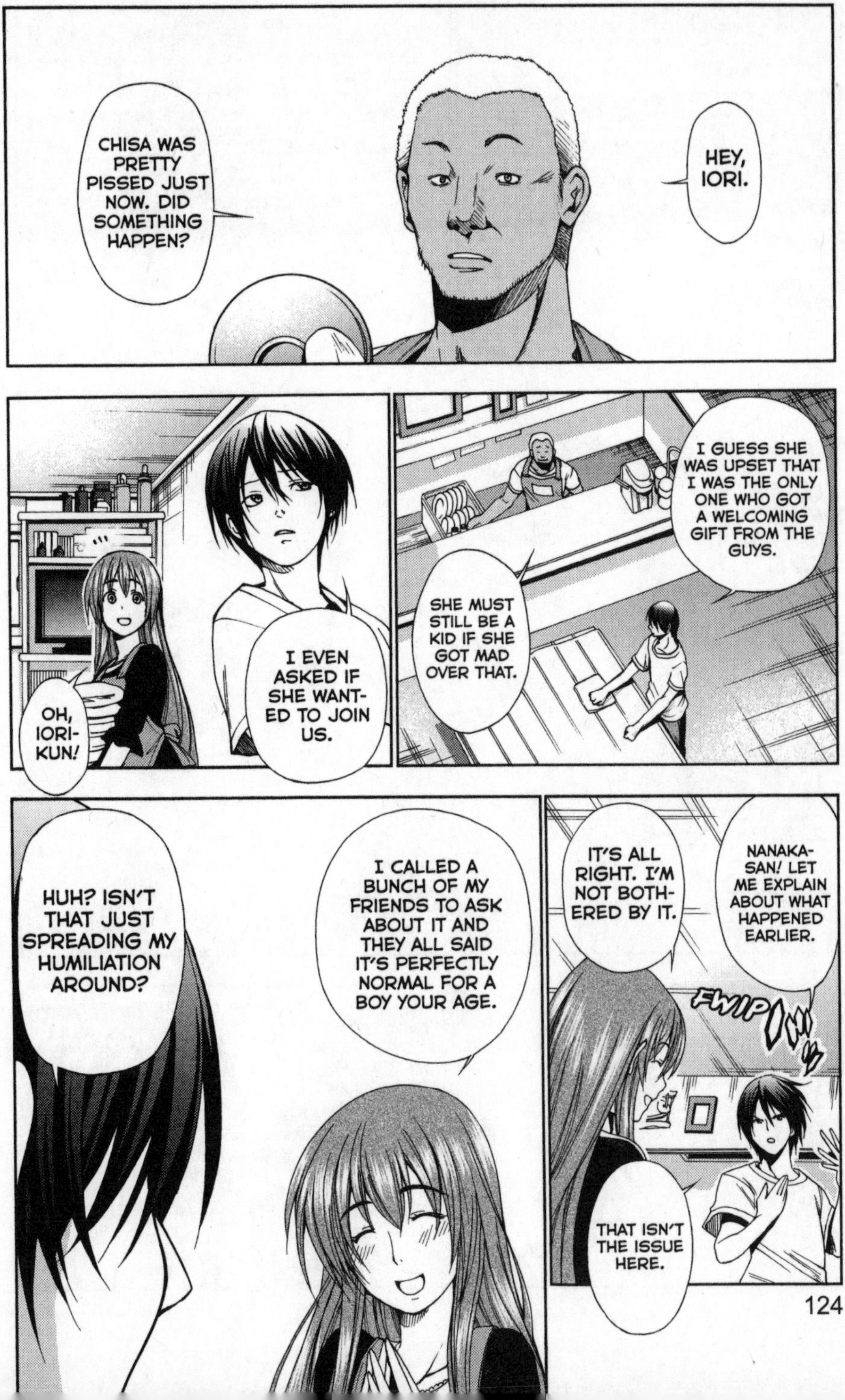
HEY, IORI.
CHISA WAS PRETTY PISSED JUST NOW. DID SOMETHING HAPPEN?
I GUESS SHE WAS UPSET THAT I WAS THE ONLY ONE WHO GOT A WELCOMING GIFT FROM THE GUYS.
SHE MUST STILL BE A KID IF SHE GOT MAD OVER THAT.
I EVEN ASKED IF SHE WANTED TO JOIN US.
OH, IORI-KUN!
NANAKA-SAN! LET ME EXPLAIN ABOUT WHAT HAPPENED EARLIER.
IT'S ALL RIGHT. I'M NOT BOTHERED BY IT.
FWIP
THAT ISN'T THE ISSUE HERE.
I CALLED A BUNCH OF MY FRIENDS TO ASK ABOUT IT AND THEY ALL SAID IT'S PERFECTLY NORMAL FOR A BOY YOUR AGE.
HUH? ISN'T THAT JUST SPREADING MY HUMILIATION AROUND?

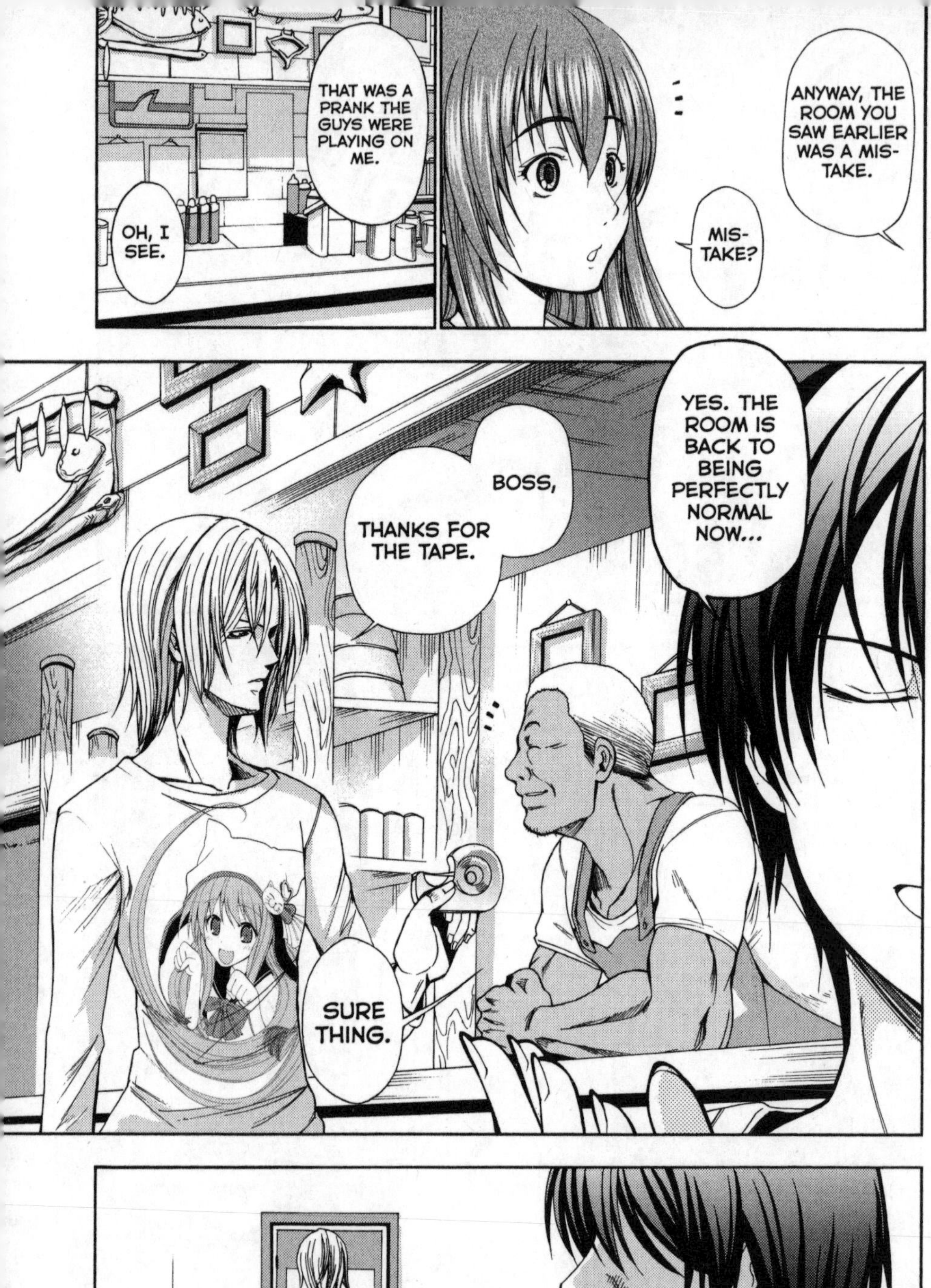
ANYWAY, THE ROOM YOU SAW EARLIER WAS A MIS-TAKE.
MIS-TAKE?
THAT WAS A PRANK THE GUYS WERE PLAYING ON ME.
OH, I SEE.
YES. THE ROOM IS BACK TO BEING PERFECTLY NORMAL NOW...
BOSS,
THANKS FOR THE TAPE.
SURE THING.

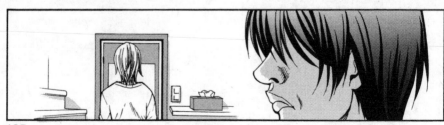

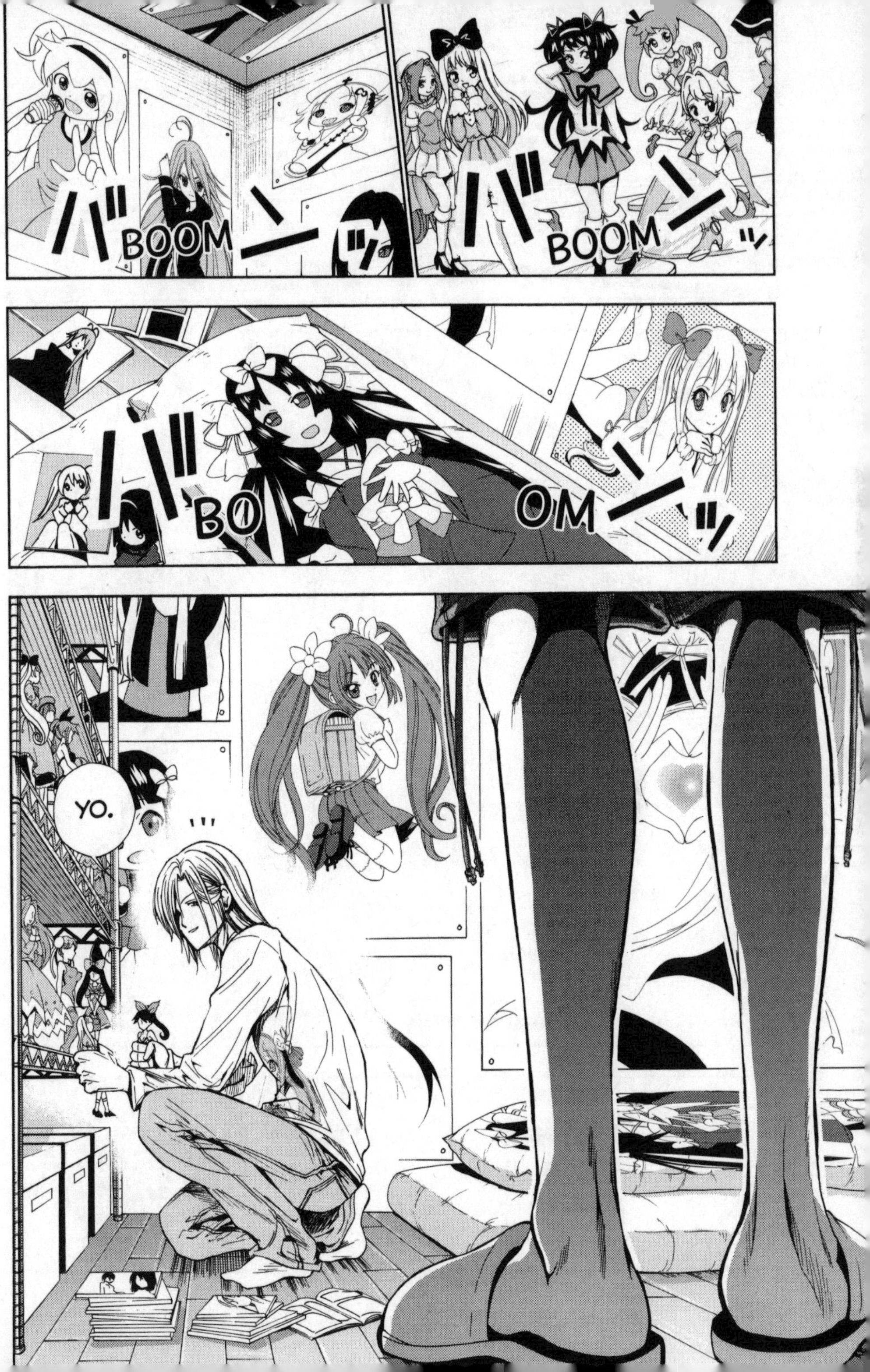

バ BOOM ーンッ
バ BOOM ーッ
バ BO OM ーンッ
YO.
!!!

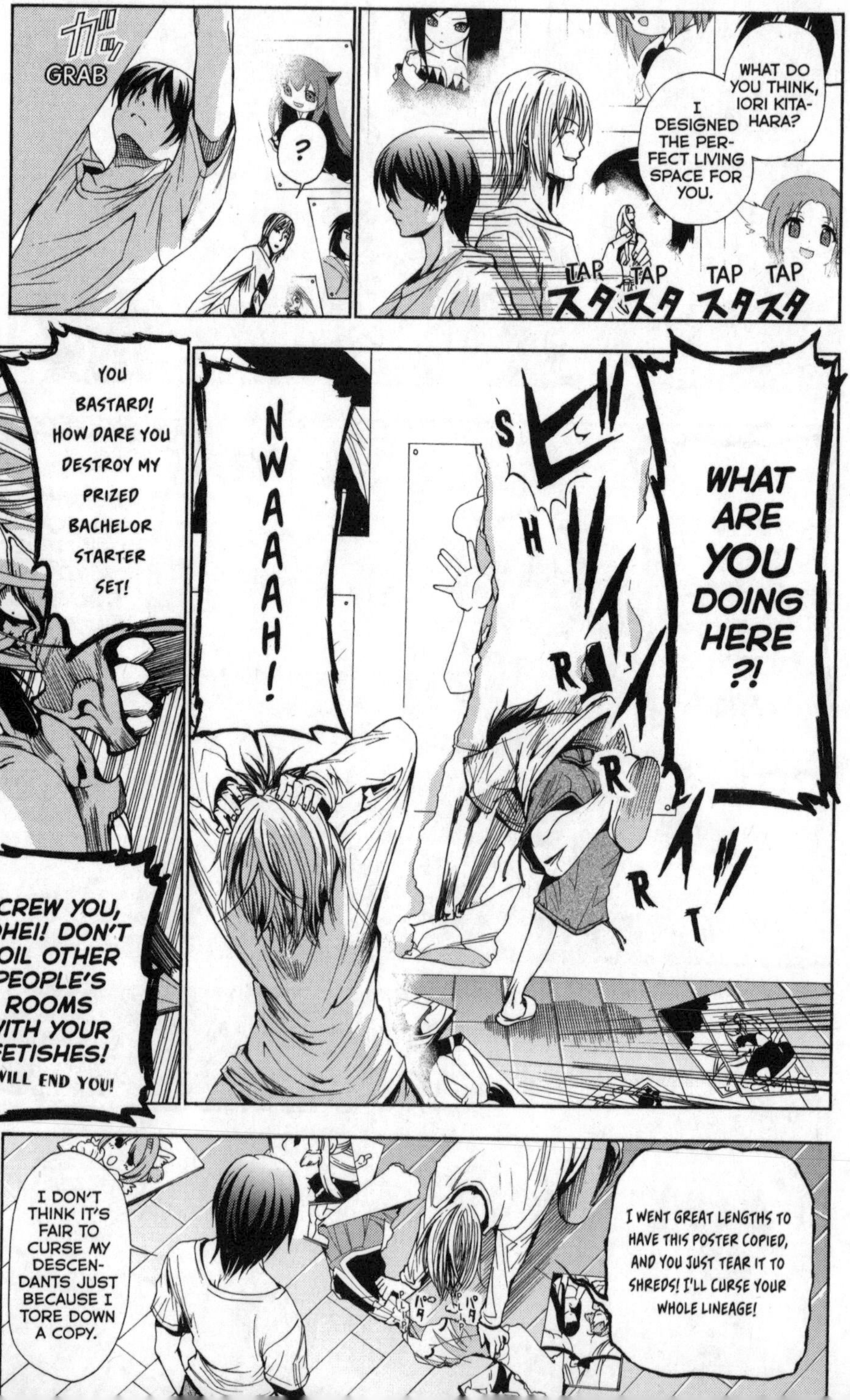
WHAT DO YOU THINK, IORI KITAHARA?
I DESIGNED THE PERFECT LIVING SPACE FOR YOU.
TAP TAP TAP TAP
スタスタスタスタ
ガッ
GRAB
?
WHAT ARE YOU DOING HERE?!
SHRRRT
NWAAAAH!
YOU BASTARD! HOW DARE YOU DESTROY MY PRIZED BACHELOR STARTER SET!
SCREW YOU, KOHEI! DON'T SOIL OTHER PEOPLE'S ROOMS WITH YOUR FETISHES! I WILL END YOU!
I WENT GREAT LENGTHS TO HAVE THIS POSTER COPIED, AND YOU JUST TEAR IT TO SHREDS! I'LL CURSE YOUR WHOLE LINEAGE!
I DON'T THINK IT'S FAIR TO CURSE MY DESCENDANTS JUST BECAUSE I TORE DOWN A COPY.

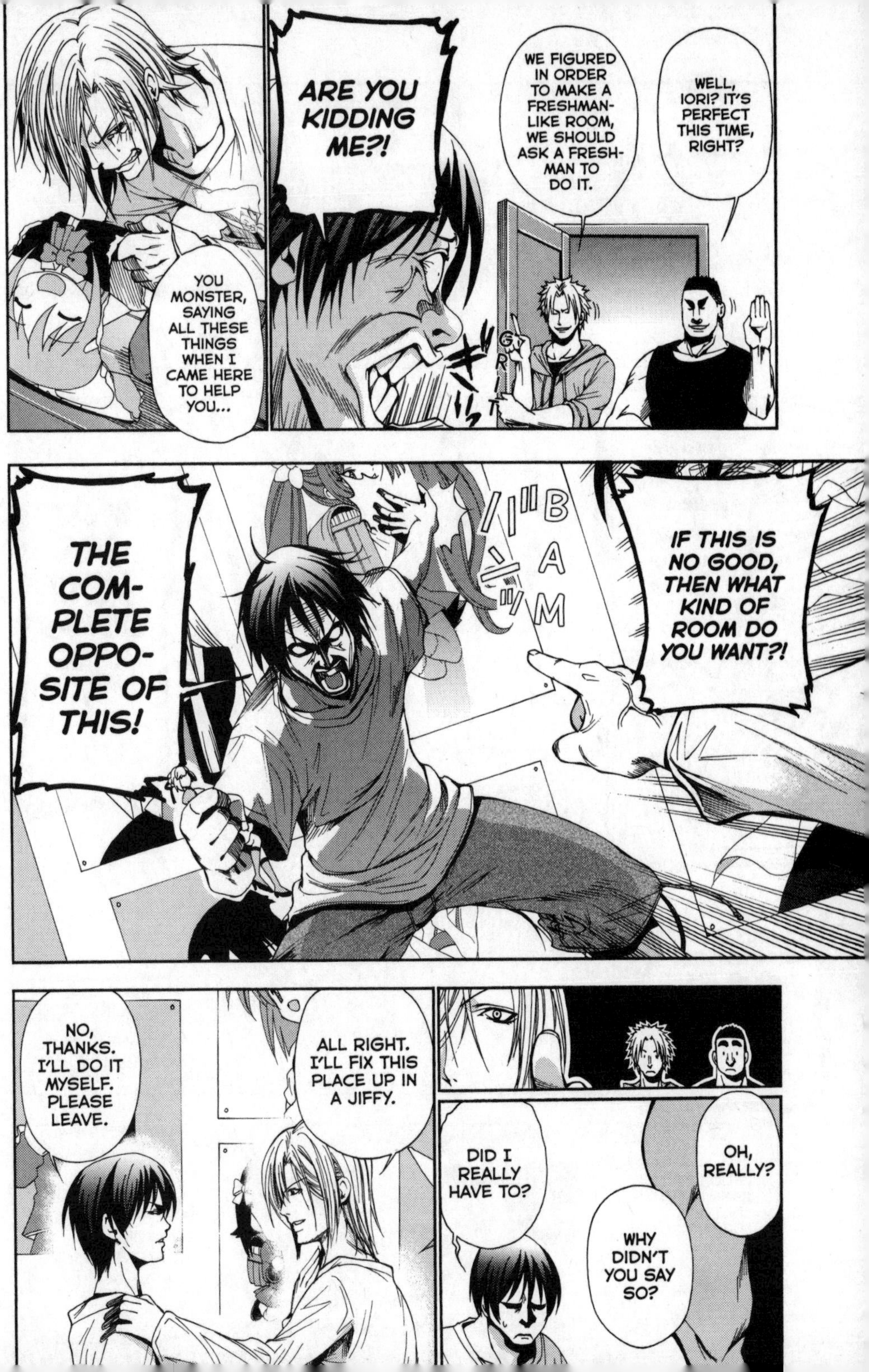
WELL, IORI? IT'S PERFECT THIS TIME, RIGHT?
WE FIGURED IN ORDER TO MAKE A FRESHMAN-LIKE ROOM, WE SHOULD ASK A FRESHMAN TO DO IT.
ARE YOU KIDDING ME?!
GRIT
YOU MONSTER, SAYING ALL THESE THINGS WHEN I CAME HERE TO HELP YOU...
IF THIS IS NO GOOD, THEN WHAT KIND OF ROOM DO YOU WANT?!
BAM
THE COMPLETE OPPOSITE OF THIS!
OH, REALLY?
WHY DIDN'T YOU SAY SO?
DID I REALLY HAVE TO?
ALL RIGHT. I'LL FIX THIS PLACE UP IN A JIFFY.
NO, THANKS. I'LL DO IT MYSELF. PLEASE LEAVE.

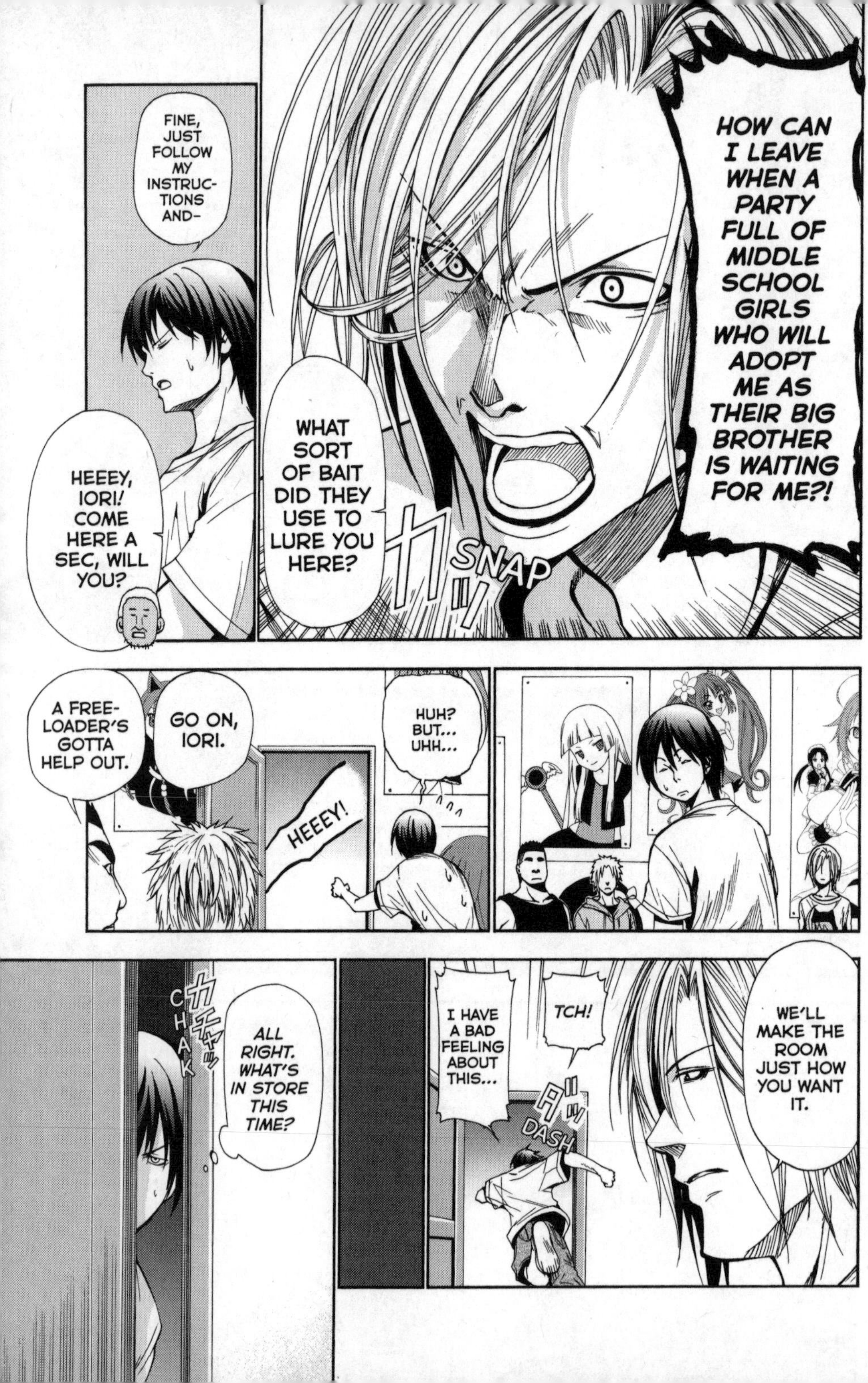
HOW CAN I LEAVE WHEN A PARTY FULL OF MIDDLE SCHOOL GIRLS WHO WILL ADOPT ME AS THEIR BIG BROTHER IS WAITING FOR ME?!
WHAT SORT OF BAIT DID THEY USE TO LURE YOU HERE?
SNAP
FINE, JUST FOLLOW MY INSTRUC-TIONS AND–
HEEEY, IORI! COME HERE A SEC, WILL YOU?
HUH? BUT... UHH...
HEEEY!
GO ON, IORI.
A FREE-LOADER'S GOTTA HELP OUT.
WE'LL MAKE THE ROOM JUST HOW YOU WANT IT.
TCH!
I HAVE A BAD FEELING ABOUT THIS...
DASH
CHAK
ALL RIGHT. WHAT'S IN STORE THIS TIME?

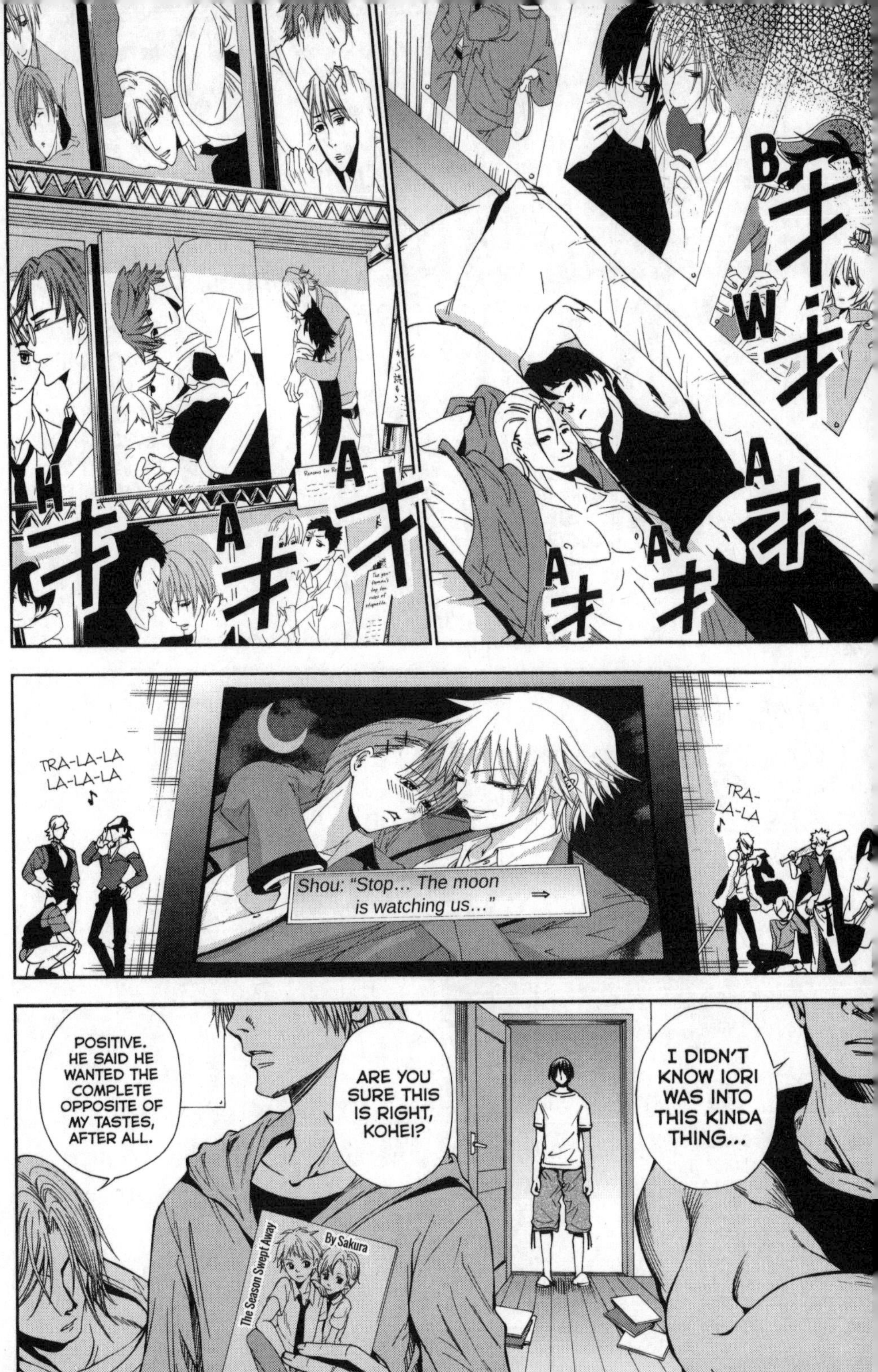
B
W
A
A
A
A
A
A
H
TRA-LA-LA
Shou: "Stop… The moon is watching us…"
TRA-LA-LA LA-LA-LA
I DIDN'T KNOW IORI WAS INTO THIS KINDA THING...
ARE YOU SURE THIS IS RIGHT, KOHEI?
POSITIVE. HE SAID HE WANTED THE COMPLETE OPPOSITE OF MY TASTES, AFTER ALL.
The Season Swept Away
By Sakura

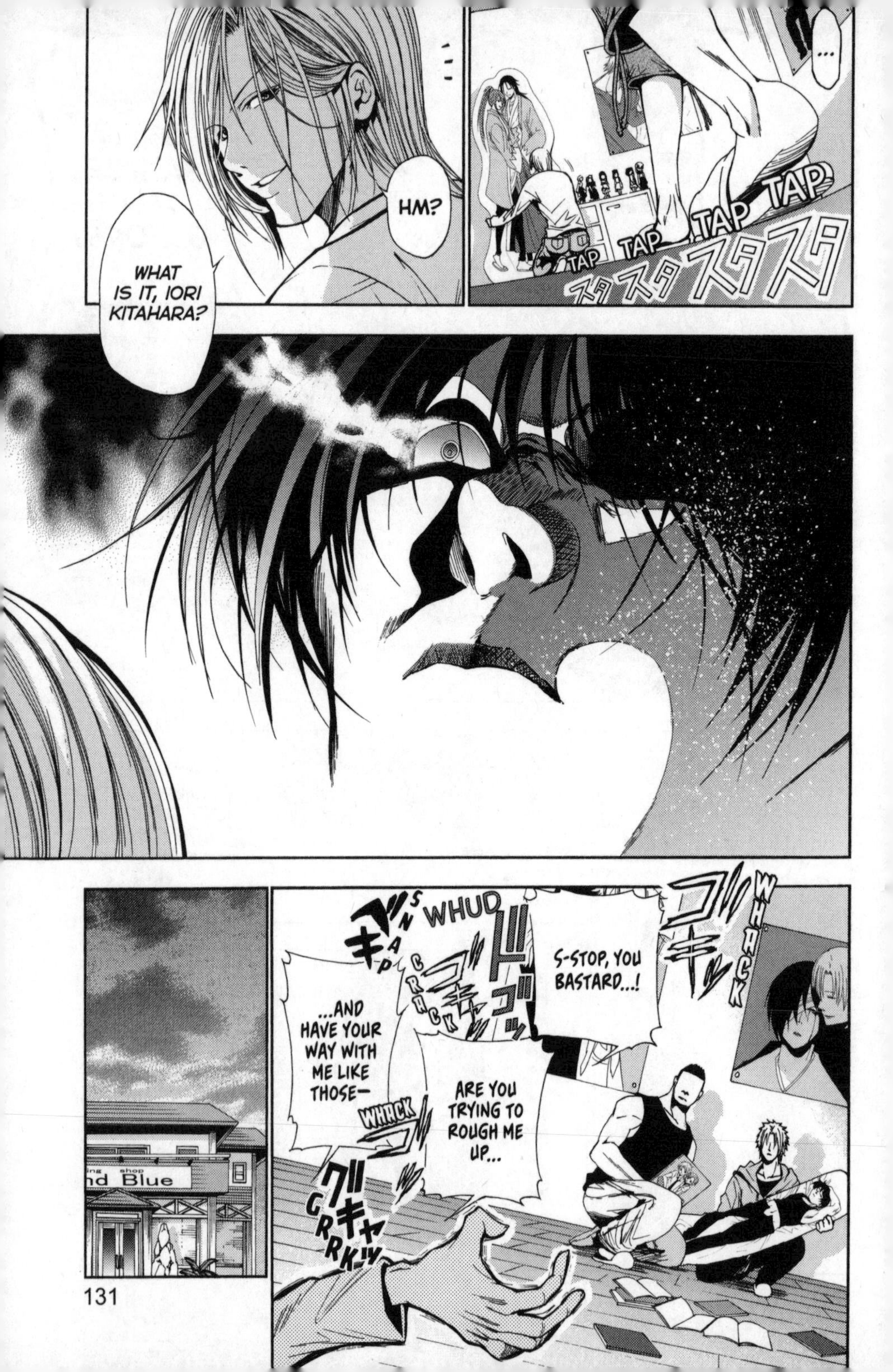
...
TAP TAP TAP TAP TAP
スタスタスタスタ
HM?
WHAT IS IT, IORI KITAHARA?
WHACK
S-STOP, YOU BASTARD...!
WHUD
SNAP
CRACK
ARE YOU TRYING TO ROUGH ME UP...
...AND HAVE YOUR WAY WITH ME LIKE THOSE—
WHACK
GRRRK
shop
nd Blue

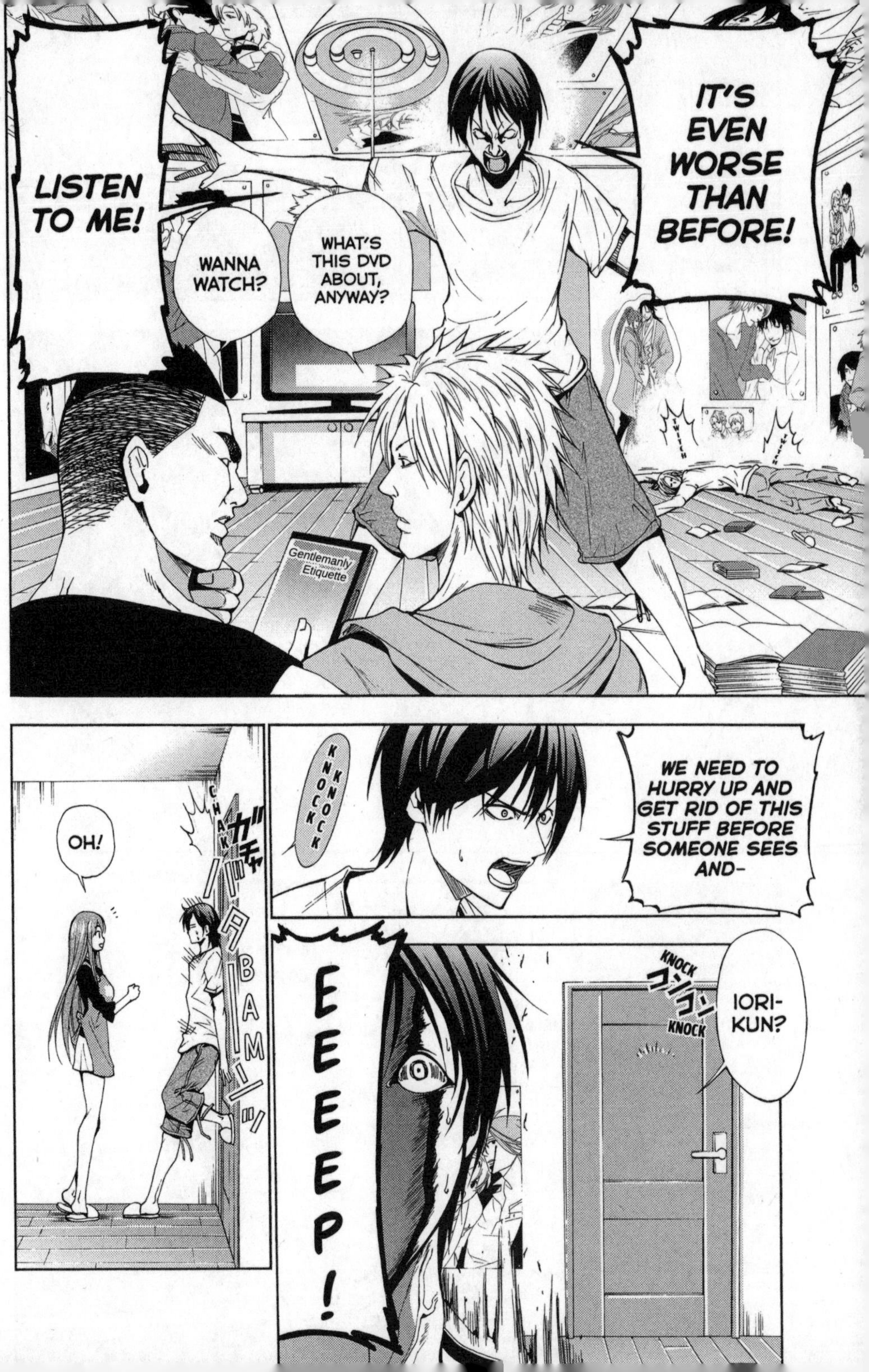

IT'S EVEN WORSE THAN BEFORE!
WHAT'S THIS DVD ABOUT, ANYWAY?
WANNA WATCH?
LISTEN TO ME!
Gentlemanly Etiquette
TWITCH
TWITCH
WE NEED TO HURRY UP AND GET RID OF THIS STUFF BEFORE SOMEONE SEES AND-
KNOCK KNOCK
IORI-KUN?
KNOCK KNOCK
EEEEP!
CHAK
BAM
OH!

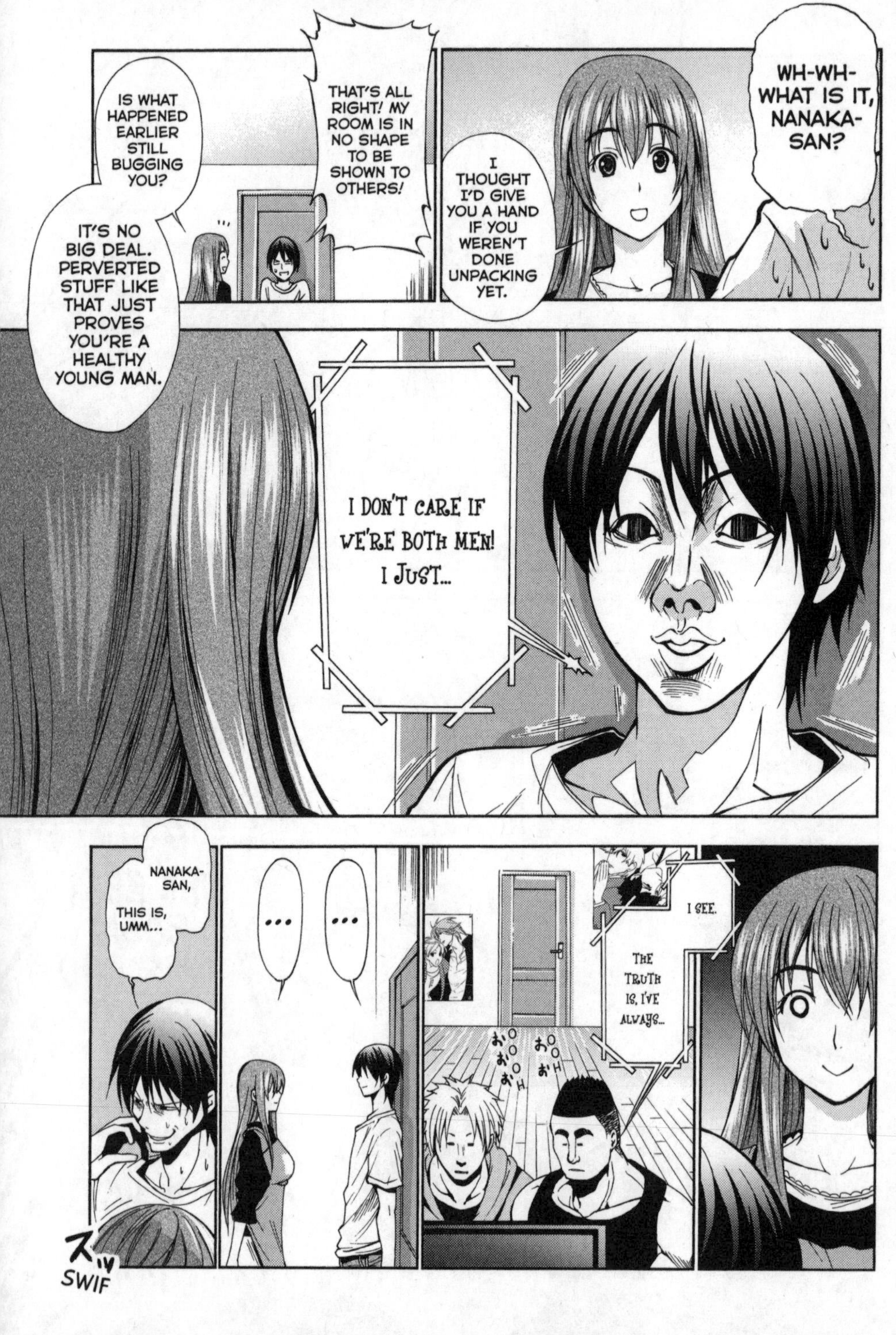
WH-WH-WHAT IS IT, NANAKA-SAN?
I THOUGHT I'D GIVE YOU A HAND IF YOU WEREN'T DONE UNPACKING YET.
THAT'S ALL RIGHT! MY ROOM IS IN NO SHAPE TO BE SHOWN TO OTHERS!
IS WHAT HAPPENED EARLIER STILL BUGGING YOU?
IT'S NO BIG DEAL. PERVERTED STUFF LIKE THAT JUST PROVES YOU'RE A HEALTHY YOUNG MAN.
I DON'T CARE IF WE'RE BOTH MEN! I JUST...
I SEE.
THE TRUTH IS, I'VE ALWAYS...
...
...
NANAKA-SAN,
THIS IS, UMM...
SWIF

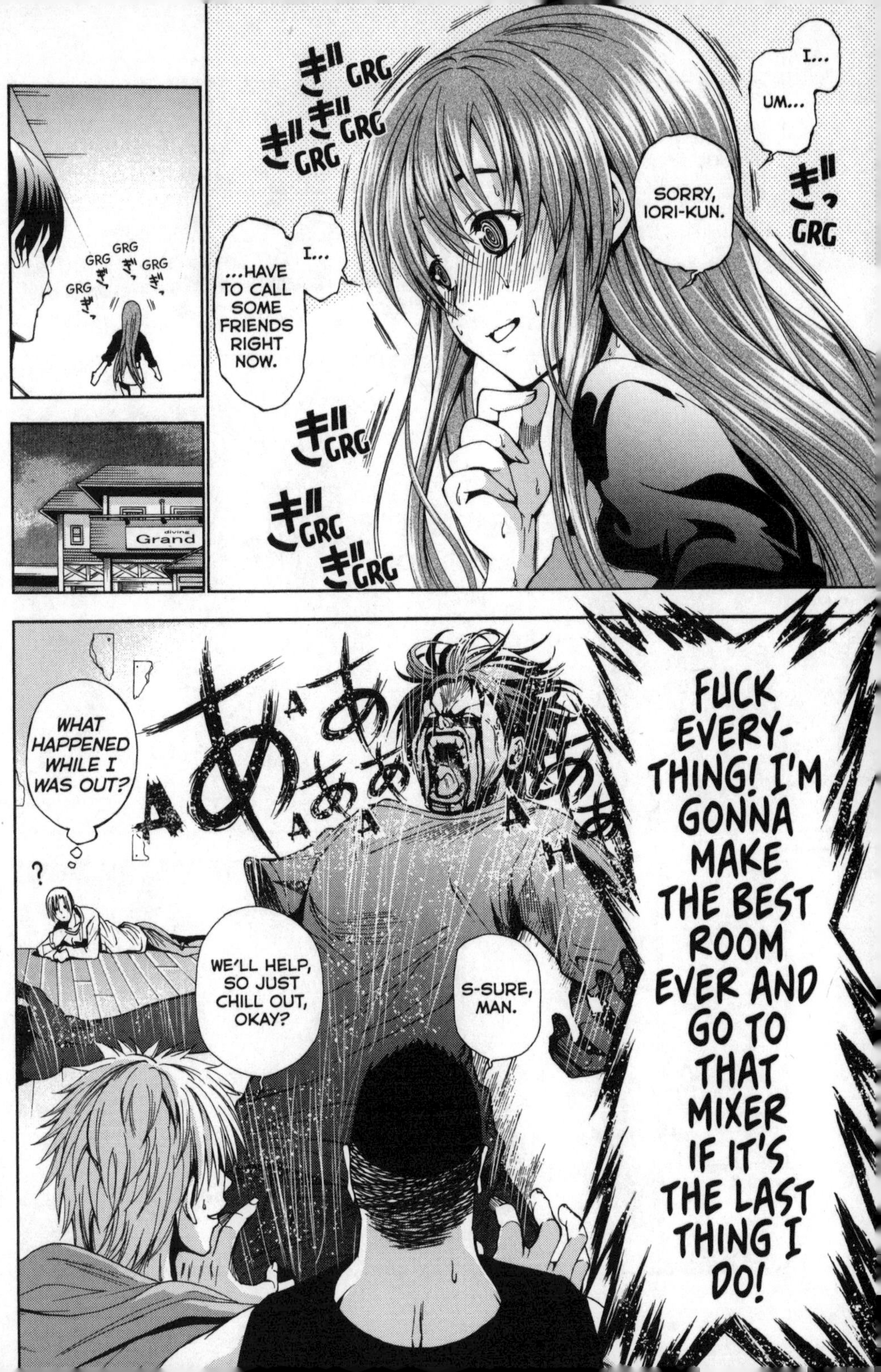
I... UM...
ぎっ GRG
SORRY, IORI-KUN.
ぎ" GRG ぎ"GRG ぎ"GRG ぎ"GRG
I... ...HAVE TO CALL SOME FRIENDS RIGHT NOW.
ぎ" GRG
ぎ" GRG ぎ" GRG
GRG ぎっ GRG ぎっ GRG ぎっ GRG ぎっ
FUCK EVERY-THING! I'M GONNA MAKE THE BEST ROOM EVER AND GO TO THAT MIXER IF IT'S THE LAST THING I DO!
あああああ AAAAAH
WHAT HAPPENED WHILE I WAS OUT?
?
S-SURE, MAN.
WE'LL HELP, SO JUST CHILL OUT, OKAY?

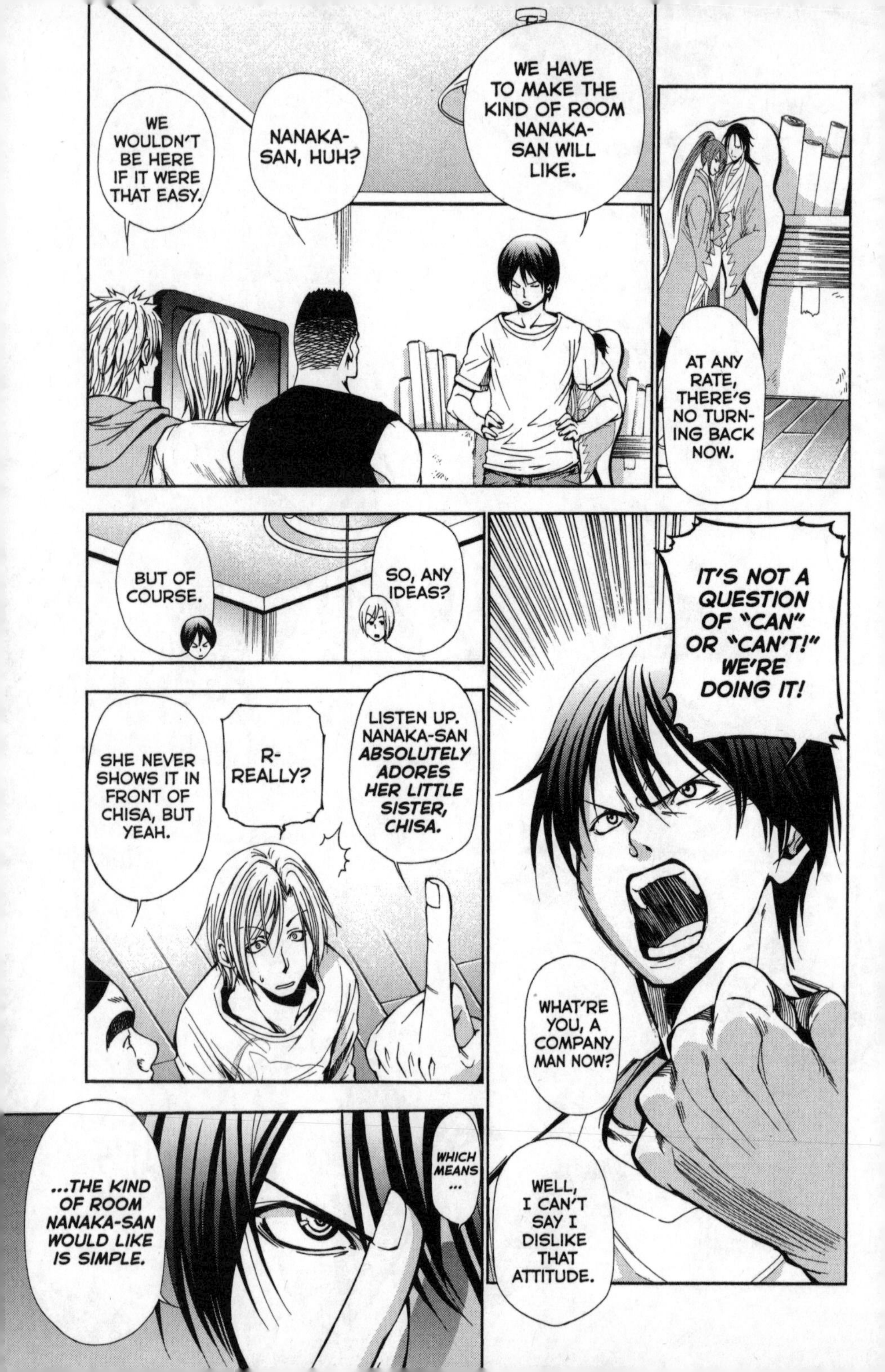
AT ANY RATE, THERE'S NO TURNING BACK NOW.
WE HAVE TO MAKE THE KIND OF ROOM NANAKA-SAN WILL LIKE.
NANAKA-SAN, HUH?
WE WOULDN'T BE HERE IF IT WERE THAT EASY.
IT'S NOT A QUESTION OF "CAN" OR "CAN'T!" WE'RE DOING IT!
WHAT'RE YOU, A COMPANY MAN NOW?
WELL, I CAN'T SAY I DISLIKE THAT ATTITUDE.
SO, ANY IDEAS?
BUT OF COURSE.
LISTEN UP. NANAKA-SAN ABSOLUTELY ADORES HER LITTLE SISTER, CHISA.
R-REALLY?
SHE NEVER SHOWS IT IN FRONT OF CHISA, BUT YEAH.
WHICH MEANS ...
...THE KIND OF ROOM NANAKA-SAN WOULD LIKE IS SIMPLE.

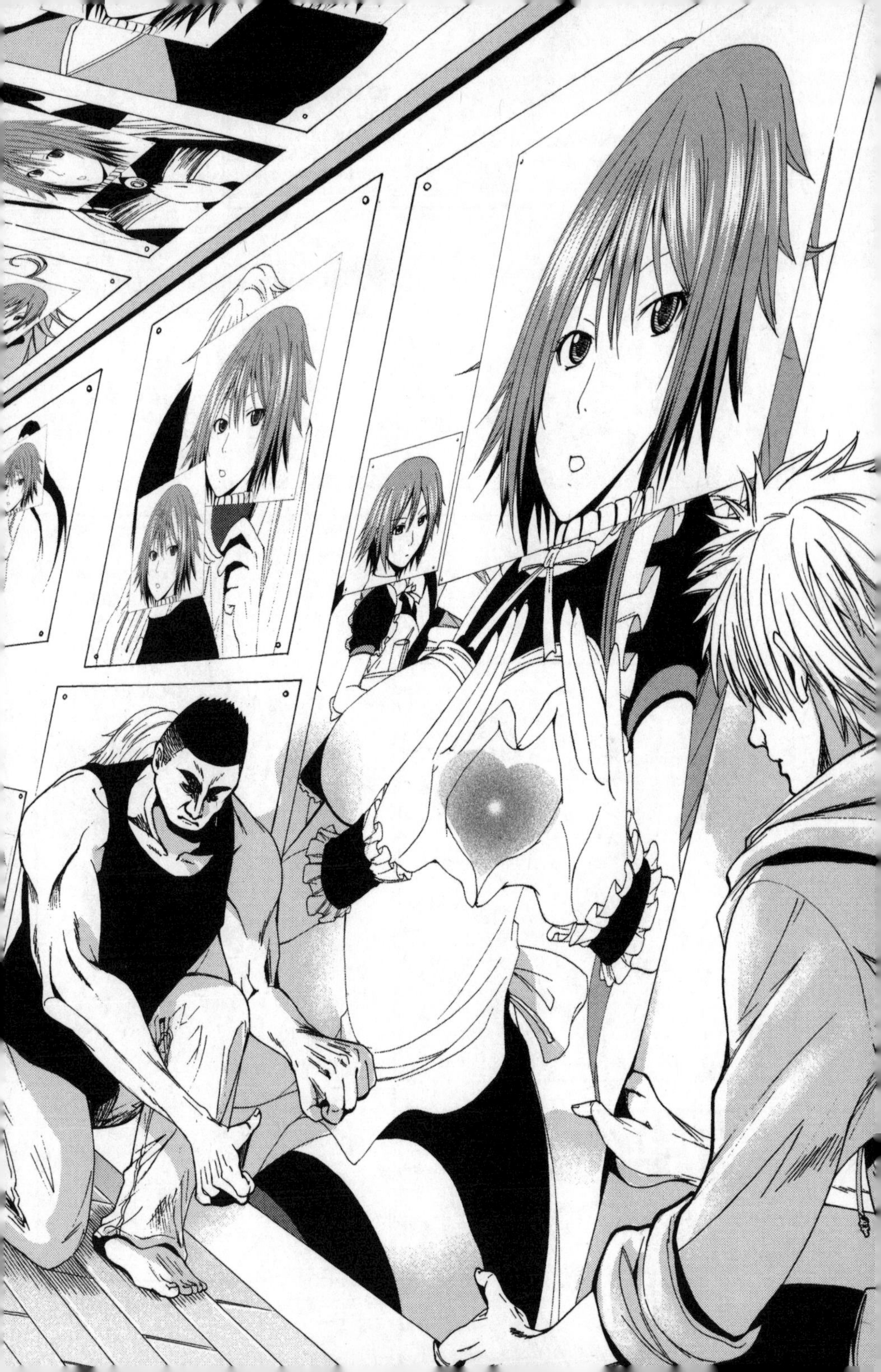

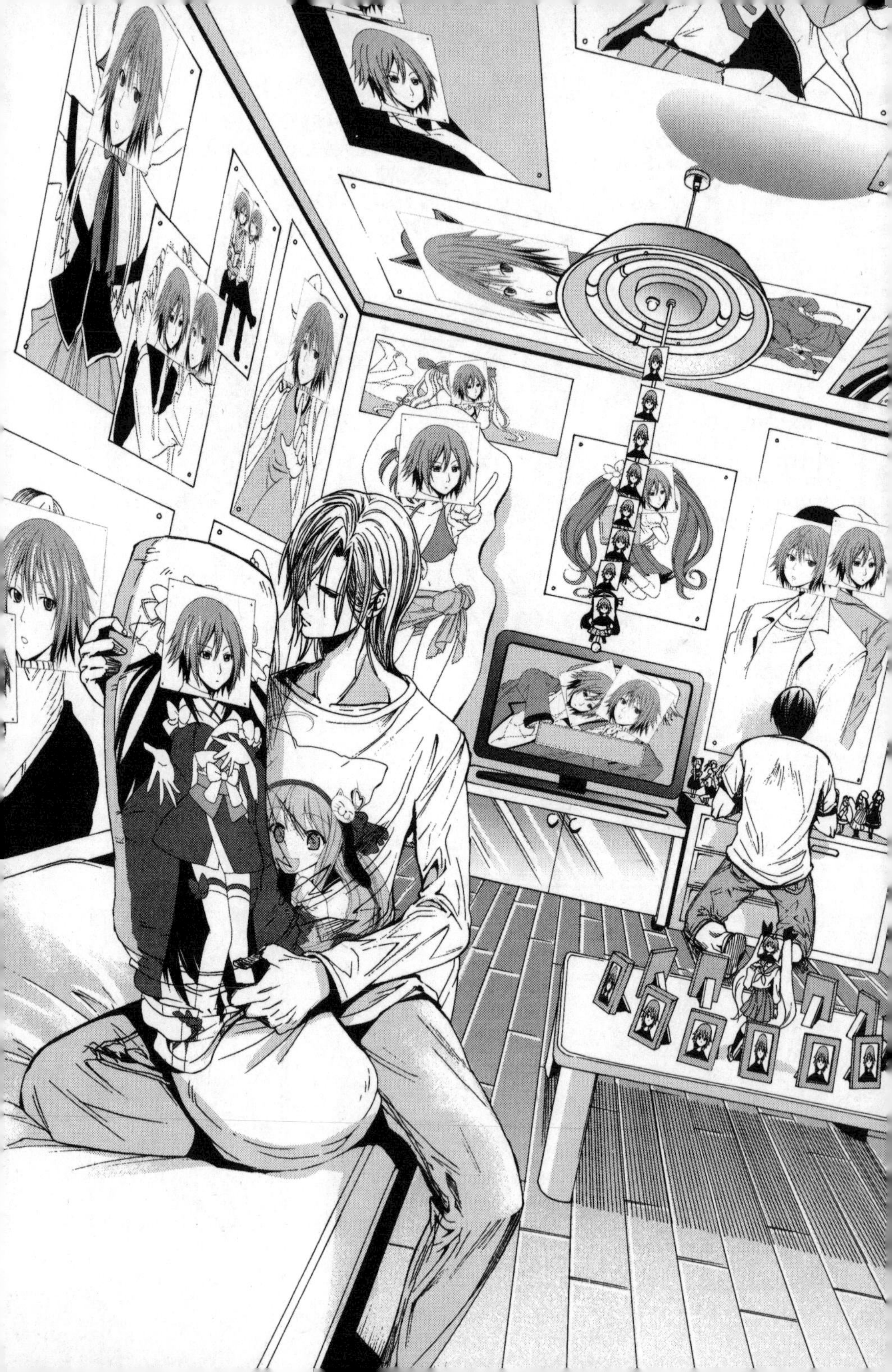

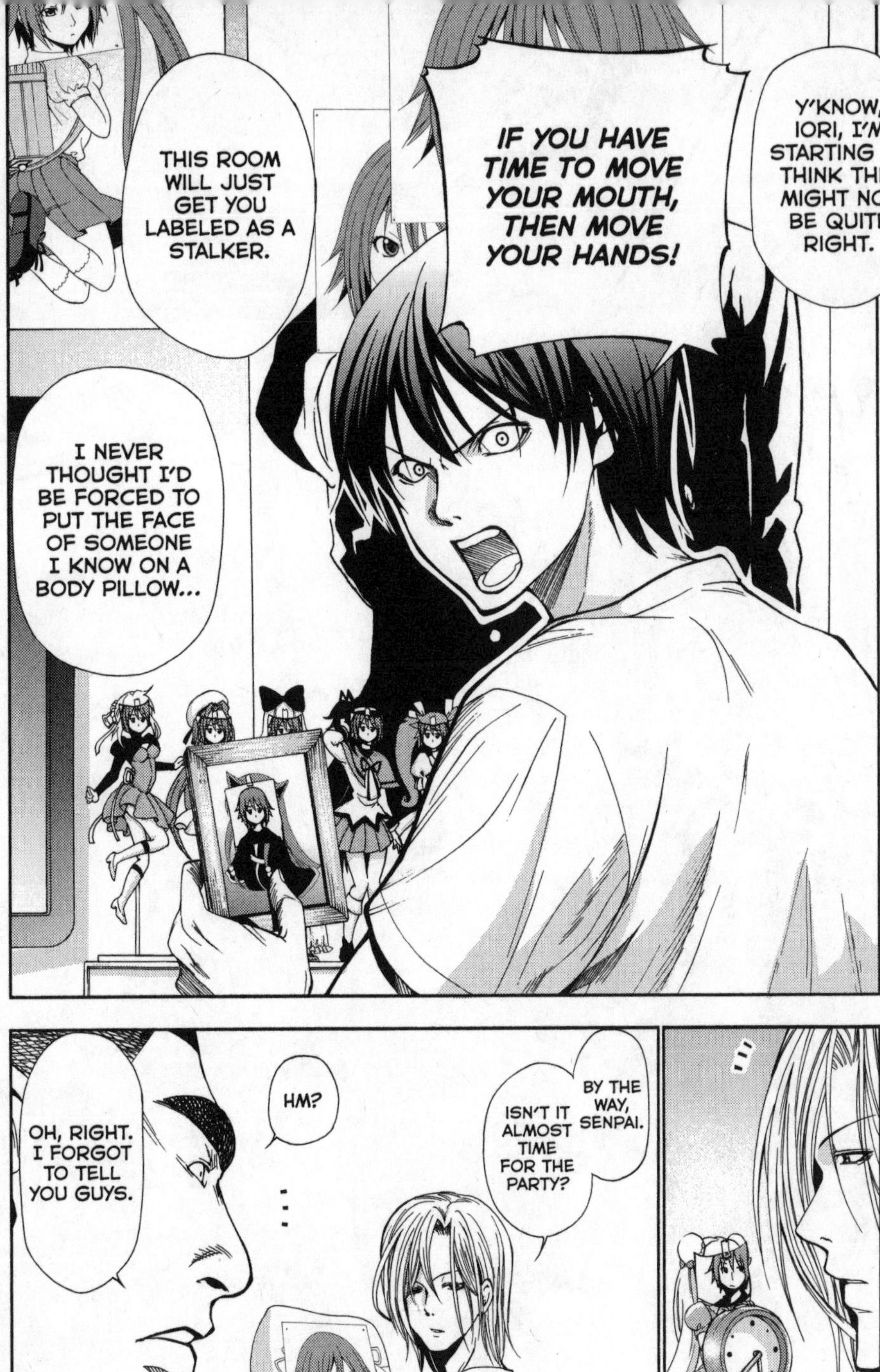
Y'KNOW, IORI, I'M STARTING TO THINK THIS MIGHT NOT BE QUITE RIGHT.
IF YOU HAVE TIME TO MOVE YOUR MOUTH, THEN MOVE YOUR HANDS!
THIS ROOM WILL JUST GET YOU LABELED AS A STALKER.
I NEVER THOUGHT I'D BE FORCED TO PUT THE FACE OF SOMEONE I KNOW ON A BODY PILLOW...
...
BY THE WAY, SENPAI.
ISN'T IT ALMOST TIME FOR THE PARTY?
HM?
...
OH, RIGHT. I FORGOT TO TELL YOU GUYS.

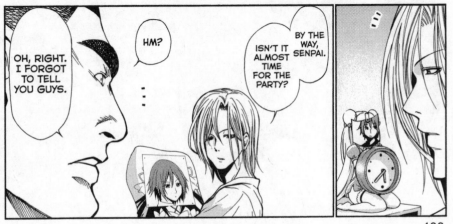

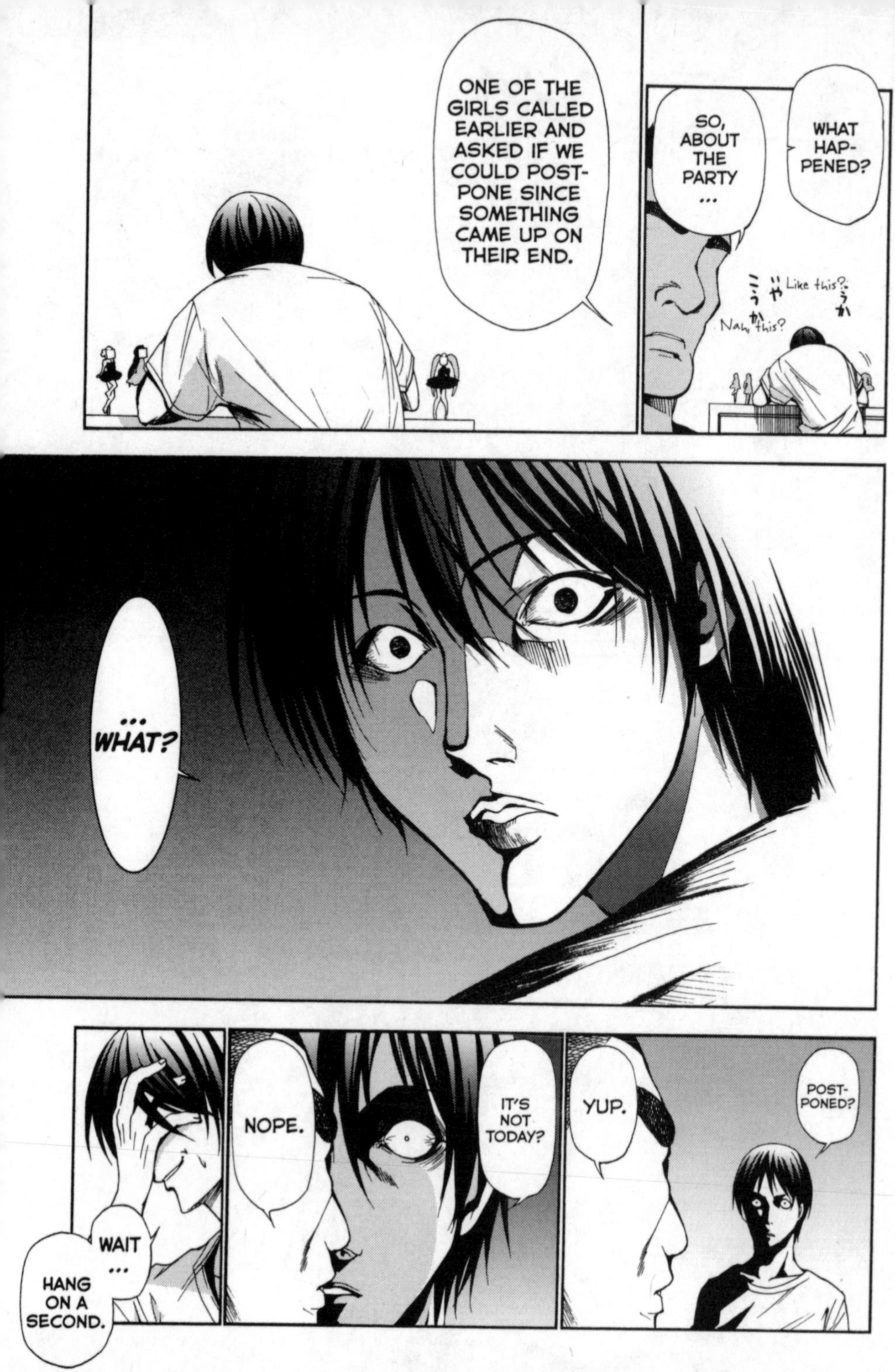
WHAT HAP-PENED?
SO, ABOUT THE PARTY ...
Like this?
Nah, this?
ONE OF THE GIRLS CALLED EARLIER AND ASKED IF WE COULD POST-PONE SINCE SOMETHING CAME UP ON THEIR END.
... WHAT?
POST-PONED?
YUP.
IT'S NOT TODAY?
NOPE.
WAIT ...
HANG ON A SECOND.

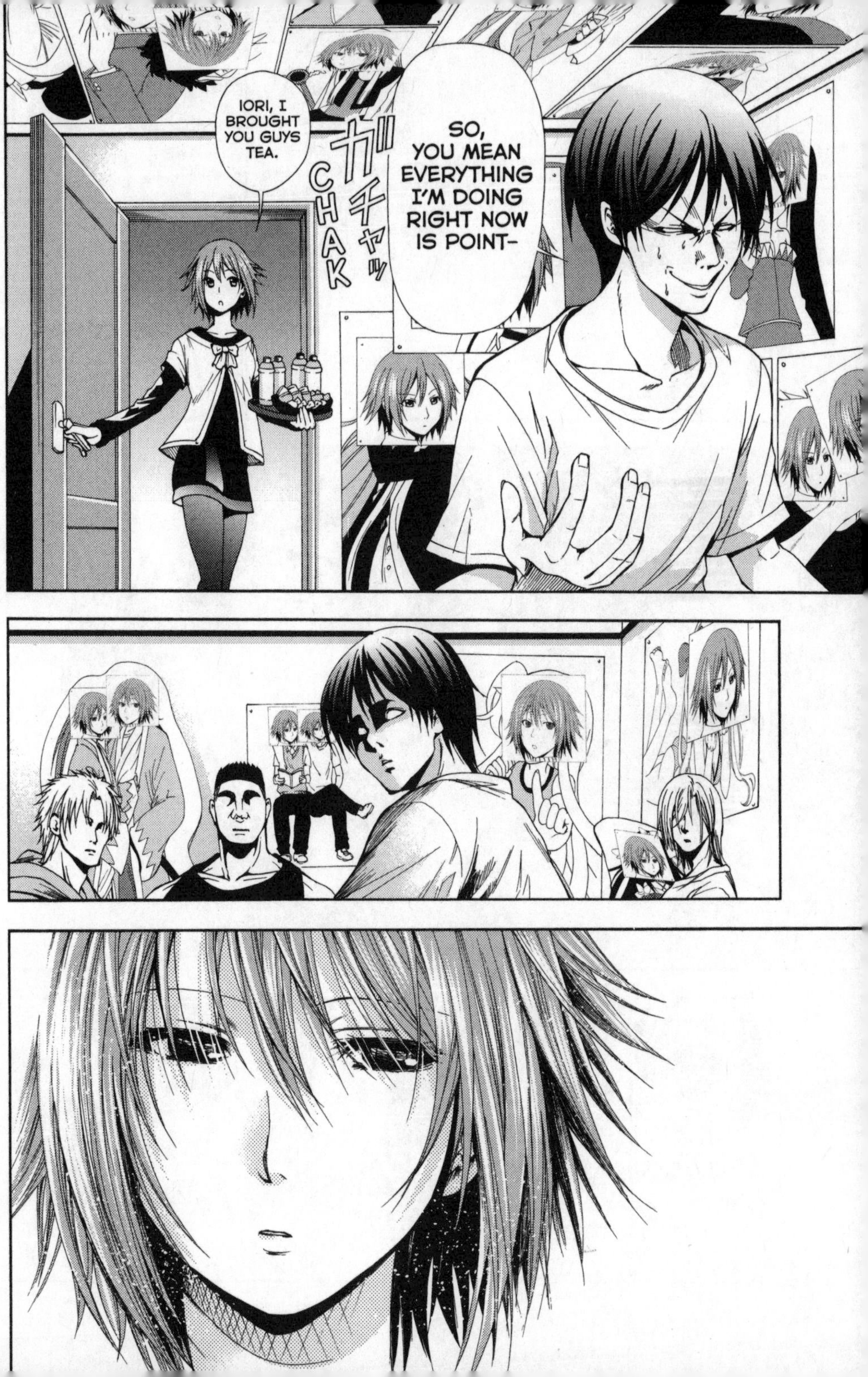
SO, YOU MEAN EVERYTHING I'M DOING RIGHT NOW IS POINT-
ガチャッ
CHAK
IORI, I BROUGHT YOU GUYS TEA.

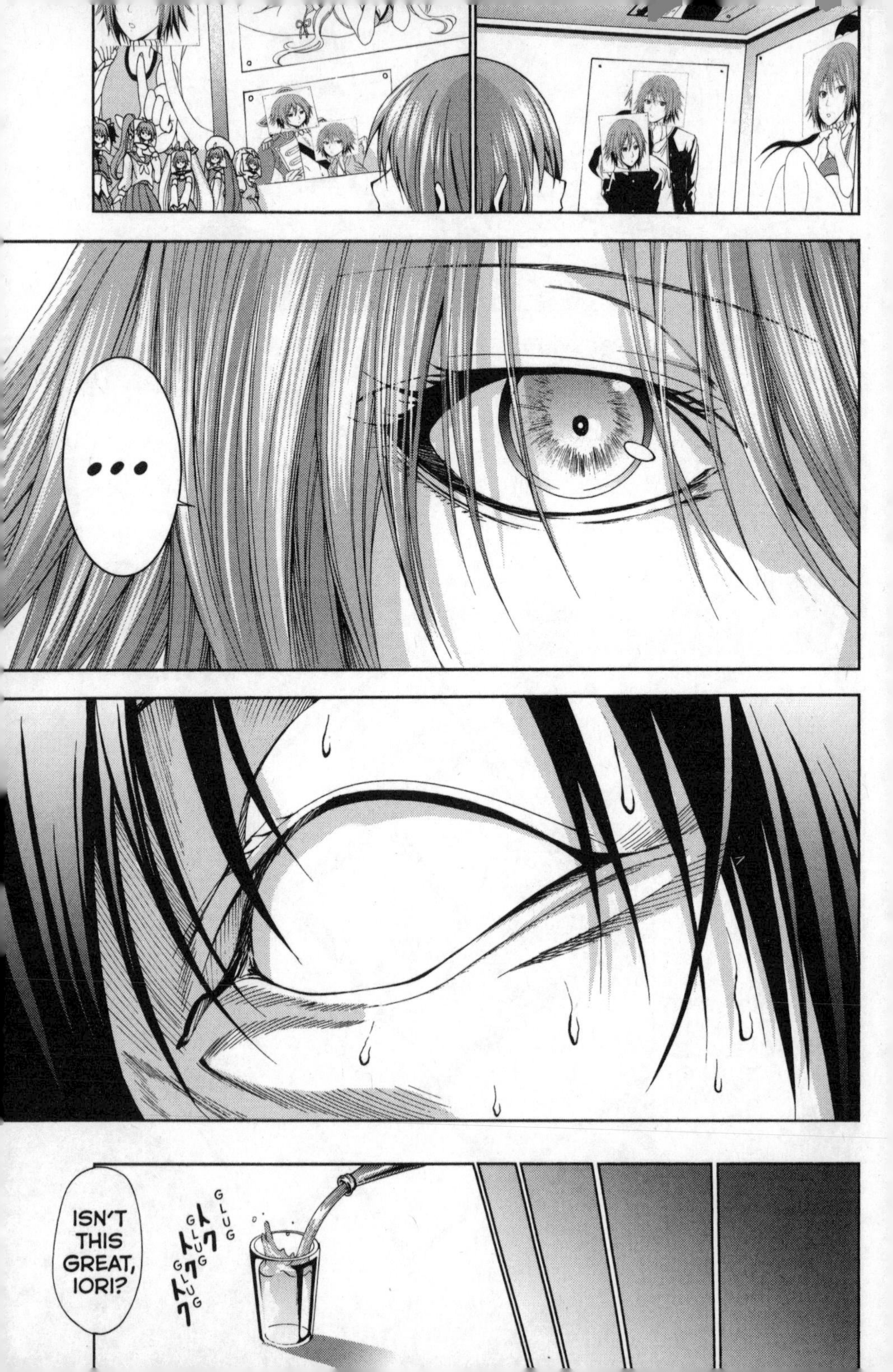
...
GLUG GLUG GLUG
ISN'T THIS GREAT, IORI?

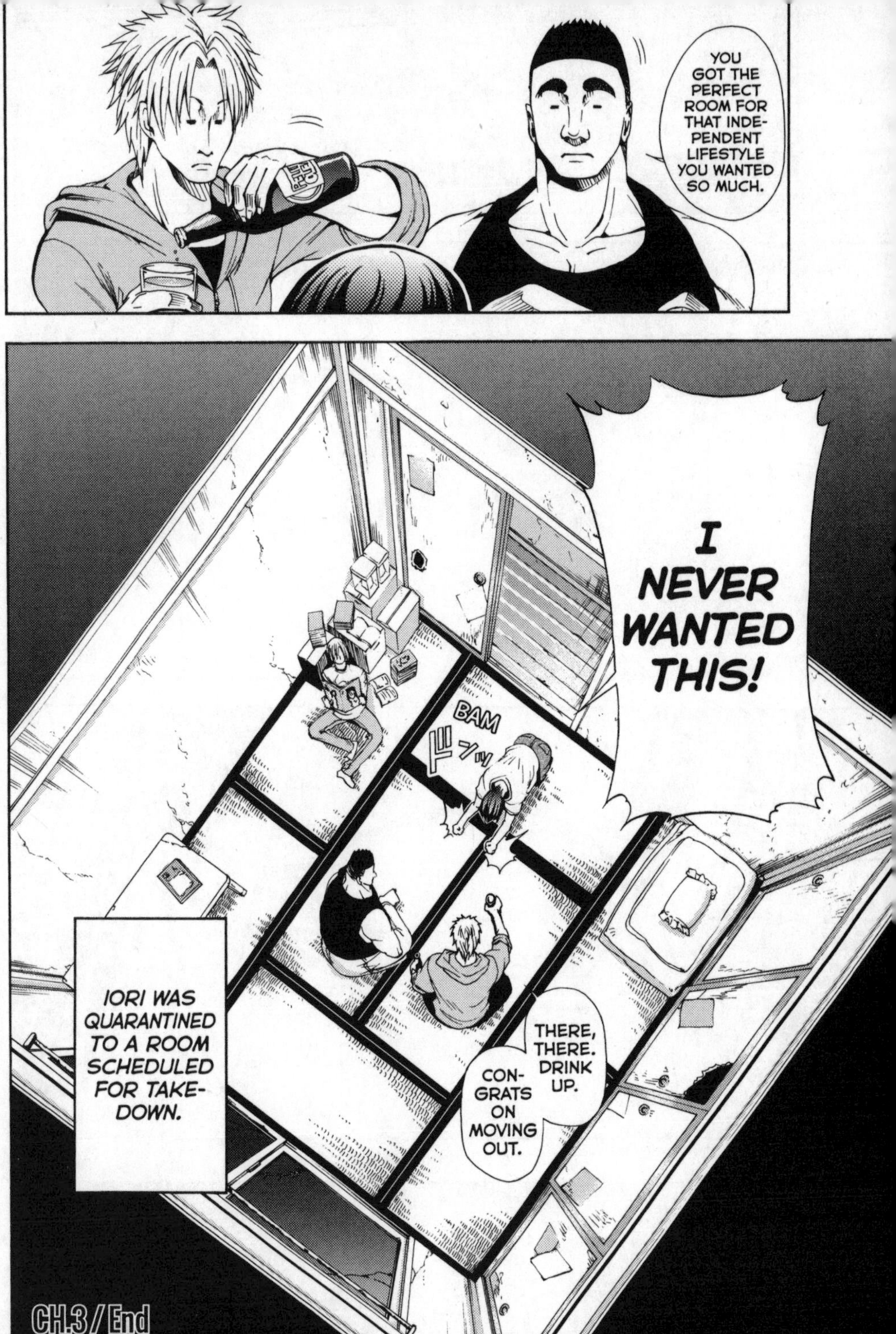
YOU GOT THE PERFECT ROOM FOR THAT INDEPENDENT LIFESTYLE YOU WANTED SO MUCH.
I NEVER WANTED THIS!
BAM
ドンッ
THERE, THERE. DRINK UP.
CONGRATS ON MOVING OUT.
IORI WAS QUARANTINED TO A ROOM SCHEDULED FOR TAKE-DOWN.
CH.3 / End

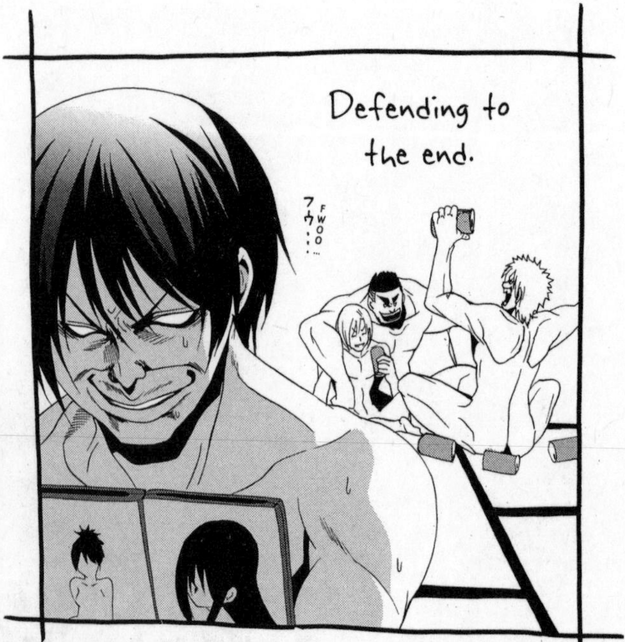
Defending to the end.
フウ… FWOO…

Grand Blue Dreaming

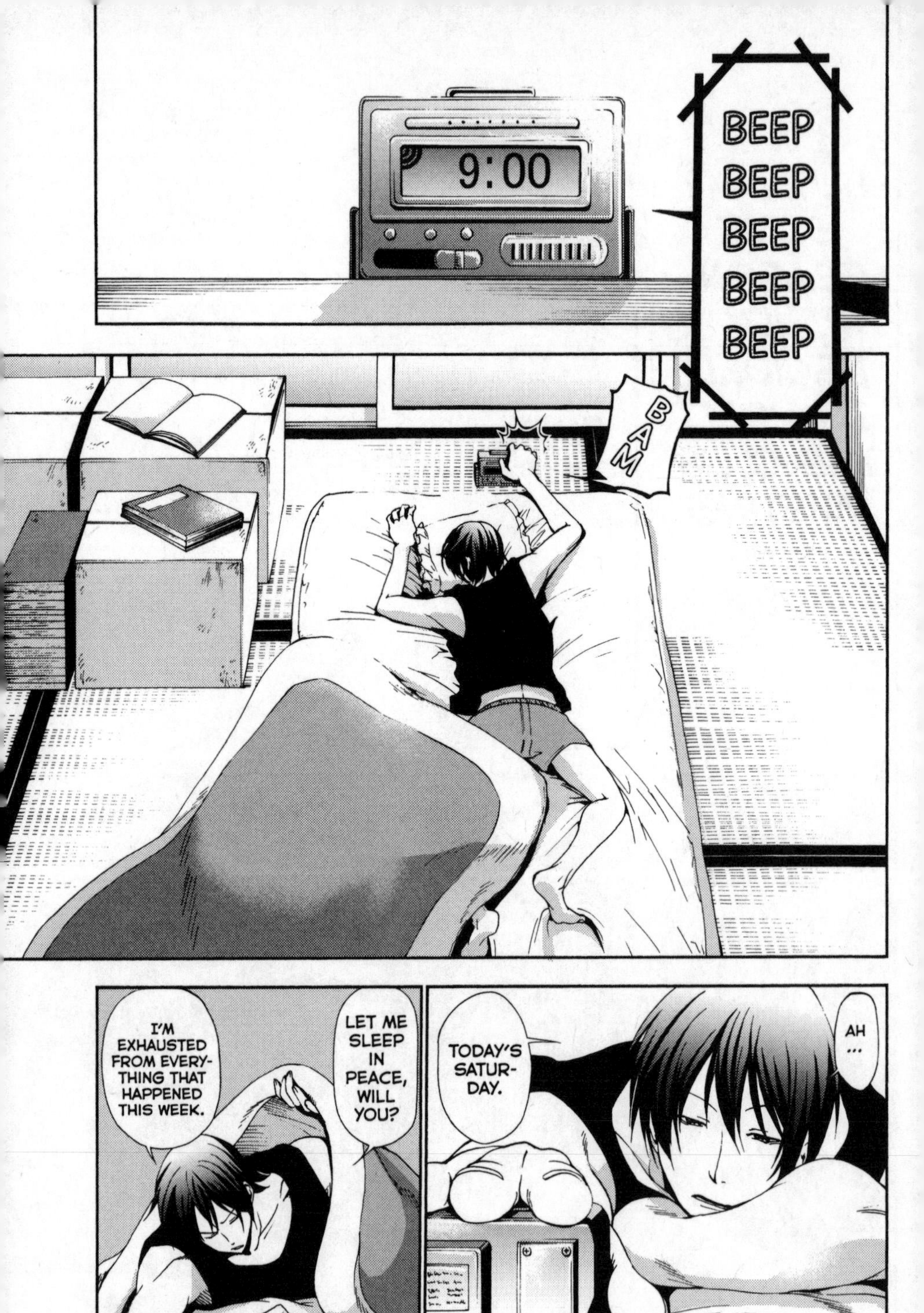
9:00
BEEP BEEP BEEP BEEP BEEP
BAM
AH ...
TODAY'S SATURDAY.
LET ME SLEEP IN PEACE, WILL YOU?
I'M EXHAUSTED FROM EVERYTHING THAT HAPPENED THIS WEEK.

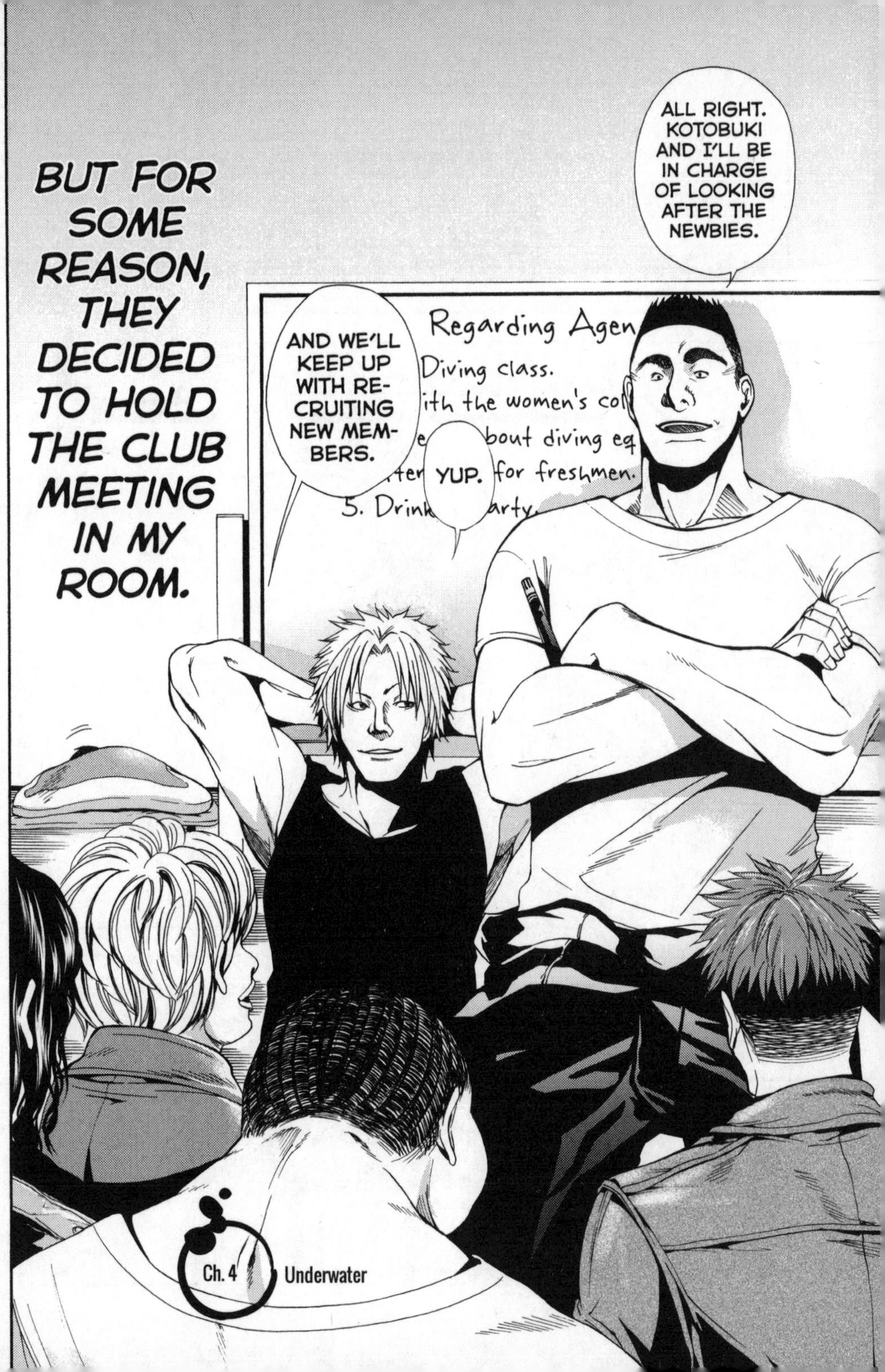
ALL RIGHT. KOTOBUKI AND I'LL BE IN CHARGE OF LOOKING AFTER THE NEWBIES.
BUT FOR SOME REASON, THEY DECIDED TO HOLD THE CLUB MEETING IN MY ROOM.
AND WE'LL KEEP UP WITH RE-CRUITING NEW MEM-BERS.
YUP.
Ch. 4 Underwater

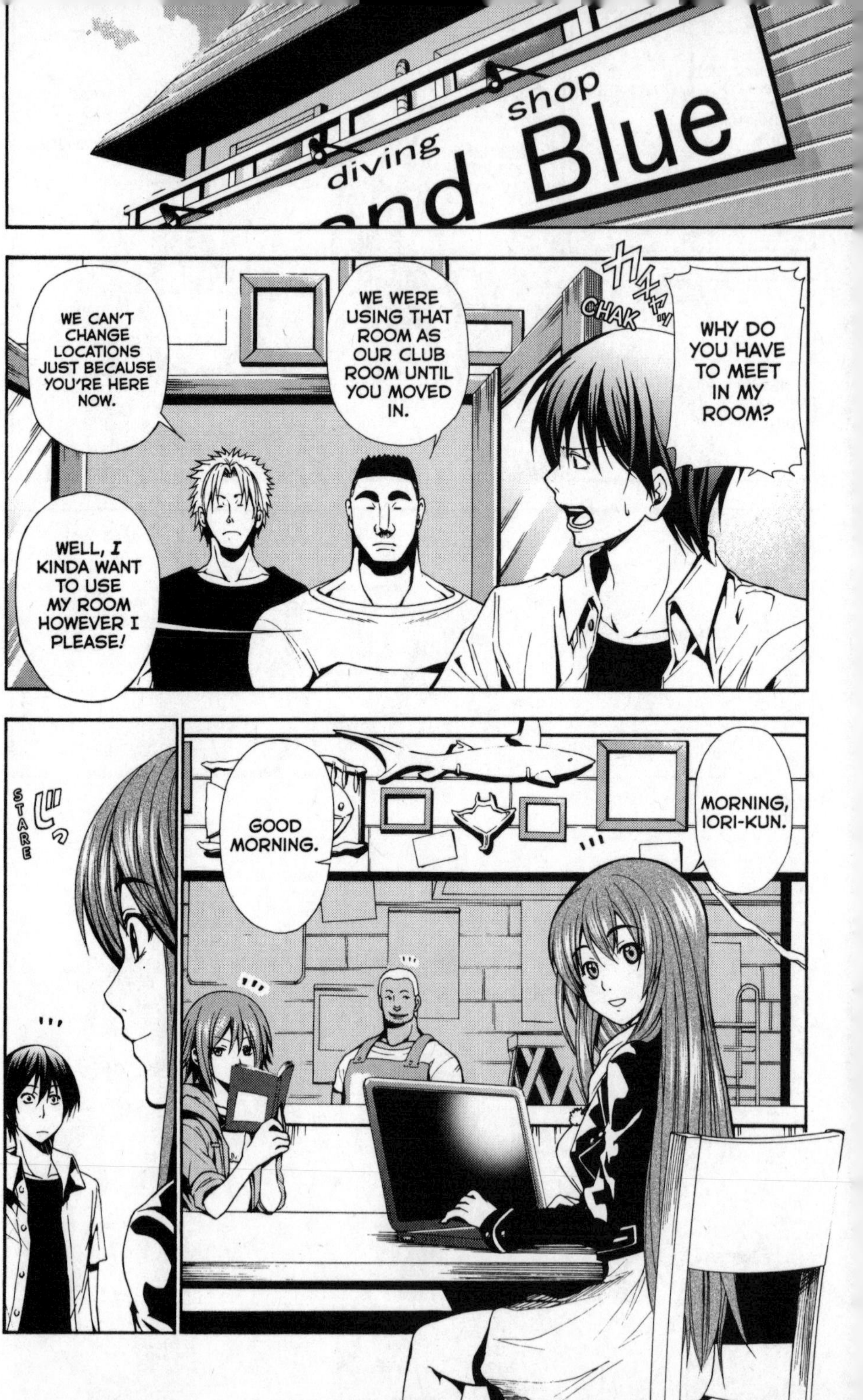
diving shop
and Blue
WHY DO YOU HAVE TO MEET IN MY ROOM?
CHAK
WE WERE USING THAT ROOM AS OUR CLUB ROOM UNTIL YOU MOVED IN.
WE CAN'T CHANGE LOCATIONS JUST BECAUSE YOU'RE HERE NOW.
WELL, I KINDA WANT TO USE MY ROOM HOWEVER I PLEASE!
MORNING, IORI-KUN.
GOOD MORNING.
STARE

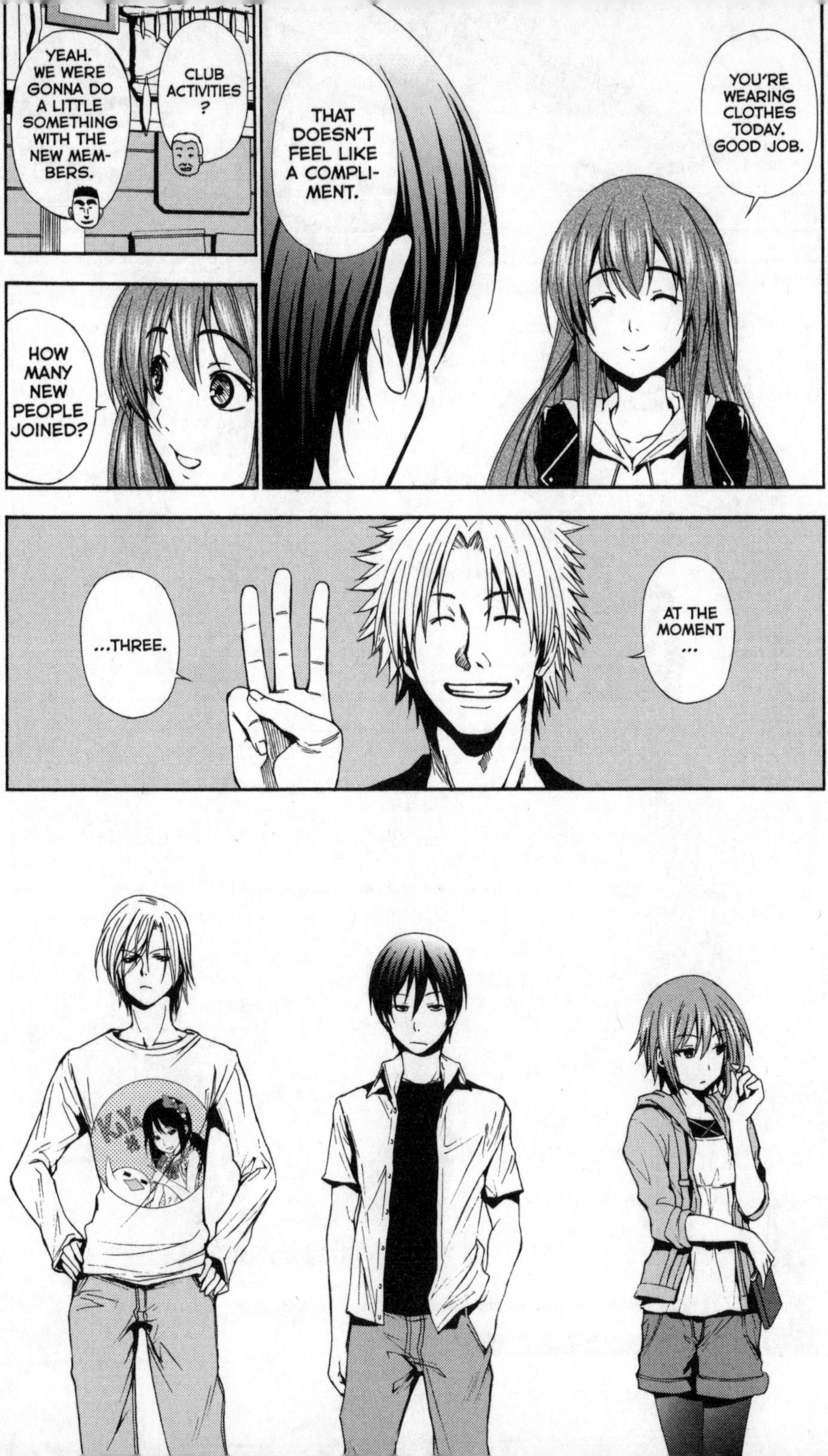
YOU'RE WEARING CLOTHES TODAY. GOOD JOB.
THAT DOESN'T FEEL LIKE A COMPLIMENT.
CLUB ACTIVITIES ?
YEAH. WE WERE GONNA DO A LITTLE SOMETHING WITH THE NEW MEMBERS.
HOW MANY NEW PEOPLE JOINED?
AT THE MOMENT ...
...THREE.

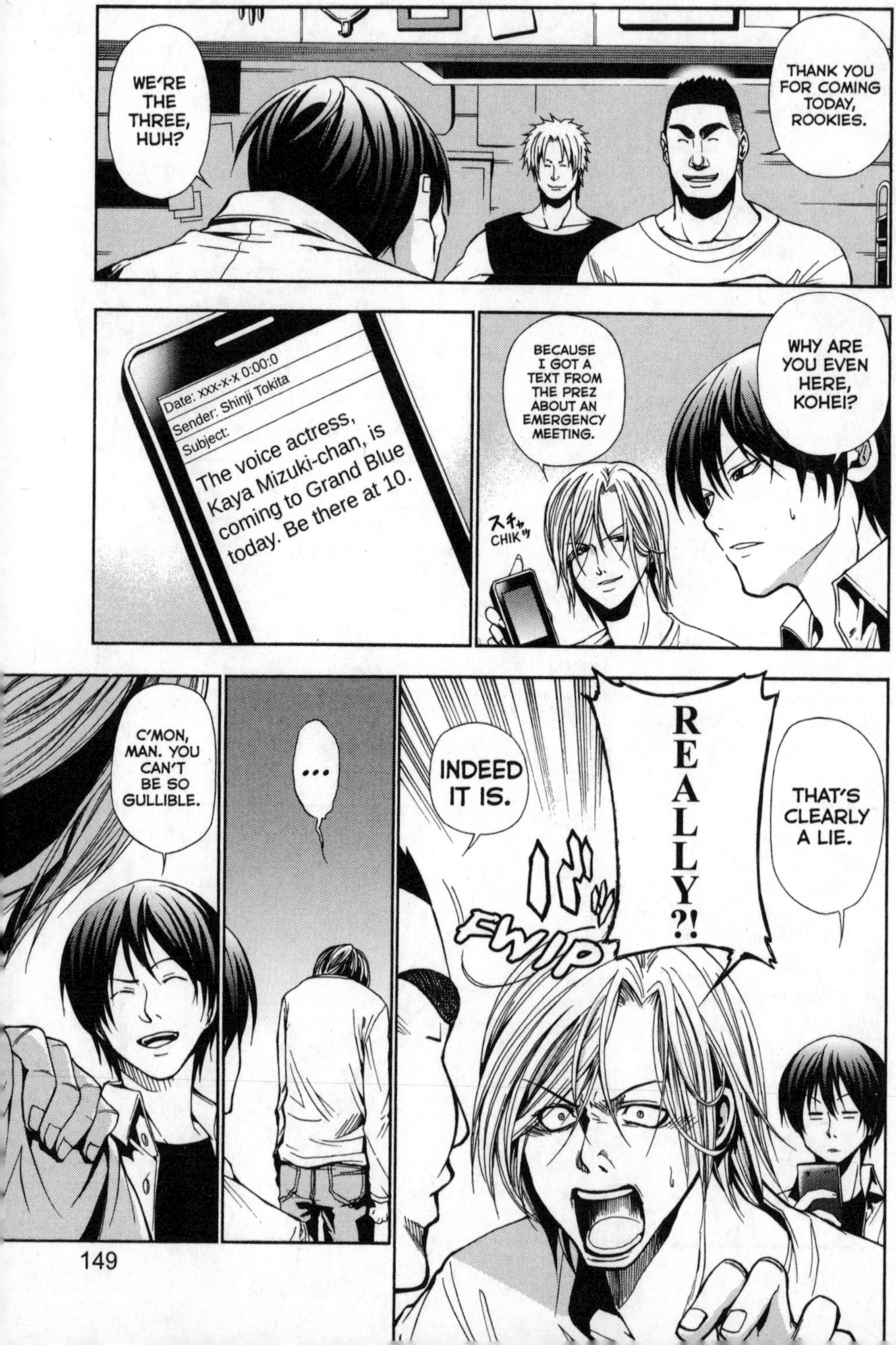
THANK YOU FOR COMING TODAY, ROOKIES.
WE'RE THE THREE, HUH?
WHY ARE YOU EVEN HERE, KOHEI?
BECAUSE I GOT A TEXT FROM THE PREZ ABOUT AN EMERGENCY MEETING.
スチャ CHIK
Date: xxx-x-x 0:00:0
Sender: Shinji Tokita
Subject:
The voice actress, Kaya Mizuki-chan, is coming to Grand Blue today. Be there at 10.
THAT'S CLEARLY A LIE.
REALLY?!
FWIP
INDEED IT IS.
...
C'MON, MAN. YOU CAN'T BE SO GULLIBLE.

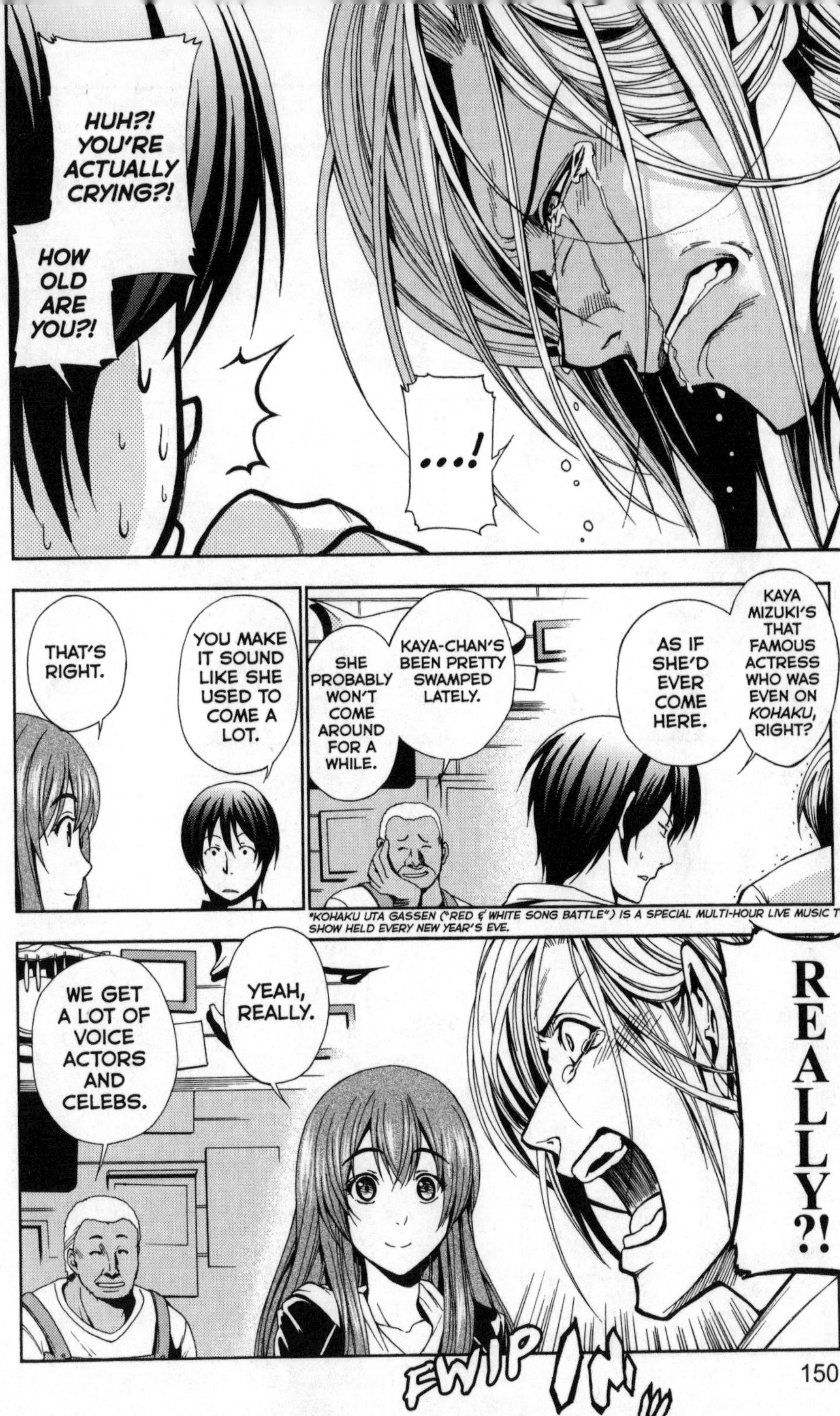
...!
HUH?! YOU'RE ACTUALLY CRYING?!
HOW OLD ARE YOU?!
KAYA MIZUKI'S THAT FAMOUS ACTRESS WHO WAS EVEN ON *KOHAKU*, RIGHT?
AS IF SHE'D EVER COME HERE.
KAYA-CHAN'S BEEN PRETTY SWAMPED LATELY.
SHE PROBABLY WON'T COME AROUND FOR A WHILE.
YOU MAKE IT SOUND LIKE SHE USED TO COME A LOT.
THAT'S RIGHT.
REALLY?!
YEAH, REALLY.
WE GET A LOT OF VOICE ACTORS AND CELEBS.
FWIP IN

**KOHAKU UTA GASSEN ("RED & WHITE SONG BATTLE") IS A SPECIAL MULTI-HOUR LIVE MUSIC TV SHOW HELD EVERY NEW YEAR'S EVE.*

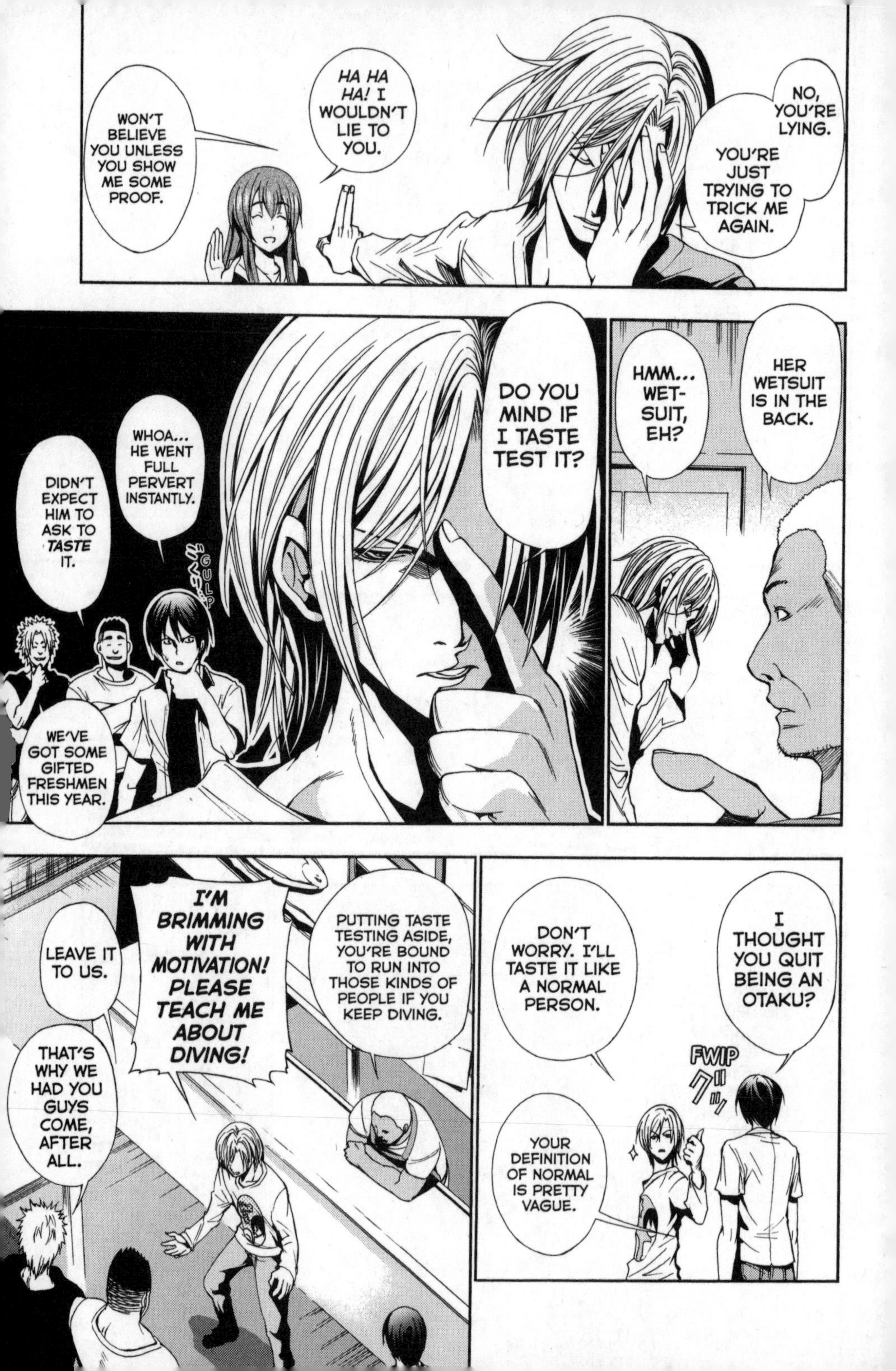
NO, YOU'RE LYING.
YOU'RE JUST TRYING TO TRICK ME AGAIN.
HA HA HA! I WOULDN'T LIE TO YOU.
WON'T BELIEVE YOU UNLESS YOU SHOW ME SOME PROOF.
HER WETSUIT IS IN THE BACK.
HMM... WET-SUIT, EH?
DO YOU MIND IF I TASTE TEST IT?
WHOA... HE WENT FULL PERVERT INSTANTLY.
GULP
DIDN'T EXPECT HIM TO ASK TO *TASTE* IT.
WE'VE GOT SOME GIFTED FRESHMEN THIS YEAR.
I THOUGHT YOU QUIT BEING AN OTAKU?
FWIP
DON'T WORRY. I'LL TASTE IT LIKE A NORMAL PERSON.
YOUR DEFINITION OF NORMAL IS PRETTY VAGUE.
PUTTING TASTE TESTING ASIDE, YOU'RE BOUND TO RUN INTO THOSE KINDS OF PEOPLE IF YOU KEEP DIVING.
I'M BRIMMING WITH MOTIVATION! PLEASE TEACH ME ABOUT DIVING!
LEAVE IT TO US.
THAT'S WHY WE HAD YOU GUYS COME, AFTER ALL.

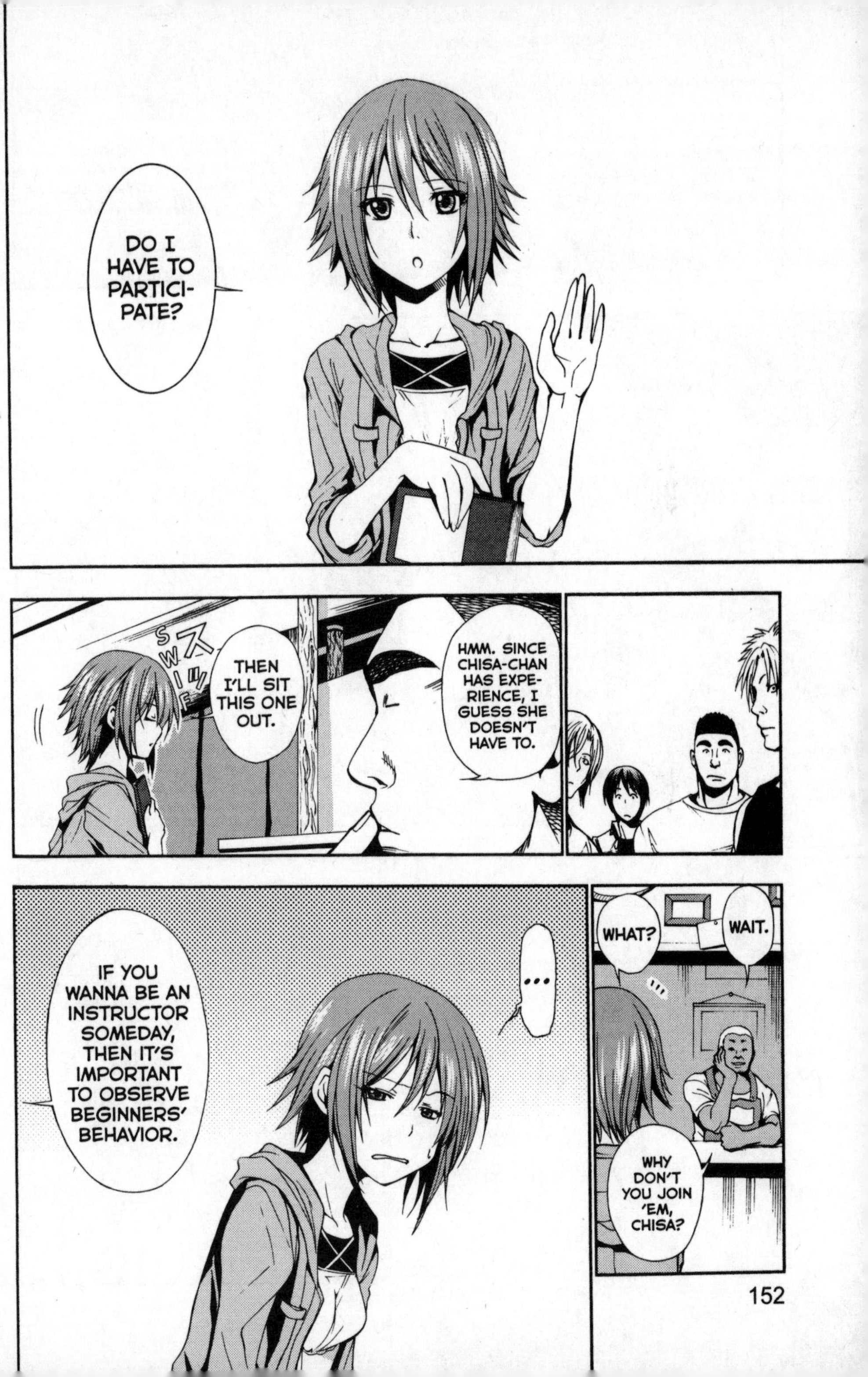
DO I HAVE TO PARTICI-PATE?
HMM. SINCE CHISA-CHAN HAS EXPE-RIENCE, I GUESS SHE DOESN'T HAVE TO.
THEN I'LL SIT THIS ONE OUT.
SWIFF
WAIT.
WHAT?
WHY DON'T YOU JOIN 'EM, CHISA?
...
IF YOU WANNA BE AN INSTRUCTOR SOMEDAY, THEN IT'S IMPORTANT TO OBSERVE BEGINNERS' BEHAVIOR.

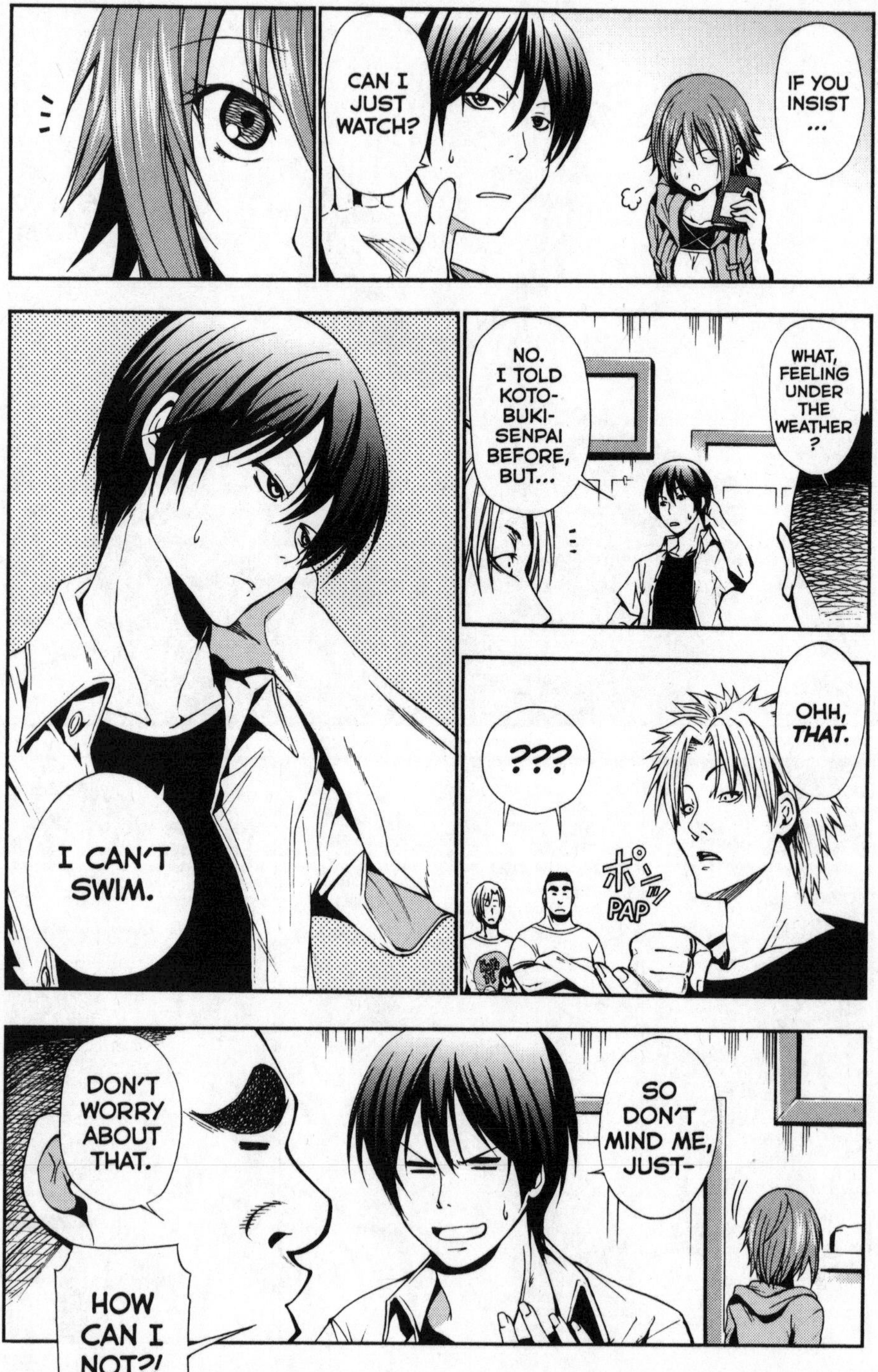
IF YOU INSIST ...
CAN I JUST WATCH?
WHAT, FEELING UNDER THE WEATHER?
NO. I TOLD KOTO-BUKI-SENPAI BEFORE, BUT...
OHH, *THAT*.
???
PAP
I CAN'T SWIM.
SO DON'T MIND ME, JUST-
DON'T WORRY ABOUT THAT.
HOW CAN I NOT?!

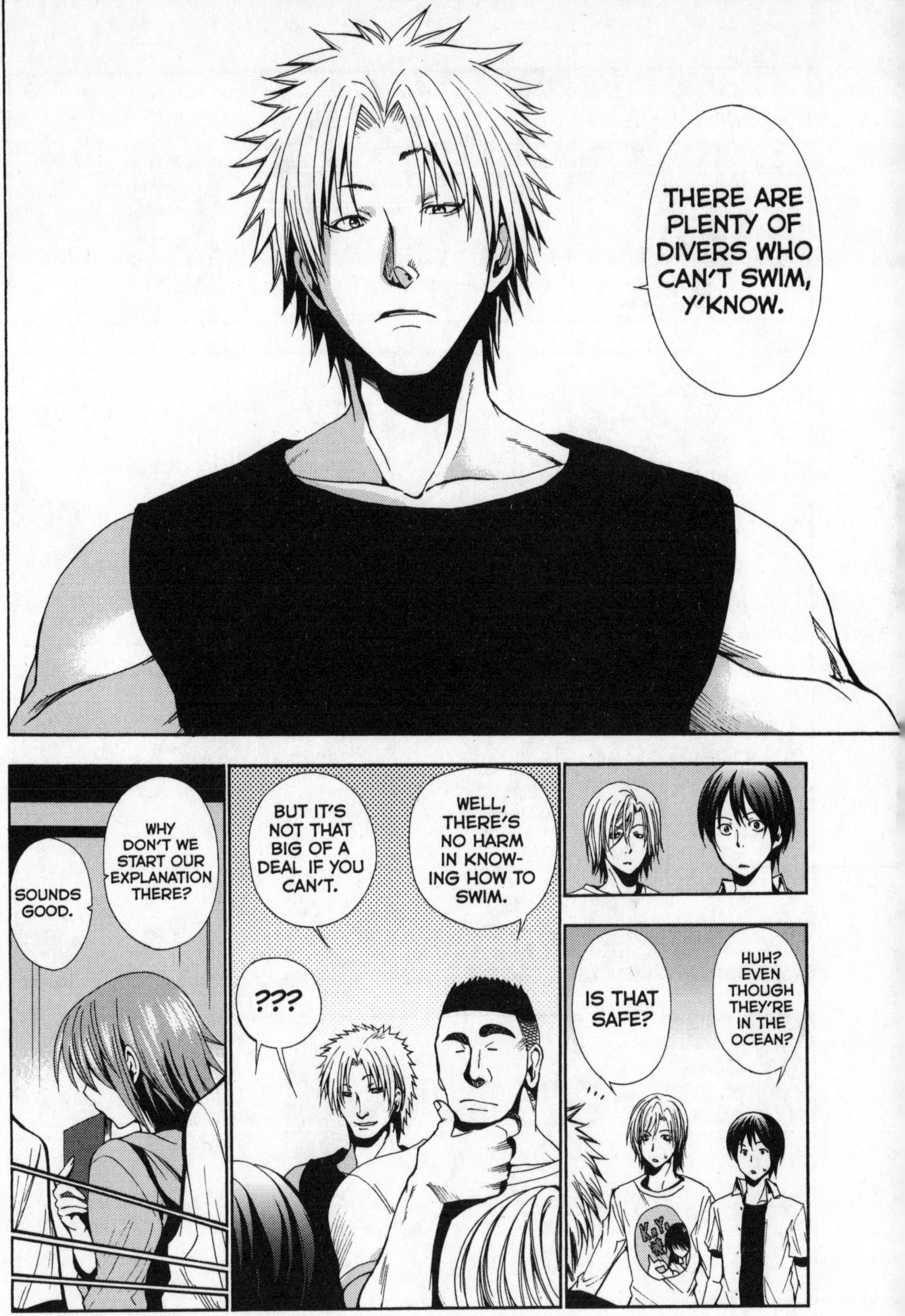
THERE ARE PLENTY OF DIVERS WHO CAN'T SWIM, Y'KNOW.
HUH? EVEN THOUGH THEY'RE IN THE OCEAN?
IS THAT SAFE?
...
WELL, THERE'S NO HARM IN KNOW-ING HOW TO SWIM.
BUT IT'S NOT THAT BIG OF A DEAL IF YOU CAN'T.
???
WHY DON'T WE START OUR EXPLANATION THERE?
SOUNDS GOOD.

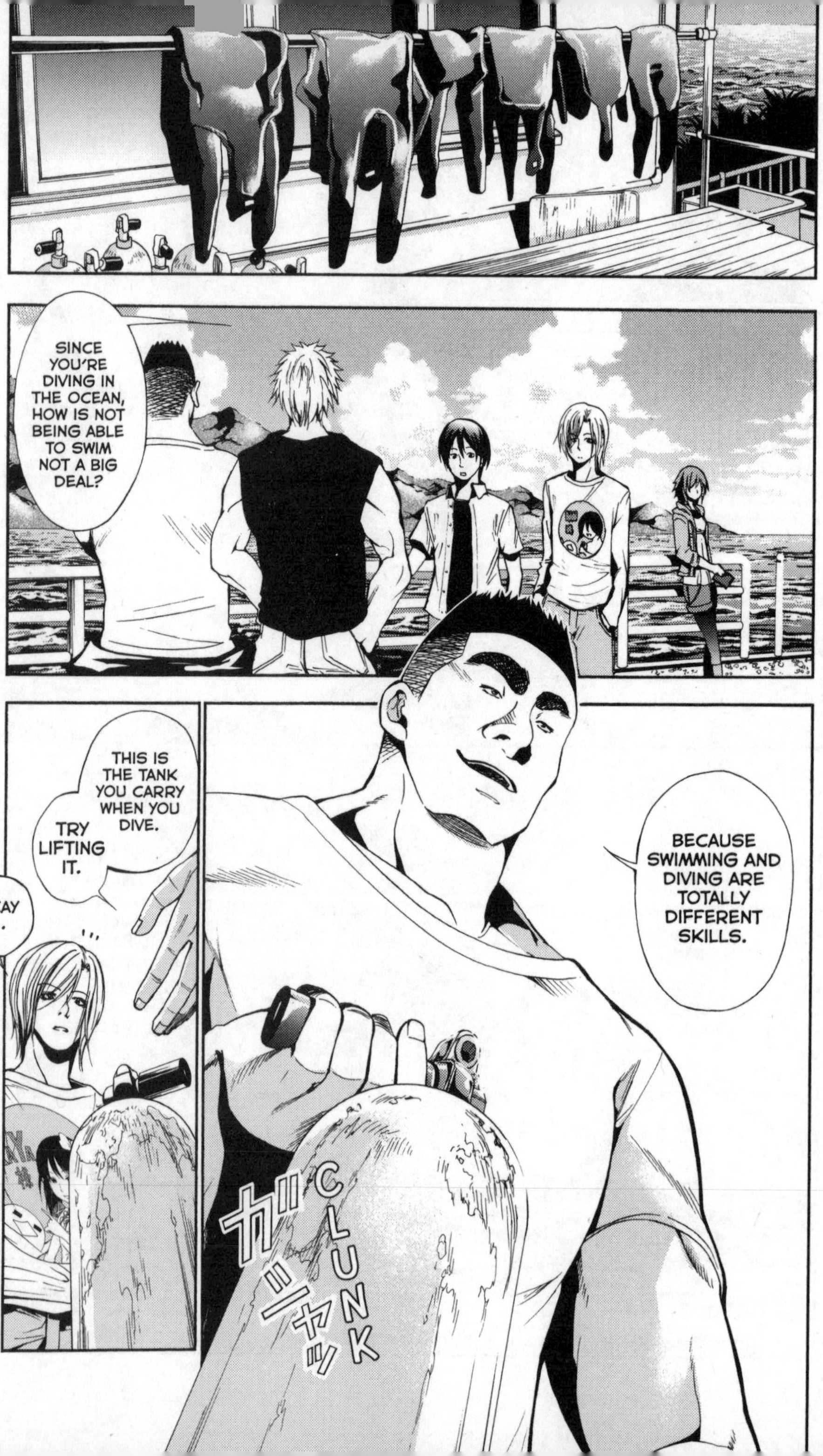
SINCE YOU'RE DIVING IN THE OCEAN, HOW IS NOT BEING ABLE TO SWIM NOT A BIG DEAL?
BECAUSE SWIMMING AND DIVING ARE TOTALLY DIFFERENT SKILLS.
ガシャッ
CLUNK
THIS IS THE TANK YOU CARRY WHEN YOU DIVE.
TRY LIFTING IT.
OKAY ...

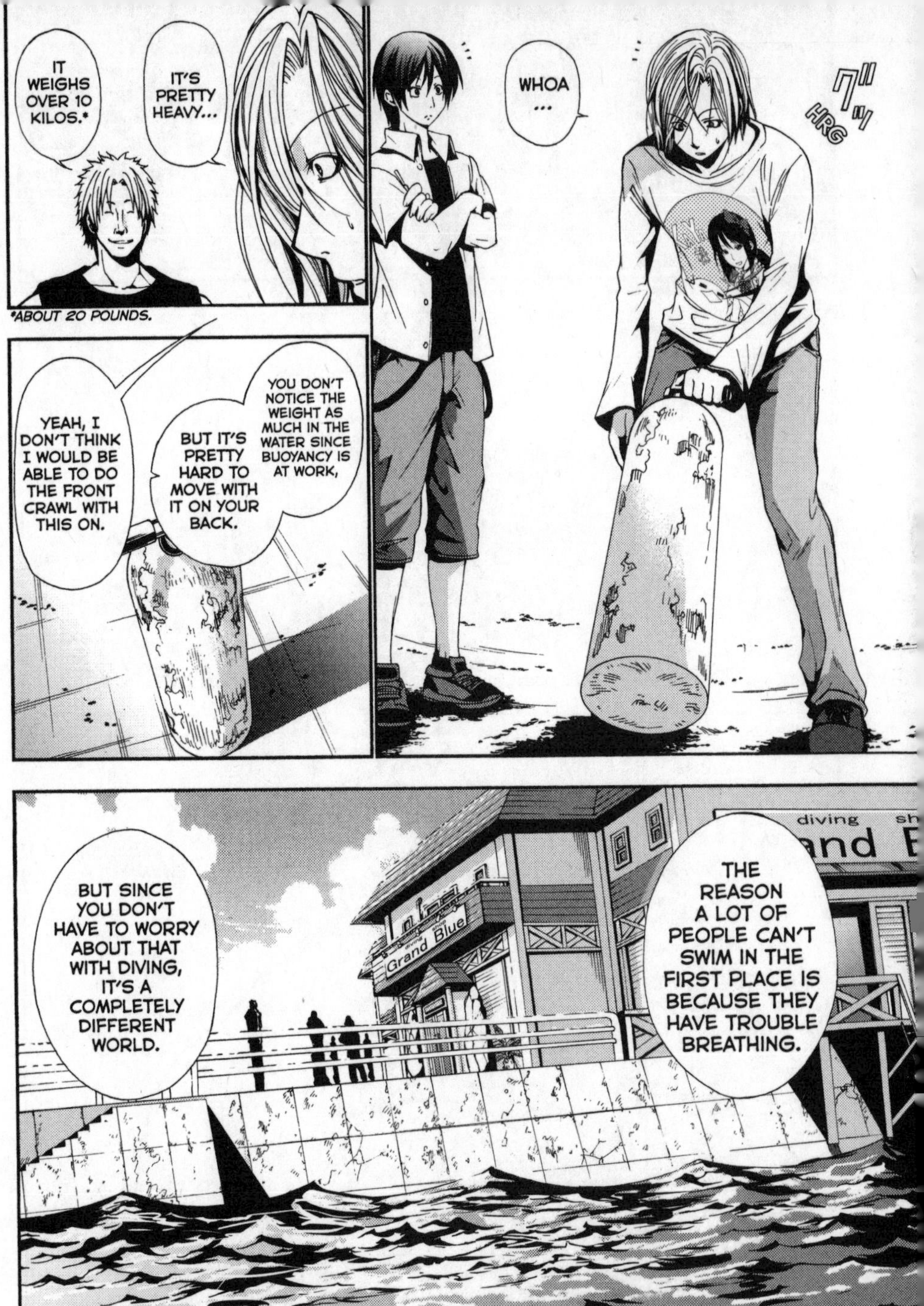
グッ
HRG
WHOA ...
IT'S PRETTY HEAVY...
IT WEIGHS OVER 10 KILOS.*
YOU DON'T NOTICE THE WEIGHT AS MUCH IN THE WATER SINCE BUOYANCY IS AT WORK,
BUT IT'S PRETTY HARD TO MOVE WITH IT ON YOUR BACK.
YEAH, I DON'T THINK I WOULD BE ABLE TO DO THE FRONT CRAWL WITH THIS ON.
Grand Blue
THE REASON A LOT OF PEOPLE CAN'T SWIM IN THE FIRST PLACE IS BECAUSE THEY HAVE TROUBLE BREATHING.
BUT SINCE YOU DON'T HAVE TO WORRY ABOUT THAT WITH DIVING, IT'S A COMPLETELY DIFFERENT WORLD.

*ABOUT 20 POUNDS.

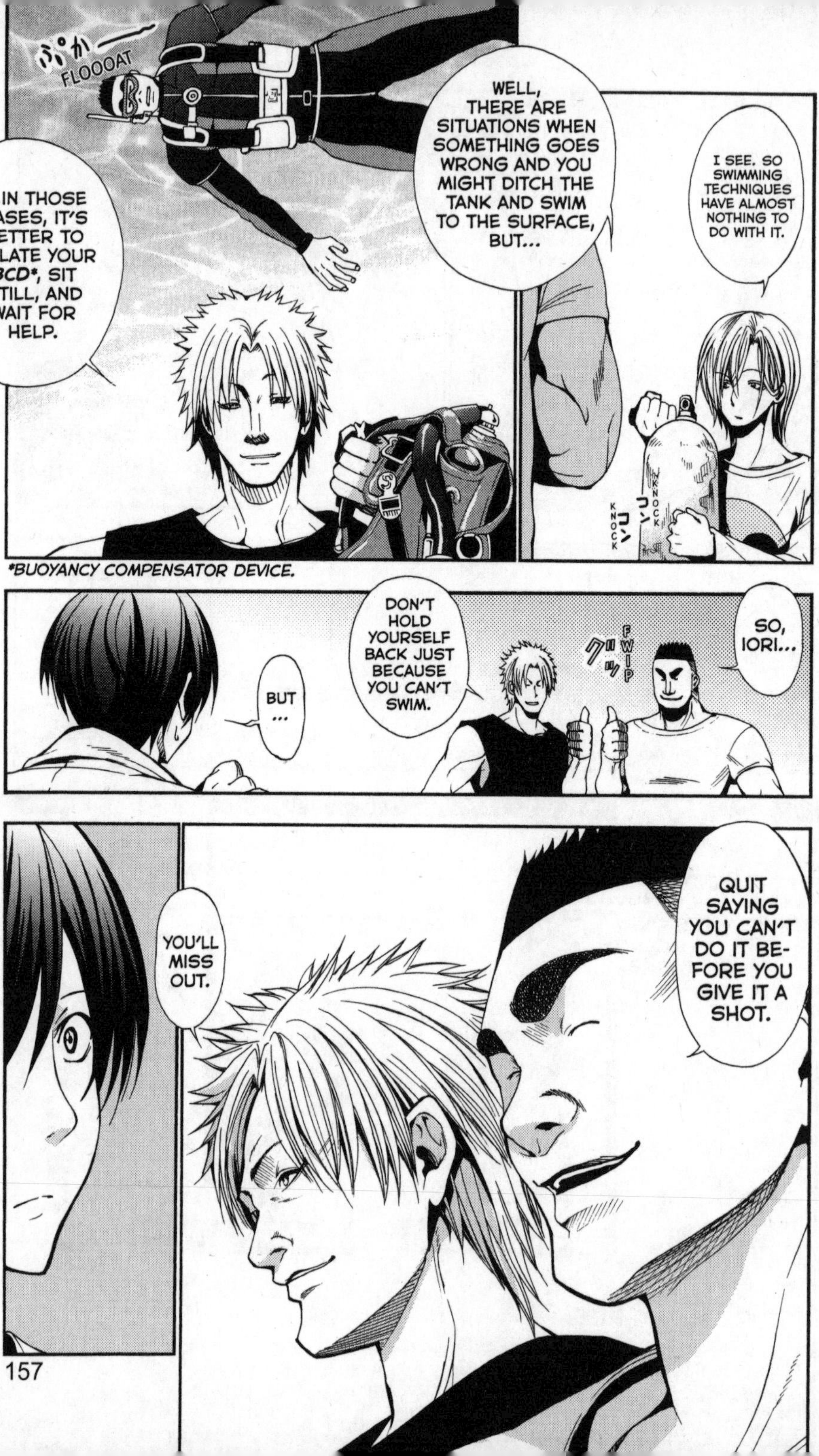
I SEE. SO SWIMMING TECHNIQUES HAVE ALMOST NOTHING TO DO WITH IT.
コンコン
KNOCK KNOCK
WELL, THERE ARE SITUATIONS WHEN SOMETHING GOES WRONG AND YOU MIGHT DITCH THE TANK AND SWIM TO THE SURFACE, BUT...
ぷかー
FLOOOAT
...IN THOSE CASES, IT'S BETTER TO INFLATE YOUR *BCD**, SIT STILL, AND WAIT FOR HELP.
SO, IORI...
グッ
FWIP
DON'T HOLD YOURSELF BACK JUST BECAUSE YOU CAN'T SWIM.
BUT ...
QUIT SAYING YOU CAN'T DO IT BE- FORE YOU GIVE IT A SHOT.
YOU'LL MISS OUT.

*BUOYANCY COMPENSATOR DEVICE.

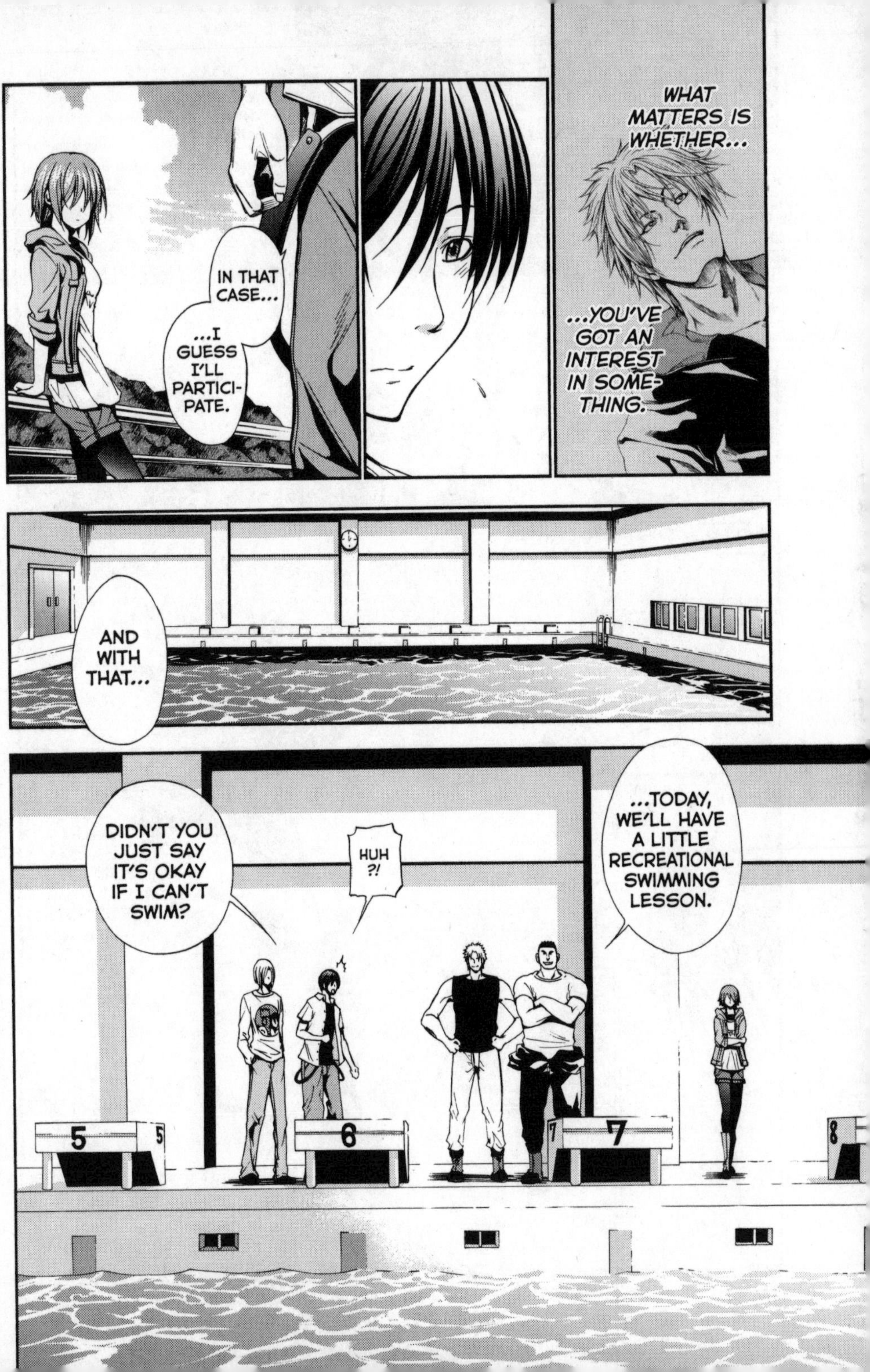
WHAT MATTERS IS WHETHER...
...YOU'VE GOT AN INTEREST IN SOME-THING.
IN THAT CASE...
...I GUESS I'LL PARTICI-PATE.
AND WITH THAT...
...TODAY, WE'LL HAVE A LITTLE RECREATIONAL SWIMMING LESSON.
HUH ?!
DIDN'T YOU JUST SAY IT'S OKAY IF I CAN'T SWIM?

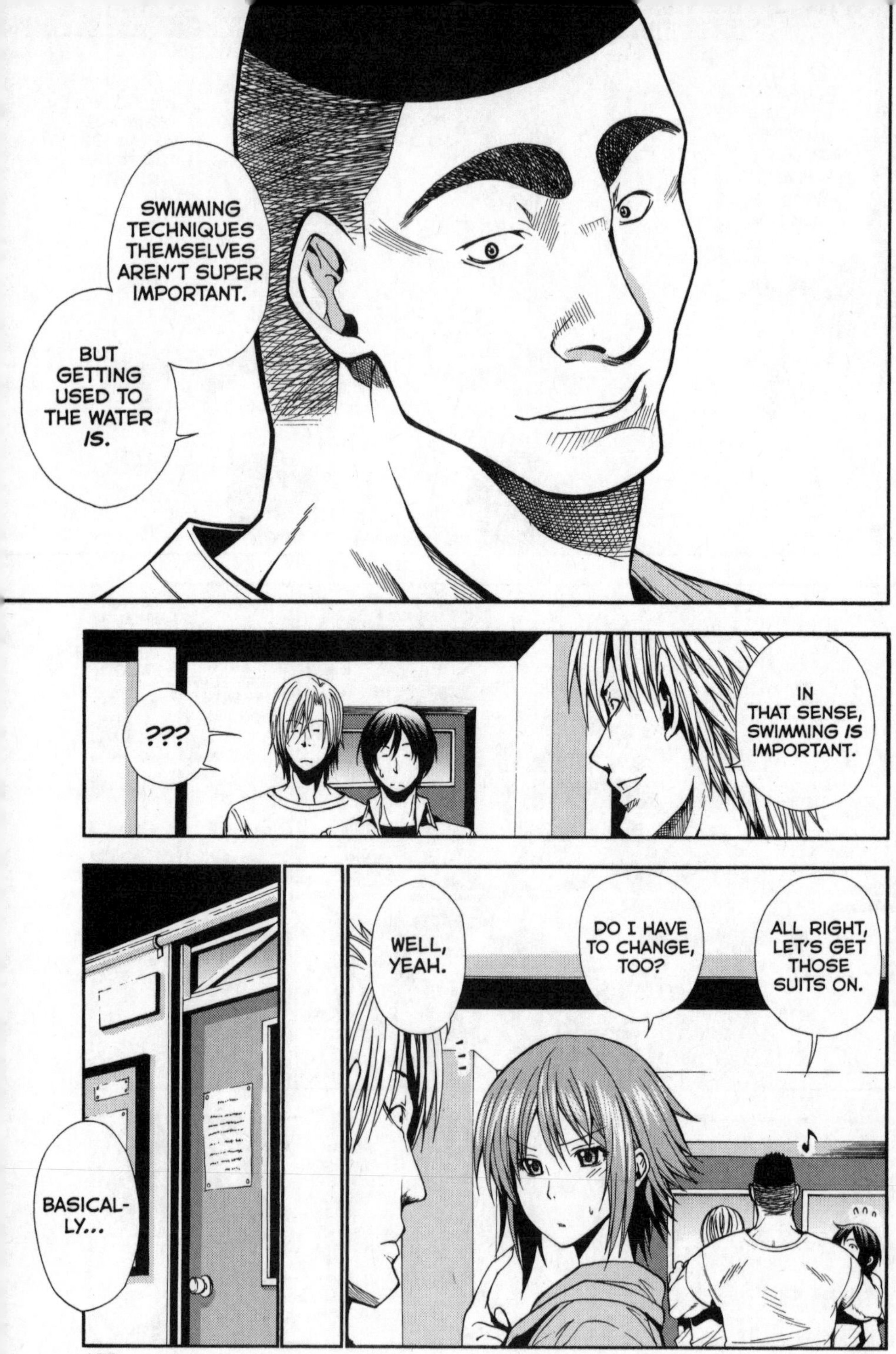
SWIMMING TECHNIQUES THEMSELVES AREN'T SUPER IMPORTANT.
BUT GETTING USED TO THE WATER *IS*.
IN THAT SENSE, SWIMMING *IS* IMPORTANT.
???
ALL RIGHT, LET'S GET THOSE SUITS ON.
DO I HAVE TO CHANGE, TOO?
WELL, YEAH.
BASICAL-LY...

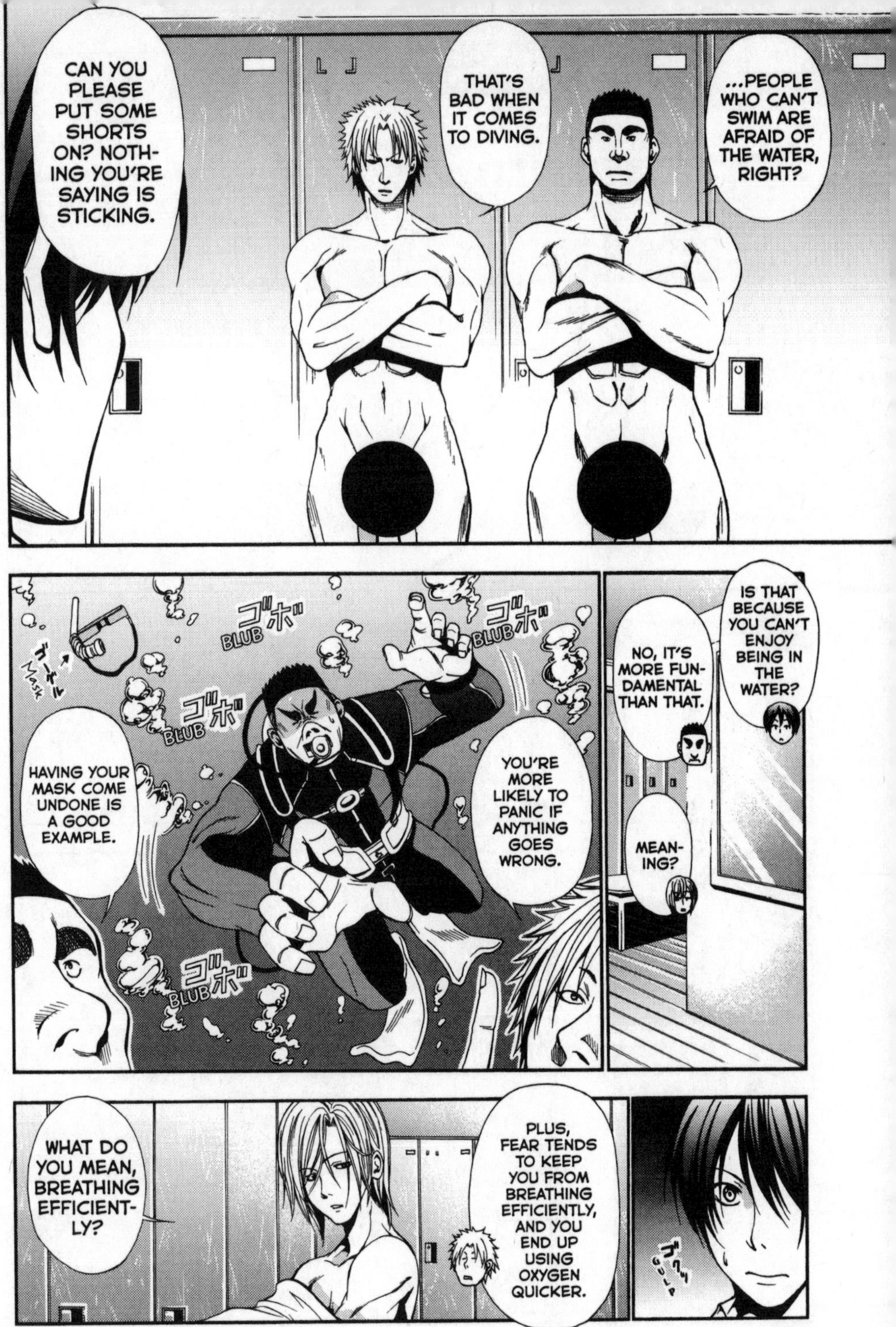
...PEOPLE WHO CAN'T SWIM ARE AFRAID OF THE WATER, RIGHT?
THAT'S BAD WHEN IT COMES TO DIVING.
CAN YOU PLEASE PUT SOME SHORTS ON? NOTHING YOU'RE SAYING IS STICKING.
IS THAT BECAUSE YOU CAN'T ENJOY BEING IN THE WATER?
NO, IT'S MORE FUNDAMENTAL THAN THAT.
MEANING?
ゴボ BLUB
ゴボ BLUB
YOU'RE MORE LIKELY TO PANIC IF ANYTHING GOES WRONG.
ゴーグル MASK
ゴボ BLUB
HAVING YOUR MASK COME UNDONE IS A GOOD EXAMPLE.
ゴボ BLUB
ゴクッ GULP
PLUS, FEAR TENDS TO KEEP YOU FROM BREATHING EFFICIENTLY, AND YOU END UP USING OXYGEN QUICKER.
WHAT DO YOU MEAN, BREATHING EFFICIENTLY?

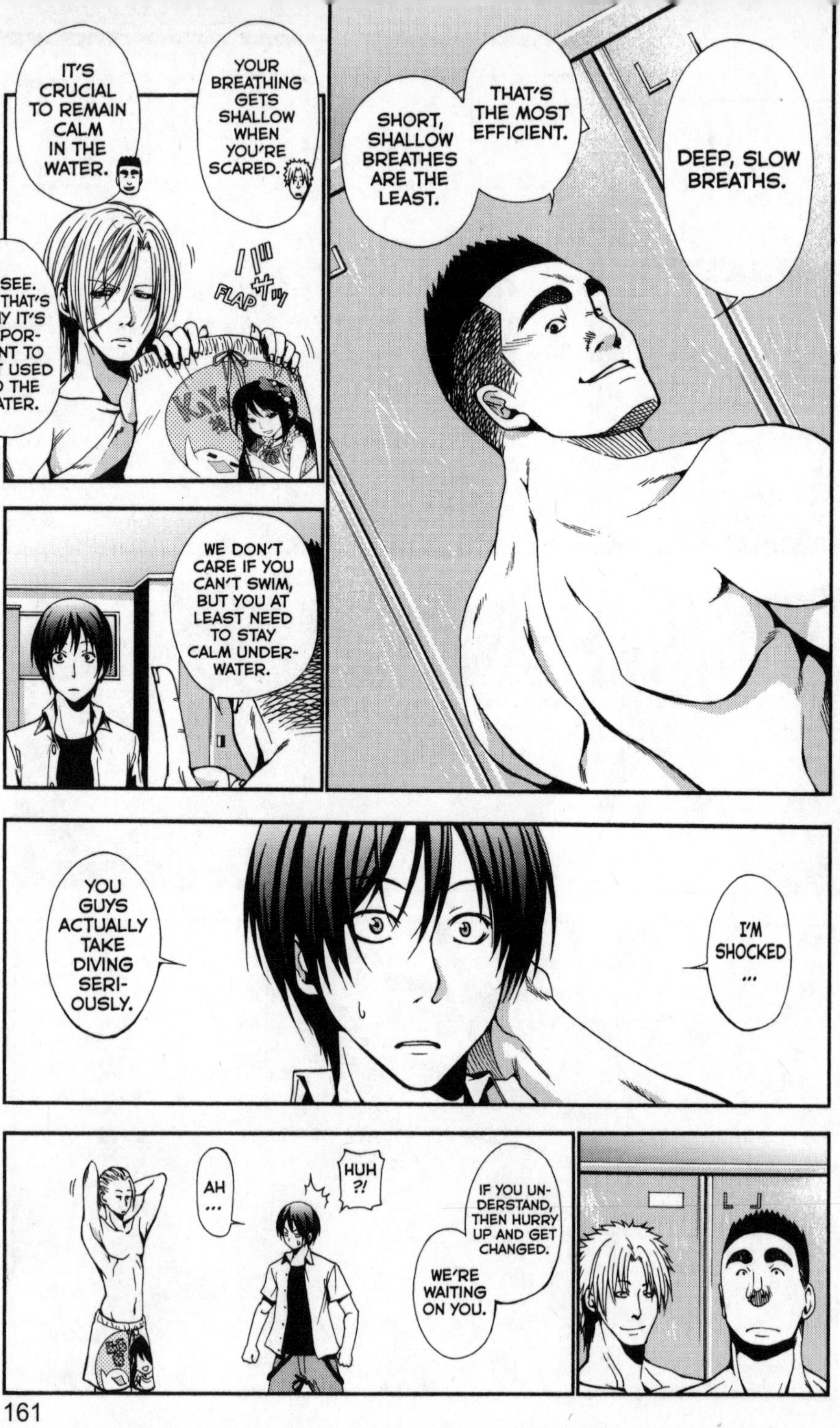
DEEP, SLOW BREATHS.
THAT'S THE MOST EFFICIENT.
SHORT, SHALLOW BREATHES ARE THE LEAST.
YOUR BREATHING GETS SHALLOW WHEN YOU'RE SCARED.
IT'S CRUCIAL TO REMAIN CALM IN THE WATER.
FLAP
I SEE. SO THAT'S WHY IT'S IMPORTANT TO GET USED TO THE WATER.
WE DON'T CARE IF YOU CAN'T SWIM, BUT YOU AT LEAST NEED TO STAY CALM UNDERWATER.
I'M SHOCKED...
YOU GUYS ACTUALLY TAKE DIVING SERIOUSLY.
IF YOU UNDERSTAND, THEN HURRY UP AND GET CHANGED.
WE'RE WAITING ON YOU.
HUH?!
AH...

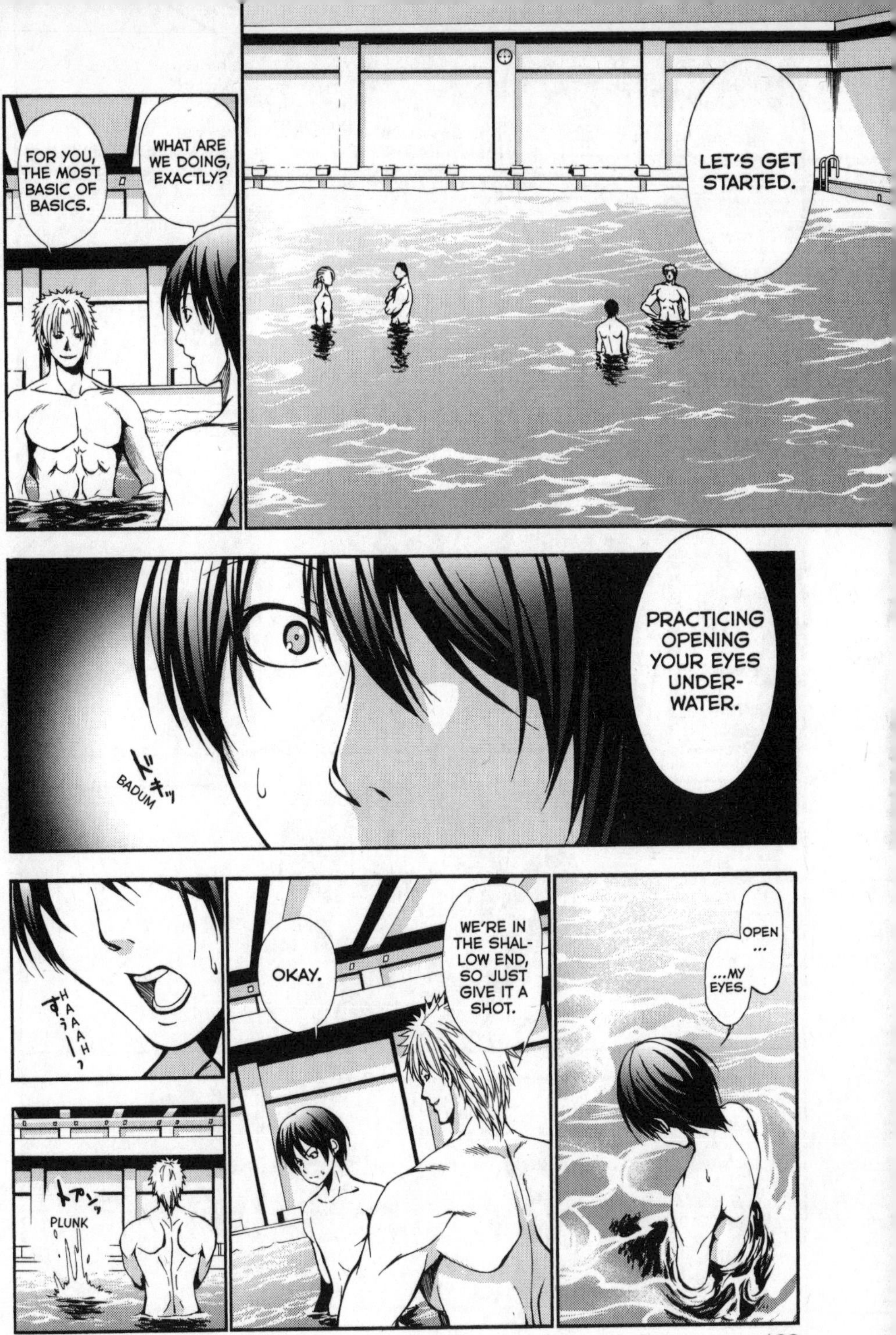
LET'S GET STARTED.
WHAT ARE WE DOING, EXACTLY?
FOR YOU, THE MOST BASIC OF BASICS.
PRACTICING OPENING YOUR EYES UNDER-WATER.
BADUM
OPEN...
...MY EYES.
WE'RE IN THE SHAL-LOW END, SO JUST GIVE IT A SHOT.
OKAY.
HAAAH
PLUNK

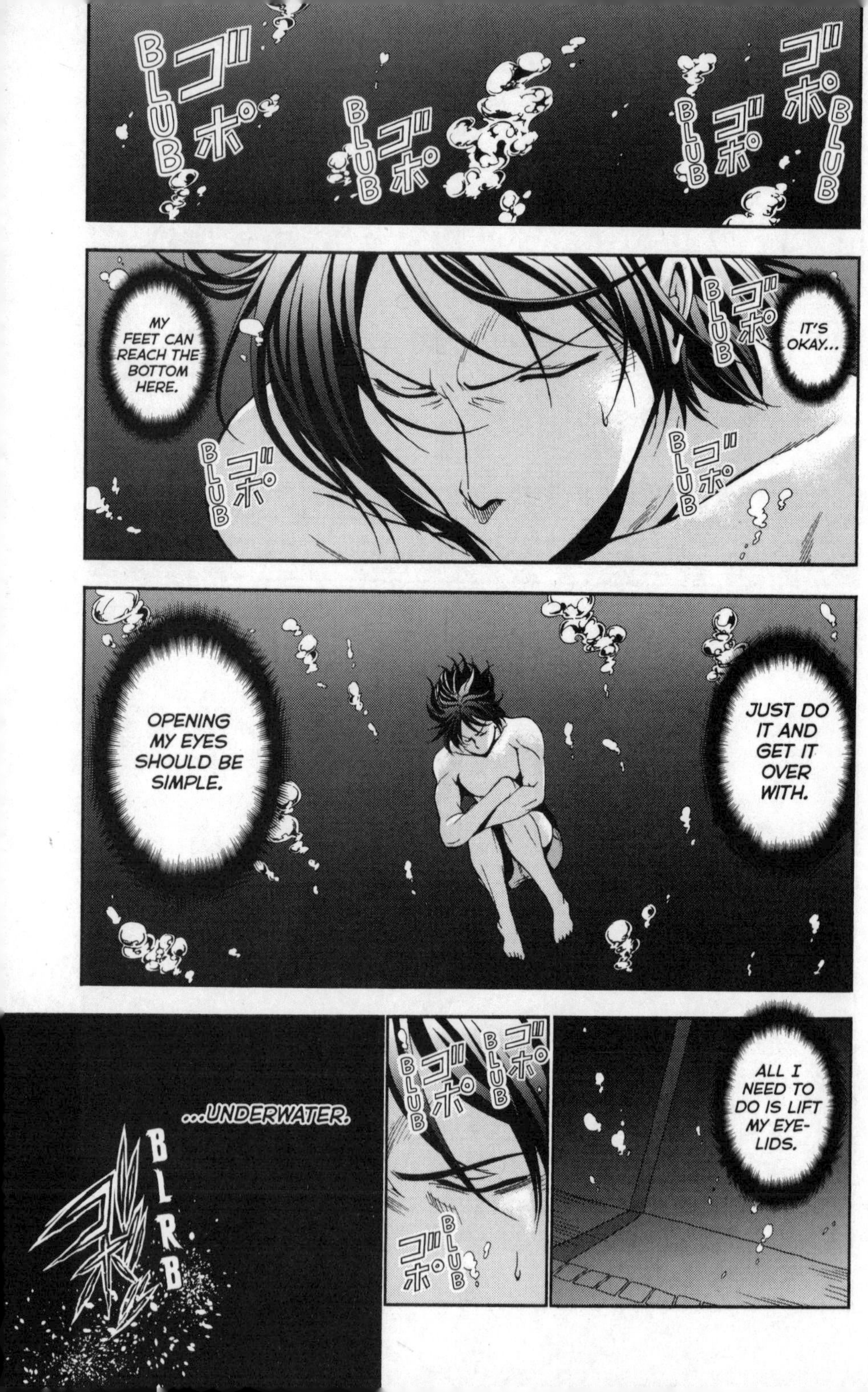
ゴポ
BLUB
ゴポ
BLUB
ゴポ
BLUB
ゴポ
BLUB
IT'S OKAY...
ゴポ
BLUB
MY FEET CAN REACH THE BOTTOM HERE.
ゴポ
BLUB
ゴポ
BLUB
JUST DO IT AND GET IT OVER WITH.
OPENING MY EYES SHOULD BE SIMPLE.
ALL I NEED TO DO IS LIFT MY EYE-LIDS.
ゴポ
BLUB
ゴポ
BLUB
ゴポ
BLUB
...UNDERWATER.
BLRB

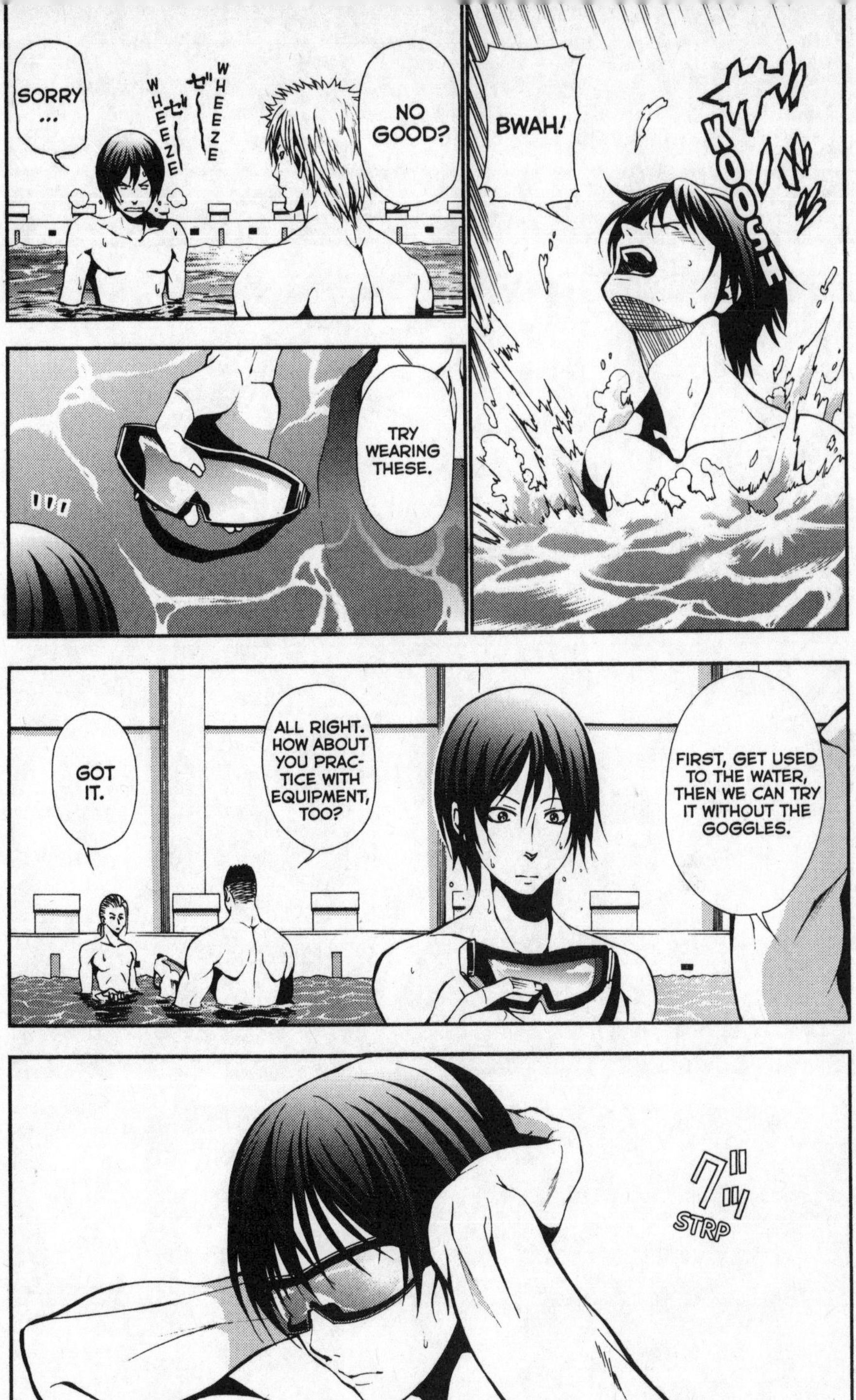
BWAH!
KOOSH
NO GOOD?
WHEEZE
WHEEZE
SORRY ...
TRY WEARING THESE.
...
FIRST, GET USED TO THE WATER, THEN WE CAN TRY IT WITHOUT THE GOGGLES.
ALL RIGHT. HOW ABOUT YOU PRAC-TICE WITH EQUIPMENT, TOO?
GOT IT.
STRP

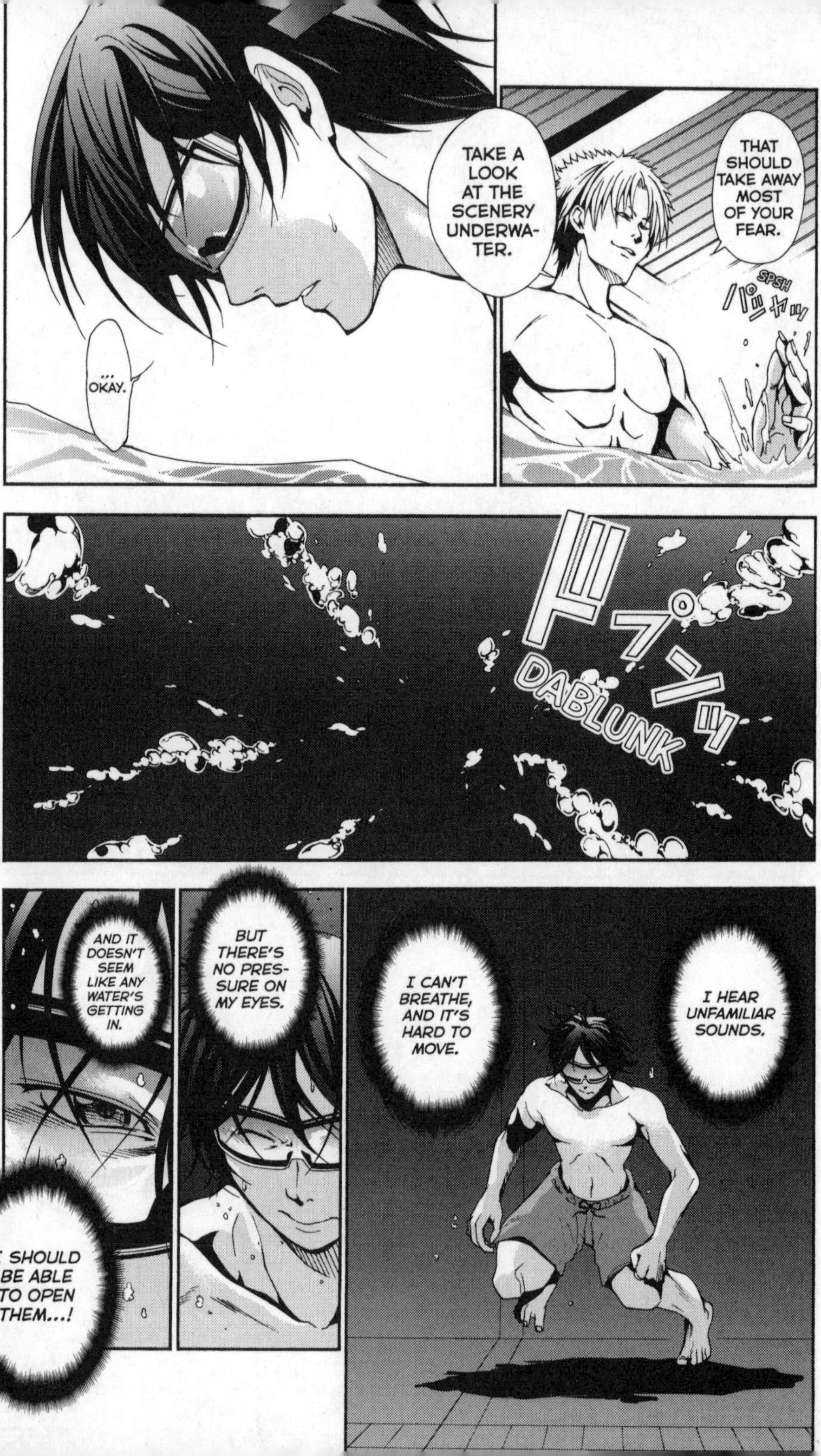
TAKE A LOOK AT THE SCENERY UNDERWATER.
THAT SHOULD TAKE AWAY MOST OF YOUR FEAR.
SPSH
...OKAY.
DABLUNK
I HEAR UNFAMILIAR SOUNDS.
I CAN'T BREATHE, AND IT'S HARD TO MOVE.
BUT THERE'S NO PRESSURE ON MY EYES.
AND IT DOESN'T SEEM LIKE ANY WATER'S GETTING IN.
I SHOULD BE ABLE TO OPEN THEM...!

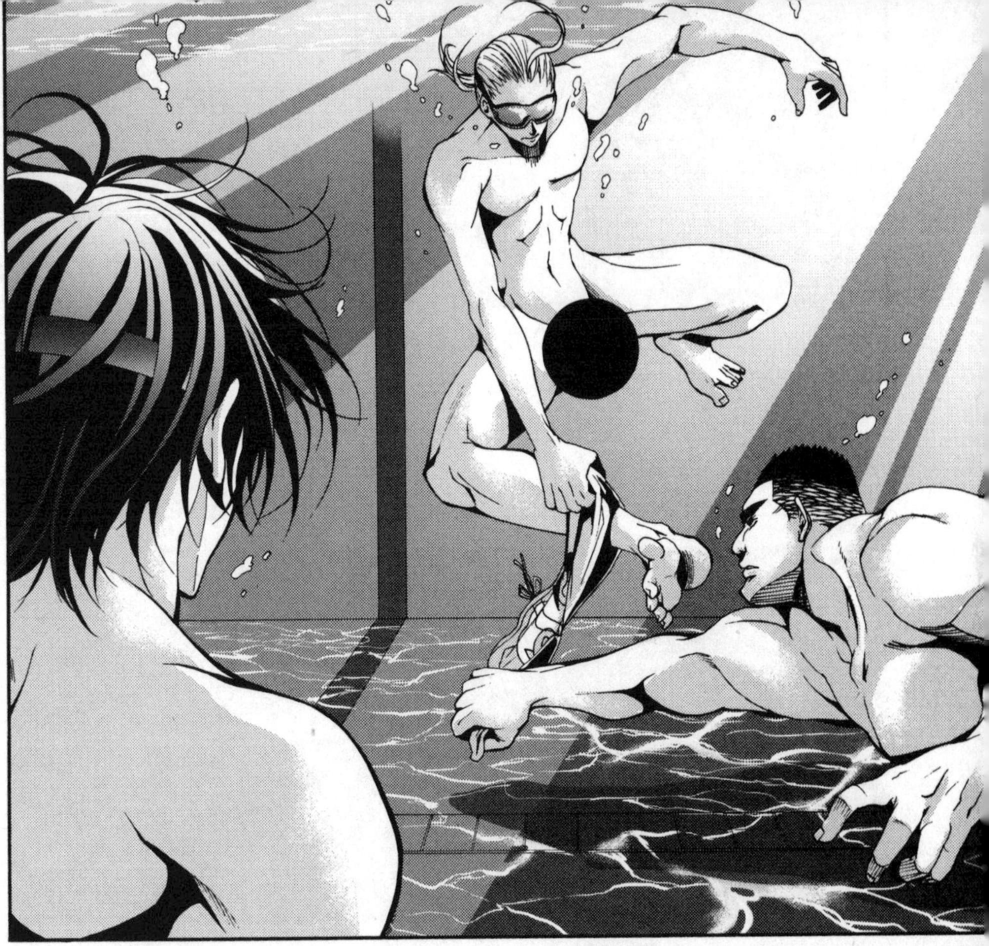

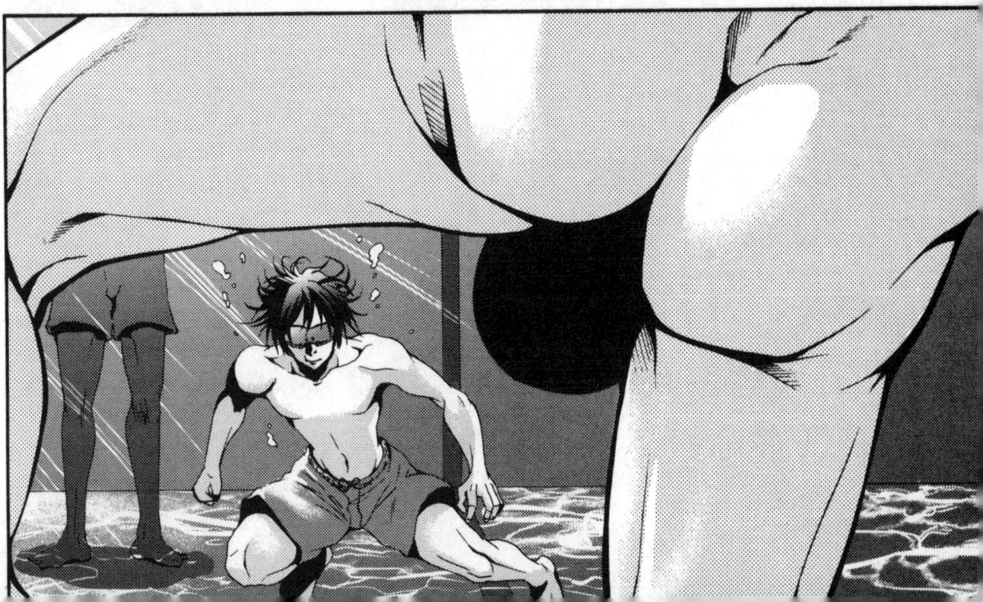

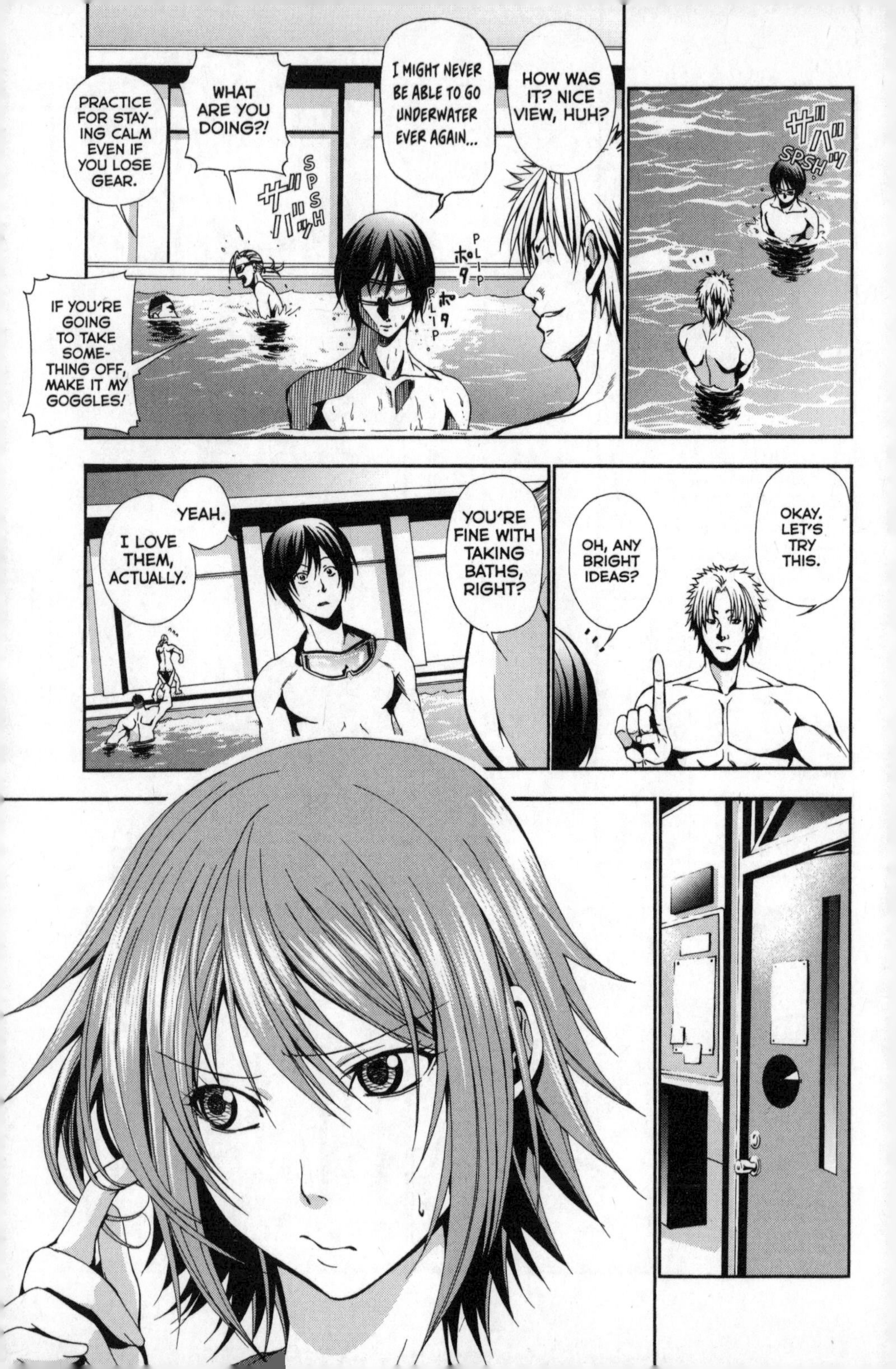
SPSH
...
HOW WAS IT? NICE VIEW, HUH?
I MIGHT NEVER BE ABLE TO GO UNDERWATER EVER AGAIN...
PLIP
PLIP
WHAT ARE YOU DOING?!
SPSH
PRACTICE FOR STAYING CALM EVEN IF YOU LOSE GEAR.
IF YOU'RE GOING TO TAKE SOMETHING OFF, MAKE IT MY GOGGLES!
OKAY. LET'S TRY THIS.
OH, ANY BRIGHT IDEAS?
...
YOU'RE FINE WITH TAKING BATHS, RIGHT?
YEAH.
I LOVE THEM, ACTUALLY.

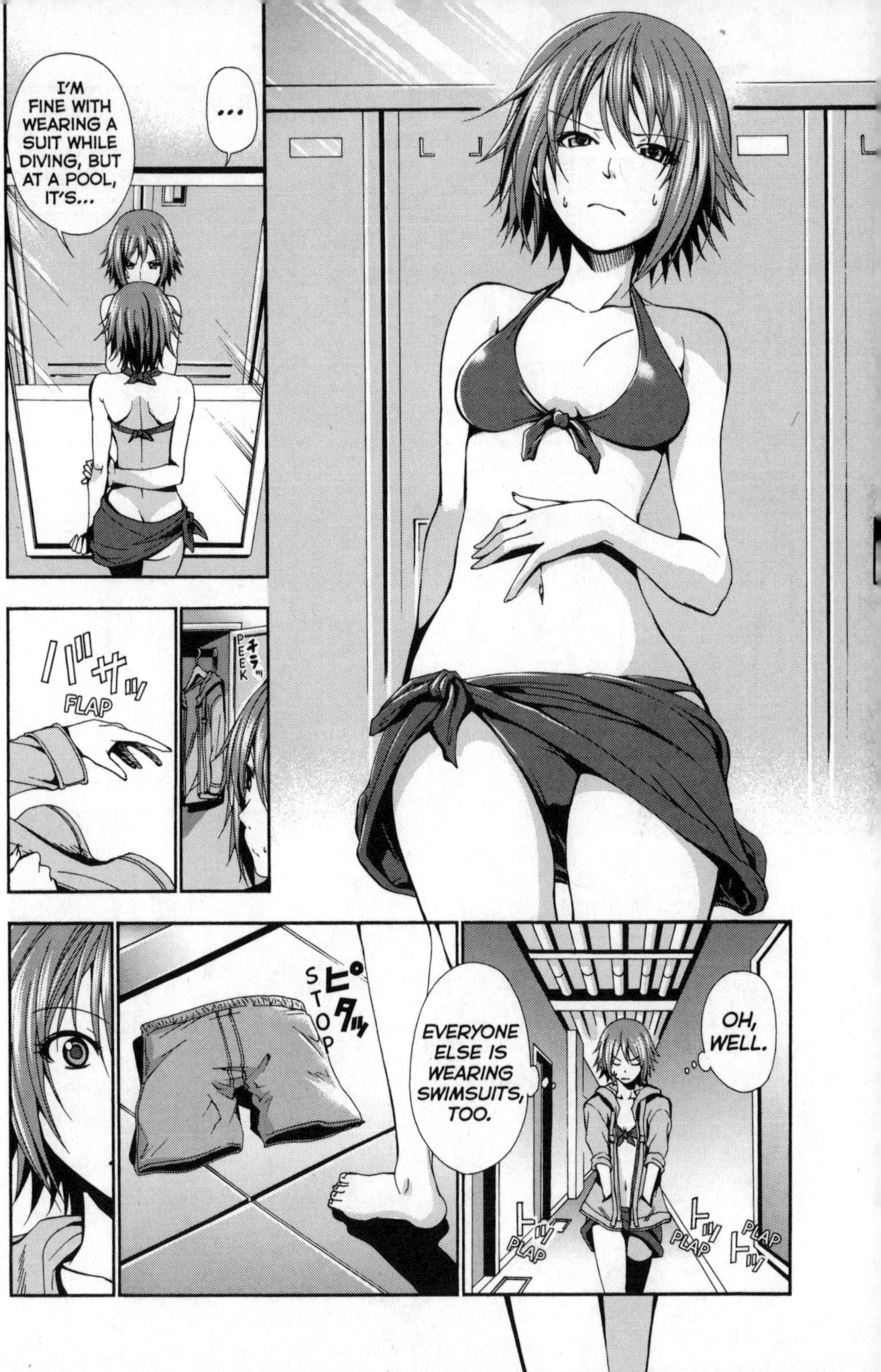
...
I'M FINE WITH WEARING A SUIT WHILE DIVING, BUT AT A POOL, IT'S...
チラッ
PEEK
バサッ
FLAP
OH, WELL.
EVERYONE ELSE IS WEARING SWIMSUITS, TOO.
トッ
PLAP
トッ
PLAP
トッ
PLAP
ピタッ
STOP

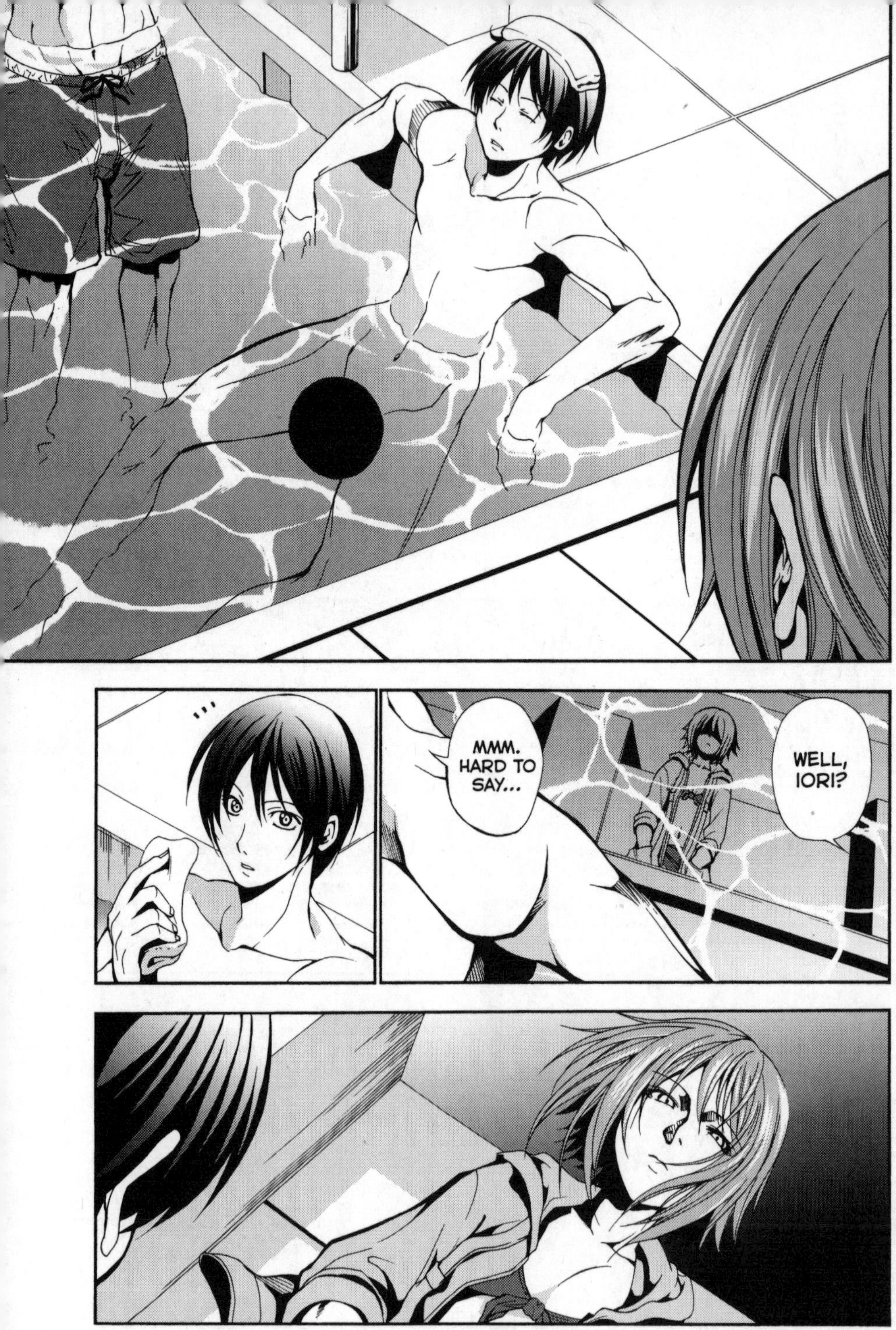
WELL, IORI?
MMM. HARD TO SAY...
...

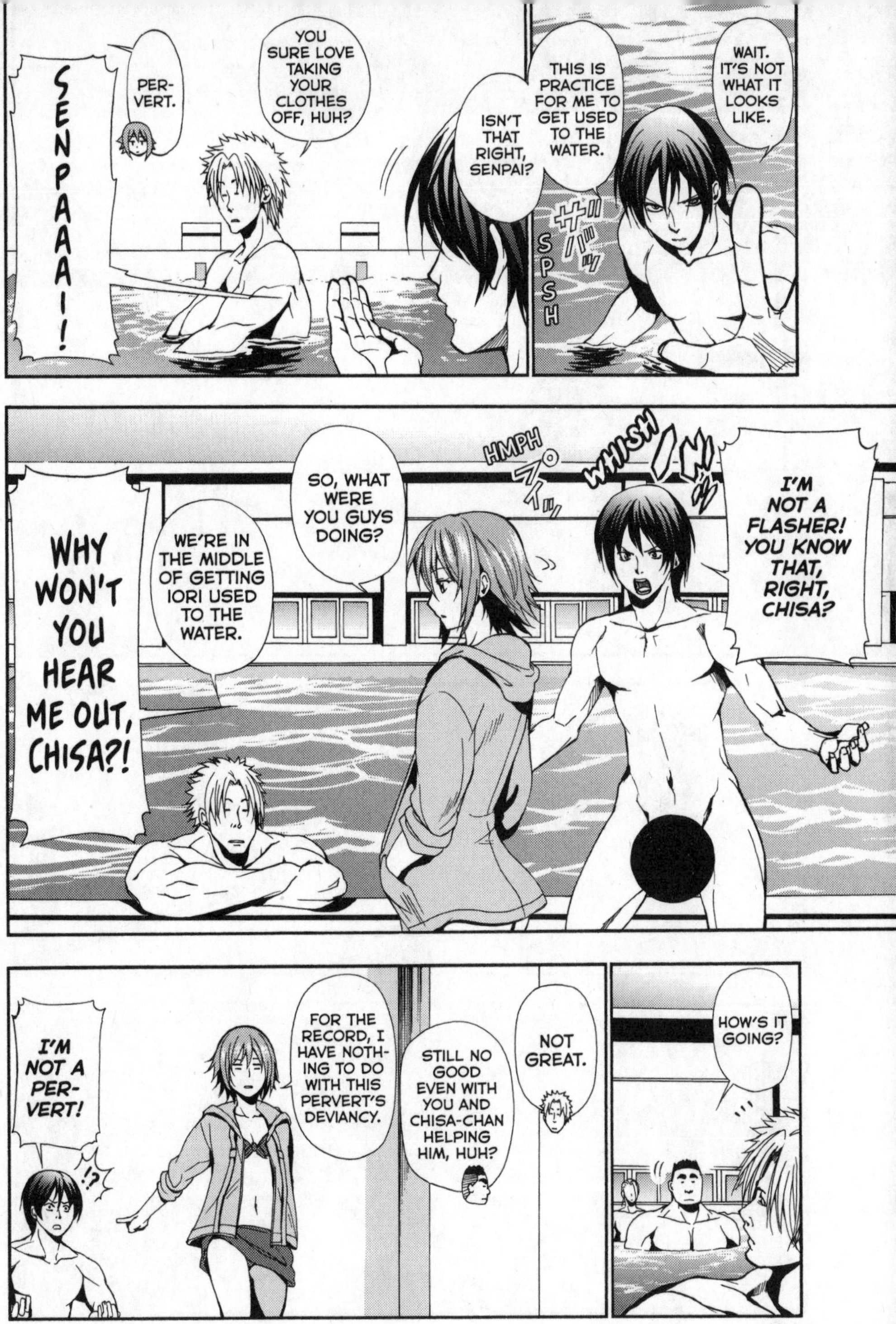
WAIT. IT'S NOT WHAT IT LOOKS LIKE.
SPSH
THIS IS PRACTICE FOR ME TO GET USED TO THE WATER.
ISN'T THAT RIGHT, SENPAI?
YOU SURE LOVE TAKING YOUR CLOTHES OFF, HUH?
PER-VERT.
SENPAAAAI!
I'M NOT A FLASHER! YOU KNOW THAT, RIGHT, CHISA?
WHISH
HMPH
SO, WHAT WERE YOU GUYS DOING?
WE'RE IN THE MIDDLE OF GETTING IORI USED TO THE WATER.
WHY WON'T YOU HEAR ME OUT, CHISA?!
HOW'S IT GOING?
NOT GREAT.
STILL NO GOOD EVEN WITH YOU AND CHISA-CHAN HELPING HIM, HUH?
FOR THE RECORD, I HAVE NOTH-ING TO DO WITH THIS PERVERT'S DEVIANCY.
I'M NOT A PER-VERT!
!?

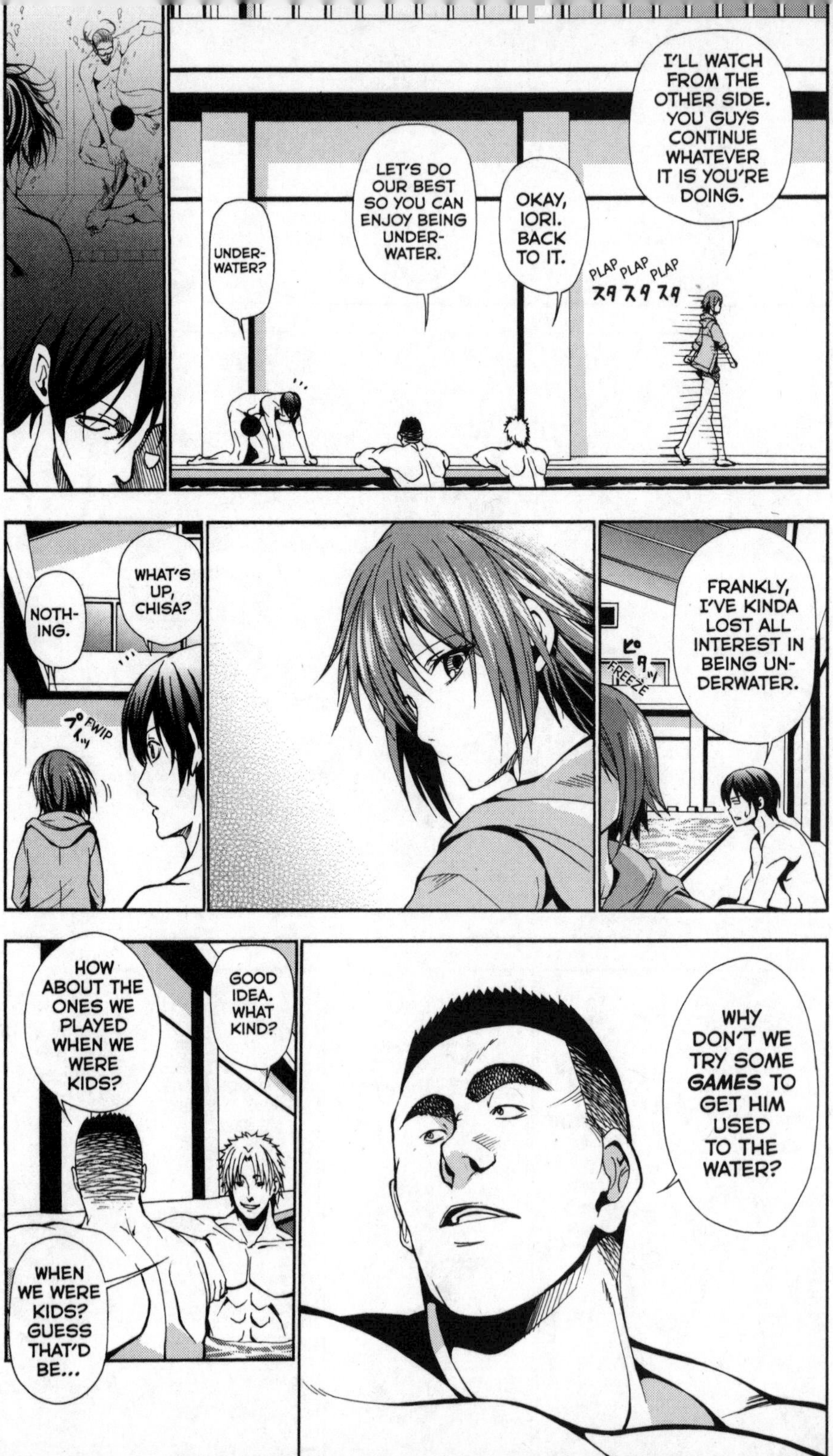
I'LL WATCH FROM THE OTHER SIDE. YOU GUYS CONTINUE WHATEVER IT IS YOU'RE DOING.
PLAP PLAP PLAP
スタスタスタ
OKAY, IORI. BACK TO IT.
LET'S DO OUR BEST SO YOU CAN ENJOY BEING UNDER-WATER.
UNDER-WATER?
FRANKLY, I'VE KINDA LOST ALL INTEREST IN BEING UN-DERWATER.
ピタッ
FREEZE
WHAT'S UP, CHISA?
NOTH-ING.
ぷいっ
FWIP
WHY DON'T WE TRY SOME *GAMES* TO GET HIM USED TO THE WATER?
GOOD IDEA. WHAT KIND?
HOW ABOUT THE ONES WE PLAYED WHEN WE WERE KIDS?
WHEN WE WERE KIDS? GUESS THAT'D BE...

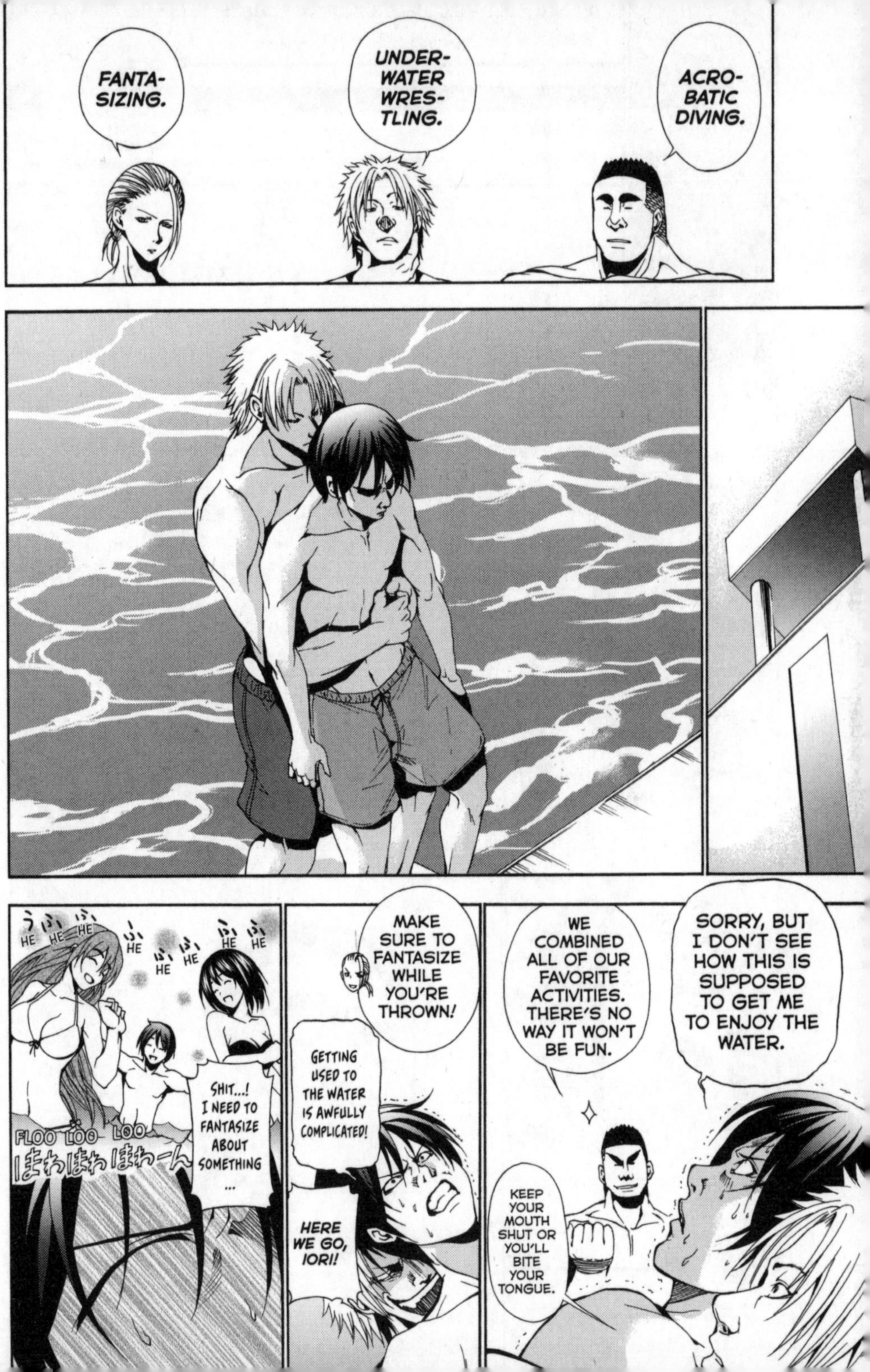
ACRO-BATIC DIVING.
UNDER-WATER WRES-TLING.
FANTA-SIZING.
SORRY, BUT I DON'T SEE HOW THIS IS SUPPOSED TO GET ME TO ENJOY THE WATER.
WE COMBINED ALL OF OUR FAVORITE ACTIVITIES. THERE'S NO WAY IT WON'T BE FUN.
KEEP YOUR MOUTH SHUT OR YOU'LL BITE YOUR TONGUE.
MAKE SURE TO FANTASIZE WHILE YOU'RE THROWN!
GETTING USED TO THE WATER IS AWFULLY COMPLICATED!
HERE WE GO, IORI!
HE HE HE HE HE HE HE
SHIT...! I NEED TO FANTASIZE ABOUT SOMETHING ...
FLOO LOO LOO
ほわほわほわーん

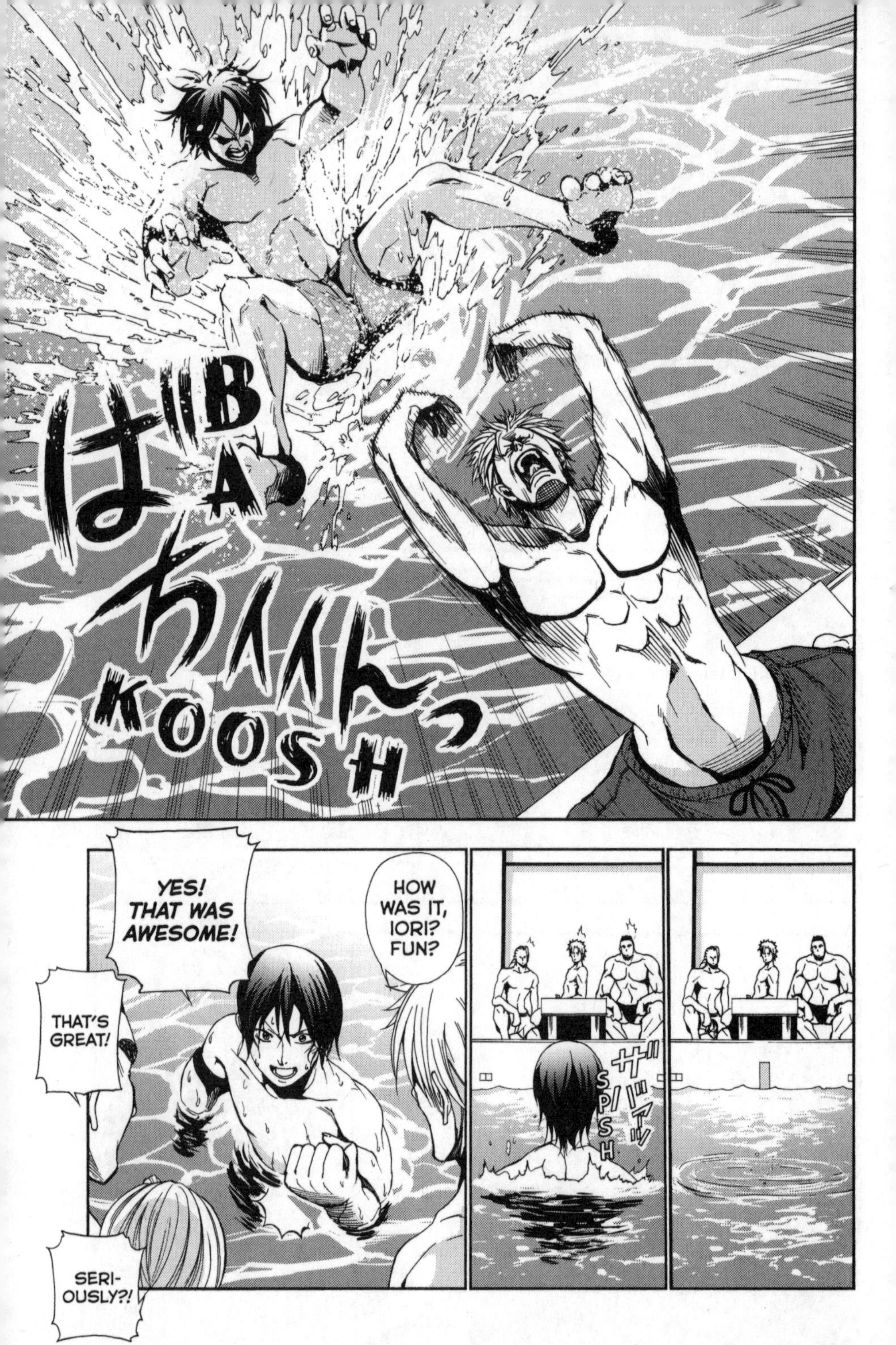
BA
KOOSH
ザバァッ
SPSH
HOW WAS IT, IORI? FUN?
YES! THAT WAS AWESOME!
THAT'S GREAT!
SERI-OUSLY?!

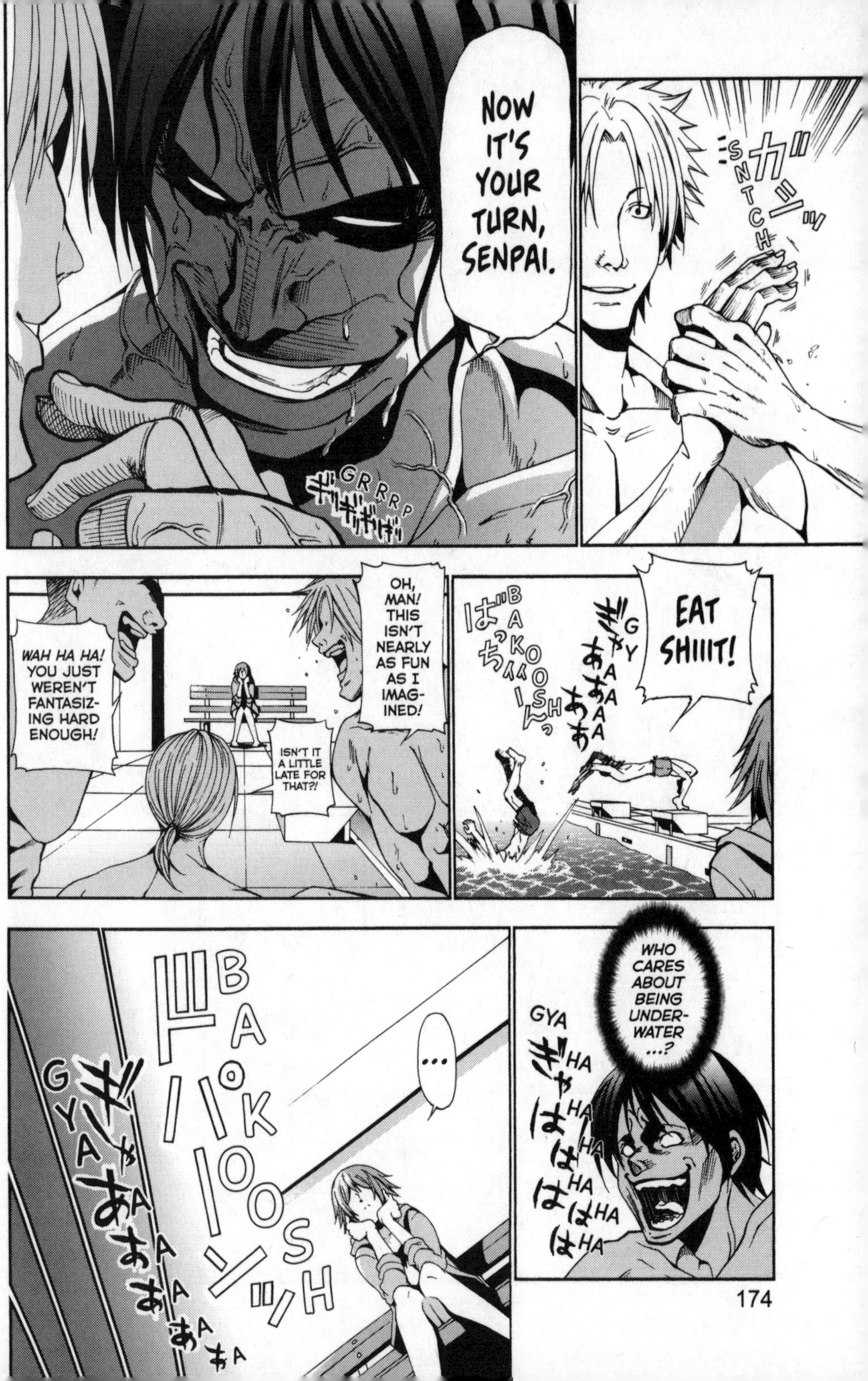
SNTCH
NOW IT'S YOUR TURN, SENPAI.
GRRRRP
EAT SHIIIT!
GYAAAA
BAKOOSH
OH, MAN! THIS ISN'T NEARLY AS FUN AS I IMAGINED!
ISN'T IT A LITTLE LATE FOR THAT?!
WAH HA HA! YOU JUST WEREN'T FANTASIZING HARD ENOUGH!
WHO CARES ABOUT BEING UNDERWATER ...?
GYA HA HA HA HA HA HA
...
BAKOOSH
GYAAAAAAA

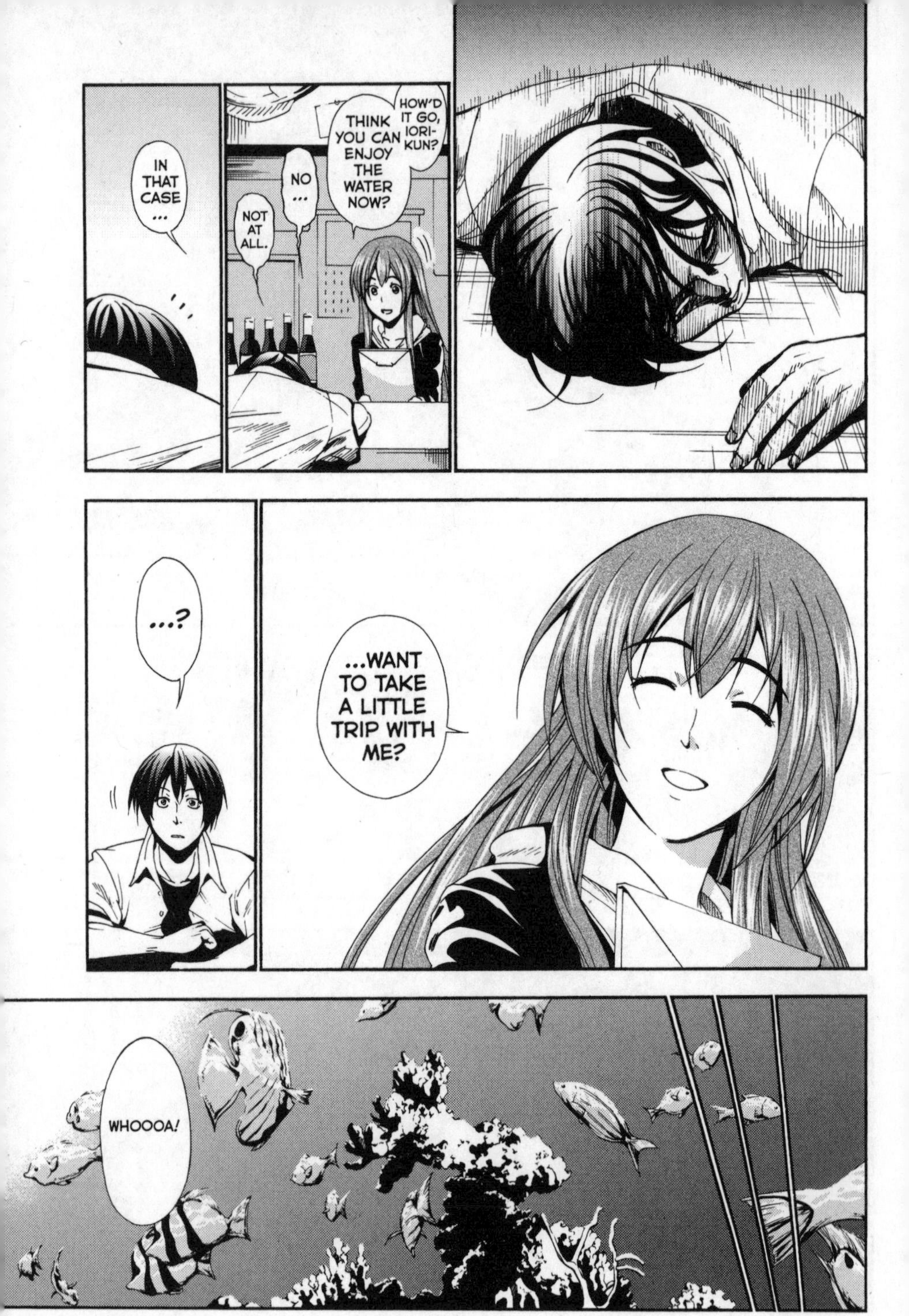
HOW'D IT GO, IORI-KUN?
THINK YOU CAN ENJOY THE WATER NOW?
NO ...
NOT AT ALL.
IN THAT CASE ...
...WANT TO TAKE A LITTLE TRIP WITH ME?
...?
WHOOOA!

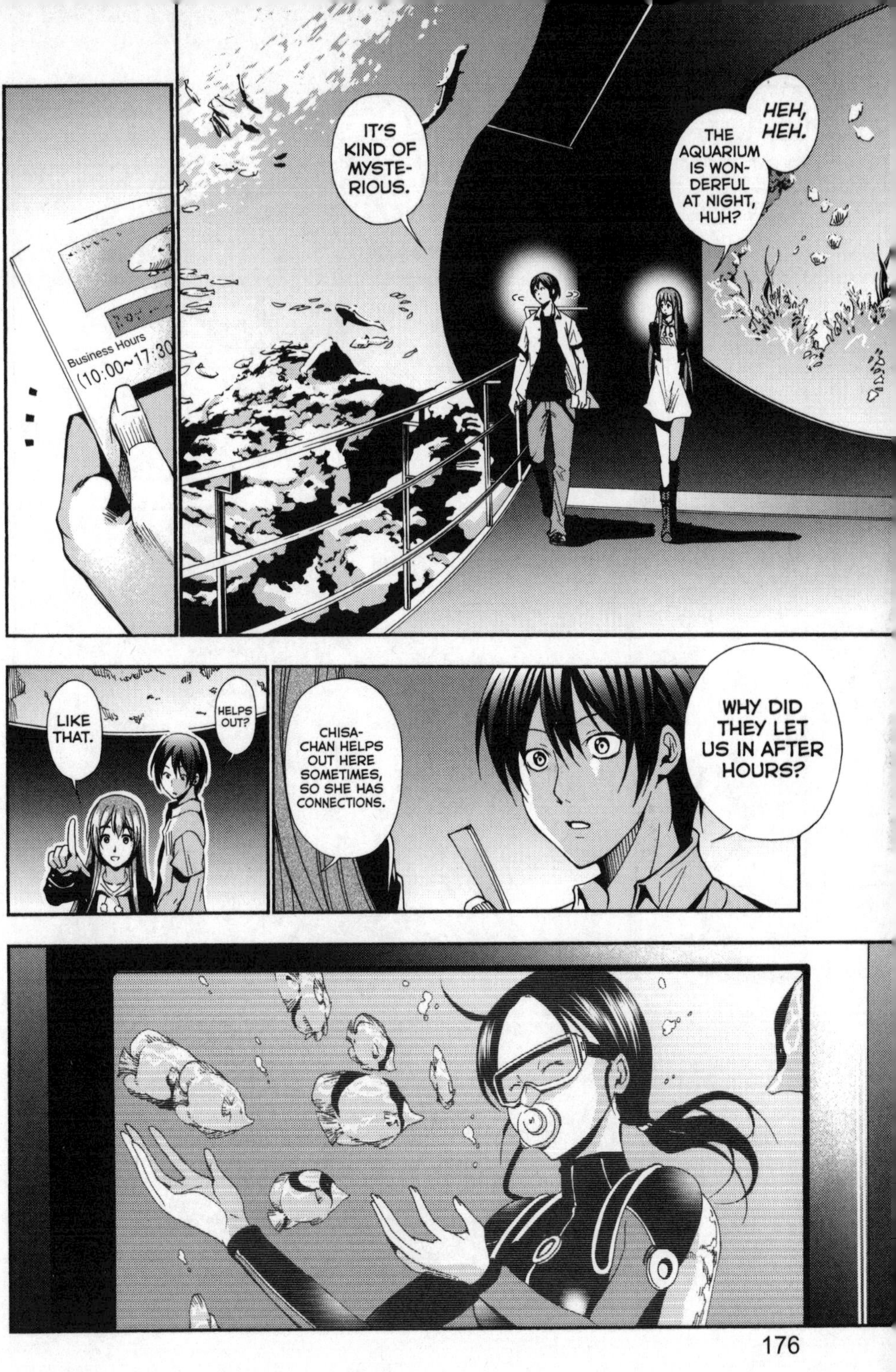
HEH, HEH.
THE AQUARIUM IS WONDERFUL AT NIGHT, HUH?
IT'S KIND OF MYSTERIOUS.
Business Hours
(10:00~17:30
...
WHY DID THEY LET US IN AFTER HOURS?
CHISA-CHAN HELPS OUT HERE SOMETIMES, SO SHE HAS CONNECTIONS.
HELPS OUT?
LIKE THAT.

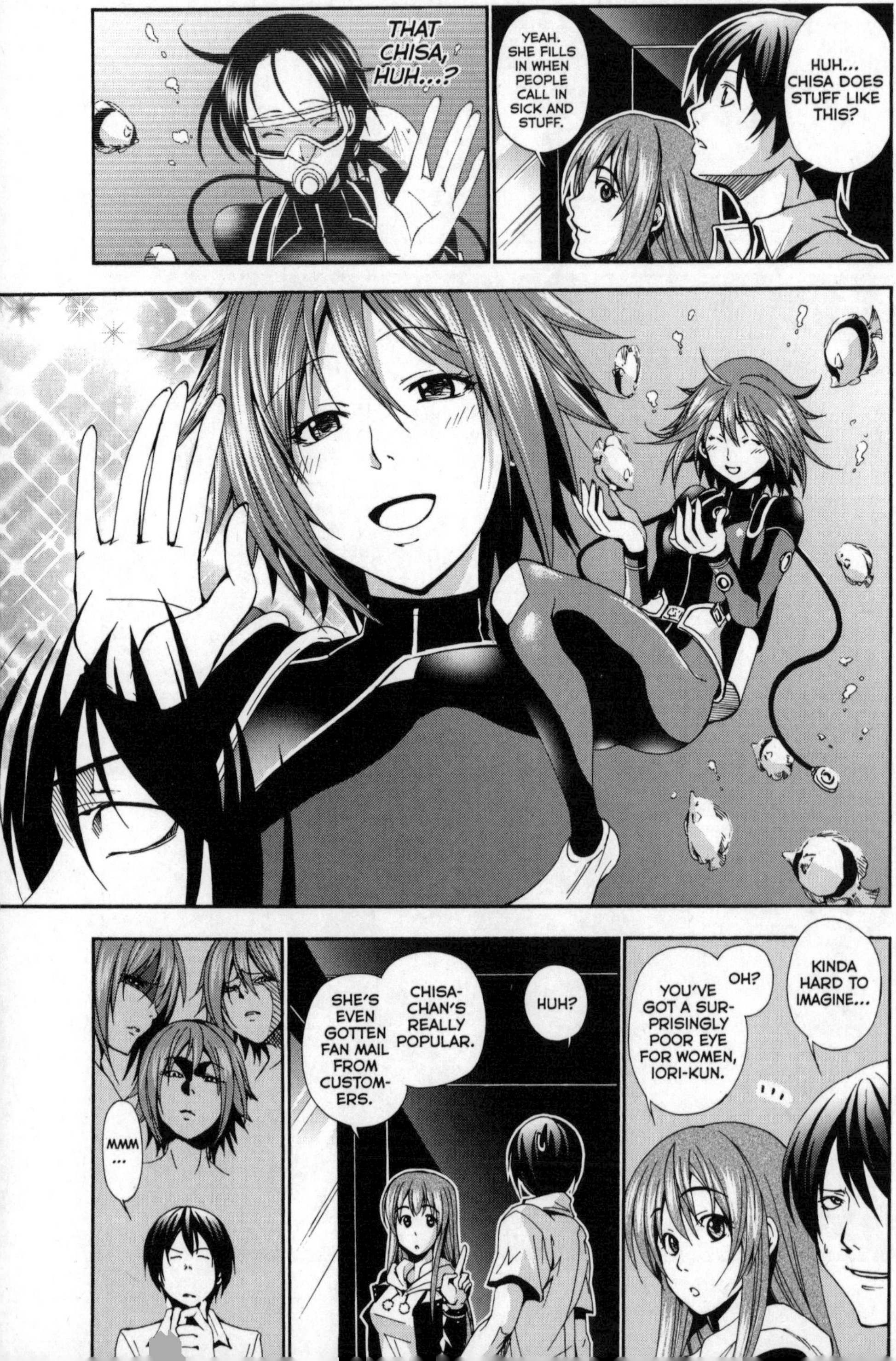
HUH... CHISA DOES STUFF LIKE THIS?
YEAH. SHE FILLS IN WHEN PEOPLE CALL IN SICK AND STUFF.
THAT CHISA, HUH...?
KINDA HARD TO IMAGINE...
OH?
YOU'VE GOT A SURPRISINGLY POOR EYE FOR WOMEN, IORI-KUN.
...
HUH?
CHISA-CHAN'S REALLY POPULAR.
SHE'S EVEN GOTTEN FAN MAIL FROM CUSTOMERS.
MMM...

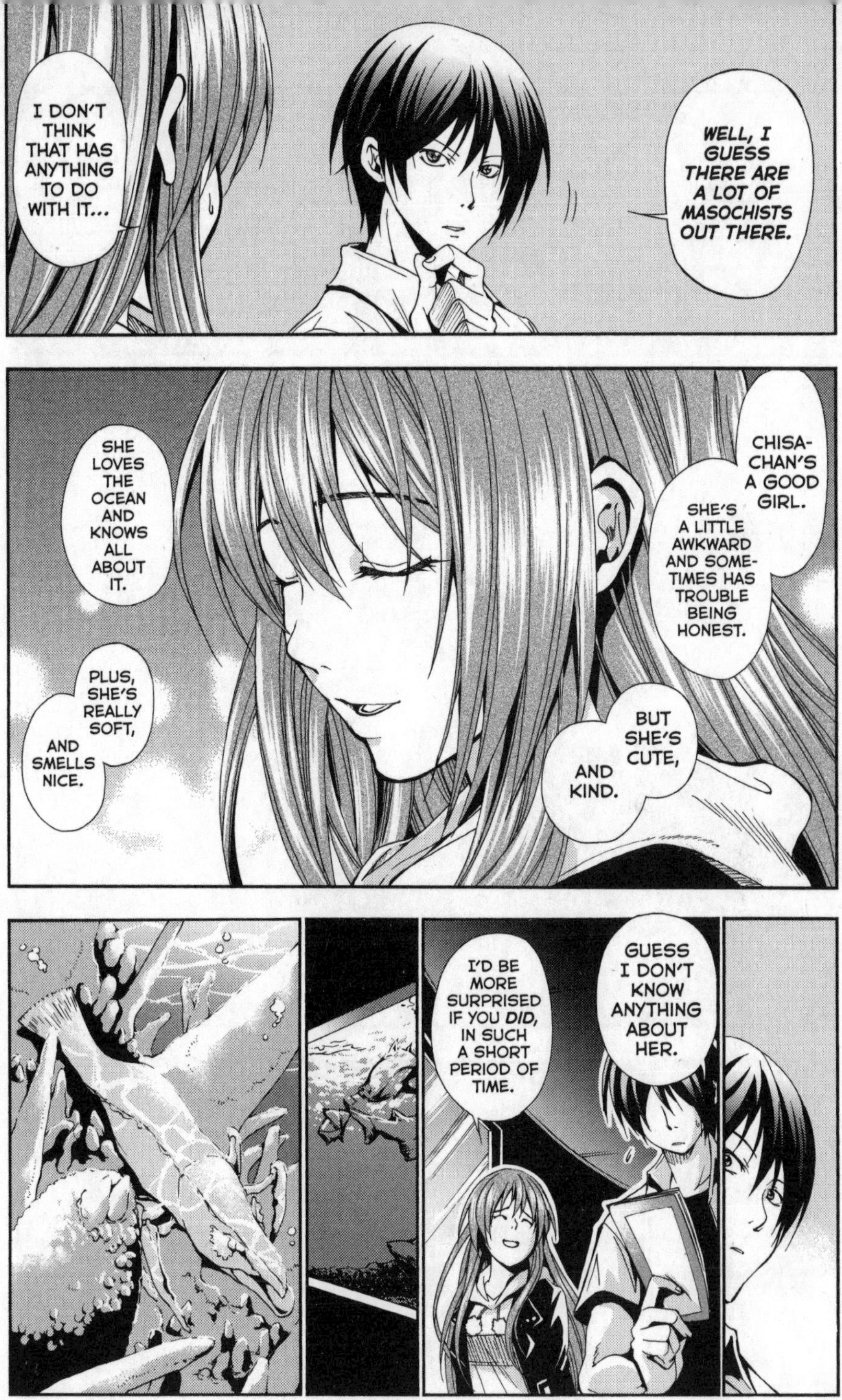
WELL, I GUESS THERE ARE A LOT OF MASOCHISTS OUT THERE.
I DON'T THINK THAT HAS ANYTHING TO DO WITH IT...
CHISA-CHAN'S A GOOD GIRL.
SHE'S A LITTLE AWKWARD AND SOME-TIMES HAS TROUBLE BEING HONEST.
BUT SHE'S CUTE,
AND KIND.
SHE LOVES THE OCEAN AND KNOWS ALL ABOUT IT.
PLUS, SHE'S REALLY SOFT,
AND SMELLS NICE.
GUESS I DON'T KNOW ANYTHING ABOUT HER.
I'D BE MORE SURPRISED IF YOU *DID*, IN SUCH A SHORT PERIOD OF TIME.

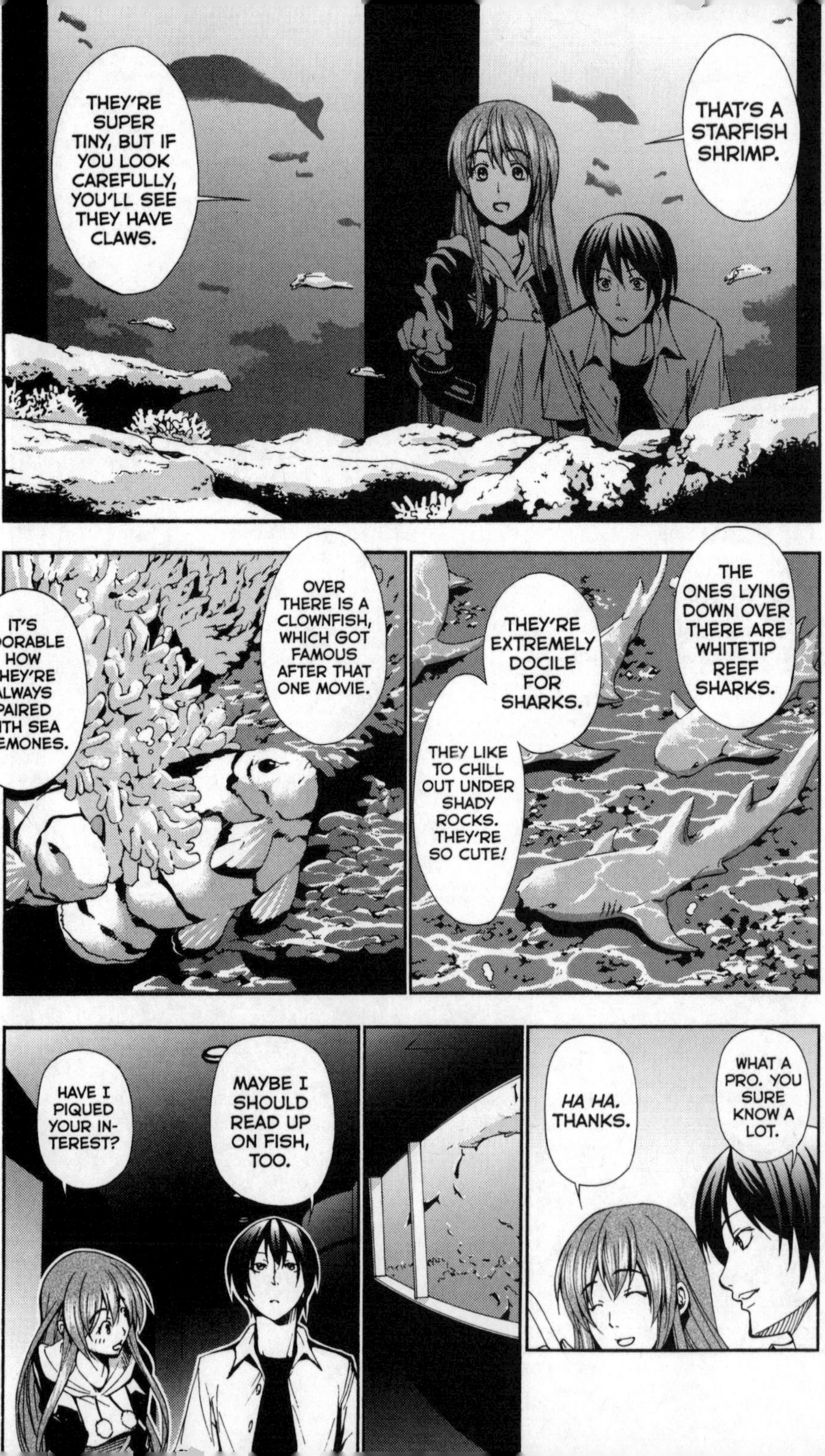
THAT'S A STARFISH SHRIMP.
THEY'RE SUPER TINY, BUT IF YOU LOOK CAREFULLY, YOU'LL SEE THEY HAVE CLAWS.
THE ONES LYING DOWN OVER THERE ARE WHITETIP REEF SHARKS.
THEY'RE EXTREMELY DOCILE FOR SHARKS.
THEY LIKE TO CHILL OUT UNDER SHADY ROCKS. THEY'RE SO CUTE!
OVER THERE IS A CLOWNFISH, WHICH GOT FAMOUS AFTER THAT ONE MOVIE.
IT'S ADORABLE HOW THEY'RE ALWAYS PAIRED WITH SEA ANEMONES.
WHAT A PRO. YOU SURE KNOW A LOT.
HA HA. THANKS.
MAYBE I SHOULD READ UP ON FISH, TOO.
HAVE I PIQUED YOUR INTEREST?

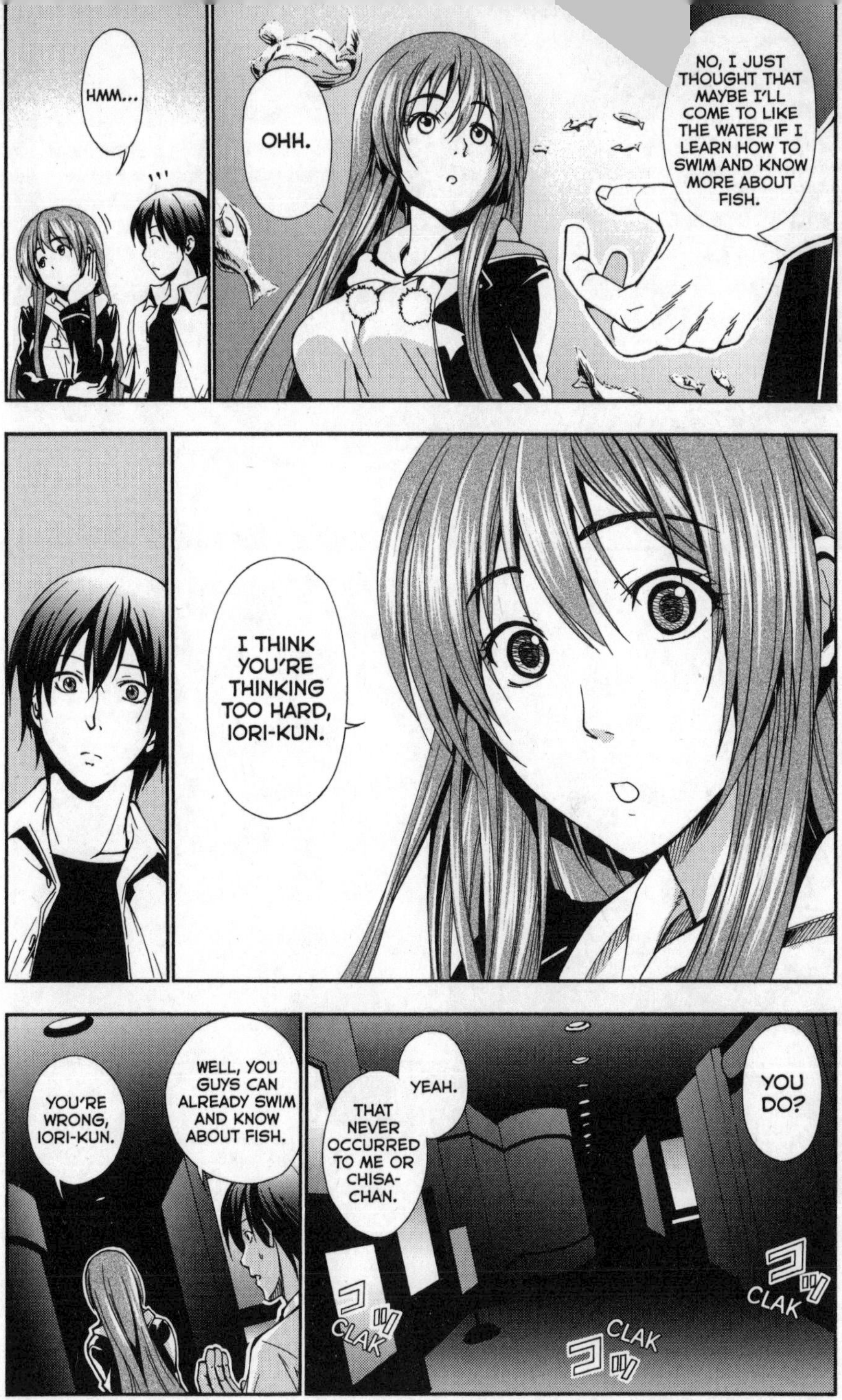
NO, I JUST THOUGHT THAT MAYBE I'LL COME TO LIKE THE WATER IF I LEARN HOW TO SWIM AND KNOW MORE ABOUT FISH.
OHH.
HMM...
I THINK YOU'RE THINKING TOO HARD, IORI-KUN.
YOU DO?
YEAH.
THAT NEVER OCCURRED TO ME OR CHISA-CHAN.
コッ
CLAK
コッ
CLAK
コッ
CLAK
WELL, YOU GUYS CAN ALREADY SWIM AND KNOW ABOUT FISH.
YOU'RE WRONG, IORI-KUN.

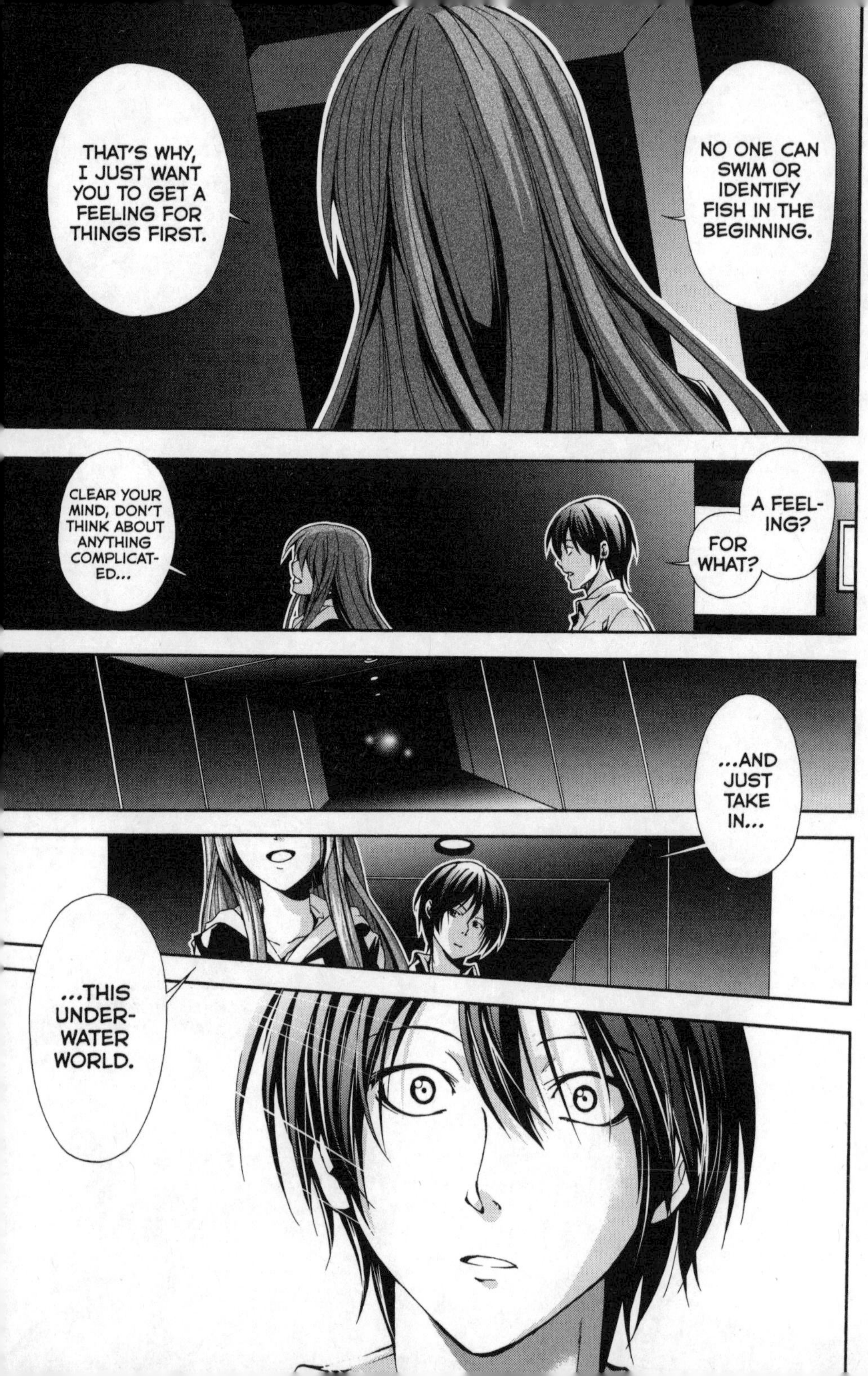
NO ONE CAN SWIM OR IDENTIFY FISH IN THE BEGINNING.
THAT'S WHY, I JUST WANT YOU TO GET A FEELING FOR THINGS FIRST.
A FEEL-ING?
FOR WHAT?
CLEAR YOUR MIND, DON'T THINK ABOUT ANYTHING COMPLICAT-ED...
...AND JUST TAKE IN...
...THIS UNDER-WATER WORLD.

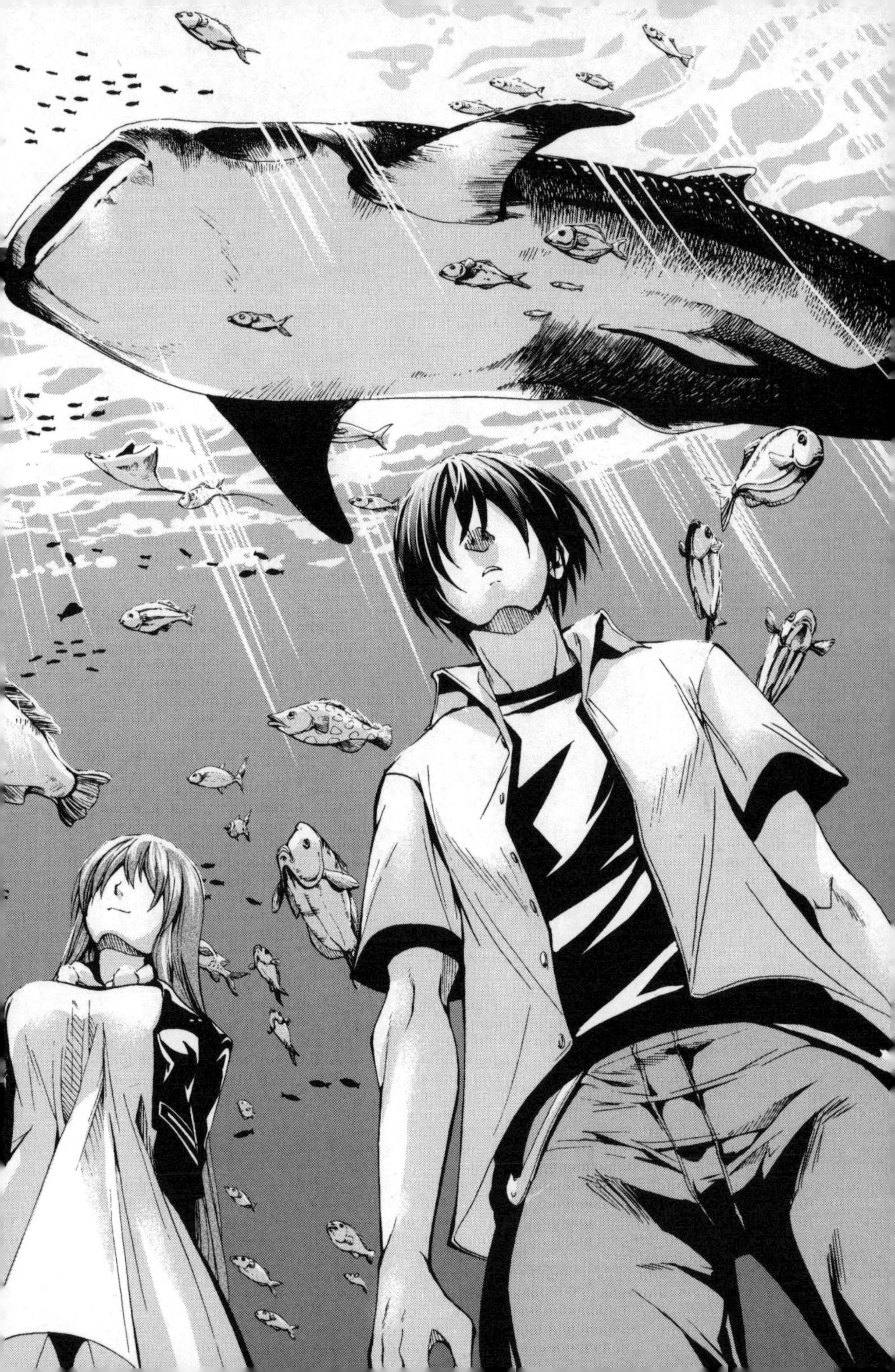

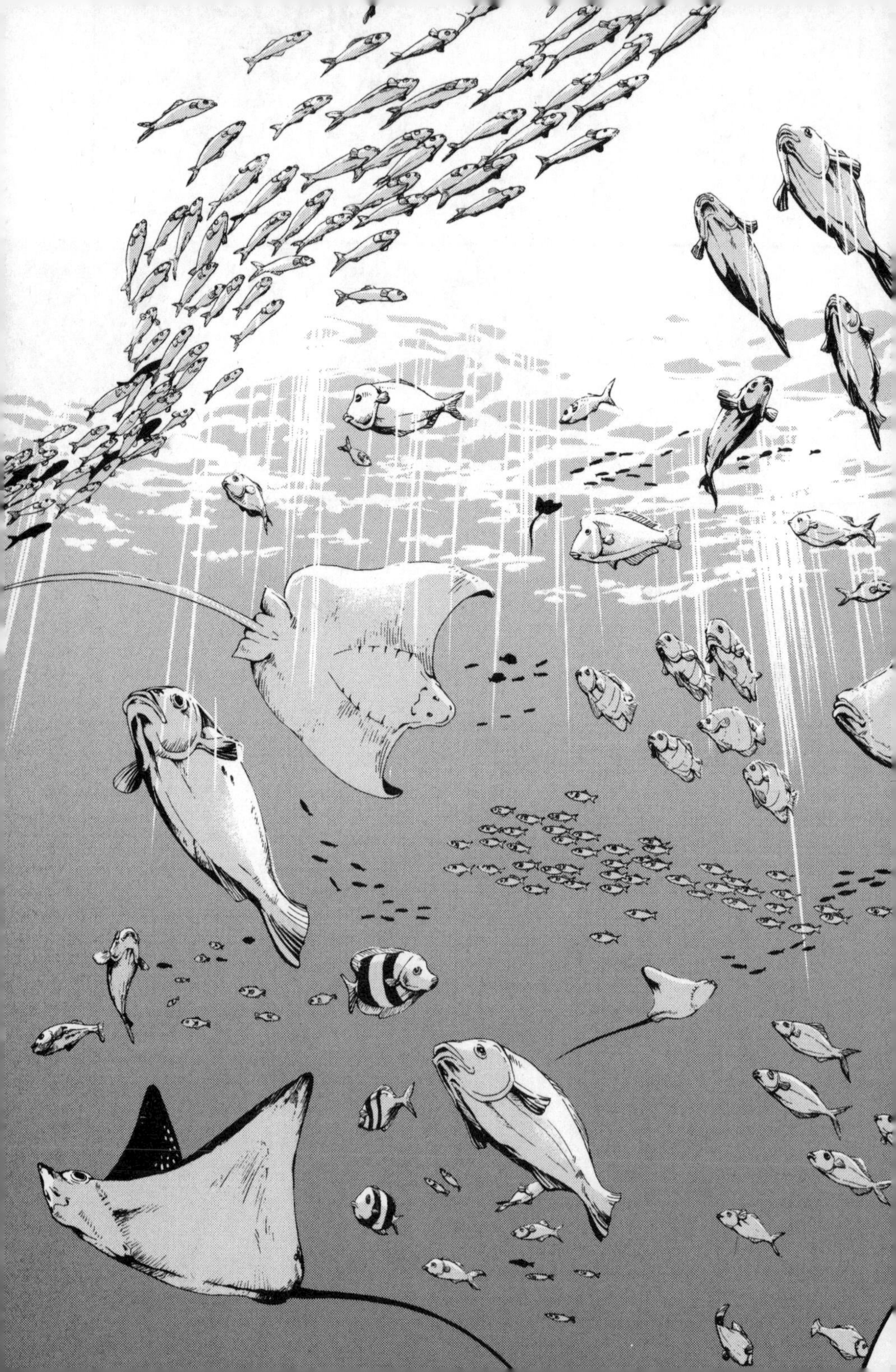

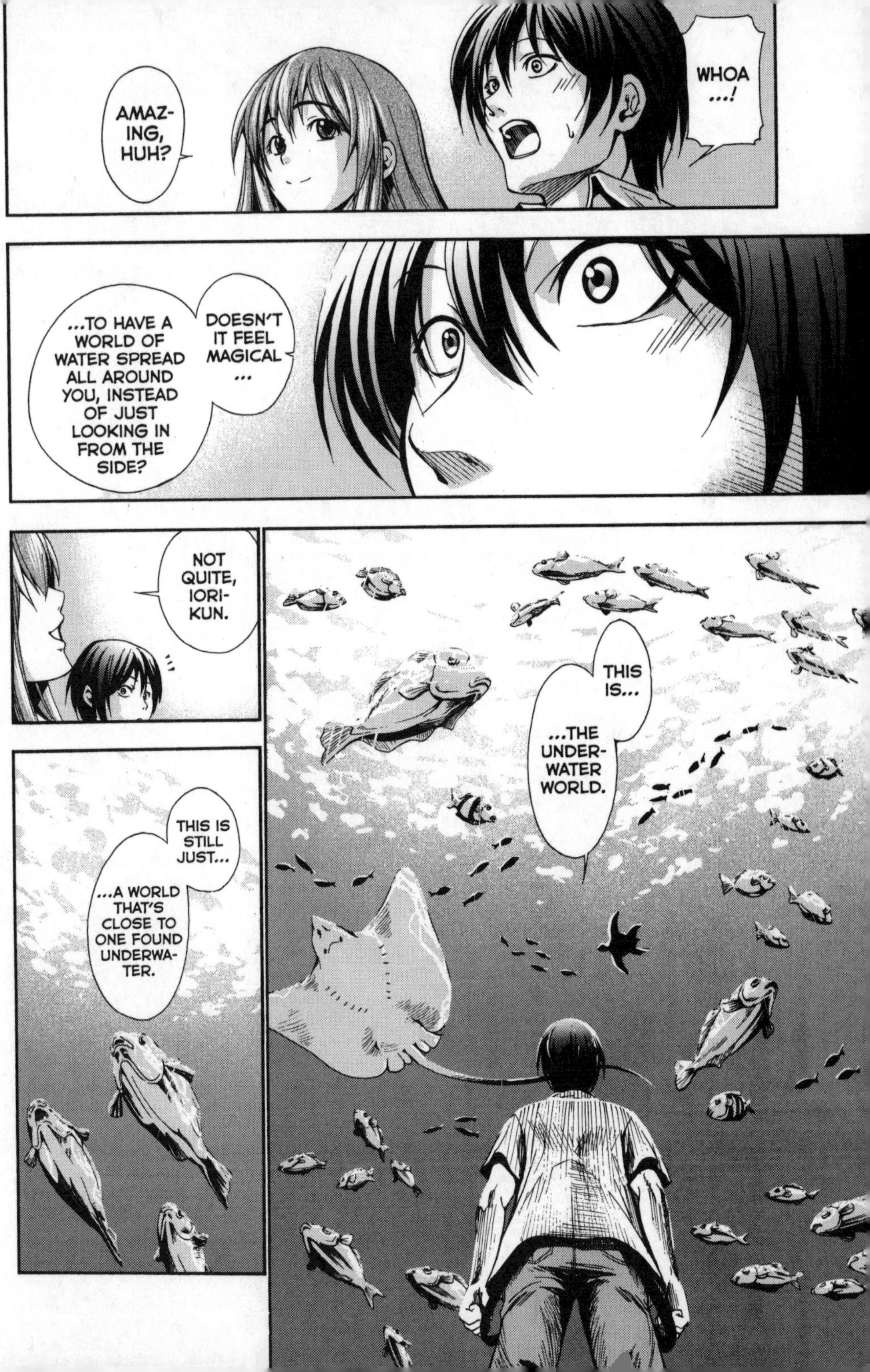
WHOA ...!
AMAZ-ING, HUH?
DOESN'T IT FEEL MAGICAL ...
...TO HAVE A WORLD OF WATER SPREAD ALL AROUND YOU, INSTEAD OF JUST LOOKING IN FROM THE SIDE?
THIS IS...
...THE UNDER-WATER WORLD.
NOT QUITE, IORI-KUN.
THIS IS STILL JUST...
...A WORLD THAT'S CLOSE TO ONE FOUND UNDERWA-TER.

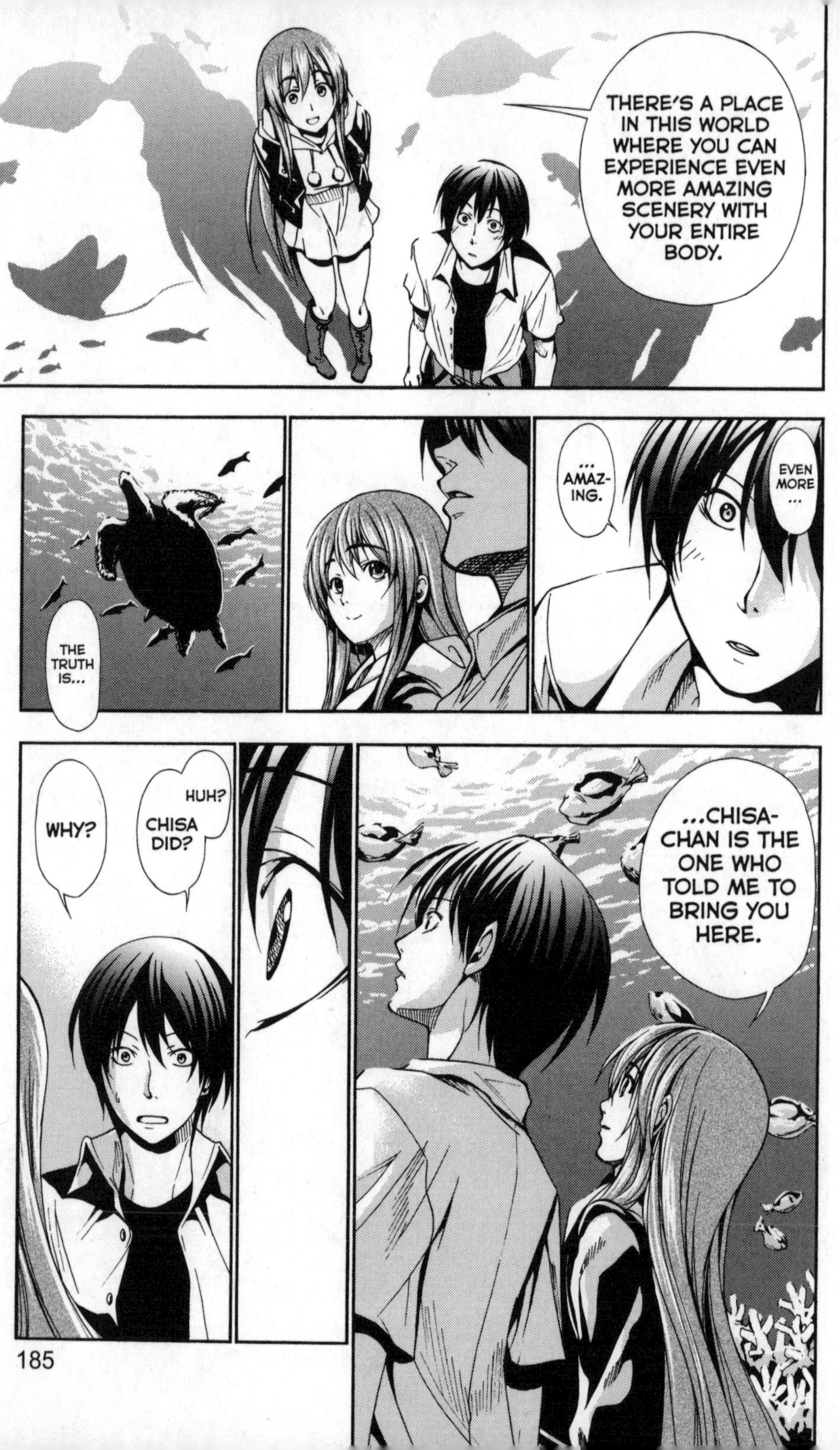
THERE'S A PLACE IN THIS WORLD WHERE YOU CAN EXPERIENCE EVEN MORE AMAZING SCENERY WITH YOUR ENTIRE BODY.
EVEN MORE...
...AMAZ-ING.
THE TRUTH IS...
...CHISA-CHAN IS THE ONE WHO TOLD ME TO BRING YOU HERE.
HUH? CHISA DID?
WHY?

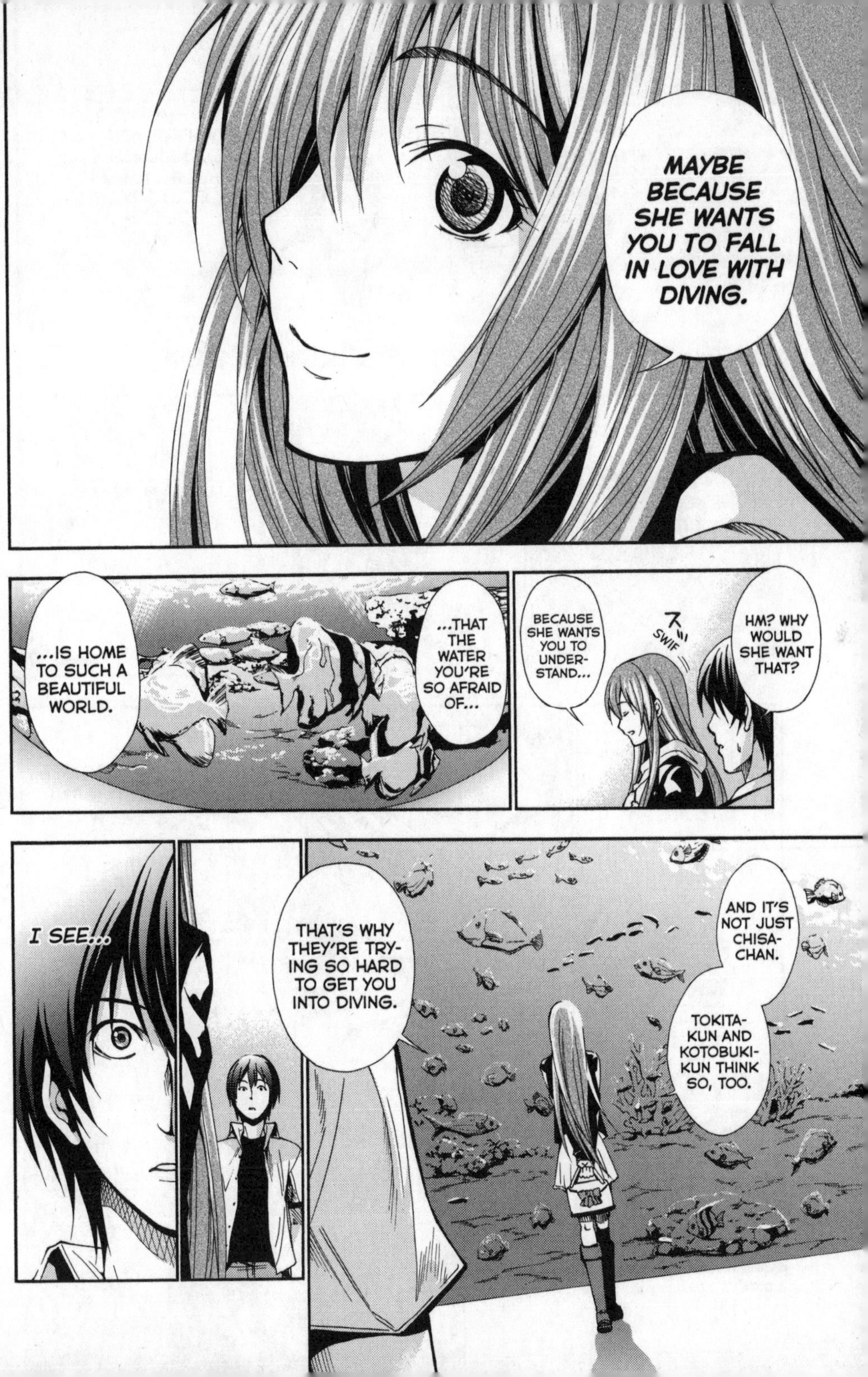
MAYBE BECAUSE SHE WANTS YOU TO FALL IN LOVE WITH DIVING.
HM? WHY WOULD SHE WANT THAT?
スッ
SWIF
BECAUSE SHE WANTS YOU TO UNDER-STAND...
...THAT THE WATER YOU'RE SO AFRAID OF...
...IS HOME TO SUCH A BEAUTIFUL WORLD.
AND IT'S NOT JUST CHISA-CHAN.
TOKITA-KUN AND KOTOBUKI-KUN THINK SO, TOO.
THAT'S WHY THEY'RE TRY-ING SO HARD TO GET YOU INTO DIVING.
I SEE...

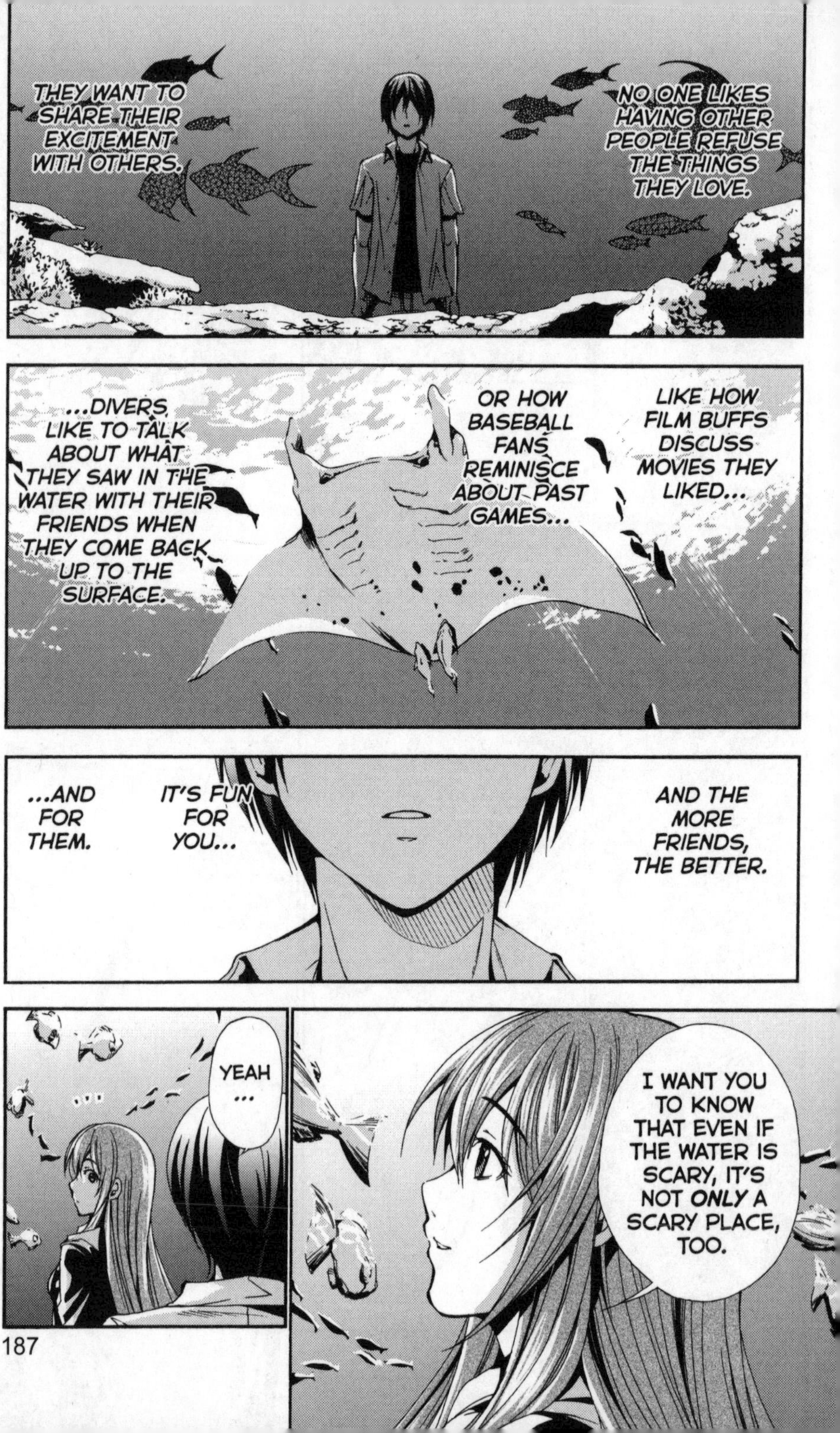
NO ONE LIKES HAVING OTHER PEOPLE REFUSE THE THINGS THEY LOVE.
THEY WANT TO SHARE THEIR EXCITEMENT WITH OTHERS.
LIKE HOW FILM BUFFS DISCUSS MOVIES THEY LIKED...
OR HOW BASEBALL FANS REMINISCE ABOUT PAST GAMES...
...DIVERS LIKE TO TALK ABOUT WHAT THEY SAW IN THE WATER WITH THEIR FRIENDS WHEN THEY COME BACK UP TO THE SURFACE.
AND THE MORE FRIENDS, THE BETTER.
IT'S FUN FOR YOU...
...AND FOR THEM.
I WANT YOU TO KNOW THAT EVEN IF THE WATER IS SCARY, IT'S NOT ONLY A SCARY PLACE, TOO.
YEAH ...
...

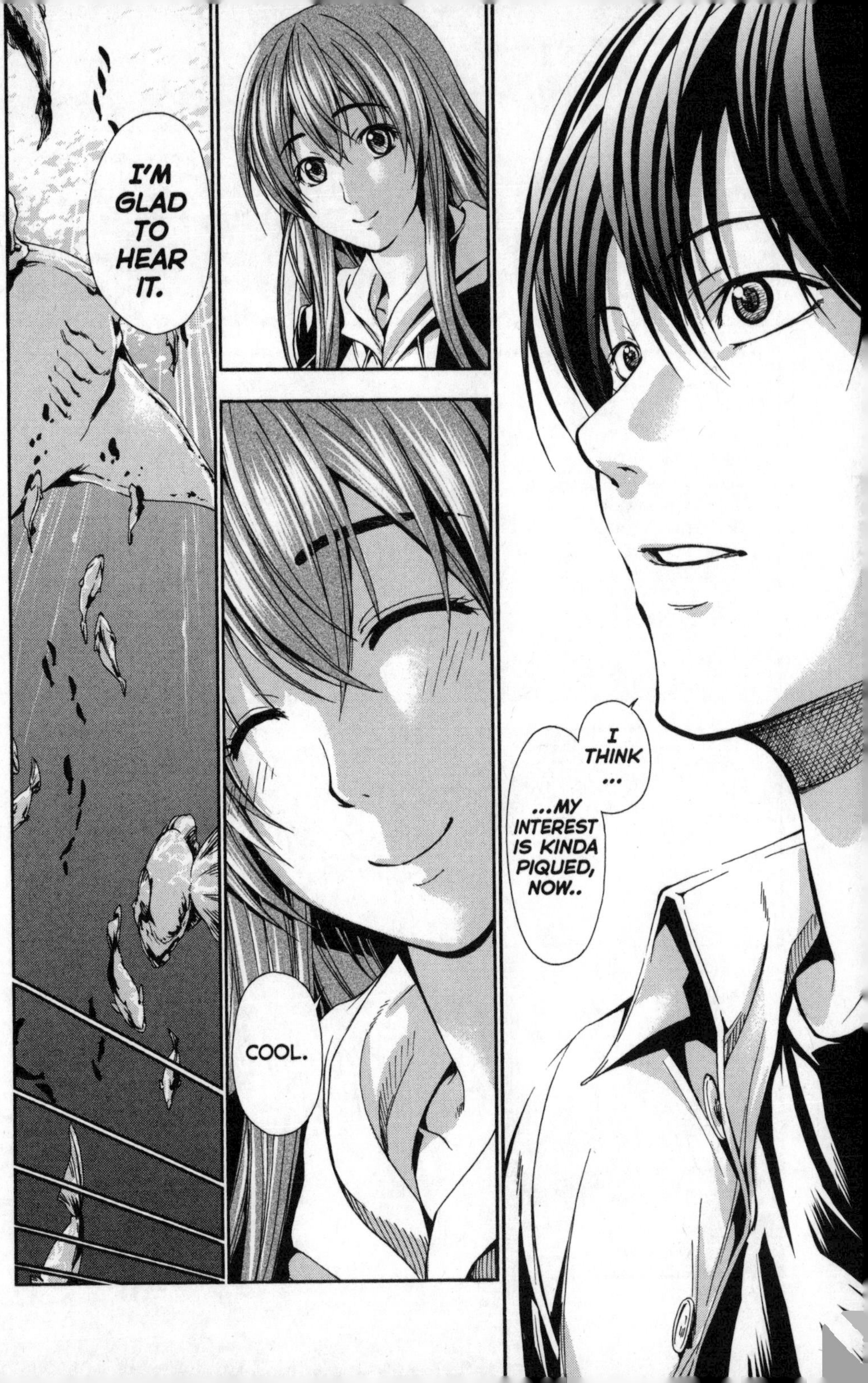
I THINK ...
...MY INTEREST IS KINDA PIQUED, NOW..
COOL.
I'M GLAD TO HEAR IT.

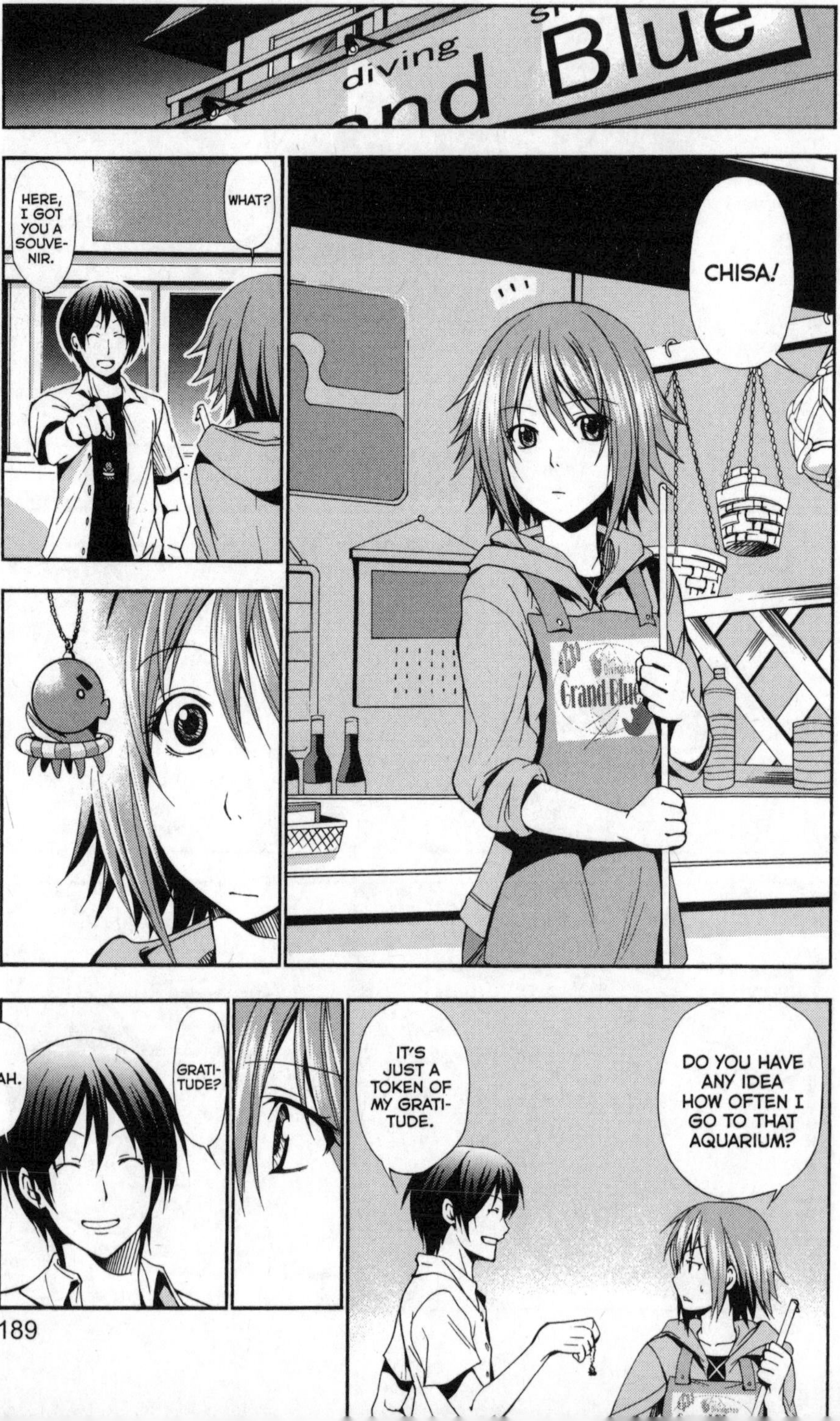
diving
Blue
CHISA!
...
Grand Blue
WHAT?
HERE, I GOT YOU A SOUVENIR.
DO YOU HAVE ANY IDEA HOW OFTEN I GO TO THAT AQUARIUM?
IT'S JUST A TOKEN OF MY GRATITUDE.
GRATITUDE?
YEAH.

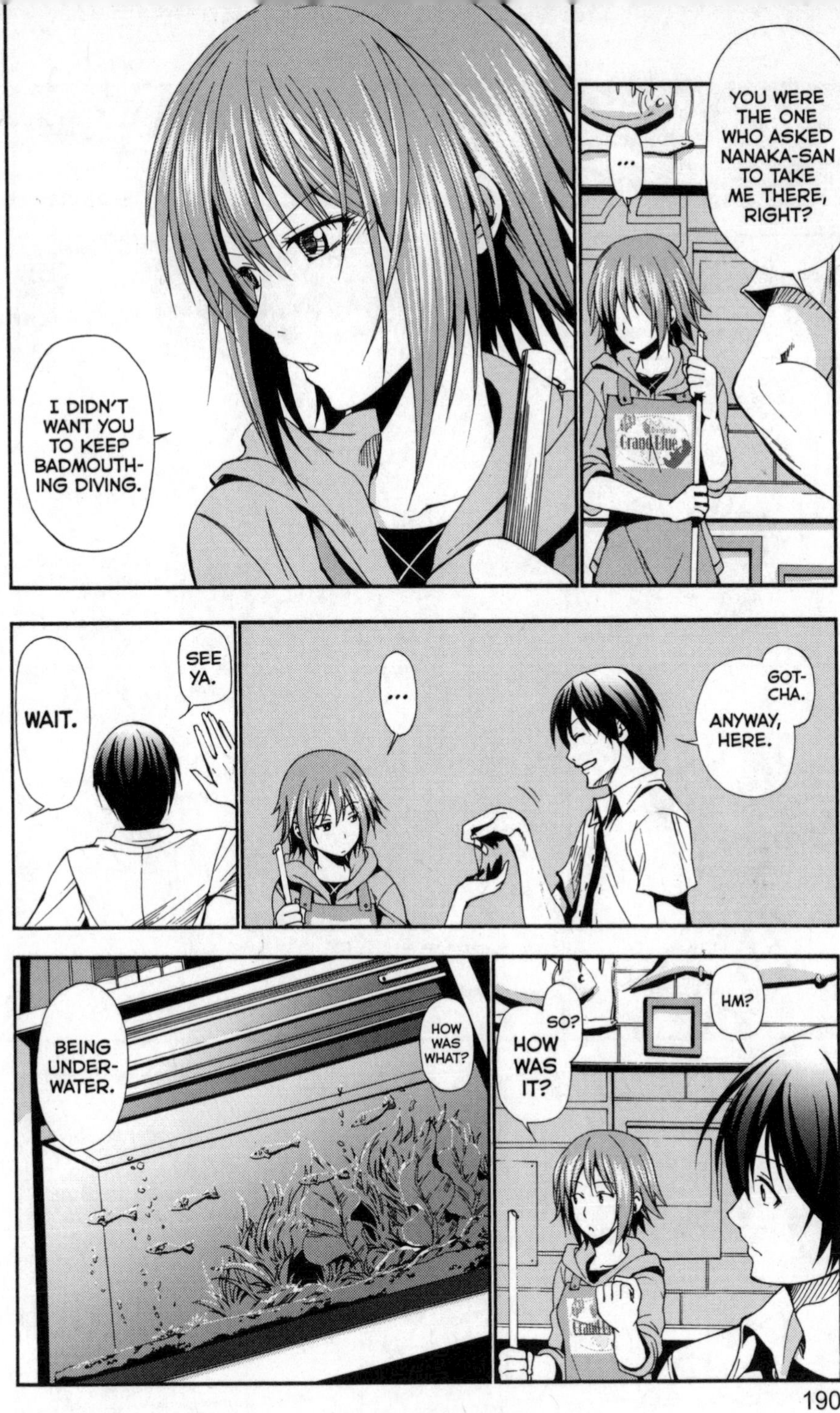
YOU WERE THE ONE WHO ASKED NANAKA-SAN TO TAKE ME THERE, RIGHT?
...
I DIDN'T WANT YOU TO KEEP BADMOUTHING-ING DIVING.
GOT-CHA. ANYWAY, HERE.
...
SEE YA.
WAIT.
HM?
SO? HOW WAS IT?
HOW WAS WHAT?
BEING UNDER-WATER.

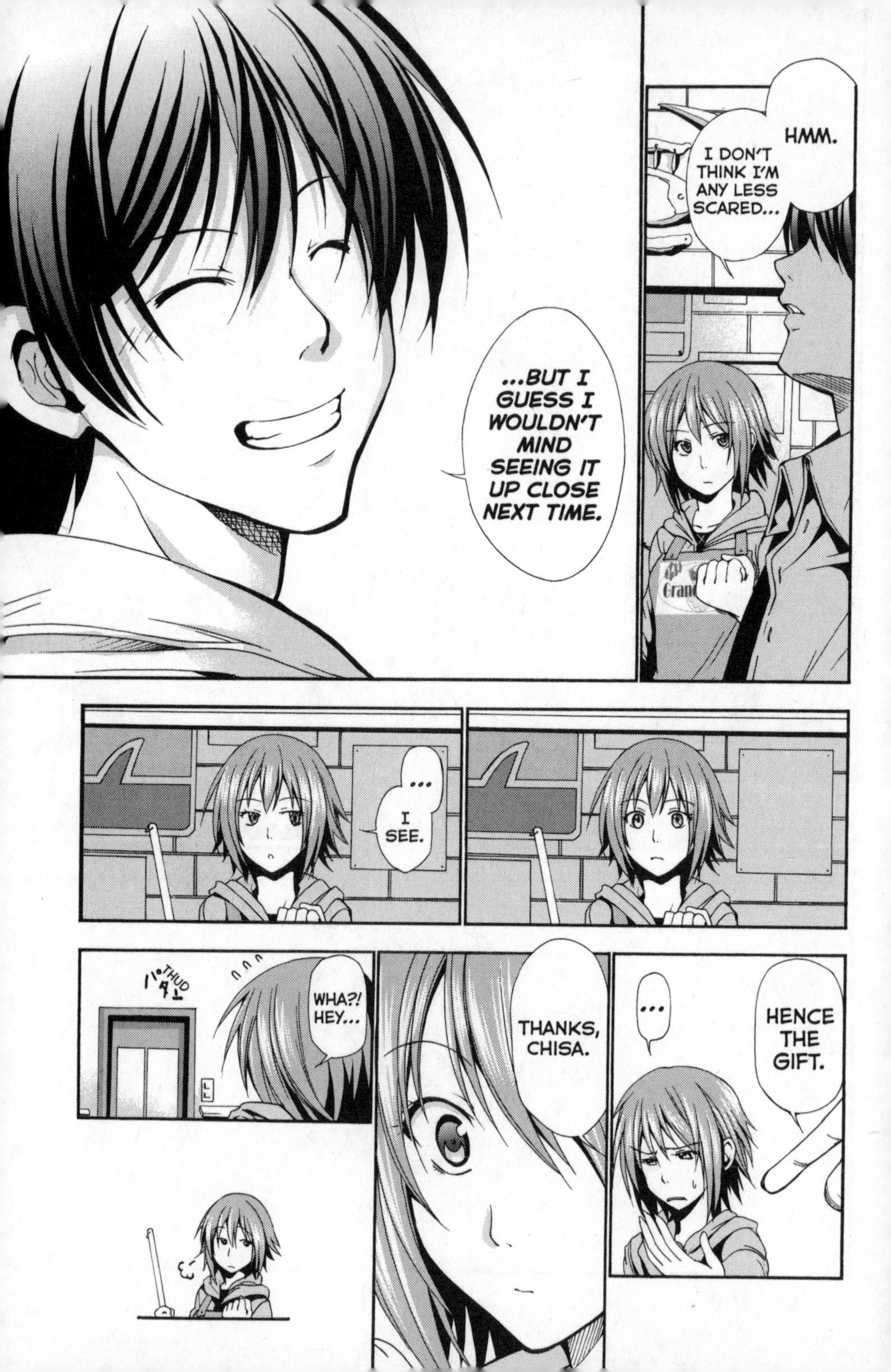
HMM.
I DON'T THINK I'M ANY LESS SCARED...
...BUT I GUESS I WOULDN'T MIND SEEING IT UP CLOSE NEXT TIME.
... I SEE.
HENCE THE GIFT.
...
THANKS, CHISA.
WHA?! HEY...
THUD

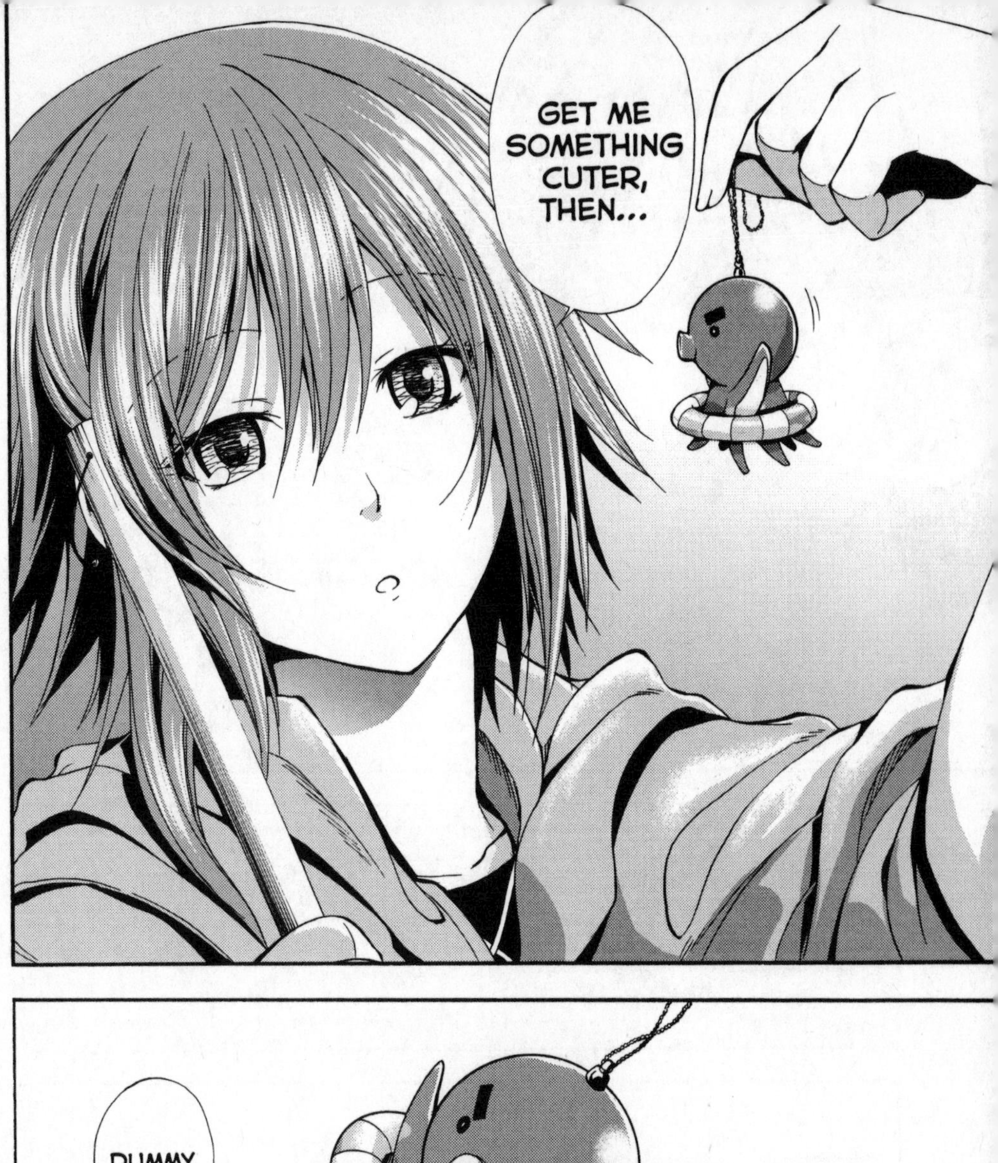
GET ME SOMETHING CUTER, THEN...

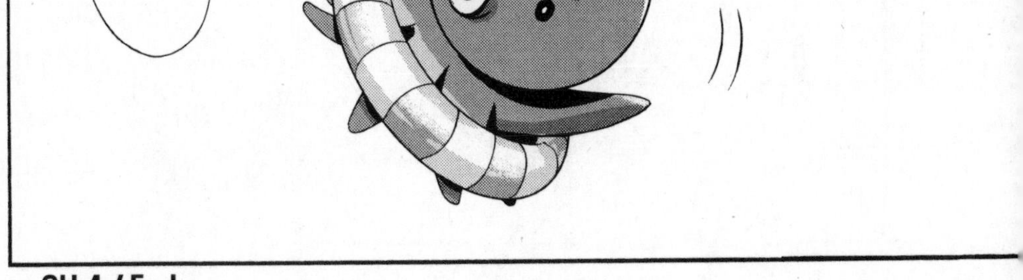
DUMMY.

CH.4 / End

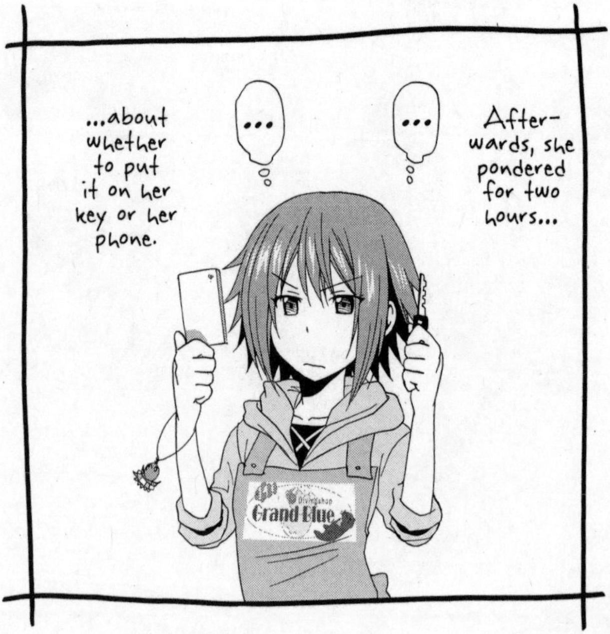
After-wards, she pondered for two hours...
...
...
...about whether to put it on her key or her phone.
Grand Blue

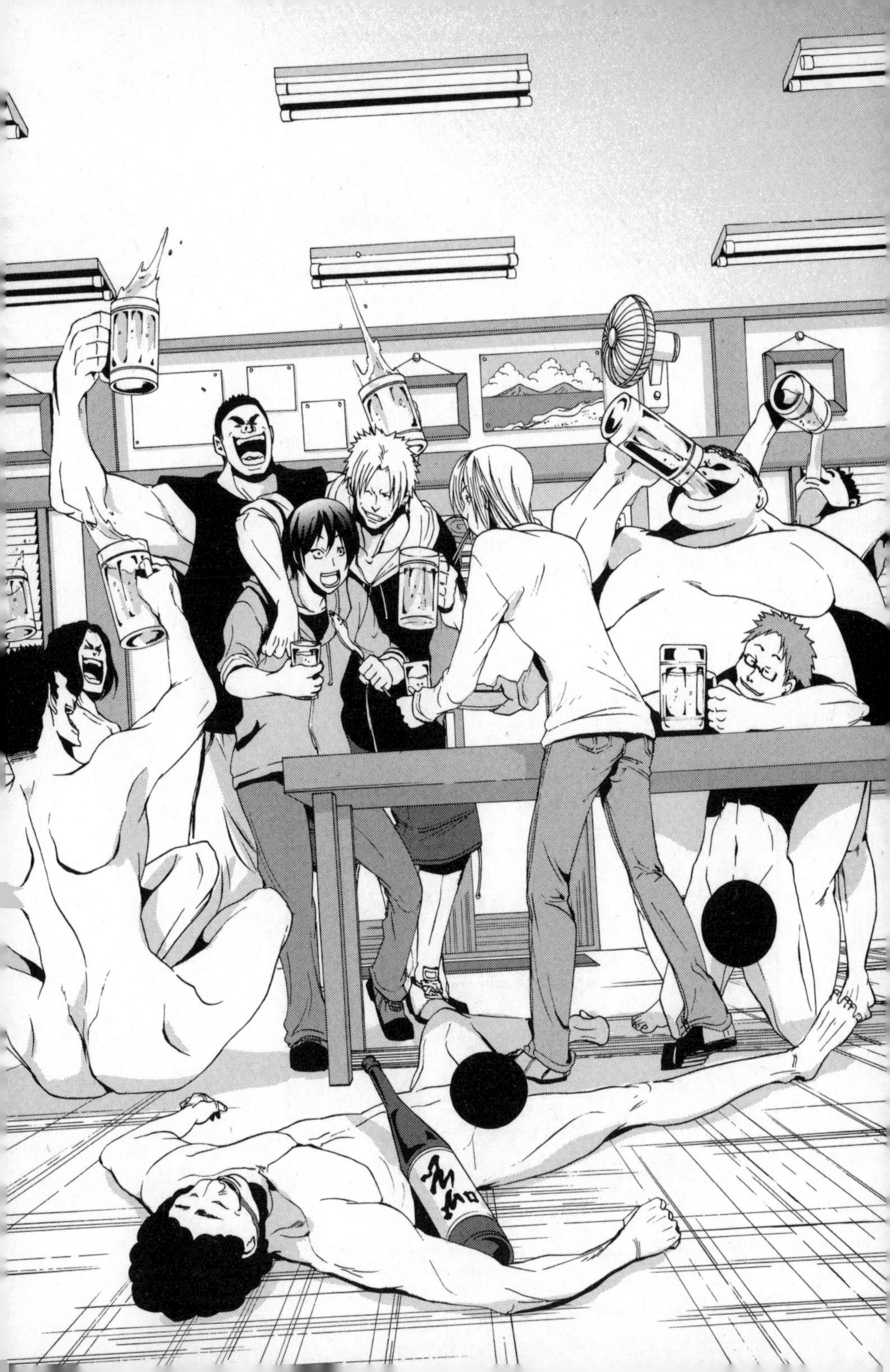

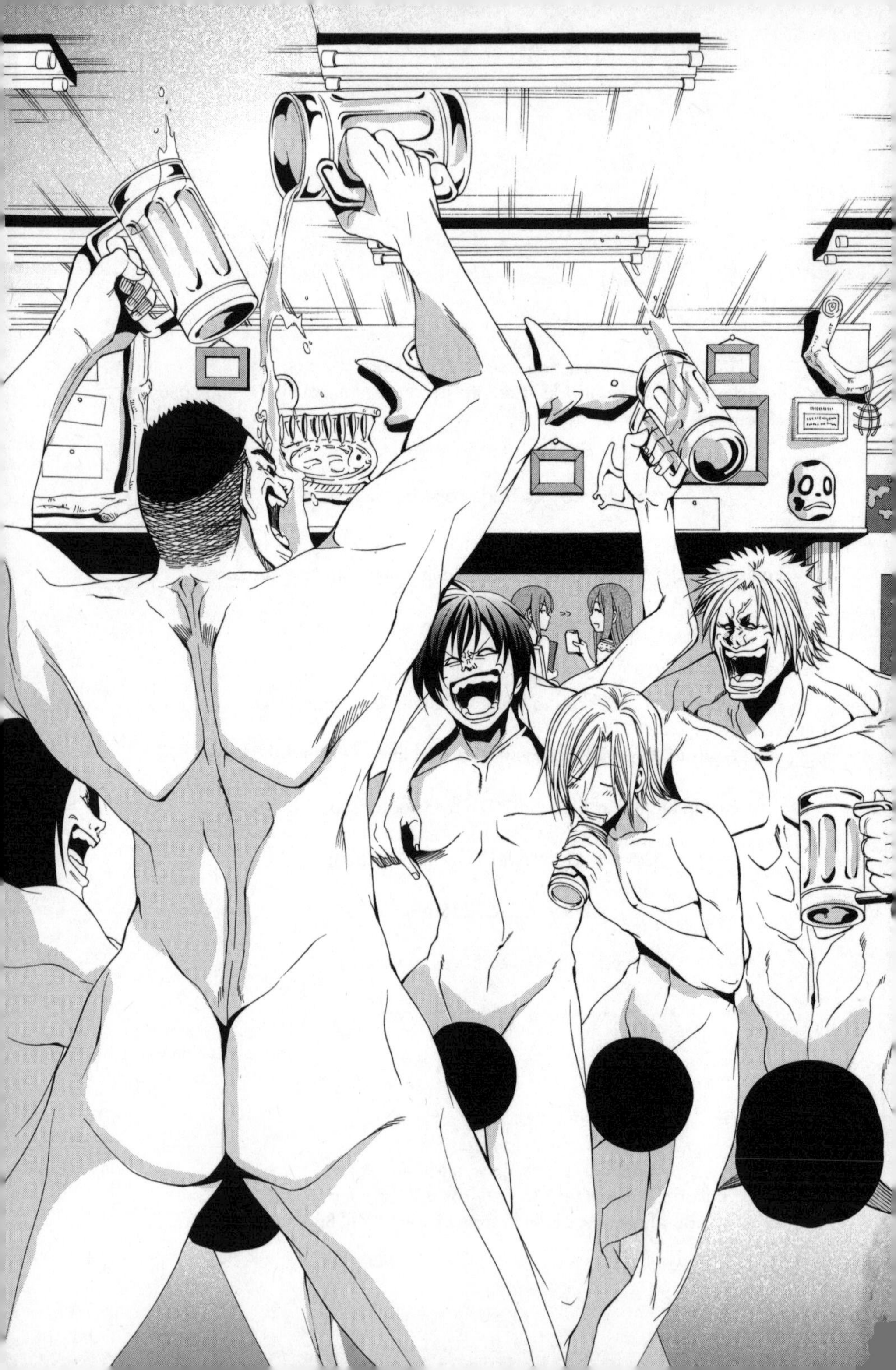

Grand Blue Dreaming volume 1 is a work of fiction.
Names, characters, places, and incidents are the products of the author's imagination or are used fictitiously. Any resemblance to actual events, locales, or persons, living or dead, is entirely coincidental.

A Kodansha Comics Trade Paperback Original.

Published in the United States by Kodansha Comics,
an imprint of Kodansha USA Publishing, LLC, New York.

Publication rights for this English edition arranged through Kodansha Ltd., Tokyo.

First published in Japan in 2014 by Kodansha Ltd., Tokyo.

Cover Design: YUKI YOSHIDA (futaba)

ISBN 978-1-63236-666-5

Printed in the United States of America.

www.kodanshacomics.com

9 8 7 6 5 4 3

Translation: Adam Hirsch
Lettering: Jan Lan Ivan Concepcion
Editing: Sarah Tilson and Paul Starr
Editorial Assistance: YKS Services LLC/SKY Japan, INC.
Kodansha Comics Edition Cover Design: Phil Balsman